When We Forgive, We Perform a Miracle Hardly Anyone Notices

We do it alone—in the private place of our inner selves.

We do it silently—no one can record our miracle on tape.

We do it invisibly—no one can record our miracle on film.

We do it freely—no one can ever trick us into forgiving someone.

But when we forgive, we heal the hurt we never deserved.

Forgive & Forget

"I recommend it to you if you are carrying a mighty wound."

—*Los Angeles Times*

"Will give help as well as comfort to those who read it."

—Madeleine L'Engle

"Helps to untangle a snarled area of human experience. Readers will find wise counsel and direct help."

—Dr. Robert McAfee Brown

"A beautiful job . . . Smedes writes eloquently."
—*Kirkus Reviews*

FORGIVE & FORGET

Healing The Hurts We Don't Deserve

Lewis B. Smedes

POCKET BOOKS

New York   London   Toronto   Sydney   Tokyo

POCKET BOOKS, a division of Simon & Schuster Inc.
1230 Avenue of the Americas, New York, N.Y. 10020

Copyright © 1984 by Lewis B. Smedes

Published by arrangement with Harper & Row Publishers, Inc.
Library of Congress Catalog Card Number: 84-47736

ISBN: 0-671-67428-5

First Pocket Books printing March 1986

14   13   12   11   10   9   8   7   6   5

POCKET and colophon are trademarks of
Simon & Schuster Inc.

Printed in the U.S.A.

TO
my sister Jessie
and
my brother Peter
"letters written not by hand, but by the Spirit"

Contents

7

A Word of Thanks

I learned about forgiving, not by reading good books, but by listening to good forgivers. Several of them appear in this volume, most behind names not their own. I thank them for sharing their struggles and their triumphs with me.

I must also mention Dr. Paul Clement, who let me teach a seminar on forgiving with him at the Fuller Graduate School of Psychology and Dr. Carol Visser, who invited me to teach a workshop on the subject sponsored by the Creative Counseling Center in Hollywood. To Jan Gathright, who with patient grace and imaginative skills converted my wretchedly scribbled drafts into flawless script, I owe much of any merit this book may have in style and clarity. To my two editors, Linda Mead of L. T. Mead & Associates and Roy M. Carlisle of Harper & Row San Francisco, who taught me more about how to write a book than I thought I needed to know, I can only say thanks for teaching me so much so fast. My wife, Doris, on the other hand, taught me a love that makes forgiving possible, and I thank her from my heart.

I wrote much of the book while I was a fellow at the Institute for Ecumenical and Cultural Research, Collegeville, Minnesota, during the fall of 1983. I could not have found anywhere a setting more pleasant and conducive to remembering and writing; so I want to thank the trustees and, in particular, Robert Bilheimer, the director of the Institute, for their hospitality to me. The trustees of Fuller Seminary generously gave me sabbatical leave to make my visit possible, and I thank them.

I must tell you, too, that I would know little about our human faculty for forgiving had I not also felt Christ's gift of forgiving love in my own life; so I thank God for inventing the way to heal the hurts we don't deserve.

An Invitation

Somebody hurt you, maybe yesterday, maybe a lifetime ago, and you cannot forget it. You did not deserve the hurt. It went deep, deep enough to lodge itself in your memory. And it keeps on hurting you now.

You are not alone. We all muddle our way through a world where even well-meaning people hurt each other. When we invest ourselves in deep personal relationships, we open our souls to the wounds of another's disloyalty or even betrayal.

There are some hurts that we can all ignore. Not every slight sticks with us, thank God. But some old pains do not wash out so easily; they remain like stubborn stains in the fabric of our own memory.

Deep hurts we never deserved flow from a dead past into our living present. A friend betrays us; a parent abuses us; a spouse leaves us in the cold—these hurts do not heal with the coming of the sun.

We've all wished at one time or other that we could reach back to a painful moment and cut it out of our lives. Some people are lucky; they seem to have gracious glands that secrete the juices of forgetfulness. They never hold a grudge; they do not remember old hurts. Their painful yesterdays die with the coming of tomorrow. But most of us find that the pains of our past keep rolling through our memories, and there's nothing we can do to stop the flow.

Nothing?

The great Jewish philosopher Hannah Arendt, toward the end of her epochal study on *The Human Condition,* shared her discovery of the only power that can stop the inexorable stream of painful memories: the "faculty of forgiveness." It is as simple as that.

Forgiveness is God's invention for coming to terms with a world in which, despite their best intentions, people are unfair to each other and hurt each other deeply. He began by forgiving us. And he invites us all to forgive each other.

Virtually every newspaper in the Western world told the story of how, one January dawn in 1984, Pope John Paul walked into a dank cell of Rebibbia prison in Rome to meet Mehmet Ali Agca, the man who had tried to kill him. The Pope took the hand of the man who had fired a bullet at his heart, and forgave him.

But the Pope is a professional forgiver; and it may be easy for such a highly placed professional to forgive when he knows ahead of time that the whole world will be watching.

It is ten times harder for an ordinary person, whom nobody is watching, to forgive and forget.

Forgiving is love's toughest work, and love's biggest risk. If you twist it into something it was never meant to be, it can make you a doormat or an insufferable manipulator.

Forgiving seems almost unnatural. Our sense of fairness tells us people should pay for the wrong they do. But forgiving is love's power to break nature's rule.

Ask yourself these questions: What do I do when I forgive someone who has done me wrong?

Who is forgivable? Have some people gone beyond the forgiveness zone?

How do I do it?

Why should I even try? Is there a pay-off? Is it fair?

I invite you to come with me in search of the answers I have found along my own journey.

The Magic Eyes
A Little Fable

In the village of Faken in innermost Friesland there lived a long thin baker named Fouke, a righteous man, with a long thin chin and a long thin nose. Fouke was so upright that he seemed to spray righteousness from his thin lips over everyone who came near him; so the people of Faken preferred to stay away.

Fouke's wife, Hilda, was short and round, her arms were round, her bosom was round, her rump was round. Hilda did not keep people at bay with righteousness; her soft roundness seemed to invite them instead to come close to her in order to share the warm cheer of her open heart.

Hilda respected her righteous husband, and loved him too, as much as he allowed her; but her heart ached for something more from him than his worthy righteousness.

And there, in the bed of her need, lay the seed of sadness.

One morning, having worked since dawn to knead his dough for the ovens, Fouke came home and found a stranger in his bedroom lying on Hilda's round bosom.

Hilda's adultery soon became the talk of the tavern and the scandal of the Faken congregation. Everyone assumed that Fouke would cast Hilda out of his house, so righteous was he. But he surprised everyone by keeping Hilda as his wife, saying he forgave her as the Good Book said he should.

In his heart of hearts, however, Fouke could not forgive Hilda for bringing shame to his name. Whenever he thought about her, his feelings toward her were angry and hard; he despised her as if she were a common whore. When it came right down to it, he hated her for betraying him after he had been so good and so faithful a husband to her.

He only pretended to forgive Hilda so that he could punish her with his righteous mercy.

But Fouke's fakery did not sit well in heaven.

So each time that Fouke would feel his secret hate toward Hilda, an angel came to him and dropped a small pebble, hardly the size of a shirt button, into Fouke's heart. Each time a pebble dropped, Fouke would feel a stab of pain like the pain he felt the moment he came on Hilda feeding her hungry heart from a stranger's larder.

Thus he hated her the more; his hate brought him pain and his pain made him hate.

The pebbles multiplied. And Fouke's heart grew very heavy with the weight of them, so heavy that the top half of his body bent forward so far that he had to strain his neck upward in order to see straight ahead. Weary with hurt, Fouke began to wish he were dead.

The angel who dropped the pebbles into his heart came to Fouke one night and told him how he could be healed of his hurt.

There was one remedy, he said, only one, for the hurt of a wounded heart. Fouke would need the miracle of the magic eyes. He would need eyes that could look back to the beginning of his hurt and see his Hilda, not as a wife who betrayed him, but as a weak woman who needed him. Only a new way of looking at things through the magic eyes could heal the hurt flowing from the wounds of yesterday.

Fouke protested. "Nothing can change the past," he said. "Hilda is guilty, a fact that not even an angel can change."

"Yes, poor hurting man, you are right," the angel said. "You cannot change the past, you can only heal the hurt that comes to you from the past. And you can heal it only with the vision of the magic eyes."

"And how can I get your magic eyes?" pouted Fouke.

"Only ask, desiring as you ask, and they will be given you. And each time you see Hilda through your new eyes, one pebble will be lifted from your aching heart."

Fouke could not ask at once, for he had grown to love his hatred. But the pain of his heart finally drove him to want and to ask for the magic eyes that the angel had promised. So he asked. And the angel gave.

Soon Hilda began to change in front of Fouke's eyes, wonderfully and mysteriously. He began to see her as a needy woman who loved him instead of a wicked woman who betrayed him.

The angel kept his promise; he lifted the pebbles from Fouke's heart, one by one, though it took a long time to take them all away. Fouke gradually felt his heart grow lighter; he began to walk straight again, and somehow his nose and his chin seemed less thin and sharp than before. He invited Hilda to come into his heart again, and she came, and together they began again a journey into their second season of humble joy.

Part 1

THE FOUR STAGES OF FORGIVING

What do you do when you forgive someone who hurt you? What goes on? When is it necessary? What happens afterward? What should you expect it to do for you? *What is forgiving?*

The act of forgiving, by itself, is a wonderfully simple act; but it always happens inside a storm of complex emotions. It is the hardest trick in the whole bag of personal relationships.

So let us be honest with each other. Let us talk plainly about the "magic eyes" that are given to those who are ready to be set free from the prison of pain they never deserved.

We forgive in four stages. If we can travel through all four, we achieve the climax of reconciliation.

The first stage is *hurt:* when somebody causes you pain so deep and unfair that you cannot forget it, you are pushed into the first stage of the crisis of forgiving.

The second stage is *hate:* you cannot shake the memory of how much you were hurt, and you cannot wish your enemy well. You sometimes want the person who hurt you to suffer as you are suffering.

The third stage is *healing:* you are given the "magic eyes" to see the person who hurt you in a new light. Your memory is healed, you turn back the flow of pain and are free again.

The fourth stage is *the coming together:* you invite the person who hurt you back into your life; if he or she comes honestly, love can move you both toward a new and healed relationship. The fourth stage depends on the person you forgive as much as it depends on you; sometimes he doesn't come back and you have to be healed alone.

CHAPTER 1

We Hurt

If you live long enough, chances are you'll be hurt by someone you counted on to be your friend. If you're like me, you may let that hurt fester and grow until it stifles your joy. When that happens, you have entered the first stage of forgiving.

I'm talking about the kind of hurts that smart and rankle within us, the kind we cannot digest as if they were only so much fiber in our interpersonal diet. Our wounds may look superficial to others, but we know better; after all, we're the ones who feel them.

I'd like to tell you a little story about a hurt I felt once, to illustrate how something that may look insignificant to outsiders can push you into the crisis of forgiveness.

It's important, to begin with, to say that I come from a long line of village blacksmiths. In fact, our family name, Smedes, is an old Dutch word for smith. From the time people first took on surnames, every male child in our family grew up to earn his living pounding on an anvil, and it was a source of family pride to be a smith worthy of the vocation.

Now on to the story. I graduated, without distinction, from Muskegon Senior High School one June Friday night. The next day I rode a Greyhound bus to Detroit, where I began work in the yards of the Smedes Iron Works, a family-run shop that my Uncle Klass built up out of a smithy he operated in a garage in his early immigrant days. Because I had neither money nor promising credentials for higher education, I was glad to accept Uncle Klass's offer to get my start in the steel business.

I was put to work out in the yard, rolling steel beams into neat stacks, cutting them with an acetylene torch into the sizes that building contractors ordered and painting them with a blend of gasoline and pitch to keep them from rusting too fast. I never did get to use the forge at which ornate forms were pounded and twisted out of red hot steel bars, the only genuine smithing still done at Smedes Iron Works.

To be honest, I was a sorry excuse for either a smith or a steelworker. I was too tall, too thin, too dreamy for any of the jobs that called for the blend of strength and talent it took to work with steel. No luster was added to the name of Smedes during my stint at the Iron Works.

My cousin Hank was different; he was born to the forge. His wrists were powerful; his hands were obedient to his mind, and he could see an artful form of steel in his mind's eye before he even put his hands to the hammer.

Hank sometimes took me along to construction sites, where we would install a gate or a fancy railing that he had crafted at the shop. He taught me how to chisel square holes into a concrete floor and set the gateposts in, pouring molten lead into the space left over. He occasionally took me into his confidence, telling me delicious family secrets about Uncle Klass and dirty jokes such as I had never heard before.

Gradually, Hank made me feel as if I were truly his friend.

But he seemed to have a dual personality. One side of him was friendly and fun; the other side was devious and cruel.

When he and I were alone, he showed me his friendly side. I accepted that part of him; it was certainly the only part that I needed.

But whenever somebody else came along while we were working—a building inspector, for instance—

Hank showed me his mean side. He turned on me, and always within earshot of the man who was watching us.

"Hey, Lew, get your skinny butt over here and do this job right for a change."

"This jackass they foisted on me as a helper doesn't know the difference between a hammer and a curling iron, but he's the boss's nephew so I have to put up with him."

"Lew, you ain't worth nothin' around here—you just better know that."

This is how Hank would talk to me, and about me, in front of the men we both wanted badly to impress as competent workmen.

He would set me up by getting me to believe that I was his friend; then he would humiliate me. I was a pushover, because at that time I needed a friend more than I needed anything else. So when Hank would show me his friendly side on our way home—even if he had made me feel like a fool that very day—I would fall for it, only to catch his scorn again the next day.

I hated Hank a lot, I suppose, and for a good while, too. And why shouldn't I have hated him? It hurts to be taken in as a friend and then treated like a stray dog. I knew in my heart that, even though I had set myself up as a sucker for the hurt Hank gave me, I didn't have it coming.

My hurt brought me into the first stage of forgiving—the critical stage at which I had to make a simple decision: Did I want to be healed, or did I want to go on suffering from an unfair hurt lodged in my memory?

We are always, all of us, pushed into this crucial stage when we feel that somebody has hurt us deeply. Will we let our pain hang on to our hearts where it will eat away our joy? Or will we use the miracle of forgiving to heal the hurt we didn't deserve?

Of course, we suffer a lot of superficial pains that nobody really needs to be forgiven for—mere indignities that we simply have to bear with a measure of grace.

We need to sort out our hurts and learn the difference between those that call for the miracle of forgiveness and those that can be borne with a sense of humor. If we lump all our hurts together and prescribe forgiveness for all of them, we turn the art of forgiving into something cheap and commonplace. Like good wine, forgiving must be preserved for the right occasion.

The hurt that creates a crisis of forgiving has three dimensions. It is always *personal, unfair,* and *deep.* When you feel this kind of three-dimensional pain, you have a wound that can be healed only by forgiving the one who wounded you.

PERSONAL PAIN

We can only forgive people, we cannot forgive nature, even though nature often hurts us. Sometimes the pain comes from what nature fails to give us— some people, through no fault of their own, are born into the world with less health, beauty, or intelligence than they want. Sometimes we simply reel from the assault of nature's fury, the way close friends of mine felt as they buried their baby the other day, a victim of the mystery called crib death. Each of us can be random victims of natural forces that strip us of our dignity and smash us without respect for merit or need.

But we cannot forgive nature. We can curse it, rage against it, blame it for all that is wrong with us, and finally surrender to its brute power. We can use science to defend ourselves temporarily against nature's whimsical savagery. Or, in faith, we can look beyond nature and rest ourselves in God's secret purpose behind nature's oddly perverse ways. But we do not forgive nature. Forgiving is only for persons.

Nor can we forgive systems. God knows that systems can hurt people. Economic systems can lock poor people in a ghetto of brutal poverty. Political systems can turn free people into slaves. Corporate systems can push people around like puppets and toss them out like trash. But we do not forgive systems. We only forgive people.

People are the only ones who can be held *accountable* for what they do. People are the only ones who can *accept* forgiveness and decide to come back to us.

Forgiving is always a personal event. It follows, then, that you should forgive *only* the persons who hurt *you*.

I do not need to forgive people who have not hurt me. In fact, I have no *right* to forgive them; only their victims have that right. I may be outraged at what they do to others. I may judge them, condemn them, and call for their heads to roll. I may, for instance, nurture a gargantuan rage at Joseph Stalin for his massive murder of Russian people. But, unless he injured me, I should not forgive him, not because he is too evil, but because he can be forgiven honestly only by the people whom he hurt. I would only cheapen the miracle of forgiveness if I claimed to forgive the great hurters of people who did not hurt me.

I do not mean that you have to feel the culprit's hands on your own throat. We often hurt most when we feel the pains of people we love. I, for instance, am almost neurotic about the way I feel the pain my children feel. If you hurt my children, you hurt me worse than if you assault me directly. In any case, we have somehow to *feel* the hurt ourselves or else we do not need the healing that forgiving was invented to give.

If forgiving heals the pains *we* feel, we have good reason to keep in touch with our own hurts.

Some of us deny the pain we really feel. It just hurts too much to acknowledge it. Sometimes it scares us; people betrayed and brutalized by their parents are often afraid to admit their pain for fear they may hate the people they most dearly want to love. So they use a thousand devices to deny their pain.

I sometimes deny my pain, not out of fear, but out of

sheer pride. I grit my teeth in heroic refusal to concede that certain people have enough power to hurt me. Just so, the betrayed wife says, "I know my husband has been playing around with that conniving little witch he calls his secretary, but I am not going to let him have the pleasure of seeing me suffer." So she shoves her pain into the dark room of the soul where feelings are not allowed to enter. And she may carry it off; she may outlast the secretary. But she will never forgive her husband as long as she refuses to admit to herself the pain she feels so deeply.

I am simplifying the scenario, of course. The story is not usually about an innocent lamb and a bad wolf. Most of us have to do our forgiving while we are being forgiven. And sometimes being forgiven gets so homogenized with forgiving that we can hardly feel the difference between them.

But in its essence, the miracle of healing happens when one *person* feels the pain and forgives the *person* who opened the wound.

UNFAIR PAIN

We always face a crisis of forgiving when somebody hurts us *unfairly*. Forgiving is love's remedy to be used when we are hurtfully *wronged* by a person we trusted to treat us right. There is a difference between suffering sheer pain and suffering painful wrongs.

It hurts to lose fifty dollars on a fair bet; it also hurts to be mugged on the street and robbed of fifty dollars. But there is a moral difference between what we lose fair and square and what we suffer in violent unfairness! It hurts a boy to be bawled out by his mother for slapping his sister; it also hurts when a child is screamed at by a drunken father for having been born. But what a difference between fair hurt and brutal wrong!

Not everybody is out to get us. Our lives are cluttered with people who wound our feelings in small ways, but who mean no real harm. We suffer some inevitable aches simply because we are vulnerable people living in a crazy world where fragile spirits sometimes accidentally collide.

For example: There was once a person in my life who did outrageous things to me. She screamed at me all through dinner; she made me jump to her service anytime, day and night, no matter how busy I was with other things; and now and then she would pee on my best slacks. To make matters worse, she got acutely sick and drove me mad because she did not tell me what was wrong. There were moments when I felt like whacking her. But I never felt an impulse to forgive her.

She was my six-month-old baby, and I did not feel a need to forgive the outrageous things she did to me, because she did not hurt me wrongfully. I loved her and I took whatever she dished out.

My example may be a little far-fetched, but it does make the point; we don't have to forgive people for every hurt we feel.

Many of us are hurt when we discover that an important human relationship we thought would last forever is, in fact, temporary. We part, we leave each other, and being left is often a very sour sorrow.

Some friendships need to be dissolved, some love affairs need to be ended. And leaving usually hurts somebody. But a wounded heart may be only the risk of love in a world where everything that comes must also go.

Perhaps the worst way for people to leave us unfairly—yet without wronging us—is to get sick and die and leave us all alone. But people die because that is the way of nature; generally, they do not die because they want to hurt us. Still, how can a child understand that the father who got cancer and died did not really *mean* to leave her all alone? How sensitive we must be with people who know better with their heads, but who still *feel* wronged by someone who died and left them just when he was needed most.

It is harder still when those we love *decide* to die in spite of how much we needed them to stay alive. When Bob hung himself, he did not tell anybody what his motives were. Did he have to end his life? Is he to blame for the awesome pain he left behind? Should his wife forgive him? I cannot tell. Only she can know.

Sometimes you can't know for sure whether you have been the victim of an unavoidable accident or whether you have been wrongfully wounded. You may need help to sort out your hurts, so you can see the difference between feeling the pain that comes from our vulnerability and the pain that comes from being the butt of an unfair attack.

I do *not* mean that pain is unfair *only* when someone *means* to be unfair. Pain is unfair when we do not *deserve* it, or when it is not *necessary*. So you do not have to prove that someone *meant* to wrong you before you can forgive. You will be shoved into a crisis of forgiveness when you are needlessly knocked around, no matter what the other person's intentions were.

I have made a little catalogue of unfair hurts that everyone feels from time to time. In no case does the hurt-giver *mean* to be *unfair*. But in every case, we *experience* the hurt as an unfair assault. Match my list of hurts with your own experience.

PEOPLE HURT US BECAUSE THEY THINK
WE DESERVE IT

Some people aim to hurt, they mean to do someone harm; but they want no more than just retribution. This is Shakespeare's Macbeth, resolved to do in his king: "I am settled, and bend up / Each corporal agent to this terrible feat." This is Booth taking aim at Lincoln in a theater. This is Lee Harvey Oswald plotting to shoot Kennedy on the streets of Dallas. This is Judas slouching into the night to betray his Master. Each one was doing what he felt his victim deserved.

I am pretty sure that almost everyone who has ever

hurt me on purpose sincerely believed I was getting what I had coming. A colleague of mine once wrote a private letter to my board to accuse me of some theological delinquencies. His letter was unfair to me, and it caused me a lot of trouble. I believe that my colleague meant to be fair. But what he meant and what I experienced were two different things. It *was* unfair, no matter if he *meant* it to be fair. And the unfairness of it threw me into a crisis: did I want to let it fester in my memory, or would I use the "magic eyes" and be healed?

Most people who mean to hurt other people believe they are being fair. They set out, teeth grinding, eyes steeled, lips tight, to do us harm in the belief that we deserve it. "It hurts me worse than it does you" is the ultimate piety of the person who intends to hurt but means to be fair. But what they *intend* does not take away the unfairness we *feel*.

When we are hurt in this way, we enter a crisis of forgiveness. We cannot relate to the person who hurt us as a friend or lover until we come to terms with the unfairness of the hurt.

PEOPLE HURT US COMPULSIVELY

Sometimes people hurt us, not because they want to do us harm, but only because they cannot control themselves.

Jack did not mean to hurt his family; he simply could not stay away from booze. Walter never intended to hurt his wife by having a sexual affair with another woman; he just could not harness his lively libido.

A year or so ago my friends Ben and Phyllis Sewall were slammed into as terrible a crisis of forgiveness as anyone has ever let me share. Their son, Roger, was idling his moped at a four-way stop on a lazy summer evening in Laguna Beach, California. Stopped, feet on the ground, he waited his turn to move on. A half-block behind him Sid Charid was gunning his Camaro down the same street in Roger's direction. He did not

27

slow down for the stop sign. Roger, hit from behind, was killed almost instantly by a car he never saw coming. The driver stopped for a moment, then drove on, hit and run.

Sid, apparently, was high on drugs. He did not *mean* to hurt anyone; he was just out of control, driven by a mind-blowing chemical. But Roger did not deserve to die; nor did my friends deserve to lose their son. It was not fair. And this grotesque unfairness created as painful a crisis as any wounded heart can bear.

PEOPLE HURT US WITH THE SPILL-OVERS OF THEIR PROBLEMS

Sometimes our personal struggles, too turbulent to contain, spill over to affect innocent bystanders. We do not mean to hurt them; they just happen to be in the wrong place at the wrong time.

Children are sometimes the most unlucky victims of the pain that washes over from grown-up conflicts.

My friend Morgan was trapped in a miserable marriage and had good reason to want to escape. But his two little children happened to be living in the same house, drenched in the backwash of adult rage, sure that it must somehow be their fault that their parents hated each other. Morgan was only trying to get out of a hopelessly bad marriage. The last thing he wanted to do was injure his children, but they got caught in the crossfire. They did not have it coming; they were *wronged* as surely as they were hurt.

PEOPLE HURT US WITH THEIR GOOD INTENTIONS

Sometimes people hurt us even when they mean to do us good. Their well-meant plans go awry, maybe through other people's knavery, maybe by their own bungling. No matter how, what they do to help us turns out to hurt us.

The most generous friend I have ever had was Alec Morton, a selfless surgeon who gave two years out of every four to healing poor people in a shanty hospital on a mission compound in Burundi. He took no pay for

28

his work; he even brought along his own medications and gave them generously to the sick. He himself flirted chronically with borderline insolvency. But he cared a lot about his children and about their education. So he took the advice of a smart broker and sank all his savings into a real estate deal that, in a few years, promised to pay off well enough to see his six children through college and his wife through any troubles.

The payoff turned out to be a worthless piece of wilderness.

Alec's mind was on suffering people in Burundi and on security for his children. He intended it to turn out well, but his generosity was turned to unfair loss.

Alec—prone to depression anyway—sank deeper and deeper into the muck of self-condemnation. One night he drove up the hill behind his home and shot himself. His suicide was the unfairest cut of all. His children did not deserve to lose *him* as well as his money; and he was terribly unfair to them, no matter how good his intentions were. I think his children needed to forgive their father even if he was a saint.

PEOPLE HURT US BY THEIR MISTAKES

Sometimes we get hurt because other people make mistakes. They may be ministering professionals and they may surely mean to help, but sometimes they bungle the job.

Not many people can hurt us by mistakes the way doctors can. We trust them to take care of us; we let them put us to sleep while they slice our bodies apart and sew them together again. But they can err, and their errors cost us a lot.

When my mother-in-law was old and very sick she needed a massive blood transfusion. Somehow they managed to pump her veins full of the wrong type of blood. Nobody in the hospital meant to hurt her. Mistakes can happen to anybody. But she almost died. Unfairly!

A young intern, trying to impress his nurse, went

ahead on his own with a new treatment, when he should have checked first with the surgeon in charge. He prescribed drugs that, once inside of his patient, clashed with other drugs that she was taking; the medic should have checked more carefully, but he was in too much of a hurry, and the consequences were very painful and very unfair.

Mistakes, all of them! Everybody makes them sometimes. But when our doctors make them, we pay. We pay in extra hospital costs. We pay in pain that could have been avoided. Once in a while we may pay with our lives. And it isn't fair, no matter what the medics meant.

But enough! My catalogue of unfair hurts should be enough to remind you that the unfairness of the hurt often lies in the experience of the victim, not in the intention of the one who causes it.

Should you forgive someone who hurts you unfairly, but who never meant to do you wrong?

Not many people ever *mean* to be unfair. Even a Mafia hit man believes he kills only people who have it coming. So if we need to forgive people only when they *mean* to hurt us unfairly, we may never need to forgive anyone on earth.

In fact, you may *feel* the unfairness of your pain even more terribly just because the person hurt you carelessly. The drunk driver who kills your neighbor's child never meant to hurt anybody. But you may feel the horror of his unfairness all the more because of its pointlessness.

Perhaps more to the point, however, is our need to forgive *for our own sakes*. Every human soul has a right to be free from hate, and we claim our rightful inheritance when we forgive people who hurt us unfairly, even if their intentions were pure.

DEEP PAINS

The third dimension of the pain that needs forgiving has to do with depth. Hurts that need forgiving are deep hurts.

"Deep" is not a precise measure when it comes to pain; depth of pain lies in the hearts of people who feel the hurt. So we cannot be exact. We know for sure only when *we* feel the bruise. But surely we can at least agree on some rough differences between the superficial wounds that we can tolerate and the deeper hurts that separate us from the person who brought them on.

Here are a few of my own experiences of hurts that are really too shallow for a falling-out.

ANNOYANCES

Our lives are sprinkled with annoyances. I can't stand the kind of shoppers who check out fifteen items in the eight-item express lane and then talk about their cat with the cashier, while I wait impatiently to pay for one carton of milk. I drive my wife crazy by switching channels mindlessly on the television set. She annoys me when she stretches the short stories she tells at dinner into full-length novels. These are nettles against our tender skin; but they are probably not deep enough to raise the issue of forgiveness.

If we were to turn every nuisance into a crisis of forgiveness, our conversations would become revolving reconciliations. Better to swallow annoyances and leave forgiveness for the deeper hurts.

SLIGHTS

Slights are snubs, not as bad as being maligned, but bad enough to make us feel as if we've lost our standing in the pecking order. We want people to respect our place in the line-up, and we hurt whenever we lose our place.

Once, when I was a graduate student in Holland, I was invited to spend a Sunday evening at the home of

31

a famous professor in Amsterdam. Monday morning, I bragged to my fellow American students and hinted that the great man and I had become close friends. A few weeks later, at a reception, I was standing with the same American friends when the renowned professor came into the room. We were all introduced to him. When he got to me, he did not remember ever having laid eyes on me before. He did not tell my friends that I was a worm, he did not spit at me or revile me. He just slighted me when I wanted badly to be noticed. I could have killed him. But I did not need to forgive.

Slights hurt because we are unsure of ourselves, needy creatures walking among people whose notice we need to support our self-esteem. We hurt when people walk by without looking at us; but we do not exile people from our lives for not noticing us. Slights are really for shrugging off, not for forgiving.

DISAPPOINTMENTS

We are hurt by people who do not do what we expect them to do for us. We invest our lives in our children; they take our investment for granted, as if they had it all coming. I was once a candidate for a cherished award; I did not get it, and I later discovered that my closest friend did not vote for me. A friend of mine stayed with his company out of loyalty when he was offered a better job somewhere else; when a position he wanted opened up his boss passed him by to promote a youngster waving a fresh M.B.A.

Disappointment! It can slap you in the face of your pride and leave you feeling cheated. Yet, though deeply disappointed, you are not betrayed and you don't need to forgive.

COMING IN SECOND

One mother gives her daughter all the advantages, more than she can afford; her daughter drops out of school and becomes a waitress while her best friend's daughter becomes an attorney. One student knocks himself out for a B while his roommate, who hardly tries, gets nothing but As. Your friend's horse prances into the winner's circle every race; your horse never manages to show.

When someone else gets the glittering prize you wanted, it smarts to come in second. The hurt is hardest to bear when the person who gets there ahead of you is a close friend. You have to put your arm around his shoulder and celebrate his good luck when you would really rather run away and drown your sorrows alone.

To be honest, we would feel better if our friends lost when we lost, their stocks tumbled when ours tumbled, and their kids failed when ours failed. But we do not quit a friendship because our friends got something we wanted, nor do we have to forgive them.

It is wise not to turn all hurts into crises of forgiving. If you need to forgive every minor bruise that you suffer in your run for a place in the sun, you will dam up the ebb and flow of all your fragile human relationships. We put everyone we love on guard when we turn personal misdemeanors into major felonies.

What sort of unfair hurt, then, does go deep enough to create a crisis of forgiveness? How do you know you have been hurt seriously enough to cause a falling-out? When does the wound require the radical spiritual surgery we call forgiving?

I will offer three examples of unfair hurts deep enough to bring us into a crisis of forgiving: *disloyalty*, *betrayal*, and *brutality*. Let me try to explain what I mean by each of them.

DISLOYALTY

I am disloyal when I belong to a person and I treat him or her like a stranger.

Most of us have several circles of people to whom we belong by personal bonds of loyalty. Inside the circle we are bonded to each other by a promise we have made to stay at each other's side. Sometimes the promise is made, head bowed, before witnesses, as a public vow. Sometimes the promise is tucked silently into what we do; a mother makes a silent commitment to care for her newborn baby simply by taking the child into her arms and two friends can vow a deep loyalty to each other without ever saying a word. Either way, our freely given promise to stay together and care for each other is the invisible fiber that holds us together; we belong to each other in the only way one human being may ever belong to another.

The promises we make *to* each other give birth to the trust we have in each other. People count on people who make promises. A baby counts on his mother to be there when he needs her. A wife counts on her husband to be there for her. A friend counts on a friend. Wherever people promise to be with us in care and support, we are bonded to them by our trust just as they are bonded to us by their commitment.

So when a father leaves his family in the lurch, he is disloyal because he has treated people who belong to him as if they were strangers. When a son makes a habit of lying to manipulate his parents, he treats them as strangers though he belongs to them by the bond of trust. A woman feels violated when she learns that her husband has played around with other women for several years because someone who belongs uniquely to her has treated her as if she were just another woman.

The loyalties of friendship may not be as binding as the loyalties of family, but if I discover that a friend let me down after he promised something to me—a favor, a loan, a blessing—let me down when I needed him badly, and only because he did not want to go out of his way for me, I feel as if the fundamental terms of our friendship had been violated. Someone I trusted to care for me as a loyal friend treated me as if he and I were strangers.

A person who breaks a promise of loyalty violates a relationship based on promise and trust. We cannot go on as usual in the relationship unless the wrong of it is healed. The hurt is too deep to go on as if nothing had come between us.

Disloyalty is not acceptable; it is offensive. We must either separate and carry the hurt alone or forgive the person who was disloyal to us.

BETRAYAL

Turn the screws a little tighter and disloyalty becomes a betrayal. My partner is disloyal to me when he treats me like a stranger, but he betrays me when he treats me like an enemy.

Peter was disloyal to Jesus when he denied that he ever knew the man. Judas betrayed Jesus when he sold him to his enemies for thirty pieces of silver. We betray people we belong to whenever we sell them out for a price.

Can anything hurt worse than a friend's betrayal?

We do not have to parlay for huge sums to be betrayers. Most betrayers are minor Iscariots, playing for petty stakes. A friend who tells another my special secret about my private shame, knowing that I may be hurt, betrays me. A husband who belittles his wife in front of guests commits minor treason. A close colleague who promises to support my bid for a promotion, but secretly signals to my boss that I am not competent to do the job, betrays me. A father who seduces his own daughter most certainly betrays her.

Caesar had his Brutus, his dearest friend who turned on him and slew him. But a friend, lover, spouse, or partner who lets others do us harm just as surely betrays us. No matter what the method is or how superficial the cut, we are betrayed.

Something lying close to our souls cannot indulge treason, not even trivial treason. We feel fouled and we feel diminished. Every human relationship built on trust is fractured by betrayal. To be friends or lovers after betrayal would be a sham. We know it is so because we feel the stab so deeply. And when we feel it, we are in the crisis of forgiveness.

BRUTALITY

As a rule, we forgive people who belong to us in

some way—spouses, children, parents, close friends. But sometimes we need to forgive strangers who bind themselves to us with a rope woven of brutality.

A stranger breaks into your home at night while you are asleep, vulnerable, alone in the ultimate privacy of your bedroom. You feel so personally violated that you cannot ever feel indifferent toward this man, not the casual way you feel indifferent toward an ordinary stranger who never got close to you. He did not touch you. You did not see his face. Yet, he came inside of your special private place where he had no right to be. He is not a mere stranger anymore; he is now, though faceless, a personal enemy.

Consider an assault far worse. A stranger rapes a woman in a dark parking lot. She is violated to her core. She does not know his name. She only felt his violence. But he can no longer be a mere stranger to her. He ravaged her and became her personal enemy; and because they are bound by violence, she is alienated by hate.

But brutal people are not always strangers. In fact, most brutal people assault those they belong to. Men who never sleep with other women beat their wives, and claim credit for fidelity. Fathers who would never desert their families batter their own children. We can be cruelest of all to people who belong to us.

There are also brutalities that never blacken an eye or break a bone. We can brutalize one another without touching. I have heard mothers tell their sons, for no good reason, that they were rotten kids, worse than worthless. I have known fathers who regularly told their daughters that they were no better than prostitutes.

At a party once, in Europe, I watched an American try to amuse his guests by coaxing his wife—who knew only Hungarian—to repeat English four-letter words that she would be horrified to speak had she known what they meant. I thought that he was brutalizing her as surely as if he had hit her. And I felt brutalized with her.

We are brutal whenever we reduce another person to less than human excellence. It may be a violent rape. It may be a degrading insult. Brutality, no matter who commits it, confronts us with one of the most agonizing crises of forgiveness.

So much, then, for the sorts of personal, unfair, and deep hurts that lead us into the first stage of forgiving.

Minor hurts that would ordinarily not call for forgiving can *become* major offenses by sheer repetition. For example, if Betty persists in an action just *because* it is annoying, and throws this petty annoyance at you regularly, she probably *wants* to demean you without having to risk too much. She wants to hurt you with her contempt, but she does not have the courage to make a frontal assault. Her annoyances then become moral injuries, and you cannot let her get away with it.

The same goes for slights. If your boss *always* forgets her appointments with you, her slight demeans you. If your father *never* takes time to listen to your troubles, his slight edges toward disloyalty. If your friend *never* calls you when he knows you are sick or in trouble, his slight slides into disloyalty because he treats you like a stranger.

How do you know when forgettable misdemeanors become insufferable felonies that need forgiveness? You can tell for sure only when you are on the scene. You cannot draw lines for others; you need to feel the difference for yourself. Some people turn all misdemeanors into felonies whenever *they* are hurt by them. Other people make themselves passive targets, inviting almost anybody to take a crack at them. But there is a difference, and one of the signs of growing up is the insight you need to tell the difference in the painful pinch of a moment when you are the victim.

CHAPTER 2

We Hate

Hate is a tiger snarling in the soul. Hate is our natural response to any deep and unfair pain. Hate is our instinctive backlash against anyone who wounds us wrongly.

But what is it that we feel when we feel hate for another human being? Especially when we hate someone we also love, or used to love?

Maybe we feel no more than a *passive* hatred—the grain of malice that robs us of energy to wish a person well.

I have felt passive hatred often—and, if the truth were known, so have other people who love at least as easily as I do. When I think about a man who once whispered lies about me, I cannot find it in my heart to hope that he will be a great success in his work. I do not wish he would die; I simply have no desire for him to do well while he lives. At the very least, I don't want him to do better than I do. I cannot raise an honest prayer that he will become a bright star in the little sky we share.

On the other hand, there is an *aggressive* fury that drives us out of our wits. A woman wishes her former husband would catch herpes, or at least be miserably unhappy with his new wife. You hope the friend who hurt you when he told your secret will get fired from the new job he found. We may settle for lesser retribution, or we may wish our enemy would drop dead. In any case, we are not only drained of the positive energy to wish someone well, we devoutly wish them ill. We are poised to attack. This is *aggressive* hate.

When you hate passively, you lose love's passion to bless. When you hate aggressively, you are driven by a passion to whip someone with a hurricane—or at least a stiff March wind—of hostility.

Passive or aggressive, our hate separates us from those we ought to belong to. It shoves them away from us. Where? Any place where no good can reach them or harm can miss them. Hate is the elemental inner violence that drives people apart.

Sometimes hate divides our own souls; one part of us hates and the other part loves. And we both hate and love the same person. A wife loves her husband for his sexy attractiveness and hates him for his savage put-downs. A husband may love his wife's devotion to their marriage and hate her for her pallid indifference to his needs. We love the father whose love we gasp for; we hate him for driving us crazy with a love he keeps just beyond our grasp, like a prize held just out of reach. Oh yes, we could play the love-hate duet infinitely.

The point is that hate's searing flame coexists with love's soothing flow; the hate that pushes us apart lives inside us right along with the love that pulls us together. Indeed, we can hate most painfully the people we love most passionately.

Hate eventually needs healing. Passive or aggressive, hate is a malignancy; it is dangerous—deadly, if allowed to run its course. Nothing good comes from a hate that has a person in its sights; and it surely hurts the hater more than it hurts the hated.

We must not confuse hate with anger. It is hate and not anger that needs healing.

Anger is a sign that we are alive and well. Hate is a sign that we are sick and need to be healed.

Healthy anger drives us to do something to change what makes us angry; anger can energize us to make things better. Hate does not want to change things for the better; it wants to make things worse. Hate wants

39

to belch the foul breath of death over a life that love alone creates.

Let me point out some things about hate that make it such a hard sickness to cure.

IT IS PEOPLE, NOT MERELY EVIL, THAT WE HATE

It is said that we are supposed to "hate the sin and love the sinner." If we manage to do this, our hate can be creative. But I must admit that I do not easily find the power to do this—the evil I hate wants to stick to the person I hate the way skin sticks to the body, and I can seldom tear them apart.

So I am not talking about hating cruelty; I am talking about hating cruel *people*. I am not talking about hating treachery; I am talking about hating *traitors*.

If David betrays me, and I hate him for hurting me, it is because my mind cannot separate his action from his person. He and his broken promise are one reality, stuck together within my hurting soul.

This is the pain, this person-directed hate; it is not health, it is not strength, it is the soul's sickness.

None of us wants to admit that we hate someone. It makes us feel mean and malicious. So we deny our hatred. We hide it from ourselves. Hate is too ugly for us; we cannot admit that we have a bucket full or even a spoonful of it in our system. We deny, we disguise, and we suppress the real hate that ferments in our souls.

But we do hate people. Only an unearthly saint or an unfeeling oaf gets far in life without hating someone, sometime—passively, at least, and now and then with the bursting belligerence of aggressive malice.

When we deny our hate we detour around the crisis of forgiveness. We suppress our spite, make adjustments, and make believe we are too good to be hateful. But the truth is that we do not dare to risk admitting the hate we feel because we do not dare to risk forgiving the person we hate.

We make believe we are at peace while the furies rage within, beneath the surface. There, hidden and suppressed, our hate opens the subterranean faucets of venom that will eventually infect all our relationships in ways we cannot predict. Hate left to itself, denied and hidden, leaves us in a cold hell behind insulated masks of warm conviviality. Hate, admitted and felt, compels us to make a decision about the healing miracle of forgiving.

Why worry about it? Why fret so much that decent people hate people who do them wrong?

The reason is that hate focused on people is very hard to heal. When we only hate the wrongness of a thing, our hate dies when the wrong we hate is righted. But when we hate people who do us wrong, our hate stays alive long after the wrong they did is dead and gone, the way the ashen smell of charred lumber lingers with a burned building long after the fire is out.

We attach our feelings to the moment when we were hurt, endowing it with immortality. And we let it assault us every time it comes to mind. It travels with us, sleeps with us, hovers over us while we make love, and broods over us while we die. Our hate does not even have the decency to die when those we hate die—for it is a parasite sucking *our* blood, not theirs.

There is only one remedy for it.

WE MOST OFTEN AIM OUR HATRED AT PEOPLE WHO LIVE WITHIN THE CIRCLE OF OUR COMMITTED LOVE

We usually hate someone who is close to us—close enough to love. We hate the person we trusted to be on our side, the person we expected to be loyal, the person we trusted to keep a promise.

We do not usually hate strangers. We get angry at strangers. At baseball games I have raged at the cross-eyed umpire and gotten mad at the loud drunk sitting near me. But I have never hated an umpire I didn't know personally, or a drunk I never saw again. The only time we really hate strangers is when they get close enough to violate us intimately.

Hate for people within our circle of committed love is the most virulent kind. It does not affect us so much

41

when we hate a person who never promised to be with us, never walked with us on our private paths, never played the strings of our soul. But when a person destroys what our commitment and our intimacy created, something precious is destroyed. Hate for people we love makes us sick.

The virus resists every antibody save one.

WE HATE PEOPLE WE BLAME

Whenever I hate someone I pronounce that person guilty of hurt in the first degree, and I hold that person responsible for hurting me personally—I blame them. I refuse to excuse Howard's brutality on the grounds of his own brutal childhood. I cannot suspend judgment on Jean's unfaithfulness on grounds that she is only a hapless victim of torrid hormones. If they have hurt me, I feel hatred for them.

Unless we are a little crazy, we hate only the people we blame for doing us wrong.

Our hatred is a compliment, in a strange sort of way. The hated person is set apart from other creatures and honored as a free person. Our hate tells us that this person has a will and he used this will to do us harm.

When we hate a person who deserves our hate we feel very righteous in our hating. The jerk has it coming. What we feel is precisely what we ought to feel. Heaven and earth would shake if we did not hate the person who meant to do us harm.

Holy hatred is the toughest kind of all to cure. Only one remedy is worth prescribing. But it comes hard. And the longer we hate, the harder it is to heal us.

I recall Michael Christopher's play *The Black Angel*, where he tells the story of Herman Engel. Engel, a German general in World War II, was sentenced by the Nuremberg Court to thirty years in prison for atrocities committed by his army. He survived his sentence and was released from prison. At the time of the play he is in Alsace, building a cabin in the woods where he and his wife intend to live out the years left to them—incognito, forgotten, at peace.

But a man named Morrieaux, a French journalist, is waiting in the wings.

Morrieaux's whole family had been massacred by Engel's army during the war. When the Nuremberg court had refused to sentence Engel to death thirty years before, Morrieaux privately condemned Engel to die. His condemnation was kept alive and hot by the fire of hate he kept kindling in his heart. Now the time had come.

Morrieaux had stoked up the fanatics in the village close by Engel's cabin. That very night, they were going to come up the hill, burn down the cabin, and shoot Engel and his wife dead.

Morrieaux, however, wanted to get to Engel beforehand. Some gaps in Engel's history plagued the reporter's need for a finished story. So he went up the hill, introduced himself to a shaken Engel, and spent the afternoon grilling the former general about the village massacre that lay like a forgotten shadow in Engel's past.

But Engel's feeble humanity—he seemed less like a monster than just a tired old man—confused Morrieaux. Besides, he was having a hard time putting all the pieces of the terrible story together; and so he was plagued by newborn doubt. His vengeance was blurred; the purity of his hate was contaminated.

Toward the end of the afternoon, as the sun fell deep and the woods became a cavern, Morrieaux blurted out to Engel that the villagers were going to come and kill him that night. He offered to lead Engel out of the woods and save his life.

But the afternoon's inquisition had brought other kinds of doubts into Engel's soul. Engel paused, eyes fixed on a cone just fallen from a black pine: "I'll go with you," he slowly said, "on one condition." What? Is he mad? Does he lay down a condition for having his own life saved? What condition?

"That you forgive me."

Forgive? Morrieaux had exterminated Engel a thousand exquisite ways in the fantasies of hate that he had played in his mind for thirty years. But face to face with the ambiguity of Engel's humanity, Morrieaux's vengeance was unsettled. He would save the man's life. Yes, he would cancel the execution.

But forgive him? Never.

That night, the enraged villagers came with sacks over their heads, burned the cabin, and shot Engel and his wife dead.

Now I ask, why was it that Morrieaux could not forgive Engel? Why was forgiving even harder than saving Engel's life?

It was too much for Morrieaux, I think, because his hatred had become a passion too long lodged in his soul. Morrieaux could not live, could no longer be the person he was without his hatred; he had *become* his hatred. His hate did not belong to him, he belonged to his hate. He would not know who he was if he did not hate Engel.

The tragedy was that only forgiveness, the one thing he could not give to Engel, could have set Morrieaux free.

Hate can be fatal when we let it grow to enormous size inside of us. The best of people can get their bellies full of it. And it is just as real whether it involves a nasty little scene between friends or a question of international immorality.

Sometimes hate only nibbles at the edges of the heart; it does not always burn out the lining of the soul. Sometimes it only asks that the hated person keep away from us for a while; it does not always go for the jugular.

But whether your hate is a carcinoma growing hell-bent for death inside your soul, or only a pesty heartburn, it will hurt you if you do not use the right remedy. Your healing may take heroic surgery of the soul. Then again, you may get by with a quick cauterization. But eventually, unchecked hate will do you in.

Such hate *can* be healed, however, and it is to the healing that I invite you next.

CHAPTER 3

We Heal Ourselves

We are ready to take our first step inside the healing heart. Pull your mind away from the person who needs to be forgiven; do not ask yet what happens to the forgiven wrongdoer. Look only at the wounded forgiver. Think only of Fouke and his "magic eyes." Never mind Hilda for the time being.

When you forgive someone for hurting you, you perform spiritual surgery inside your soul; you cut away the wrong that was done to you so that you can see your "enemy" through the magic eyes that can heal your soul. Detach that person from the hurt and let it go, the way a child opens his hands and lets a trapped butterfly go free.

Then invite that person back into your mind, fresh, as if a piece of history between you had been rewritten, its grip on your memory broken. Reverse the seemingly irreversible flow of pain within you.

The first gift we get is a new *insight*.

As we forgive people, we gradually come to see the deeper truth about them, a truth our hate blinds us to, a truth we can see only when we separate them from what they did to us. When we heal our memories we are not playing games, we are not making believe. We see the truth again. For the truth about those who hurt us is that they are weak, needy, and fallible human beings. They were people before they hurt us and they are people after they hurt us. They were needy and weak before they hurt us and they were weak and needy after they hurt us. They needed our help, our support, our comfort before they did us wrong; and they need it still. They are not *only* people who hurt us; this is not the deepest truth about them. Our hate wants to cloak them, top to bottom, only in the rags of their rotten deed. But the magic eyes of forgiving look beneath the tattered rags and let us see the truth.

New insight brings *new feeling*.

When forgiving lets us see the truth about our enemies, it gives us a new feeling toward them.

When we talk of feeling, the word "irrelevance" may help. When you forgive me, for example, the wrong I did to you becomes irrelevant to how you feel about me now. It does not matter, does not count, has no bearing, cannot be figured into your attitude toward me, the person you hated until now. The pain I once caused you has no connection with how you feel toward me now.

Of course, we cannot pry the wrongdoer loose from the wrong; we can only release the person within our *memory* of the wrong. If we can peel the wrong away within our forgiver's memory, we can see the person who really lives beneath the cloak of the wrongdoing.

Forgiving, then, is a new vision and a new feeling that is given to the person who forgives.

The Bible talks the same way when it describes how God forgives. In the ancient drama of atonement, God took a bundle of human sins off a man's back and tied it to a goat. He gave the goat a kick in the rear and sent it off, sin and all—a scapegoat—to a "solitary land," leaving the sinner free of his burden. Or, as the poet of the Psalms put it, he wipes our sin away, as a mother washes grime from a child's dirty face; he removes it from us as the East is removed from the West, and "ne'er the twain shall meet."

A scapegoat? A washed face? It is poetic language for what God does *within his own mind*. He changes his memory; what we once *did* is irrelevant to how he *feels* about what we *are*.

It is like that when *we* first forgive someone. When you forgive your friend Linda, you may be the only person healed. You do not have power to woo Linda back into your life. She is out of your control. It could be that she does not give a fig for your forgiveness; maybe she would prefer your hate, maybe your hate for her justifies her hate for you. So when you forgive you must often be content with the editing of your own memory. It is the editing of your memory that is your salvation.

If you cannot free people from their wrongs and see them as the needy people they are, you enslave yourself to your own painful past, and by fastening yourself to the past, you let your hate become your future. You can reverse your future only by releasing other people from their pasts.

Forgiving is an *honest* release even though it is done invisibly, within the forgiver's heart. It is honest because it happens along with honest judgment, honest pain, and honest hate. True forgivers do not pretend they don't suffer. They do not pretend the wrong does not matter much. Magic eyes are open eyes.

How can you tell when it happens?

If the first stage of healing is release, and if release happens in your vision of the person who hurt you, is there an early sign that your healing has begun? Is there a clear symptom of the onset of forgiveness?

You will know that forgiveness has begun *when you recall those who hurt you and feel the power to wish them well*.

Forgiveness is love's antidote for hate, beginning with passive hate, the loss of energy to wish people well. So, when we feel the slightest urge to wish that life would go well for them, we have begun to forgive; we have started to release those who hurt us from the blight of the harm they did to us.

This sign of the healing stage of forgiving was made clear to me as I talked with my friend Myra Broger about forgiving her former husband.

Myra is a beautiful woman, an actress, who was

47

almost killed by a hit-and-run driver a few years ago. She was left crippled, but still gorgeous and luminous. Her husband, a TV and film star, stayed with her only until she recovered from the accident. Then, coldly and quickly, he took off and left her alone.

I asked Myra if she had been able to forgive him. She said she thought so. I asked her what made her think so. "I find myself wishing him well," she said. I bore down. "Suppose you learned today that he had married a sexy young starlet, could you pray that he would be happy with her?" I expected her to bristle at my pushy insensitivity. But she responded almost casually, "Yes, I could and I would. Steve needs love very much, and I want him to have it."

I was skeptical. She sounded far too simple and sweet. But I came to know that her forgiveness was genuine, and that she was living within the free flow of a healed memory. She really did wish him well!

A modest beginning, to be sure. Not yet an Olympic plunge into a new relationship. I do not know whether her magic eyes make any difference in the life of her former husband, but they make all the difference in the world to Myra's life. The hate is gone; and when the mortar of hate goes, the wall eventually crumbles.

The act of forgiving, at this stage, has not achieved its climax. It is not yet the embrace of two people simultaneously released from the grip of a painful past.

Many profound thinkers do not want the healing of the memory—short of climax—to count as forgiveness. Take the late American theologian Paul Tillich, for instance; he says that "genuine forgiveness is participation, reunion overcoming the power of estrangement." In Tillich's opinion forgiving does not really happen unless people are brought together in a renewed relationship—close, intimate, mutually accepting. Forgiveness completed, fulfilled in the coming together of two people, is the only genuine article.

I think Tillich was wrong; I think we can have reality even if we do not have the whole of it. We can have a great experience climbing a mountain even if we never reach the peak.

Sex can be good—if not all we want—even if orgasm escapes us; forgiving can be real even though the person we forgive is out of our reach. We need not deny ourselves the healing of incomplete forgiving; we can forgive and be free in our own memories.

But forgiving does create a momentum that, left unbraked, can carry a healed person back to the one who wounded him.

Let us move on to the next stage, then, the new beginning, the place where we who are separated come together again.

CHAPTER 4

We Come Together

I have always liked the way Scottish theologian H. R. MacIntosh talked about forgiveness. Forgiveness, he said, "is an active process of the mind and temper of a wronged person, by means of which he abolishes a moral hindrance to fellowship with the wrongdoer, and reestablishes the freedom and happiness of friendship."

Abolishing the "moral hindrance to fellowship"— this is the key to complete forgiving.

Remember that it is what people *do* to us that creates the "hindrance" to our getting together, really together, in spirit as well as in space. When people hurt us unfairly and deeply, the *wrong* they do comes between us. They make us feel wronged in a way we cannot easily brush aside. And we know in our heart of hearts that things will never be right between us if we ignore the *wrong* that separates us.

If we ignore the "moral hindrance" as if it did not really matter, we take our first step into an opiated life where nobody really gives a damn.

It is not a matter of our being too touchy; we are not overloading on peevishness and pique. We are only holding on to respect for what we are and for what has to be right between us if the two of us are going to have honest love between us.

Only the magic eyes can take away the "moral hindrance" in the heart and mind of the forgiver.

Now let's say that your magic eyes have done their healing work in your mind and heart. You have emptied out your hate and doused your lust for getting even. You no longer need the sour satisfaction of revenge.

But what will it take to *"reestablish the freedom and happiness of friendship"*?

Both parties—the wronged and the wrongdoers—must bring about an honest coming together. Magic eyes cannot do this part alone.

You hold out your hand to those who did you wrong, and you say: "Come on back to me, I want to be your friend again."

But when they take your hand and cross over the invisible wall that their wrong and your hate built between you, they need to carry something with them as the price of their ticket to your second journey together.

If they cannot or will not pay their fare, you will have to settle for your own healing, your private freedom from hate, your own inner peace.

What must they bring?

They must bring truthfulness. Without truthfulness, your reunion is humbug, your coming together is false. With truthfulness, you can make an honest new beginning.

But what is truthfulness?

Truthfulness is a state of mind; it has to do with your real intentions. You must want your words to carry your real intentions. What you say must vibrate with what you feel in your heart. Harmony between the message you give to the outside world and the feelings you keep on the inside.

But there is one thing more about truthfulness, just one thing. You must at least try to bring both your heart and your words in tune with reality.

This is the truthfulness those you forgive must bring with them as their entrée back into your life.

To be specific, you must expect those who hurt you

to be honestly in touch with the reality of your falling-out, your pain, and their responsibility for them.

FOR ONE THING, THEY MUST TRULY UNDERSTAND THE REALITY OF WHAT THEY DID TO HURT YOU

They need to *know* that the pain you suffered at their hands was unfair to you. You did not deserve to feel the hurt; no matter what was meant by it, you suffered what you should not have had to suffer.

They also need to know that the hurt they caused you went *deep*. Deep enough for you to feel that you could not go on as before unless something happened to remove it. They may be dumbfounded that their little lance could have sliced so close to your heart. Never mind. People are always surprised at how much their "little" faults can hurt other people. The point is that you felt it so deeply that you could not let them come near you and share what was left of your heart in the same way it was shared before. And they must, with their mind, feelings, and words, reflect the truth of your hurt.

You cannot expect them to agree with you about every little detail. No two people in the history of personal misunderstandings have ever remembered their painful experience in the same colors and the same sequences, because no two people have experienced the same hurt in precisely the same way. So, if you want total recall, blow for blow, insult for insult, hurt for hurt, you will never get what you need.

But they must be truthful about what happened in the eye of the storm of your sad falling-out. And you need to believe that they are truthful before you can let them all the way back into your life.

THEY MUST BE TRUTHFUL WITH THE FEELINGS YOU HAVE FELT

To be truthful with your feelings, they must *feel* the hurt that you feel. What they know intellectually must percolate to the bottom of their heart. It is not enough to admit that they hurt you; they must feel the very hurt they hurt you with. Their feelings need to be one with your feelings.

How can they feel your pain? They can feel your pain as it echoes deep within them. You felt their disloyalty as an unfair cut that made you hate them enough to turn them into partial strangers. Now they must feel as if their *real* selves are strangers to the persons they were when they hurt you; they must hate themselves for what they did to you.

Their pain and your pain create the point and counterpoint for the rhythm of reconciliation. When the beat of their pain is a response to the beat of yours, they have become truthful in their feelings. Their feelings are moving to the tempo of your feelings. They have moved a step closer to a truthful reunion.

THEY MUST BE TRUTHFUL IN LISTENING TO YOU

They cannot give you truthfulness in their words alone. The truthfulness of a soliloquy is never enough to reunite two people. So, in your coming together, their honesty must be born in listening. The price of their ticket into your life is an open ear; an open mouth gets them only half way.

They must listen to you until they *hear* your claims and your complaints and your cries. At first they will filter your message through the screen of their own desires and fears. They will want to reshape every little syllable you speak until it suits the message they want to hear you speak. So you must make sure they have listened long enough.

And you must also listen to their response, to make sure that they really did hear you. You must lure them into a response, several times over, seduce them into many repetitions, until you can be sure that they are truly hearing you, and hearing your needs as you reveal them. This is the only way you can know they are being truthful.

53

THEY OUGHT TO BE TRUTHFUL ABOUT YOUR FUTURE TOGETHER

For two people who are coming together again after a falling-out, truthfulness requires a promise made and a promise meant to be kept. Those who hurt you must return to you with a promise that they will not hurt you again; and you need to believe that they intend to keep the promise they make.

They promise to be there for you in the future, when you need them, to be there in a style that lives up to the kind of relationship you have together.

You should not ask for a lot more; but you should ask for no less. They cannot offer you a guarantee; they cannot be depended on the way you might rely on a computer or a well-trained dog. They are ordinary, fallible human beings; they are not God. You lay a bet on them; you need to take a risk. But if they are truthful, they *intend* to keep their promise. And their honest intentions tilt the odds in their favor.

You don't have to have total truthfulness before you can *begin* to forgive them. The forgiving you do to heal the wounds in your memory has no strings attached; it is your free act of grace, done for yourself within the innermost cells of your soul. The demand of truthfulness is for the *fulfillment* and *climax* of your forgiving, the coming together again of two people who once belonged to each other and were separated from each other in their spirits.

We have been speaking of the requirements for reconciliation. Now we can shift our focus and talk about the *realistic limits* of every coming together.

We come together within the unrelenting boundaries of our time and of our circumstances.

Time shapes all our reunions with a mastery that not even the miracle of free forgiveness can loosen. We cannot turn our calendars back to a happier day. Time does not let us come together as if nothing had happened between our falling-out and our forgiving. We change personally, and we take on new roles; we cannot simply abandon our new places in life the moment a friend is forgiven and invited back into our lives.

If you have forgiven another person and want that person back in your life, you must be realistic enough to ask this question: What has happened to each of us between our falling-out and our forgiving?

Sometimes, I know, the time has been mercifully brief and our roles unchanged. A woman forgives her husband for his blundering infidelity. He wants terribly to come home to her; he has languished in the loneliness of his true love's unsatisfied needs. She opens her arms. Chances are he will sail back to her on the frenzied winds of recharged eros. Their coming together may be a sexual crescendo, ecstatic, enough to make them both playfully grateful for the separation that rekindled their stormy hankering after each other.

Not always so. Maybe she has forgiven her husband a hundred times for putting her down in the presence of handsome young women. She forgives him and takes him back again, not with a voluptuous bedding down, but with a muted sigh that whispers nothing more seductive than, "Well, let's get on with it then." But they do get on, and they bind their lives together with the invisible thread of loyalty, strong enough at least for a new beginning. Not a rapturous embrace; but better, no doubt, when all is said and done, than staying strangers separated by hate.

Sometimes, given the way things have stacked up since the falling-out, you have to do with a very limited sort of reconciliation. My friend's husband wronged her so badly that she found no way to go on with him. They had a spiteful divorce, and afterward she hated him lavishly for leaving her out in the cold while he found warm love nestled in the lap of a woman twenty years younger. But that was four years ago, and she has since forgiven him; she released him as she let her hate go away, and as she was able to see him for the needy person he really was. So she invited him back into her life. But he could not come far.

He has been married for three years, to the woman

he loved too much while he was still married to my friend. So their coming together will have to leave them at a distance. He can be a friendly *former* husband, and she will wish him well with the woman she hated him so much for loving. Maybe they will talk on the telephone and trade stories about the kids; maybe the children will get them together for an hour on Christmas Eve.

We cannot breathe back all the old life; we forgive and reunite on the terms that time and circumstance make available to us.

I know a splendid woman who is struggling to forgive her father and wants some sort of reconciliation with him. Her father is a fundamentalist preacher who knows right from wrong in every nook and cranny of everyone else's life. He proclaims the judgment of an angry Almighty for every infraction of any of his rules; his ways are very narrow and his gates very straight. Nonetheless, he sexually abused my friend when she was a little girl, convincing her that a father who lived close to God could do no wrong. She left home at seventeen to get away from him and swore she never wanted to be near him again.

Now, after fifteen years of alienation, she is freed from her hate, and wants him to be her father again. But she knows she cannot take him back into her life as a little girl welcomes her daddy home. She cannot be a child to him again.

Their roles will be reversed; she may have to take care of him and let him be a child to her. In any case, she cannot have her deepest wish—to crawl back into his lap, resting in his strong arms, finding the loving care he once betrayed by twisting love into cruel abuse. If it is possible for them to come together again at all, she knows it will have to be a reunion that cannot give back her lost childhood.

Here is a sad little story that is heard more and more these days. Jack and Jan were more than good friends once, but Jack was married and Jan was not. The sexual part of their friendship eventually destroyed the rest of their friendship altogether. Jack made promises he could not keep and then cut the knot quickly, crudely, cruelly, leaving Jan very empty. She filled the void with hate. She was badly wounded, and for two years raged against Jack for using her. Then ever so gradually, and to her own surprise, she forgave him. She was healed.

But she could not bring Jack back to their true love of three years before. Their reunion, honest as it is, must be long-distance—letters, a Christmas card, a conversation on a busy corner, concern for each other's well being, no more. Reunion within the bounds of reality.

We practice love's high art framed and fringed by the boundaries of time and place. We heal the wounds of our painful pasts, but the healing is limited by things that have happened to us during the time since our falling-out began. We make our new beginnings, not where we used to be or where we wish we could be, but only where we are and with what we have at hand.

Accepting limits is its own kind of honesty. Wine out of water, OK—but, please, not out of Elmer's glue! New beginnings must fit within the arena of one's own circumstances. The only day we ever have to forgive each other in is *this* one, the day we have at hand; and with the options we have on this particular day we must make our new starts on the adventure of reconciliation.

We start over, too, in the semidarkness of partial understanding. We will probably never understand why we were hurt. But forgiving is not *having* to understand. Understanding may come later, in fragments, an insight here and a glimpse there, *after* forgiving. But we are asking too much if we want to understand everything at the beginning.

You must start over again in your mysteries. He is a mystery to you. And you want to be a mystery to him.

There is a lot more to you than meets his eyes, he must know that. So you can share each other's private demons and secret angels, and leave yourselves room for wonder at one another. As long as you are ready to move on with him without first unraveling his mystery, your shared mysteries can unfold as you go.

CHAPTER 5

Some Nice Things Forgiving Is Not

When you forgive the person who hurt you deeply and unfairly, you perform a miracle that has no equal. Nothing else is the same. Forgiving has its own feel and its own color and its own climax, different from any other creative act in the repertoire of human relationships.

Forgiving gets its unique beauty from the healing it brings to the saddest of all the pains. We need to do it at all only because we live in a world in which human love can be fractured by unfair suffering. It has something in common, in this respect, with the beauty of artful surgery. But precisely for this reason, as the healing of wounds left open from our painful pasts, we should not let it slip into a sloppy blend of several other nice things people can do for each other in unpleasant situations. We need to develop a fine taste for the distinctive quality of the forgiving art.

So let us go on from here and test our sense for the subtle difference between the miracle of forgiving and other things we need to do in order to get along well together in our unfair world.

FORGIVING IS NOT FORGETTING

When we forgive someone, we do not forget the hurtful act, as if forgetting came along with the forgiveness package, the way strings come with a violin.

Begin with basics. If you forget, you will not forgive at all. You can never forgive people for things you have forgotten about. You need to forgive precisely because you have not forgotten what someone did; your memory keeps the pain alive long after the actual hurt has stopped. Remembering is your storage of pain. It is *why* you need to be healed in the first place.

Forgetting, in fact, may be a dangerous way to escape the inner surgery of the heart that we call forgiving. There are two kinds of pain that we forget. We forget hurts too trivial to bother about. We forget pains too horrible for our memory to manage.

We don't remember every trivial hurt, thank God, not *all* the bruises we have felt from people along the way; if it doesn't go deep, we let it heal itself and we forget. An old friend came to me not long ago to ask me to forgive him for something he did to me that I could not remember, not even when he tried to stir my recollection. He needed to be forgiven, he said. I persuaded him that I felt for his needs, and that I would be his friend just as if he had never told me, but that I could not forgive him. If he had brought back old pain by bringing back my memory, I should have forgiven him. But as it was I could not really forgive him; I could only love him and by loving him heal the separation that he felt, though I did not.

The pains we *dare* not remember are the most dangerous pains of all. We fear to face some horrible thing that once hurt us, and we stuff it into the black holes of our unconsciousness where we suppose it cannot hurt us. But it only comes back disguised; it is like a demon wearing an angel's face. It lays low for a while only to slug us later, on the sly.

Forgetting can be Russian roulette, the same sort of game a woman plays when she "forgets" the little lump she felt on her breast a month ago.

Enough, then, to light up a warning sign: never mistake forgetting for forgiving.

Once we *have* forgiven, however, we get a new

freedom to forget. This time forgetting is a sign of health; it is not a trick to avoid spiritual surgery. We *can* forget *because* we have been healed.

But even if it is *easier* to forget after we forgive, we should not make forgetting a *test* of our forgiving. The test of forgiving lies with healing the lingering pain of the past, not with forgetting that the past ever happened.

True, the Bible says that God promises to forgive us *and* forget. Jeremiah speaks for God: "I will forgive their sins, and will remember their sins no more." But does he forget the way we forget when we can't remember where we left our keys? Of course not. God does not have amnesia; to say that God forgets is to say that he *feels* about us the way he *would* feel if he *had* forgotten.

We are the same. Can you stop your memory on a dime, put it in reverse, and spin it in another direction the way you can reverse direction on a tape recorder? We cannot forget on command. So we just have to let the forgetting happen as it will; we shouldn't rush it, and we certainly should not doubt the genuineness of our forgiving if we happen to remember.

The really important thing is that we have the power to forgive what we still do remember.

I will say more about forgetting later on, and about a healing way to remember bad things. But enough for now: forgiving and forgetting are not the same.

EXCUSING IS NOT FORGIVING

Excusing is just the opposite of forgiving. We excuse people when we understand that they were not to blame. Maybe the devil made them do it. Maybe there were extenuating circumstances. They were not to blame. So why should we forgive them? We forgive people for things we blame them for.

We excuse people because we understand why they

had to do what they did. A French proverb says, "To understand all is to forgive all." But this is not quite right. We only *excuse* all if we understand all.

It takes no saving grace to excuse someone. All excusing takes is a little insight.

We all need a lot of excusing. All of us are what we are partly because of what other people have made of us—our parents, our teachers, our ancestors.

We were dealt a hand of cards when we were born, and we have had to play our game with those cards. Some of our cards were strong; we were blessed. But there were some jokers in the hand as well. Surely we do not need to be forgiven for the weak cards that were in the hand that was dealt to us, cards we did not ask for and have never wanted. All we can be blamed— and forgiven—for is how we played the hand we were dealt.

Think of the reasons you could submit to show someone that you were not to blame for the rotten thing you did.

Your genetics. An X got where a Y was supposed to be in your chromosomic building blocks; your genetic structure is shaky. The fault lies in your DNA. You do not need forgiving; you need to be re-engineered!

Your psychic conditioning. You had a crazy upbringing; your father was passive-aggressive and your mother was manic-depressive. Together, they made you what you are today. You do not need forgiving, what you need is therapy.

Your culture. Your culture made you what you are. You were conditioned to do whatever in your culture gave you pleasure and to avoid whatever in your culture caused you pain. We do not have to forgive you for anything; if we want to help, we can change the culture that made you.

You see, there is no grace needed. All it takes is a little savvy about how human beings work.

But when you finally say, "There is no explaining what they did," we have, at that moment, admitted the mystery of their free choice and we have come to where the crisis of forgiving lies.

Sometimes, frankly, the difference is a matter of very delicate shading. Frank Kooster and Leo Sedman come floating out of my boyhood to show how subtle the difference between excusing and forgiving can sometimes be.

First, Frank. One summer in Michigan I was picking cherries from one of those tall, rickety stepladders that get you high enough to reach the top branches of a cherry tree. A few trees away, I could hear Frank Kooster saying terrible things about me to a stranger. He couldn't see me, but I heard it all; and I felt as though I had died.

Frank had become my special friend. Every summer, when I was ten or so, my mother took me to visit some old friends of hers, people she had known back in the old country, who lived on a farm about fifteen miles up a gravel road from our house in Muskegon, Michigan. Three days on that farm were our summer's vacation. They were my idyll, the more so as I got to the age when farm boys did men's work.

When it actually came to doing the jobs, though, I was badly miscast, badly enough to make a farmer thank the Almighty he had no son with my lack of aptitude. I really did fail farming.

But Frank, a real farmer's farm boy, embraced me and took me in. I felt like an insider with Frank; we had sat on the ample seat of a tractor for hours in the fields, had walked on the same path as we flanked the cows coming in for milking, had pitched new mown hay side by side. I felt we were bonded by our hours of silence in the sun, by the secrets of the soil we shared, the nest of baby rabbits we almost plowed under but skirted around instead because Frank had an eye for the slightest variation in the ground's make-up, the bucket of baloney sandwiches we ate together for lunch in the shadow of a MacIntosh apple tree at ten in the morning. Oh yes, we were bonded all right.

That day in the orchard he was picking cherries too, with a farmer friend his own age, a few trees from where I was picking, hidden from view, but not out of earshot.

He was gossiping about his parents' friends from the city—us. I heard it all. Pete and Wes, my brothers, were fine, good guys. But Lewis is good for nothing, he said. "He wouldn't know enough to come in out of the rain if it was hailing coconuts. He's worthless."

Me? Yes, Frank was bad-mouthing *me*. The one person, above all others in the world, I wanted to like me was telling a stranger that I was a bust, a fizzle, a wash-out, a piece of wasted creation. I felt stabbed.

Yet, as I remember the moment now, I find myself excusing Frank for making me feel outcast. He was only sizing up reality as he saw it, through the only lenses he had available to him—the lenses of a farmer. He was not interested in the possibility that I might survive as a traveling salesman, or a jazz singer, or maybe a preacher. He judged me as a farmer, the way a baseball scout sizes up the potential of a bush-league third baseman. Who cares if the guy can do calculus if he can't hit a curve ball?

So, Frank is excused; he is almost blameless in my eyes.

Leo Sedman is different; he needs to be forgiven. Leo was the coach of the Muskegon High School football team, the Big Reds, when I was a skinny kid trying to run through the obstacle course of what they smirkingly called physical education.

What did they care if a kid was ashamed to show his skinniness in the locker room? I hated my body. I hated the bony bumps where other kids were smooth and round. More than anything else, I hated the hip bones, the pointed nubs that jutted from my sides like swords sticking out from twin scabbards beneath the flesh.

The moment of painful truth came to me at the end of every gym period, when the curtain went up on my side-bones. Shower time! Twice each week, my side-bones were flung on center stage in the boys' locker room! Every kid in the class would look at the bones and—I knew it in my heart—would laugh inside and be glad he was not made like me.

So I cheated. I would get undressed, open my locker door, fiddle with it, and wrap a towel around the hip bones. I would shuffle, cagey, over toward the showers, hang around just outside them for a minute or two, whistling, eyes on the locker room door, just in case the coach walked through, with the towel casually draped over the bones. Then I would amble back over to my locker, unshowered, and sneak my clothes back on over my sweaty body.

Mostly I got away with it.

One day big Leo caught me; he waddled right up to my locker, the very head coach of the Big Reds, standing right alongside me. Leo was big, really big; hipbones cushioned under three layers of the most beautiful fat a toothpick kid could covet. He must have weighed 300 pounds. And there he was, looking me over, hard-eyed, tight-lipped, tough. He had been watching me, he bawled. Well I had better believe him, buddy boy, that I was not going to get away with it. He would teach me not to cheat on the shower. Off with my clothes, and into the shower, while everybody gawked.

A crowd of kids came around, like a bunch of people at a curb where a man lies bleeding. They were all looking at me, grinning, waiting for me to bleed and die. Good show.

Leo knew what he was doing. He was out to hurt a kid who was ashamed of his body. He was a college graduate, trained in the human behavior of skinny kids, six feet tall. Somebody could put up a case for him, I suppose; maybe a fat man needs to be reassured that fat is nicer than skinny. But I think he knew what he was doing. And I cannot excuse him.

You were guilty, Leo Sedman, and I hated you. Boy, did I hate you. All I can do with you is forgive you.

Forgiving is tough. Excusing is easy. What a mistake it is to confuse forgiving with being mushy, soft, gutless, and oh, so understanding. Before we forgive, we stiffen our spine and we hold a person accountable. And only then, in tough-minded judgment, can we do the outrageously impossible thing: we can forgive.

FORGIVING IS NOT THE SAME AS SMOTHERING CONFLICT

Some people hinder the hard work of forgiving by smothering confrontation. When they are in charge of the shop, they never let people heal conflict through forgiving; they stage-manage conflict so that people never get a chance to forgive.

Some parents are dedicated to smothering conflict. They shush us and soothe us and assure us that whatever makes us mad is not worth raising a fuss about. They get between us and the rotten kid who did us wrong, always protecting, always pinning down the arms of our rage, forever pacifying. Their "now thens" and "there, theres" keep us from ever unloading our anger and from ever forgiving. They say, "Forgive and forget," but what they mean is: "Don't make a fuss, I can't stand the noise."

Ministers tend to be compulsive managers of conflict. The church needs controversy no more than Arkansas needs a tornado. So if the vestryman's wife is involved in hanky-panky with the organist, and somebody threatens to blow the lid, smother it, keep it out of sight until we can get the mess swept under the rug of churchy discretion. If a deacon is put down by the chairman of the board and wants to thrash it out at the next meeting, smother it, get the deacon to see that nobody will like him if he raises a hullabaloo. We must have no confrontation.

There is a lot to be said for managing conflict. Goodness knows not many of us are good at it. My meager message here is only that we should not confuse the technique of smoothing things over with the high art of forgiving those who transgress against us. Quieting troubled waters is not the same as rescuing drowning people, and smothering conflict is not the same as helping people to forgive each other.

ACCEPTING PEOPLE IS NOT FORGIVING THEM

We accept each other *because* we *are* acceptable *in spite of* blemishes that sometimes make it hard. People come to us with a cluster of unacceptable qualities; but we accept them as our friends anyway. We spot fine people slouching behind a brush of disagreeable traits. So we accept them *because* of what they are, or can be, to us—in spite of what we have to get through to find them.

Accepting a person can feel a lot like forgiving. But it is not the same.

The difference between accepting and forgiving is very simple. We accept people *because of the good people they are for us*. We forgive people *for the bad things they did to us*. We accept people for the good they *are*, and we forgive them for the bad they *did*.

It will help us see the difference if we look at three ways we have of accepting people. First, *social* acceptance. Second, *professional* acceptance. And, third and most difficult, *personal* acceptance.

We accept people *socially* when we embrace them inside of our community. Some of their customs may be odd and distasteful to us. Their lifestyle may stick in our craw. We may not take to their ways at all. But we accept them, not necessarily as people we want as friends, but as people whom we reckon deserve a place of respect within our group.

We accept them socially because they qualify socially. We have no call to forgive them for anything; they have not hurt us unfairly. We just accept them within our group even though there may be things about them that we do not much like personally.

We accept people *professionally* because we need to accept them in order to help them. The really nifty people-accepters are our friendly therapists. We can spill all our beans to them without having to worry that they will throw us out. "Hmm, you would like to shoot your mother-in-law through the head. Interesting. Oh, you want to sleep with your sister-in-law? Yes, of course, I understand. No, no, I don't think it is terrible for you to want to sleep with her. Do you?"

Our broad-spirited counselors ignore all our oddities, overlook our weird inclinations, and treat us with unconditional regard. They make us feel accepted, unjudged, secure.

But what is happening is *not* forgiveness.

For one thing, we did not hurt *them*. They would need to forgive us if we were trying to seduce their spouse, or if, God forbid, we refused to pay their bill. But, in their *professional* relationship with us, they accept us "in spite of" our neuroses, and they do not confuse this acceptance with forgiving. So much for the technique of accepting people for professional reasons.

We accept people *personally* as our friends or our lovers because they are worth a lot to us in spite of a lot of things about them we would rather do without.

A wife accepts her husband in spite of his odd need to tell dirty jokes in company once he has had a drink or two. And he has to accept her compulsion to hover over him like a mother hen to see that he does not drink too much, or eat too much, or pick his nose in public.

No marriage could last, no friendship survive, no family endure if we could not see each other as people worth accepting beneath our crazy-quilt patterns of kinks and cranks. We accept the people we love partly because we are committed to them, no doubt, but also because, on balance, tolerating their quirky habits is a decent trade-off for the good things they bring to our lives.

When we forgive a person we do more than over-look a blemish for the sake of the beauty behind it. A woman who forgives a lover for betraying her secret knows that when she forgives him she does something very different from what she does when she accepts him in spite of his bad breath.

There is one right word for the amazing moment when we release a person who dug a deep hurt into our lives. The right word for this moment is not acceptance. The right word is forgiveness.

FORGIVING IS NOT TOLERANCE

Forgive me and you heal yourself. Tolerate everything I do and you are in for a lot of trouble.

You can forgive someone almost anything. But you cannot tolerate everything.

Whenever people try to live or work together, they have to decide on the sorts of things they will put up with. The group that puts up with everything eventually kills itself.

Take my friend Joe, a squatty, balding Italian who sold bargain bread out of a tired old store in a nervous neighborhood on the border of blight. We used to buy bread from Joe at half the supermarket price, and kids came from a mile around to buy sweet rolls from him with a good chance of getting a sugar-sprinkled dough-nut thrown in. Joe turned second-day bread into a symbol of a neighborhood trying hard for a second time around.

One afternoon, near closing time, three neighbor-hood kids walked into Joe's store, pulled a gun, cleaned out the cash, and then, for no reason, one of them—a kid named Sam—shot Joe in the stomach. He almost died.

While Joe was in the hospital, the parents of the kid who shot him came to see him. They were decent, devout folks, poor like most people in the neighborhood, and now bent heavy with shame. One night they brought Sam; nobody ever thought they could get him to come.

Joe forgave Sam. He decided he was going to look at Sam as a weak human being who needed a chance instead of as the rotten kid who shot him in his stomach. In fact, he talked with Sam's parents about giving him a chance to earn a little money cleaning out the store.

But Joe never meant to put up with shooting people in the stomach. Nor was his neighborhood ready to tolerate what Sam did.

So when Sam came to trial, Joe was a sad but convincing witness for the prosecution.

Sam spent a year at a juvenile detention center.

Take Pastor Gambit, a man with an enormous appetite for human adoration, especially female, preferably up close, and prone if at all possible. He cultivated quite a knack for parlaying spiritual counseling into erotic campaigns, and before long he had more than a few adoring women singing ecstatic doxologies in response to his secret ministrations. So many, in fact, that he could not keep them all quiet about it. The upshot: Gambit became the center of scandal.

He was charged with ministerial malfeasance in the court of the church.

Some of Gambit's colleagues (who knew that there, but for the grace of God, went they) made a pitch for the court to forgive him, in the style of Jesus, who once turned to a woman guilty of a like sin and said to her: "Neither do I judge you, go and sin no more."

But the kindly clergy were getting forgiving mixed up with tolerance. Gambit needed forgiveness all right, from somebody. But the court's job was not to decide whether Gambit could be forgiven, but whether the church could tolerate what Gambit had done.

Take a different sort of situation, one where no one offends morality, but where a bad judgment threatens efficient procedure.

Dr. Harry Den Best runs an elite surgical team at Atlantic Medical Center where he is head heart surgeon and where the brightest and best young surgeons on the East Coast get their start toward the brilliant career they assume is their birthright. But the limits of tolerance for goofs in Den Best's operating room are so narrow that few students make it through residency at Atlantic without a chronic case of terror.

Some mistakes are tolerable—*once*. Anybody using a tough technique for the first time can fumble. Even a second time, though, they had better come up with a good excuse. A third time? Better start thinking of a residency in Sioux Falls. But there is one error that Den Best does not tolerate even once: an intern or resident surgeon does not initiate a new medical procedure for a Den Best patient without consulting him first.

Dr. Fred Bush, a brilliant but arrogant young resident, was in the unit one night when one of Den Best's patients in intensive care took a turn for the worse about twelve hours out of surgery. Something had to be done, but it was 2 A.M. and Bush knew Den Best had to be in the operating room again at five. Why wake him up? So Bush wheeled the patient back into the O.R., where he, on his own, patched her up brilliantly.

Ten minutes after Den Best arrived at Atlantic that morning, Dr. Bush's career, like Den Best's patient, took a quick turn for the worse. The best hope Bush has now is a secure residency at a general hospital in central Iowa.

Den Best could have personally forgiven Bush; but he could not tolerate what Bush had done. Bush had gone beyond the tolerable even though he was well within the range of the forgivable.

Every group has to decide what it will put up with and what it cannot tolerate. But what we need to remember is this: we don't have to tolerate what people *do* just because we forgive them for doing it.

Forgiving heals us personally. To tolerate everything only hurts us all in the long run.

Let me put together the sum and substance of what I have been saying in this chapter.

You do not *have* to forget after you forgive; you may, but your forgiving can be sincere even if you remember.

You do not excuse people by forgiving them; you forgive them at all only because you hold them to account and refuse to excuse them.

You do not forgive people by smothering conflict; if you forever smother people's differences, you rob them of a chance to forgive.

You do not forgive people merely by accepting them; you forgive people who have *done* something to you that is unacceptable.

You do not have to tolerate what people do when you forgive them for doing it; you may forgive people, but still refuse to tolerate what they have done.

Part 2

FORGIVING PEOPLE WHO ARE
HARD TO FORGIVE

A wonderful woman recently told me how, long ago, some men she never saw and whose names she never knew had done a thing so terrible to her that it changed her life forever. Her story helped me to see how hard some people are to forgive.

She was a dark Armenian beauty, with black eyes that bore into mine as if she were trying to seduce from my eyes what my words were not giving her: release from her painful memory of the worst thing any human being could do to another. How could I give her a key to freedom from the hate that possessed her for almost a half century, glowing like incense on the altar of holy vengeance?

Whom did this splendid lady need to forgive? She needed to forgive men with no faces and no names, a gang who invaded her home one late night in Teheran and slaughtered everyone in her family. She had grown up in Iran, early in the century, moderately upper class. One night five terrorist Turks with hoods over their heads came to her house and tied up her husband and her two children, her father and her mother, dragged them out of the house and outside the city and butchered them all. She lived only because, unlike most any other night, she was away on an errand for the prep school where she taught Iranian children.

"Tell me," she softly demanded, "tell me how I can forgive people who have no faces, no names, no numbers, but were real enough to murder my children?" I felt an awesome turbulence moving inside her gentle confrontation.

Her problem was the faceless anonymity of those who did evil against her. Can you forgive the invisible people, the ones whose faces you cannot see, but who do you terrible wrong?

I have told you about my gentle interrogator so that she could lead us into what we must talk about next: people who are very hard to forgive.

It is hard to forgive people we cannot see, or touch, or maybe even know.

It is also hard to forgive people who do not care whether we forgive them or not.

It is hard to forgive some people because they seem too evil to be forgiven.

And it may be hardest of all to forgive ourselves.

But what about God? Some of us have wondered, in tough times, why God let us down when he could have helped us? Can we forgive God? Do we dare ask?

I invite you to explore with me the lives of some of these people, the kind that are very hard for us to forgive even when we want both to forgive and forget.

CHAPTER 6

Forgiving the Invisible People

Some people invade our lives for a tragic hour or a sad lifetime, leave us with hurting memories, and then move away where we cannot see them. They are invisible, people whose reality is now woven from the thin fabric of a time that no longer is. They are not less real to us than people we see before us, people with faces and names and bodies to touch. They are only harder to reach with our hands and with our forgiveness.

People become invisible when they die before we can forgive them. Or when they hide their faces behind the masks of corporations. People become partially invisible, too, when they do not leave a clear picture of themselves in the minds of their victims—mentally handicapped people, and children, hurt by people whose faces they can only dimly see.

Walk with me slowly through a few fields of the most fragile feelings that can haunt a human memory.

THE PARENT WHO DIED

I know a woman who hates her father for inflicting her life with a bad memory of the perverted sex games he made her play with him when she was too young to say no to Daddy. Now he is dead.

She hates him. But she hates herself even more.

She is sure she cannot free herself from the hatred

she feels for herself until she forgives her father. But how does she forgive a father who is not here to say, "I'm sorry"?

Most of our mothers and fathers were ordinary people with ordinary flaws. They do not need to have been savage slatterns or raging bulls to make them hard to forgive. Morally straight parents who could not love their children may be as hard to forgive as morally bent parents who molest their children. But once they become invisible, they are all terribly hard for us to forgive.

No matter, then, whether we were walloped by a hot-tempered father or hung out to dry by a cold-hearted mother—why is it so hard to forgive parents who pulled a fast one on us by dying before we got the freedom to forgive them?

Dead parents are hard to forgive for the simple reason that they are so far out of reach. We cannot hug them after we forgive them. We can't crawl on their laps and let them love us now the way we needed it then; and they cannot tell us how sorry they are. They cannot do any of the reconciling things that make forgiving a little easier.

Dead parents are hard to forgive, too, because something in us does not want our departed parents to need forgiving. We want to remember a saintly mother and a noble father, and to forgive them means to catalogue them with ordinary folk. It isn't nice to hate someone—and then to forgive someone—who sacrificed so much to get us to make something of ourselves. Especially if they have died and gone to heaven.

Still, hard as it is, a lot of us need to forgive dead parents if only for the sake of peace within our own living selves. And we can do it.

Keep in mind these facts when you try to forgive your dead parent.

NO PARENT IS PERFECT

No parent is a god, few mothers are saints, and

hardly any fathers deserve to be idols. Even "ideal parents" are at best gentle folk, and gentle people do cruel things. You will not shake the foundations of life if you admit that your father could have been cruel to you and your mother could have left you in the cold.

Once they are dead, we want our parents to be sheer light, with no darkness in them at all; and we feel a little foul if we allow shadows to darken our memory. We don't want them to *need* forgiving; because if we forgive them, we must have found fault with them first, maybe even hated them. I still shudder when I think about forgiving my mother. She gave her body and soul to put food in our stomachs and steer us toward godliness and a steady job. You could go to hell, I thought, for hating a mother like her. Yet, she had a shadow side, as every parent does. And I learned that hate does not have to cancel love, that I could love her as much as I ever did, and still hate and forgive one part of her.

If you feel a need to forgive a dead parent, you must face up to the reality that your father or mother could truly have done you wrong.

OUR PAINFUL FEELINGS ARE VALID

You may remember childhood hurts, and one part of you may hate the parent you blame for them; but you do not dare to *feel* the pain and do not dare to *feel* the hate. We do not dare let ourselves follow our feelings into their depths because we are afraid the pain will be unbearable and the hate too ugly for us to admit.

There is a flow to feeling that can, if you follow it, carry you to its own deep well. It will carry you to the depths if you are willing to put away your defenses.

If you let them, your feelings can take you into terrible nights of awesome sadness. You will feel again the loneliness of your childhood struggle to be loved. You will feel again the dread of not being good enough for a parent's love. You may feel as if you are lost, without hope and without light, such feelings as you would hardly dare admit to your best friends.

And they can take you into an ugly place where you will feel the heat of your hate. Even hatred for a saintly mother or a beloved father! They may lead you into your own private hell. But there is no freedom to forgive your dead parents unless you let yourself *feel* the pain you need to forgive them for.

Your feelings, of course, may be exaggerated. They may also be distorted. No matter. They are *what you feel*. So they are valid. And you find freedom to forgive your dead parents when you admit the validity of your feelings about them and when you let yourself *feel* the pain you want to forgive them for.

YOU NEVER COMPLETELY FORGIVE A DEAD PARENT

You can't finish the four stages of forgiving when you forgive a dead parent. Perfect forgiving ends in a reunion of two people estranged by hurt and hate. But when death intervenes, this happy ending is postponed for a time beyond all earthly relationships. You must be satisfied for now with a healing of memory.

You may not even complete your *own* healing; the cure may need to be repeated many times. Forgiving dead parents works a lot like quitting smoking; you may need to start over again several times before you finally pull it off.

YOU NEED TO FORGIVE YOURSELF EVEN AS YOU FORGIVE YOUR DEAD PARENTS

The hurt we get from parents almost always makes us feel guilty or ashamed of ourselves; I have never met a person who hated his father or mother who did not also hate himself.

Most people who try to forgive their dead parents have a frightened hunch that they deserve the miserable feelings their parents left them with. Ask a woman who was sexually molested by her father what the worst effect of it is. She will probably tell you that the worst part of it is the way it made her hate her own self.

Even if our parents were saints, they could get us to hate ourselves by infecting us with the hatred they felt for themselves. My own saintly mother developed self-accusation into a fine art. The fact is that she had little time and less energy to do much hard-core sinning. Yet she remembered every little sin she did manage to sneak into her life, and she ruminated over it and inflated it until she felt like one of the great sinners of the age.

To us she was both holy and heroic; but her goodness only made things worse for us. If a saintly mother could not forgive herself, how could moral midgets like us ever forgive ourselves?

I discovered after she died that I could forgive the mother who nurtured my self-hatred only when I forgave the self I hated. But I honestly do not know which came first, forgiving her or forgiving me.

But dead parents are not the only invisible people.

THE INVISIBLE MOTHER WHO GAVE HER CHILD AWAY

Here is a conversation we have heard at our house more than once:

"Why should I?"

"Because I asked you to."

"Why should I do what you ask me to do?"

"Because I am your mother."

"You are not my mother."

"I am your mother and I love you."

"You *never were* my mother and I *hate* you."

The angry young lady in the conversation was our daughter Cathy, a flaming hothead of sixteen at the time, a beautiful lady of twenty-six now, and our best friend. The woman she was raving at was my wife, Doris.

As we look back on those rip-roaring domestic tempests and as we enjoy our friendship now, we are sure that the toughest challenge for adopted children is their struggle to forgive the invisible birth-mother who gave them away.

When Cathy was a little girl we put the best possible face on it for her: "She gave you away because she loved you too much to keep you." Maybe so. But somewhere in her heart, Cathy wondered whether it wasn't just the other way around; maybe her birth-mother gave her away because she was not worth keeping. Besides, if she loved her *that* much, Cathy suspected, she could have kept her if she had really *wanted* to; what she probably wanted was to get rid of a baby who could only get in the way of what she really wanted out of her own life.

In any case, Cathy had to hate somebody. She had every right. Being given away and adopted can be a crummy way to be smuggled into a family nest. And since the invisible birth-mother who gave her away was not around to hate; why not hate the visible parents who were all too close at hand? *Our* love was only a reminder to her that somebody else had let her go. So she carried a double load of hate.

The only remedy for the pain of her hate was her power to forgive.

But how do you forgive a mother who has no face, no name, no address? How *does* an adopted child forgive an invisible mother?

I will share my sense of how Cathy came to be healed by the power of forgiving. I do not mean to suggest that every adopted child has to move toward forgiveness along Cathy's route. But it can't be *wholly* unique to her.

One thing Cathy did was to get *some* information about her biological parents. Not everything. She did not track them down and meet them face to face, as some adopted children do. But she learned enough about them to get a feel for their personal reality: they were very young, they were poor, they belonged to religions that did not seem to mix, and, of course, they were not married. *And* she learned that her birth-mother was Italian, a delightful "explanation" for the romantic spirit in Cathy that her sober Dutch parents could never tame. Her birth-mother became a more *real* person to her, even though she was still invisible.

Then Cathy learned more, and in a new way, about the agonies a young woman goes through before she decides to give her baby for adoption. One of her special friends became pregnant and, after upheavals of fear and doubt, gave her child to a childless couple for adoption; Cathy loved her friend deeply, shared her terrible conflict, and was sure that, all things considered, her friend did the right thing for her child. She came to feel in a new way how her own birth-mother was probably a wonderful person who was caught in a terrible conflict and really did give her away because she loved her too much to keep her. Cathy was too smart to believe that it was *all* love and no self-interest; but she came to see that there could have been *enough* love to make it true that she was given away because she was loved too much to be kept. Her new empathy with her natural mother did not wash out all of Cathy's hatred, but it did bring it down to forgiving size.

Cathy's next move was the most important one of all. She came—with help—to see herself as she really was, a splendid, strong, intelligent, and valuable person. Having been given away as a baby could not diminish her own superb worth as a woman. But here too, she was smart enough to see herself as a mixed bag. She needed forgiveness as much as she desired to be applauded.

Finally, she came to believe that God forgave her invisible mother, for whatever wrong she did. And if *God* could forgive her birth-mother, why shouldn't *she* forgive her too? And, for that matter, why shouldn't she forgive herself in the bargain?

I do not want to give the impression that Cathy walked an easy and straight line to freedom and peace. But she did it; she managed one of the toughest jobs in the whole arena of forgiving: she forgave the invisible person who brought her into the world and then gave her to us.

Doris and I have muddled through the rearing of three adopted children. They have handled the forgiving challenge in their own ways. Not one of them has done it the same way as the others. But each has proven to me that forgiving is the only remedy for the hurt of being given away as a child.

THE INVISIBLE GHOST BEHIND THE ORGANIZATION

People sometimes hide behind organizations and hurt us with institutional systems.

Their faces are hidden from us by desks and boardroom doors, secretaries' smiles, and minutes of committee meetings.

They are the invisible people we need to forgive when the organization hurts us and we hate the organization for doing it.

For Bob it was the textile factory where he worked in Boston for twenty-five years, without a day's work lost for sickness; the company "released" him without a pension when it moved to cheaper labor in South Carolina.

Charlie was promoted to a job that gradually got too big for him to do. He had put in twenty years, the best years he had to give. But they fired him at an age when no other company was likely to pick him up. And they hired two people to replace him at the job they had asked him to do alone.

For some, it is something much worse.

Organizations have little grace. They can knock you down, drag you across a bed of nails, throw your remains into the street, and, just before you hit the pavement, hand you a ten-dollar plaque with your name on it to show the company's gratitude. Organizations are amoral; they can leave you bleeding in the street with no breathing human being around to accept the blame: it is all company policy.

So you end up hating an impersonal organization.

What do you do when you hate the organization and your hate is tarnishing your golden years, turning you into a crotchety, maybe surly, but surely wounded old soul?

What you have to do is find yourself a living, breathing, responsible *person* in the organization and forgive that person (or persons, if more than one were involved).

If you were thrown out of your job before your time by a callous company policy, you must not try to forgive the impersonal company. You will never pull it off. You need to find a vice-president or a personnel manager, someone who could have seen to it that you were treated fairly. And, if you can, you should make an appointment for a confrontation. He or she will probably put you off with a reasonable explanation. But it is better to forgive someone whose name you know and who may not be solely to blame than to be saddled for the rest of your life with the pain caused by an impersonal system.

You shouldn't waste your soul's vitality trying to forgive an organization. The secret to peace is: get to a person behind the corporate facade.

Chances are he or she will tell you the system was to blame. You mustn't let the company's spokesman off the corporate hook too quickly. You must declare him or her guilty of second-degree hurt, at least, and then you can use the power that God gives you to hold your hand out to the vice-president or the foreman and say, "I forgive you." After that, you are on the way to healing. Only *on the way*. But it is enough for starters.

PEOPLE BADLY OUT OF FOCUS

Some people cannot get a clear picture of the culprits who did them harm because the "cameras" in their brains are out of focus. But they, too, need to forgive those who wrong them.

I wonder how mentally retarded children forgive people whose identity is always fuzzy in their eyes. Is a Down's Syndrome child equipped with special powers to forgive?

When I wonder how intelligent a person has to be to forgive someone, I always think about Toontje. I am not proud to tell it, but I want to tell it so that I can show how easy it is to hurt somebody who cannot get a firm fix on the person doing the hurting.

In our graduate student days, I was living with Doris on the grounds of a large mental hospital outside a village called Bennebroek, in Holland, where we had splendid rooms in a rambling Dutch mansion. The grounds of the hospital were landscaped like a park, with winding walks lined by oaks and dotted with patches of hyacinths, tulips, and daffodils. The beauty of the place encouraged me to take a snappy walk every morning through the hospital grounds and alongside the flowered fields.

It was on my walks that I met Toontje, close to noon every morning. Toontje ("Little Tony" in English) was microcephalic; his brain was too small to organize his world or learn the alphabet.

But Toontje learned to perform one useful service. He had a smallish cart with two large buggy wheels for easy steering, a straight handle for pushing, and two legs behind the wheels so the cart could stand almost upright when Toontje parked it. He also carried a stick about three feet long, with a sharp point on one end for stabbing pieces of paper along the sidewalks of the hospital grounds.

You could see him every morning jabbing at crumpled cigaret packages or chewing gum wrappers, carrying them to his cart, pulling them off his stick, and cautiously laying them there, one by one.

If he walked a ways without finding any litter to pick up, he would provide his own. He would stop his cart, lift out a piece of paper, carry it to the edge of the sidewalk, drop it to the ground, walk back to the cart for his spear, stalk the piece of paper, pierce it through, carry it back, and soberly deposit it back into his barrow. Toontje was exercising his human right to be useful.

How, you may ask, did Toontje know when it was time to call it a morning and head back to Building Nine for his lunch? Simple. He had learned to ask one question and to recognize the one answer that gave him his signal. He learned to ask: *"Hoe laat is't?"* ("What time is it?"). When he heard one answer— *"Twaalf Uur"*—he knew it was time to turn the cart about and head home. So, with his respectful, squeaky drawl, he asked everybody he passed on the hospital walks: *"Hoe laat is't?"* Everybody, every morning— same question.

One sunny Dutch morning I spotted Toontje poking his studded stick through another crumpled cigaret pack, and I felt a nasty impulse of the sort that leads decent persons to do very mean things.

What would Toontje do if I asked *him* his own question?

My timing had to be exquisite. I had to catch Toontje on the very verge, lips puckered for the H in *Hoe,* and then sneak in my question before he had a chance to ask his.

"Hoe laat is't, Toontje?"

He froze. His hand dropped limp from the handle of his cart, his eyes gaped, fixed on blank space, and he began to shake, first his hands, then his head, and his entire body quaking, while from his mouth came inchoate stuttering sounds. He shook for all of fifteen horrible seconds and then he gradually put his hands back on the handle of his cart and pushed it past me, not looking, not saying anything.

I knew the evil I had done the moment I saw him shake. In the conceit of my temptation I thought it was a harmless game, maybe even a psychological experiment. But after I did it, I knew what it really was that I had done: I had demeaned a person who had no tools to play my unfunny game with me. I had betrayed my brotherhood with this man, and hurt a child of God who did not have it coming.

Could he forgive me? Were my chances of forgiveness less with Toontje than with a nasty Ph.D.? Could this man with a brain too small to count change get a clear enough focus on me and what I did to him, even to sense that I needed forgiving? Or is it possible that a large heart made up for his small brain?

I do not know whether Toontje, and all other people who are short-changed on cerebral skills, are given a special power to forgive. Toontje died some time ago. In heaven, I'm sure, Toontje learned what a wretched thing I had done to him that April morning twenty years before. He also got a clear profile of me as the person who did it. And I am sure he forgave me, though I never deserved it.

When we meet maybe he will teach me how people with small brains forgive people with small souls.

I think we are all like Toontje in our own ways. Everyone is at bottom a mystery to me, just as I was a mystery to Toontje. I can never get a perfectly clear fix on anyone. The difference between the partial way we all understand each other and the partial way Toontje understood me is really not all that great.

We all see and know each other in part, as through a glass darkly.

So we forgive in part, too.

CHAPTER 7

Forgiving People Who Do Not Care

The scenario of forgiving does not always end in a happy reunion. Sometimes the story is suspended in mid-air, where the response to our forgiveness is, "I couldn't care less."

A person who hurts us and does not care digs the first wound deeper and makes the miracle of forgiving ever so much harder.

We do not want to forgive someone who laughs at our pain. For that matter, we do not rush to forgive someone who just shuffles off and leaves us alone to suture the cuts he sliced into our life.

When someone hurts us meanly, we want him to suffer too. We expect this clod to pay his dues; we want him to grovel a little. The old-fashioned word for what we want is *repentance*.

But the people who hurt us do not always come through.

The question is: should we forgive them anyway? Does it even make sense to forgive someone who would rather we keep our forgiveness and feed it to the dog?

Before we decide, we should make sure of what we want. What do we want people to do for us when we ask them to repent?

Not every hurt calls for repentance, any more than every cut needs stitching. In the cross-town traffic of human relationships we have limitless chances to rub people the wrong way, thoughtlessly, carelessly, and stupidly. But we do not dig a ravine between each other every time we get hurt. Mini-wrongs can be soothed with a modest gesture that falls well short of repentance.

An *apology!*

Apology? What a conversion that word has had! In the old days, an apology meant a plea of innocence against a dreadful charge. Today we apologize when we plead guilty to a trifle.

The other night my wife came home in a stew about a crude male who shoved his way into her place at the gas station. It was raining, hard. Doris was fourth in line at the self-service lane, where there was one diesel pump that could be gotten at from either side. Three cars were lined up ahead of her. When it was finally her turn at the pump, she got out of the car, put her back to the pump while she spun off the gas cap, and then turned to reach for the nozzle. But a new station wagon full of family splashed up in the other lane; the driver sprang out of the front seat, grabbed the nozzle just as Doris reached for it, and then took the cap off his own tank and whistled while he filled it with diesel fuel.

My wife watched him, buffaloed, and then pulled herself together to make her counterattack. "You saw that I had been waiting in line for this pump before you got here." "That makes no difference to me," he said. "I think what you are doing is contemptible." "I don't give a damn what you think." "Your children are watching; do you care what they think?" "Look, lady, I told you I don't care what *you* think."

She recycled the dialogue to me as if I stood for every rude macho driver in the world: "He would never have dared to do that to me if I had been a man!" Probably not.

Would an apology do? Suppose she met the man next week at the same pump and he offered to let her move ahead of him and said, "Sorry about last week, the kids had been driving me mad, I was in a dreadful hurry to get home, and I was terribly late." I think

Doris would have gulped and grudgingly indulged him. His apology would have done the job.

Apologies keep life oiled when the bearings begin to wear. Nicely timed and sincerely meant, the graceful apology is a curtsy to civility, a gesture that helps crowded citizens put up with each other with a smidgin of courtly humor, a modest bow to keep the hassle within tolerable bounds.

All the more reason, then, to see that apologies do not try to do the job that only repentance can do.

Powerful and sneaky people use apologies as end runs around repentance. They betray a trust; and, when they have been found out, they say they are sorry for "mistakes in judgment." They smile through their oily apologies when their crime calls for quakes of repentance. They get by only because we have lost our sense of the difference between repentance for wrong and apologies for bungling.

Ordinary people do it too. We do something painfully wrong, but when we are called to account we try to slide through our fault on a slippery apology: "Oh, my dear, you *are* exaggerating. But if you insist, I'll say I am sorry, so let's forget it." A quick maneuver around the pain of penitence!

We should not let each other get away with it. A deep and unfair hurt is not a mere *faux pas*.

We cannot put up with everything from everyone; some things are intolerable. When somebody hurts us deeply and unfairly an apology will not do the job; it only trivializes a wrong that should not be trifled with.

If Jackie apologizes for having betrayed you, you must call her bluff and throw her "Sorry about that" into the garbage disposal. If Fred lies about you after he promised to be your friend, you must accept no apologies from him; you must tell him to face up to the truth or leave you alone.

Well now, if some wrongs are matched only by the sorrow of repentance, we must get a clear picture of what we want when we ask a person to repent.

Repenting is a four-storied mountain. We must pass

through all four levels before we are finished. Let me name them.

THE LEVEL OF PERCEPTION

The first awakening moment dawns when you see your own action through another's eyes. You perceive that their feelings about what you did are true. You have reached the level of interpersonal perception.

You do not need to see every detail of your falling-out precisely the way they see it. You will probably never, even after a thousand explanations, agree on exactly how it all happened. No matter. You see that they are right when they say that what you did to them was mean and unfair and insufferable.

THE LEVEL OF FEELING

You move now from perception to pain. Here you *feel* the pain that you made someone else feel. You share the hurt that you inflicted.

You somehow enter another's soul and share his suffering. Once there, you feel as if you are out in the cold, barefoot in the snow, stuck for a while in the inner hell of your own deserved condemnation. The family name of this pain is "guilt."

THE LEVEL OF CONFESSION

When you can tell those you hurt that you realize what you did was intolerable and that you share their pain, you reach the level of confession. If they believe you, your separate sadnesses begin to melt into one.

When you confess *this* way, you do more than *admit* your blame. Criminals are sometimes trapped into admitting what they can no longer deny; lawyers call this a "confession," but it isn't what I am talking about. Terrorists break their necks to claim blame for the worst sorts of brutalities; but they do not confess in our sense of the word.

Confession is different, too, from spilling the beans. Celebrities are not confessing when they hire ghost writers to tell their private stories. Confession is not for payoffs; it is for healing.

When you confess to another person, you do not merely admit that you did something; you tell the person you hurt that you hurt too, with the very hurt that you hurt them with, and that you want terribly to be forgiven.

It is awesomely hard to confess to friends, I know—a lot easier to confess to God than to a wounded brother. And the deeper you hurt them, the harder it is to confess to them.

When you confess, you put yourself helpless in the hands of the person you wronged, trust him with your very self, bringing nothing with you but your hope for a sign of love. Confession is the rumbling of a crumbling heart.

THE LEVEL OF PROMISE

If you know and genuinely feel the wrongness of what you did, you also feel a passionate desire not to hurt again. So you make a promise.

Why should you expect anyone to take your confession seriously unless you promise that you do not intend again to foul your relationship with still more of the same unfair pain?

You can give no guarantee; the best of us go back on promises. But anyone who has been hurt should expect a sincere *intention*, at least.

These, then, are the four stories of the mountain of repentance: *perception, feeling, confession,* and *promise*.

It seems right that people who want you to forgive them should give you a signal that they repent.

Most of us who have read the story of the Prodigal Son feel good when the son says to his forgiving father, "I am not worthy." But try changing the scenario. See the son swaggering home and hear him say: "I've decided to do everybody a favor by coming back to my old place in the family circle." We will not have it that way. We want him to stick to the original script: "I don't deserve even to be a hired hand."

Take Marmelodov. Dostoevski tells us about him in *Crime and Punishment*.

Marmelodov was a wretched lush who ruined everyone who loved him. He pushed his angelic daughter Sonia out on the street to sell her body to keep him on the bottle. He stole grocery money from his long-suffering wife, Katerina.

But Marmelodov fully expected to be embraced in the end by the loving arms of a merciful God. Decent folk mocked his hopes, chided him, louse that he was, for presuming on the mercy of the Lord. Where did he get off, the most loathsome rat in the sewer, thinking that he could deserve a mansion in heaven prepared for him?

Ah, said Marmelodov, that is just the secret: he *knew* he didn't deserve it. He had had a vision in which God welcomed home all the prodigals of the world. " 'Come forth ye drunkards, come forth, ye weak ones, come forth, ye children of shame!' And we shall all . . . stand before him. And he will say to us, 'Ye are swine . . . but come ye also.' And the wise ones . . . will say, 'Oh, Lord, why dost thou receive these men?' And this is what the Lord will say to his critics: 'This is why I receive them, oh ye wise, this is why I receive them, oh ye of understanding, that not one of them believed himself to be worthy of this.' "

The art of getting back into fellowship after we have done someone dirt is knowing we don't belong there. We must *know* we are not worthy. And, like Marmelodov, we need to say so. If we are the ones who hurt someone, we should repent; repentance is the only honest entrée to forgiveness.

But supposing we are the ones who have *been* hurt. Must we *demand* repentance *before* we forgive the person who hurt us? Should we hold back on forgiving when the other one holds back on repentance?

God takes the tough line, it seems, from what we read in the Bible. When Jesus sent his disciples to tell the world that God forgives, he also told them to ask people to *repent*. Following this lead, St. Peter put the cards on the table: "Repent so that your sins can be forgiven."

Why? Why do we have to repent when we want to be forgiven?

I don't believe God wants us to grovel just to give him the pleasure of watching us sweat.

My own guess is that God asks us to repent, not as a condition he needs, but as a condition *we* need. What God wants is not only that we *be* forgiven in *his* heart and mind, but that we should also *feel* forgiven in *our* heart and mind. He wants an *honest* coming together with his children. Asking for repentance was only a way of asking for *truthfulness*.

What about us mortals?

Should *we* waste our forgiving on someone who does not want it? Or admit he needs it? Pearls before swine? Pardon for the unrepentant? Let's have another look.

Realism, it seems to me, nudges us toward forgiving people who hurt us whether or not they repent for doing it.

For one thing, time does not let people stay near us forever. They may die before they have gotten around to repenting. But we need to forgive them anyway.

And, second, there is a matter of letting others take responsibility for themselves. We cannot *make* them repent; we cannot pull them back to us like a dog on a leash. Let them be responsible for staying away from us. But why should we let them keep us from healing ourselves?

So we need to forgive the unrepentant for our own sake. We need to forgive people who do not care if only so that we do not drown in our own misery. Let the other guy take care of himself.

I love a Jewish sentiment found in an ancient document called the *Testaments of the Twelve Patriarchs:* And "if a man sin against thee . . . if he repent and confess, forgive him. . . . But if he be shameless, and persisteth in his wrongdoing even so forgive him from the heart, and leave to God the avenging."

Leave the avenging to God—that, I think, is the way for us to cope with people who hurt us and do not seem to care.

The climax of forgiveness takes two, I know. But you can have the reality of forgiving without its climax. You do not always need a thing whole to enjoy it at all. A blossom has real beauty even if it never becomes a flower. A climb can be successful though we do not reach the summit. Forgiving is real even if it stops at the healing of the forgiver.

Should you sentence yourself to the escalator of hate simply because the person you need to forgive does not want your forgiveness?

Back to fundamentals! Forgiving is a process. One stage is the healing of the forgiver's memory. If the people you forgive want to stay where they are, let them. You can make a solo flight to freedom.

CHAPTER 8

Forgiving Ourselves

Do you dare release the person you are today from the shadow of the wrong you did yesterday?

Do you dare forgive yourself?

To forgive yourself takes high courage. Who are you, after all, to shake yourself free from the undeniable sins of your private history—as if what you once did has no bearing on who you are now?

Where do you get the right—let alone the cheek—to forgive yourself when other people would want you to crawl in shame if they really knew? How dare you?

The answer is that you get the right to forgive yourself only from the entitlements of love. And you dare forgive yourself only with the courage of love. Love is the ultimate source of both your right and your courage to ignore the indictment you level at yourself. When you live as if yesterday's wrong is irrelevant to how you feel about yourself today, you are gambling on a love that frees you even from self-condemnation.

But there must be truthfulness. Without honesty, self-forgiveness is psychological hocus-pocus. The rule is: we cannot really forgive ourselves unless we look at the failure in our past and call it by its right name.

We need honest judgment to keep us from self-indulging complacency.

Let me recall the four stages we pass through when we forgive someone else who hurt us: we hurt, we hate, we heal ourselves, and we come together again.

We all hurt ourselves. Unfairly, too, and sometimes deeply.

God knows the regrets we have for the foolish ways we cheat ourselves. I smoked cigarettes too long, and while I puffed away on my pack-a-day, I feared the time that I would say: you fool, you fool, dying before your time, and you have no one to blame but yourself. Then there are the opportunities spurned, disciplines rejected, and addictions hooked into—they all can haunt you with a guilty sense that you did yourself wrong.

But the hurt your heart cries hardest to forgive yourself for is the unfair harm you did to others.

The memory of a moment when you lied to someone who trusted you! The recollection of neglecting a child who depended on you. The time you turned away from somebody who called out to you for help! These are the memories, and thousands like them, that pierce us with honest judgment against ourselves.

We do not have to be bad persons to do bad things. If only bad people did bad things to other people we would live in a pretty good world. We hurt people by our bungling as much as we do by our vices.

And the more decent we are the more acutely we feel our pain for the unfair hurts we caused. Our pain becomes our hate. *The pain we cause other people becomes the hate we feel for ourselves. For having done them wrong.* We judge, we convict, and we sentence ourselves. Mostly in secret.

Some of us feel only a *passive* hatred for ourselves. We merely lack love's energy to bless ourselves. We cannot look in the looking glass and say: "What I see makes me glad to be alive." Our joy in being ourselves is choked by a passive hatred.

Others sink into *aggressive* hatred of themselves. They cut themselves to pieces with a fury of contempt. One part of them holds its nose and shoves the other part down a black hole of contempt. They are their own enemy. And sometimes, in the ultimate tragedy, their self-hatred is acted out in self-destruction.

Of course, your inner judge may be an unreasonable nag, accusing you falsely, and flailing you unfairly. On the other hand, your better self often sweeps real guilt under a carpet of complacency. You con yourself just to save yourself the pain of confrontation with your shadowy side.

In any case, you shouldn't trust your inner judge too far.

Still, he *is* your toughest critic, and you have to come to terms with him.

So let us move on *to love's daring response*.

What happens when you finally do forgive yourself?

When you forgive yourself, you rewrite your script. What you are in your present scene is not tied down to what you did in an earlier scene. The bad guy you played in Act One is eliminated and you play Act Two as a good guy.

You release yourself today from yesterday's scenario. You walk into tomorrow, guilt gone.

Again, the word that fits the case best is "irrelevance." Look back into your past, admit the ugly facts, and declare that they are irrelevant to your present. Irrelevant and immaterial! Your very own past has no bearing on your case. Or how you *feel* about it.

Such release does not come easy. The part of yourself who did the wrong walks with you wherever you go. A corner of your memory winks at you and says, "Nice try old chap, but we both know the scoundrel you really are, don't we?" It takes a miracle of love to get rid of the unforgiving inquisitor lurking in the shadows of your heart.

Perhaps nobody has understood the tortured route to self-forgiveness better than the Russian genius Dostoevski. In his novel *Crime and Punishment*, he portrayed the inner struggle of self-forgiveness in the soul of a murderer named Ilyon Raskolnikov.

Raskolnikov did something as evil as anyone can do. He brutally murdered a helpless woman, an old pawnbroker—a miserable woman to be sure, and miserly, and mean, but innocent still. His guilt was stupefying.

No soul can bear such guilt alone, not for long. Sooner or later one must tell. Raskolnikov found a girl, an angel, Sonia, and he confessed to her. He told her everything.

She persuaded him to admit everything to the police, and he finally did. He was sent to prison in Siberia.

The loving Sonia followed him there and waited for him to forgive himself so that he could find the freedom to accept her love.

Raskolnikov could not forgive himself. He tried to excuse himself instead.

He came to grief, he said, "through some decree of blind fate"; he was destined to kill the old woman. Besides, when you come right down to it was his act really *that* bad? Did not Napoleon do the same sort of thing and do they not build him monuments? In clever ways like this he excused himself by finding deep reasons why he was not to blame.

Raskolnikov did not *dare to be guilty*.

"Oh, how happy he would have been," wrote Dostoevski, "if he could have blamed himself! He could have borne anything then, even shame and disgrace."

Yet, now and then, Raskolnikov did get a glimpse of "the fundamental falsity in himself." He knew deep inside that he was lying to himself.

And finally it happened. How it happened he did not know. He flung himself at Sonia's feet and accepted her love. "He wept and threw his arms around her knees." He finally had the power to love. And his power to love revealed that the miracle had really happened; he had forgiven himself.

He forgave himself? For such a crime as coldblooded murder? Yes. "Everything, even his crime, his sentence and imprisonment seemed to him now . . . an external strange fact *with which he had no concern.*"

Release! Release by a discovery that his terrible

past was irrelevant to who he was now and was going to be in the future. He was free from his own judgment and this was why he was free to love.

Raskolnikov stands out in staggering boldness to show us that even the worst of us can find the power to set ourselves free.

Finally, the climax of self-forgiving; it comes when we feel at one with ourselves again. The split is healed. The self inside of you, who condemned you so fiercely, embraces you now. You are whole, single; you have come together.

You are not being smug. You care very much that you once did a wrong. And you do not want to do it again. But you will not let your former wrong curse the person you are now. You take life in stride. You have let yourself come home.

It does not happen once and for all. The hate you felt comes back now and then, and you reject yourself for doing what you did. But then you come back to yourself again. And again. And again.

To forgive your own self—almost the ultimate miracle of healing!

But *how* can you pull it off?

The first thing you need is honesty. There is no way to forgive yourself without it. Candor—a mind ready to forego fakery and to face facts—this is the first piece of spiritual equipment you need.

Without candor you can only be complacent. And complacency is a counterfeit of forgiveness. Some people are superficial, there is no other word for it. Drawing on the top layer of their shallow wits, they pursue the unexamined life with unquestioning contentment, more like grazing cows than honest human beings.

The difference between a complacent person and a person who forgives himself is like the difference between a person who is high on cocaine and a person who has reason for being really happy.

Then *you need a clear head to make way for your forgiving heart.*

For instance, you need to see the difference between self-esteem and self-forgiveness.

You can gain esteem for yourself when you discover that you are estimable, that you are in fact worth esteeming. To esteem yourself is to feel in your deepest being that you are a superb gift very much worth wanting, God's own art form, and a creature of magnificent beauty.

Sometimes you gain self-esteem only after you come to terms with the bad hand you were dealt in life's game.

I know a man who has what is cruelly called the Elephant Man syndrome; a tough hand to play, but the only hand he has. He has learned to see the beautiful person he is beneath his thorny skin, and he esteems himself—*because* of what he is. Kim, on the other hand, is a beautiful adopted child whose birth-mother dealt her a genetic disease. Kim has chosen to accept herself as an incredibly splendid gift of God because of what she is, and in spite of the tough hand she was dealt.

Blessed are the self-esteemers, for they have seen the beauty of their own souls.

But *self-esteem* is *not the same as self-forgiveness.* You esteem yourself when you discover your own excellence. You forgive yourself after you discover your own faults. You esteem yourself for the good person you are. You forgive yourself for the bad things you did.

If you do not see the difference, you may shout a thousand bravos at yourself and never come to the moment of self-forgiving. So you need a clear head about what it is you are doing.

You also need courage. Forgiving yourself is love's ultimate daring.

The reason it takes high courage to forgive yourself lies partly with other people's attitudes toward self-forgivers. Self-righteous people do not want you to forgive yourself. They want you to walk forever under the black umbrella of permanent shame.

I understand these people; I am one of them. There is something inside me that wants a wrongdoer, especially a famous wrongdoer, to keep a low profile, to take the last place in line, to speak with a meek voice; I want him to grovel a little. Maybe a lot.

So, when you walk and talk like a person who has sliced your sinful past from your present sense of selfhood, you will need courage to face the self-righteous crowd.

Then *you need to be concrete*.

You drown in the bilge of your own condemnation for lack of specificity. You will almost always fail at self-forgiving when you refuse to be concrete about what you are forgiving yourself for.

Many of us try, for instance, to forgive ourselves for being the *sorts* of persons we are. We are ugly, or mean, or petty, or given to spouting off; or, on the other hand, we are too good, a patsy, everybody's compliant sucker, humble servant to all who want to get something out of us.

But people who try to forgive themselves for being wholesale failures are not humble at all; they are really so proud that they want to be gods. John Quincy Adams, not the greatest, but a very good President, could not forgive himself. "I have done nothing," he wrote in his diary. "My life has been spent in vain and idle aspirations, and in ceaseless rejected prayers that something should be the result of my existence beneficial to my own species." The last words spoken by the great jurist Hugo Grotius, the father of modern international law, on his deathbed, were: "I have accomplished nothing worthwhile in my life." Such people sound humble with their moans about being failures in life; but they are really crying because they had to settle for being merely human.

You must call your own bluff: precisely, what is it that you need forgiveness for? For being unfaithful to your spouse last year? Good, you can work on that. For being an evil sort of person? No, that is too much; you cannot swallow yourself whole.

Most of us can manage no more than one thing at a time. "Sufficient unto the day is the evil thereof," said Jesus. When we overload ourselves with dilated bags of undifferentiated guilt we are likely to sink into despair. The only way we can succeed as self-forgivers, free from the tyranny of a tender conscience, is to be concrete and to forgive ourselves for one thing at a time.

Finally, you need to confirm your outrageous act of self-forgiveness with a reckless act of love. How can you know for sure that you gambled with guilt and won unless you gamble your winnings on love?

"She loves much because she has been forgiven much"—this was Jesus' explanation for a woman who dared to barge into a dinner party uninvited, plunk herself at Jesus' feet, and pour out a small cascade of love.

Love is a signal that you have done it, that you have actually released the guilt that condemned you. You won't always know exactly when you have forgiven yourself. It is like reaching the top of a long hill on a highway—you may not be sure when you have reached level ground, but you can tell that you have passed the top when you step on the gas and the car spurts ahead. An act of love is like quick acceleration. A free act of love, to anyone at all, may signal to you that you do, after all, have the power that comes to anyone who is self-forgiving.

You can buy her a gift! Invite him to dinner! Visit someone who is sick! You can put your arms around a friend you never touched before! Write a letter of thanks. Or tell Dad that you love him. All ways of confirming that we performed the miracle of forgiving ourselves.

Yes, love gives you the right to forgive yourself. And it gives you the power as well. At least to begin. Healing may come slowly, but better a snail's pace than standing still, feet sunk in the cement of self-accusations.

To forgive yourself is to act out the mystery of one

person who is both forgiver and forgiven. You judge yourself: this is the division within you. You forgive yourself: this is the healing of the split.

That you should dare to heal yourself by this simple act is a signal to the world that God's love is a power within you.

CHAPTER 9

Forgiving Monsters

There are monsters who do such evils as ordinary people dare not dream of. They may be towering titans who trample whole populations. They may be crawling worms who seduce little children into prostitution. Whether giants or punks, they hurt people so badly that they may disqualify themselves forever from forgiveness by a fellow human being.

What makes their evil seem too awful for forgiveness? Sometimes it is the pointlessness of it—the gang on a drugged joy-ride that kills a child playing hopscotch on the sidewalk. Sometimes it is the unimaginable enormity of it—the Jim Jones who brainwashes a whole community to the point of mass suicide. There may be other reasons why any person could be too horrible to forgive; these are enough to make us wonder.

Are some people unforgivable? How can we tell?

There is at least one persuasive reason for leaving terrible evildoers unforgiven.

If we forgive the monstrous evils of the world, it is feared, we will shrink their horror. Forgiveness may reduce them so that a tolerant human society begins to swallow and digest evil while it gets on with business as usual.

Out of her passion for honesty, novelist Cynthia Ozick says that forgiving monsters "blurs over suffering and death. It drowns the past. It cultivates sensitivity toward the murderer at the price of sensitivity toward the victim."

Cynthia Ozick puts the matter precisely where it belongs: at the bar of honesty with those who suffer. But I honestly believe there is another way of looking at it.

Forgiving does not reduce evil. Forgiving great evil does not shave a millimeter from its monstrous size. There is no real forgiving unless there is first relentless exposure and honest judgment. When we forgive evil we do not excuse it, we do not tolerate it, we do not smother it. We look the evil full in the face, call it what it is, let its horror shock and stun and enrage us, and only then do we forgive it.

Besides, the greatness of evil is not simply a matter of *quantity*.

Pain is not measured only by the *number* of people who suffer it. If there are two people in a room, and one of them has a splitting headache, you would not double the amount of headache pain if the other person gets a headache too.

If you are betrayed, you feel *all by yourself* the pain that all the betrayals of human history bring into the world. We cannot add up the pain of a hundred betrayals any more than we can divide up the pain between the people betrayed. Each solitary victim feels the full measure of the betrayal even though a million people are also betrayed.

A woman who has been raped does not ask whether a man bad enough to rape one hundred women is forgivable. She asks whether she can forgive the man who raped *her*.

And if evil were measured in numbers, how would we know when a criminal has crossed the forgiveness zone? By instinct? Would we appoint a United Nations Commission on the forgivableness of atrocities? Maybe consult a panel of Harvard philosophers? Not on your life! Better consult anyone at all, anyone who has never gone to school, but who has been deeply hurt and later healed of unfair pain.

Besides, if we say that monsters are beyond forgiving, we give them a power they should never have.

107

Monsters who are too evil to be forgiven get a strangle-hold on their victims; they can sentence their victims to a lifetime of unhealed pain. If they are unforgivable monsters, they are given power to keep their evil alive in the hearts of those who suffered most. We give them power to condemn their victims to live forever with the hurting memory of their painful pasts. We give the monsters the last word.

Another, final, irony is this: when we refuse to forgive monsters we give them exactly what they want.

Monsters do not want to be forgiven. They want to be left alone to vindicate themselves in the eyes of the world. Virtually every Nazi big-wig dreamed—even as he was convicted at Nuremberg—that one day Germans would build a statue in his honor.

The self-defeating upshot is: if we disqualify giants of evil from forgiveness, we are cruelest to their victims and we give the monsters exactly what they want.

Consider, from just one more point of view, how we defeat our own purpose when we say that a monster is too evil to be forgiven.

When we declare an evil person to be beyond the pale of forgiveness, we create a monster who does not even *need* to be forgiven—a monster is excused from judgment by the fact that he or she is beyond humanity. This is the paradox of making any human being *absolutely* evil.

Let us mull it over a little while—to make sure the point gets through.

Take Adolph Eichmann, for instance: a master-architect of the holocaust. Eichmann engineered an evil so horrendously huge that none of us has yet felt its full horror. Found guilty of crimes against humanity by an Israeli court, he was hanged in Jerusalem.

Was Eichmann forgivable?

Hannah Arendt went to Jerusalem to report on the Eichmann trial. She watched this man, listened to him, researched him, studied him, and then wrote a book that she called *Eichmann in Jerusalem: A Report on the Banality of Evil.*

Banality? Of *this* evil? Banality calls up words like stupid, trite, flat, vapid, empty, and boring. How could she talk this way of Eichmann and his monstrosities?

Arendt was *not* saying that the evil Eichmann did was not all that bad. She was trying to say that Eichmann was not superhuman, not even a superhuman monster; he was a stupid, boring, flat, ordinary man who used his human freedom to become a human tool of the Nazi machinery.

Some people were outraged by Dr. Arendt's words—the "banality of evil." But I ask whether they fell to another temptation. Did they superhumanize Eichmann's evil? Did they made Eichmann an evil god?

I think they superhumanized Eichmann's evil. Eichmann was made into a concentrated core of undiluted evil, an absolute version of evil's very essence, equal with the devil himself. Eichmann became an evil god, his humanness became a mere mask that covered the kind of pure evil that only gods can be or do.

By turning Eichmann into an unforgivable monster, we set him beyond human accountability, *beyond good and evil*. Nobody forgives the devil. Why not? It is because he is *beyond* the struggle between good and evil; he is only pure evil, and therefore we set him outside the possibility of being forgiven.

The paradox!

So we exterminate Eichmann. We swat him like a deadly mosquito. We shoot him down like a vicious beast prowling through our village. We do not judge him as a merely accountable human being, we liquidate him as a *non*human.

The truth of the matter is: very ordinary people do extraordinary evil. We need to judge them, surely, and forgive them, if we can, because they are responsible. And because we need to be healed.

If forgiving is a remedy for the wounds of a painful past, we cannot deny *any* human being the possibility of being forgiven lest we deny the victim the possibility of being healed through forgiving.

Love makes forgiving a creative violation of *all* the rules for keeping score.

But what of the victim's *ability* to forgive? *Can* the victim of monsters really forgive them? That is another, very different question.

The answer is not blowing in the winds for everyone to hear. It can only come straight from the heart of the person who, for some hellish moments or years, was brutalized by a monster. The answer cannot come from me, nor from anyone who is not a survivor of the evil that monsters have done. It can come only from those who have seen the monsters with their own eyes and felt the monsters' evil in their own lives.

Perhaps the answer of power cannot come from the mind. Perhaps it comes only from the pain-wracked heart. And, finally, from the heart possessed by hope.

CHAPTER 10

Forgiving God

There is an old, old story about a tailor who leaves his prayers and, on the way out of the synagogue, meets a rabbi.

"Well, and what have you been doing in the synagogue, Lev Ashram?" the rabbi asks.

"I was saying prayers, rabbi."

"Fine, and did you confess your sins?"

"Yes, rabbi, I confessed my little sins."

"Your little sins?"

"Yes, I confessed that I sometimes cut my cloth on the short side, that I cheat on a yard of wool by a couple of inches."

"You said that to God, Lev Ashram?"

"Yes, rabbi, and more. I said, 'Lord, I cheat on pieces of cloth; you let little babies die. But I am going to make you a deal. You forgive me my little sins and I'll forgive you your big ones.'"

The Jewish tailor grabbed hold of God and held him to account.

Rabbi Harold Kushner suffered the inexpressible pain of watching his son die of old age before he was fifteen. In his book *When Bad Things Happen to Good People,* he opens our heart's door again to this question: Where is God and what is he doing when decent people are hurt, deeply and unfairly? Kushner does not believe it is God's fault when bad things happen to us; we can't expect one God to handle *everything*. So we can excuse God. And yet he challenges us to forgive God anyway:

Are you capable of forgiving . . . God . . . when he has let you down and disappointed you by permitting bad luck and sickness and cruelty in His world and permitting some of these things to happen to you?

You may react automatically: God cannot be blamed for anything, so he cannot be forgiven for anything. The Psalms say, "The Lord is just in all his ways, and kind in all his doings." Being God is never having to say you are sorry.

When it comes to God, our instinctive piety rushes to defend him against our own complaints.

Maybe so. But we should not smother the primal screams of those who feel as if God has left them dangling in the winds of pain. Would it bother God too much if we found our peace by forgiving him for the wrongs we suffer? What if we found a way to forgive him without blaming him? A special sort of forgiving for a special sort of relationship. Would he mind?

Let us try; let us talk a little, reverently but honestly, about forgiving God. Recall the four stages of forgiving? The first two are our *hurt* and our *hate*.

FIRST, THE HURT

Focus on hurts you feel are unfair and deep. Don't try to forgive God for not having made you smarter or more beautiful. Don't forgive him for not giving you wealthier parents with star-quality genes. Nobody gets everything in life.

And it stands to reason that you should not try to forgive God for lumps you give yourself. If you smoke two packs of cigarets a day for twenty years, you do not have to forgive God if you get lung cancer.

But sometimes we suffer a lot for no good reason, while folk of smaller virtue get along fine. One woman prays for ten years to have a child and never gets one;

a teenage girl playing around with sex skips off to an abortion clinic to get rid of what that woman wants more than anything else in life. One man obeys all the rules of good health and dies of a brain tumor at thirty-five; his friend smokes and drinks and grows a massive potbelly and lives to be eighty-five. A little help from God would have come in handy.

Sometimes God would have to do hardly anything at all.

Harry Angstrom, in John Updike's novel *Rabbit Run*, left the house in a huff one night; his wife Janice stayed home with the baby and got a little drunk. Janice gave the baby a bath. In the bathtub. But the baby's body was slippery with soap and Janice's mind was not managing her hands. She grabbed but she had trouble getting a good hold; she kept grabbing, but she could not find the right handles.

A contorted sense of horrible danger seized her confused mind, and then she knew "that the worst thing that has ever happened to any woman in the world has happened to her."

Harry came home several hours later and learned the terrible truth.

He went to the bathroom. The water was still in the tub, so he rolled up his sleeve and pulled up the stopper by jerking the chain that held it to the faucet.

Harry groaned: "how easy it was, yet in all his strength God did nothing. Just that little stopper to lift."

You can hear Harry's moan almost everywhere. The stoppers do not get pulled sometimes, and when they do not get pulled we feel naked against the icy blasts in the wintertime of our soul.

We need to look on the bright side, too, of course. Most of the time our babies do not drown in the bathtub. Our children get over the flu, ride their bikes home through busy traffic, evade the drug pushers, and escape child molesters. Mostly we do not get cancer; usually we tuck ourselves into bed and wake up in time to risk our lives in the next day's outing.

But when the bricks fall on us, we do not feel like balancing out our batting average by remembering all the happier days; we want to know why something could not have been done to prevent this one horrible hurt.

THEN, WE HATE GOD

It takes a tough soul, maybe somebody slightly mad, to hate God. Who is a big enough fool to wish God bad luck? Job did not have the bravado to follow his wife's advice: "Curse God, and die." Nor would I. Curse God? Not on your life!

But we do hate God sometimes. All of us, I think. On the sly.

If we dare not hate the Giver, we do dare hate his gifts. We hate his world. Or we hate ourselves. When we shut our eyes to every reason we have for being glad to be alive, when we resent good things that happen to our friends, when our hearts stifle every happy impulse, we are nurturing a passive hatred of God.

Maybe it takes an atheist to dare hate God head-on. I think of Graham Greene's Sarah, the woman in *The End of the Affair* who believed in God with such a frenzy that she just closed her eyes and jumped into faith. She loved people the way she believed God— with a trust that had no stops. But Sarah died too soon, unreasonably soon for someone who loved as well as she did and who had lately found a man who loved her too.

He hated God, her lover did, and he dared to throw his malice straight in God's face.

With your great schemes you can ruin our happiness like a harvester ruins a mouse's nest. I hate you, God, I hate you as though you existed.

True believers are more like the prophet Jeremiah. We do not dare to hate God, so we hate life instead.

When Jeremiah really felt let down by God, he turned his hatred on himself:

> Cursed be the day on which I was born!
> The day when my mother bore me, let it not be blessed.
> Cursed be the man who brought the news to my father,
> "A son is born to you," making him very glad.

Hating God's most precious gift is a believer's sneaky way to hate God.

You may hate him because you feel as if your most important friend has become your worst enemy. He could have pulled the rubber stopper, but he watched the baby drown. An ancient Jew said it a long time ago in the Book of Lamentations: "The Lord has become like an enemy, . . . he has multiplied . . . mourning and lamentation."

NEXT, WE DEFEND GOD

We plead his case against our own accusations.

Your believing mind wants to rush to God's defense against your frightening feelings of hate. And any thinking person can find good reasons why God does not pull the stopper that could have saved us from our troubles.

You can, if you think hard, look at your pains as flecks on a large screen of eternal harmony. God-haters take a cramped view of things; their pain blinds them to the large scene. Believers see things in perspective.

Walk into any large shopping plaza, and you will see the mish-mash of grey and white and black tiles that make up the floor. They don't seem to be arranged in any pattern at all. But get up on a balcony, high above the plaza, and look at the whole floor. Now the splendid mosaic comes to view. Your scrambled little corner looks good within the grand design.

You should not judge a Rembrandt painting by one darkish corner of a portrait. Step back. See the whole. The shadow only lets the light seem brighter.

So too with God's work; the dark shadows only underscore its shining glories. We will see—from the high place—that God makes all things fit together. All our pains will make his later mercies seem more tender.

There is a balm, I am sure, in this philosophical faith. It helps some people to believe that even the worst of their deep and unfair pains are really minor chords within God's great concerto.

But I would not say this to my neighbors across the street, who mourn for their twelve-year-old son Howard as he dies of a cancer that began in his testicles a few months ago and then worked up through his intestines where it intends to kill him soon. I dare not tell them that Howard's cancer will one day look good on the human canvas, like a shadow on a Rembrandt painting.

When I think I have found good reasons why we never need to forgive God, I think of Elie Wiesel. I think of him watching a little boy hang, almost but not quite dead, from a gallows at Auschwitz. In his unforgettable true story, *Night,* Wiesel tells us what he saw:

One day when we came back from work, we saw three gallows rearing up in the assembly place. . . . Three victims in chains—and one of them the little servant, the sad-eyed angel. . . .

The three victims (were) mounted together onto chairs.

The three necks were placed at the same moment within the nooses. . . .

At a sign . . . the three chairs tipped over.

Total silence throughout the camp. . . .

Then the march past began. The two adults were no longer alive. . . . But the third rope was still moving; being so light, the child was still alive.

For more than half an hour he stayed there, struggling between life and death, dying in slow agony under our eyes. And we had to look him full in the face.

Behind me, I heard [a] man asking:

"Where is God now?"

And I heard a voice within me answer him:

"Where is He? Here He is—He is hanging here on this gallows."

What voice did Wiesel hear inside his soul telling him where God was? Was it the voice of the brain? No. It was the voice of his heart!

The voice of the heart was the only voice he could listen to at that terrible moment. How cold, how cruel, any brain-contrived defense of God would have been!

Yet there are *some* things my mind tells me about God that seem reasonable in the face of my doubts. They do not prove that the hurts I feel all fit into a splendid pattern. But they may help me feel that God is my friend even when I suffer more than I deserve.

Let me speak of them.

Afterward, I will let my *heart* speak.

FIRST, I REALIZE THAT GOD GIVES ME THE KIND OF WORLD I WANT TO LIVE IN

I really want to be the sort of creature who can get hurt. I do not want to be an angel. I like being a body with nerve endings that give me pleasure when a woman touches them gently. But if she can give me pleasure by her tender touch, I must take the risk that she could hurt me with a brutal word.

He also made us free spirits in a world of free spirits. I like this part too. I would not change it for a world where people were nice to me because they had to be. But if I want to live among free people, I take the risk that some of them will sometimes do me wrong.

Pain comes with the territory. And I like being here. So why should I forgive God?

I do not feel much like forgiving someone for my suffering when he suffers as much as I do, maybe a lot more. When I complain to God: "Where were you when I needed you?" I think he says, in a still small voice, "I was there hurting with you."

Jesus wondered where God was when he was dying on the cross: "My God, My God, why have you let me down?"

But *had* God forsaken him? In retrospect, we know where God was while Jesus was hanging on the tree. God was not on leave of absence. He was in Jesus, suffering the pains of vulnerable love.

When I wonder where God is and what he is doing when I get hurt, one answer may be that he is *in me* and that my pains hurt him more than they hurt me. He is suffering with me, maybe to heal a small corner of his world through me. Maybe he suffers with us while he is working to bring about a new world where justice and peace embrace, and unfair pain is gone forever. This thought helps when I wonder if I should forgive God.

I BELIEVE THAT GOD FORGIVES

What does God do when bad people hurt innocent people for no good reason? One answer is: he forgives them.

I think of a conversation between two brothers, Ivan and Alyosha, in Dostoevski's novel *The Brothers Karamazov*. Ivan was an atheist. Alyosha was a believer. Ivan had seen some terrible things in his time; he had seen a little boy fed to a lord's wild dogs while his father and mother had to look on, all because the boy had eaten some fruit off the lord's trees. And a lot more. How can we believe that God could let bad people do such horrible things to innocent children?

Alyosha had no answer. He could think of only one thing to say. "There is one being who can forgive everybody everything because he shed his innocent blood for everyone and everything."

Did Alyosha really answer his brother? Not directly. But he did raise another question more serious than the one Ivan asked: Why should you forgive God when it is he who must forgive the people who are really responsible for doing the terrible things?

Something in me bends to Alyosha's answer.

These are some things I think about when I wonder where God is when people suffer. They help me feel him as a fellow-suffering friend of sufferers, not someone I need to forgive.

But they do not solve everything. The heart still wonders.

It helps to know that pain is a necessary shadow in the sunlit world in which I want to live. But does it have to hurt *so much?* It helps to know that God suffers with us when we suffer unfairly. But could he not heal it a *little faster?* It helps to know that God is willing to forgive people who hurt us. But could he not *prevent* some of the evil people from doing as much harm as they do?

I think we may need to forgive God after all. Now and then, but not often. Not for his sake. For ours!

So let us talk of healing ourselves as we forgive God.

Something happened to Doris and me once that forced me to come to terms with forgiving God. I am going to talk about it, though I know that what happened to us was not nearly as bad as a lot that happens to many, many other people; I mention it only because it was *our own* watershed time for forgiving God.

Doris and I had decided early on that we would have children as soon as I finished studies. But it didn't work. Doris did not get pregnant.

We went to fertility clinics everywhere we lived—in Amsterdam, in Oxford, in Illinois, in New Jersey, and in Grand Rapids, Michigan. We made love whenever the thermometer told us the time was at hand. We played our parts in the unromantic comedy of artificial insemination. We prayed in between.

And Doris finally did get pregnant, a little late in time, but really and roundly pregnant. What we wanted most was going to happen to us. Four months went by, and then another, and another. The seventh month began.

One night, getting towards ten, I was fixing crackers and cheese in the kitchen and Doris was muttering something sleepy from the sofa about getting herself to bed when, with the sentence only half out, she yelled my name. I knew instinctively that something bad was happening. It was. A dam had broken inside of Doris and she was flooding the davenport with an amniotic downpour.

Call the doctor. I fumbled my trembling index finger into the right holes of the telephone dial and finally got Ed Postma, our obstetrician, and heard from him a message I wanted terribly not to hear.

"Listen carefully. Put Doris in the car and get down to emergency. But I need to tell you something first so that you can tell Doris before you get here: the baby is going to be malformed, badly."

I got Doris wrapped in swaddling clothes and nestled her, legs bent high, into the back seat of our rusted-out red Plymouth sedan.

And I dropped the horrible reality like a horrid lump into her frightened mind.

Badly malformed.

Can you live with it? Yes, I think I can. Can you? I don't know.

Our doctor was waiting for us in the emergency room.

We got Doris admitted and wheeled into the space for women on their joyous passage to the wonder of life-giving.

After several hours, time enough for us to come to grips with what was happening to us, her intervals of pain signaled that the hour of deliverance had come. I carried my vacant terror to a little sitting room where a truck driver, ten years younger than I, was waiting for his wife to give him a third perfect offspring. "God, I am not ready for this."

120

A couple of hours later Ed Postma came in, green-smocked, face mask still hanging over his chin, with a grin on his face that looked obscene to me. But his words were wonderful to hear. "The baby is fine," he said. "We were mistaken. Everything seems to be OK. A boy. Come on, we'll have a look."

We had a look. Offspring of my loins, soul of my soul, flesh of my flesh, hair of my hair, he lay, body wrinkled, eyes, nose, mouth pushed into three inches of crimson face, fingers like wee spindlings wrapped into fists the size of two red marbles, and he screamed. I was what I wanted to be; the blood father of a normal man-child.

I drove home in a joyous delirium that comes from a belief that the best thing that could possibly happen to anyone had just happened to me. I got a few hours of sleep, woke up and made plans to call some friends with my good news.

Before I had a chance to call anybody, however, our pediatrician called me from the hospital. I knew from his inflection that the milk of God's mercy was suddenly turning sour. The baby was not breathing well. I should come.

I drove back to where I knew there would not be a second miracle.

While Doris was still in the hospital I buried the baby. Doris never had a chance to see what he looked like. She brought him alive into the world while I waited outside and I brought him dead into the ground while she waited inside.

Then I began to feel the hurt. The hurt was the loss of what we had waited for, for so long, and wanted more than we wanted anything else. But it was also the teasing meanness of the crazy game that made us dizzy with pain. Why, after the night of getting ready to love a deformed child; why, after the surprise that even doctors called a miracle; why, miracle done, was death the punch line? I felt as if I were the butt of a cruel divine joke.

Would I end up hating God? I knew I would never have the courage to bring my hate up front, where God could see it. I would turn my hate, as Jeremiah did, on life.

But we healed ourselves more quickly than we thought we could. I wasn't aware of it then, but I know now that what we did for healing was something like forgiving God.

We leaned on each other for strength; and we soon began together to feel a strange sense of our life's goodness in spite of this one rotten thing about it that had come upon us one cruel night when we felt we had a right to something very good. The feeling came to us; we did not arrive at it as a thinker finds his answer to an intellectual problem. We just sat there on her bed, and we cried, wondered, loved, grieved together, and, in our all-aloneness, hardly thought straight about anything at all.

We *felt together,* never wondering whether it hurt one of us more than the other, only sensing that we were together in our grief and our emptiness and our confusion. And that was good. Our life was good in our *shared* hurt!

In our strange euphoria about life's goodness, I felt God again as the giver, not the taker of life. As the God I know in the suffering Jesus, not a god who pointlessly makes us suffer.

I knew that I could not feel this goodness and also think that God took my child away. I knew my mind would forever say "I don't know" when my heart asked why little babies die. I heard my heart tell me that God was with us, "dying" a little along with our baby.

I understand no more today than I did then about how God was involved within the crazy game Doris and I had to play that March night. But I am sure that I shall never throw it up to him or remind him of the time he let us down.

Did I forgive God? In a way I suppose I did.

But there is a difference between forgiving God and forgiving an enemy. When you forgive your enemies, they may stay your enemies even after you forgive them. When you forgive God, you just live in the silence, and grope toward the goodness of life, and believe that, in spite of everything, he is your friend.

Part 3

HOW PEOPLE FORGIVE

Forgiving is love's revolution against life's unfairness. When we forgive, we ignore the normal laws that strap us to the natural law of getting even and, by the alchemy of love, we release ourselves from our own painful pasts.

We fly over a dues-paying morality in order to create a new future out of the past's unfairness. We free ourselves from the wrong that is locked into our private histories; we unshackle our spirits from malice; and, maybe, if we are lucky, we also restore a relationship that would otherwise be lost forever.

Forgiving is a miracle, however, that few of us have the magic to perform easily. Never underestimate the demands that forgiving puts on an average person's modest power to love. Some skeptics, when they heard Jesus forgive people, challenged: "Who can forgive sins, but God alone?" The English novelist Charles Williams remarked that forgiving is really a game; we can only play at it, he said, essentially we cannot do it.

Nobody seems to be born with much talent for forgiving. We all need to learn from scratch, and the learning almost always runs against the grain.

We talk a good forgiving line as long as somebody else needs to do it, but few of us have the heart for it while we are dangling from one end of a bond broken by somebody else's cruelty.

Yet, people *do* forgive—ordinary people, not saints—and they do heal themselves of terrible pain.

I invite you to see how ordinary people work out their own ways of forgiving. They do not have to be your ways, not in detail, certainly. But it may help to watch how other people do it. Don't expect gimmicks or techniques; look for signals and hints. Remember, nobody said it was going to be easy.

CHAPTER 11

Slowly

It takes time. A lot of time for some. Sometimes you struggle with it so long that you cannot remember the moment you finally did it; you just wake up one day and, on thinking about those you want to forgive, are a little shocked to realize you have already begun to forgive them. You know it because you find yourself wishing them well.

As a boy, C. S. Lewis, the British Christian scholar who wrote marvelous children's fantasies, was badly hurt by a bully who made a living as a teacher in an English public school. This sadist turned the lives of his boys into a living hell. Lewis could not forgive this teacher, not for most of his life, and being a failure at forgiving troubled him. But not long before he died, maybe just a few months, he wrote a letter to an American friend.

Dear Mary,

. . . Do you know, only a few weeks ago I realized suddenly that I had at last forgiven the cruel schoolmaster who so darkened my childhood. I'd been trying to do it for years; and like you, each time I thought I'd done it, I found, after a week or so it all had to be attempted over again. But this time I feel sure it is the real thing. . . .

Yours,
Jack

It was the real thing, no doubt. But maybe, if he had lived, Lewis would have had to do it a few more times. The hate habit is hard to break, harder than any, I think. And, as we do with other bad habits, we usually break it many times before we finally get rid of it altogether.

I joined two old friends recently in a lunch to commemorate the thirtieth anniversary of a great academic debacle. They were the heroes of the piece, professors at the seminary where I had been a student. We saw them then as young men with a dream, injecting a new vision into a bone-weary academic body. Others saw them as cocky threats to a great orthodox tradition. So, while the world outside knew little and cared less, they began a battle for the mind and heart of that school.

A classic struggle was joined between scholarly vitality and academic rigor mortis. Rigor mortis won. My friends were fired. And deeply hurt! Gallant all the way, but out on the street nonetheless.

Thirty years later, I raised the one question that I thought was worth asking my old teachers: "Have you forgiven the people who got you fired?"

One of them answered, "Come to think of it, I have been forgiving them for a long time. I slowly got it through my head that I needed forgiving as much as they did. What's more, it gradually dawned on me that the other men were about equally as decent and about as sneaky as I was. So about ten years ago I found myself wishing them well. We never became friends, but if our situations had been different we might have. So, I guess I have forgiven—and I think I've been forgiven. It took me a long time, too long, but I'm glad it's been done."

The worse you've been hurt the longer it takes to forgive. Minor bruises can be handled quickly. But when you've been sliced and diced inside your being, you'd better count on a longer process.

Sometimes we do it so slowly that we pass over the

line without realizing we have crossed it, as children pass from childhood to adulthood not knowing just when they crossed over.

Sometimes you seem to slide into forgiving, hardly noticing when you began to move or when you arrived. But after a long dry desert of trying, you gradually get a feeling that somewhere along the way you crossed the line between hating and forgiving.

At the beginning of the process, it helps to make a firm decision—one way or the other, fish or cut bait, here and now, and that's that—just to get going.

I remember a delicious hate I tasted a year or so ago that I would probably still be sucking on if I hadn't made a hard decision to spit it out. Let me tell you about it.

One warm June day, in midafternoon, a cop in our little town of Sierre Madre, hot with zeal to keep village pot smoking under control, brutalized my youngest son, John, in front of my own house. He was large, 250 pounds or so of vigorous lawman, and he threw all his violent bulk against my slender 140 pounder who, unknown to the officer, had a liver ailment that made hard physical contact a hazard to his life. In any case, the policeman roughed up John excessively and then charged him with resisting an officer.

The charge was quickly dismissed.

But I did not so quickly dismiss my bitterness. I took my anger down to city hall and tried to persuade the chief to rebuke the officer, just a bawling out, if you please, to help keep brute force in check. I offered signed statements by witnesses to the assault. But the chief of police in our peaceful village was not moved to criticize his own. He said he would look into the matter, but he never gave me reason to believe that he did. Case closed.

I did a secret dance of rage for several days, and the blue notes of anger gradually rose to cymbal-clanging hate. I controlled myself too well to knock anybody's block off, but I hated, passively at least; there was not an ounce of energy in me to wish the Sierra Madre police force well.

My hate almost became an instant addiction; I was infected by its virus, and I spread it to everyone who got close to me. To bring my hate to a spiritual crisis, I had a date coming up to preach a sermon on the grace of God at a Presbyterian church in Burbank.

Before Sunday came, I confided my feelings to a good friend, expecting her to add female indignation to my male malice; we would, I thought, sing a doleful duet of rage.

But she was on to me.

"Why don't you practice what you preach?"

I was trapped.

I had to decide then and there whether I really wanted to kick my hate before it got to be a habit. So I did. I opted out of hate.

But how could I make it work on the spot? I tried a technique that everything in my temperament resisted. I thought about how a priest gives instant absolution to a penitent, right off the bat, in the confessional booth. And I decided to give this cop absolution. It wasn't my style. I like to take my time when I solve my spiritual crises. But I tried it.

"Officer Milando, in the name of God I hereby forgive you. *Absolvo te*—go in peace." I said it out loud, at least six times.

Well, it worked enough to get me going anyway. I felt myself pry a couple of inches off my hate. And I was on my way.

A beginning. I am not finished with it yet. But I think that a clear-cut choice for forgiving was what I needed to set me in motion.

For some people, one definite decision is enough. For most of us, it is only a start on a long forgiving journey.

CHAPTER 12

With a Little Understanding

A little understanding makes forgiving a lot easier. If you understand *everything*, of course, you don't have to forgive at all. But it helps to understand *something* when forgiving comes very hard.

When we get hurt we are half-blinded by our pain. There is always more going on in an encounter with pain than meets the eye of somebody freshly hurt; it takes a while to see it. Even longer to understand it.

Sometimes, by understanding *some* of what was really going on inside the person who hurt you, you make forgiving a little bit easier for yourself, even though you still have to plow by hand through a thick crust of hurt and hate.

Careful, though; you are not going to understand *everything*. Those who hurt you did not really have to do it; they could have acted differently. To that extent, you will always be left with mystery; you can never fully understand evil *freely* chosen.

But if you can understand what might have influenced them, and understand a little bit of how they could have hurt you, you'll take a first step toward forgiving.

The hardest person for me—ever, in my whole life—to forgive was Mrs. Broutmeier. Mrs. Broutmeier lived in a yellow frame house across the street from the smallish house my father built with his own hands for us to live in just before I was born. This woman was unbelievably cruel to my mother and her memory has plagued me for years.

131

My parents shipped off third-class to the United States from Friesland, a province up in northernmost Holland, as soon as they were wed. My father lived just long enough to see five children born and to get his own house almost built on Amity Avenue in Muskegon, Michigan. Then he died, only thirty-three years old and hardly underway. I was the last of the five.

Left alone, with few skills and no money, my mother put bread on our table and clothes on our bodies by cleaning other people's houses and washing other people's clothes in a secondhand Maytag that broke down every other Monday.

On Amity, every house had its own splendid maple at the curb; too big around for climbing, they provided fine shade for sitting on the wooden swing that hung from the ceiling of each front porch. Our houses were all perpendicular to the street, none of your rambling ranches there: livingroom up front and a kitchen out back, with a dining room tucked in between them. You could shoot a rifle from the back stoop of the kitchen straight through the front door without hitting anything. Sometimes, if they were set just right, you could stand at your back door and look through your house all the way through the house across the street. The houses looked at each other, bay window to bay window, like poker players in a stare-down.

Our own house stood eyeball to eyeball with the Broutmeiers'.

I should explain that the Broutmeiers were our "betters." What made them "better" was partly that Mr. Broutmeier had a steady job and Mrs. Broutmeier stayed home and kept her children's noses clean. (You were a high-class kid in our neighborhood if your mother never let your nose get snotty.) But their "betterness" came out most plainly in the accent factor; they spoke English like real Americans. They were second-generation people; they had been around, they knew how to live, and, more than anything, they knew how to talk.

Mrs. Broutmeier, in all her true American betterness, became a monster. She had a co-monster next door, too, and the two of them set up a neighborhood CIA to keep an eye on the subversive goings-on at our house. She and her fellow monster drew straws at dusk every day to see which of them would report the delinquencies of her grubby kids to my mother as she came home from that day's scrubbing.

Once they both came across Amity to deliver to my mother the well-considered counsel of her betters that she should give her two youngest children—my brother Wesley and me—away as orphans, the reason being that my mother lacked the money and the savvy to care for us all in a proper manner. I remember getting word once that Mrs. Broutmeier had decreed that I should not cross Amity street to play with her children; I was exiled to the north side of the street on grounds of a dirty nose. It seemed to us, in fact, that the Broutmeiers had us staked out, night and day.

Mrs. Broutmeier and her confederate pressed the advantage of second-generation Americanism to the moral edge; they wore my mother down with shame. They got her to feel that it was a shameful thing for a woman with a brood of little children to let her husband die so young and an immoral thing to be talking to real Americans with a foreign accent on her tongue.

But my mother dipped her shame into a cup of heroic wrath. Deep down, where God's gift of dignity was simmering in her soul, she raged, she seethed. She was a goddess with fire in her bosom.

One Saturday night, done in, as if life had tied the terrible tiredness of all six working days in a bundle and given her one final blow, the latest Broutmeier slap at one of her children popped the safety valve on her fury.

We were, all six of us, in the kitchen, waiting for a pot of brown beans to finish baking, when, driven by the furies inside of her, she left the stove and strode head down, face red, fists tight, through the dining room, the livingroom, and out the front door. With apron strings fluttering behind her, she stalked across

Amity and up the Broutmeier front stoop to lay siege on the monster. The hosts of heaven never had a chance to stop her.

The five of us huddled around our bay window; we could see it all from there.

She pounded on the front door and, when Mrs. Broutmeier opened it a wedge, she pushed it aside and walked into the devil's lair. Face aflame, eyes brimming with tears, finger cocked straight at the shocked Broutmeier eyes, the widow Smedes launched a frenzied defense of her beloved brood.

Mrs. Broutmeier retreated to the dining room and took up a protected position on the other side of a round oak table with its blue Dutch teapot holding at the center. My mother used the table as a pulpit, pounding on it with her fist as she delivered her furious, inspired, but unrecorded prophecy against Broutmeier and on behalf of her own children. Mrs. Broutmeier sputtered something about the police, about calling them, and about being attacked by a woman gone crazy.

The word "crazy" seemed to bring my mother to her humiliated senses. Was she crazy? Maybe she was. She didn't know. If she was crazy, she was the more to be shamed. Better get out of there just in case. She left by the front door.

She walked, head still down, face white now, back across Amity, up our front porch, into the living room, past her children clustered at the window; she didn't look at us, didn't say anything to us, but strode straight ahead, through the dining room and kitchen, into the bathroom, and vomited. Then she wept. I do not remember when she came out or what she said to us when she did.

What I do remember is that we were sure Mrs. Broutmeier had done us all in. Our cup of shame was full. We would never have a friend in the neighborhood again.

I grew up hating Mrs. Broutmeier. I wanted her house to burn down. I hoped her children would fail in

134

school and get into a lot of trouble. I wanted them all to go to hell. My boyhood cup of aggressive hate was full.

Have I forgiven her?

I am still in the process of forgiving her. I enjoyed my hate too long, but I started to heal a long while ago and I am well on the way.

But I could never have forgiven her at all if I had not also tried to understand her.

I learned something about people who were born Americans, but from the womb of an immigrant. The Broutmeiers were second-generation immigrants with second-generation problems; they felt second-class to third-generation Americans, *their* "betters"—the "real" Americans. I learned how an ignorant woman with pride and ambition could think of a family like ours as a pool of inferiors in whose reflection she could see herself as almost equal to her own betters. I came to understand that our "inferiority" was a stool she stood on to lift herself to the level of the people a rung above her. In short, I came to see her as a weak, needy, and very silly woman who was using cruelty as a way of coping.

But I do not understand everything. I do not understand how Mrs. Broutmeier could freely choose to be so cruel. She was not driven by demons or dispatched by destiny to make my mother's life miserable. So even if I understand some of her circumstances, something about her cruelty is still beyond my grasp. She freely *chose* to hurt a decent woman, a neighbor who badly needed a friend, and such a choice is never to be completely understood.

Understanding your enemies helps bring them down to size. When we first feel the raw smart of an unfair assault, we draw a bloated caricature of that person— twice as large, twice as powerful, and twice as evil. Rotten to the core.

It also helps if you can understand *yourself* a little better, as the following story illustrates.

One night, right after Walter Cronkite had signed

off, Lena Brusbeck's husband Ben blurted out that he was in love with a woman half his age, had been for three years, and wanted to marry her.

What? For three years? The three years Lena had slept with him, nursed him, protected him from his nosey parents, kept track of his schedules, got him to work on time, made him look good and smell good, and, in general, made straight the highway for Ben and his trollop to get together? Those three years?

Lena's very virtue was her undoing. She trusted; he betrayed. She gave; he stole. She was true; he was a liar. She was faithful; he was faithless. Her only fault was the blindness of her pure love. Virtue had made a sucker of her.

Certain that any fool of a judge would see the rightness of her case, Lena hired a lawyer and sued for divorce. But Ben got himself the devil's own barrister, and he pulled Lena naked across the barbed wire of his inquisition and twisted her words into a testimony against herself. She began to look like the sharp-toothed culprit and Ben the guileless victim.

But the worse the lawyer made her look, the purer Lena felt.

She spent the next three years scourging her soul with replays of Ben's assault on her innocent devotion. She was insecure enough in her righteousness to risk some counseling with a view to getting psychological support for her malice. But her hate was undermined instead. As she found new insight into herself the bitter pleasure of her hate lost its edge. The long and short of it was that Lena began to see herself as a tarnished angel.

Ben did not deceive her; she deceived herself. She had really known all the while; but she did not dare to admit that to herself. The truth hurt too much, so she denied the plainest evidence. She wore the blinders of her own fear, more coward than fool. Her first eye-opener—insight into her dishonesty with her own self.

She also came to see that she had not been the self-giving lover she thought she had been. She really wanted security more than she wanted Ben, and she counted on Ben's commitment to give it to her. She bet everything on his morality. Ben was the sort of character who would stick with what he was stuck with. All she needed to do was remind him to be a good boy and she had him where she wanted him.

When she could see herself as she was—some good, some not so good—she made an opening for forgiveness to squeeze through.

Self-understanding reduced the act of forgiving to a minor miracle that even she could manage. She discovered herself wishing Ben well, and she felt free to be a more honest person the next time around.

With a little time, and a little more insight, we begin to see both ourselves and our enemies in humbler profiles. We are not really as innocent as we felt when we were first hurt. And we do not usually have a gigantic monster to forgive; we have a weak, needy, and somewhat stupid human being.

When you see your enemy and yourself in the weakness and silliness of the humanity you share, you will make the miracle of forgiving a little easier.

CHAPTER 13

In Confusion

Forgiving is wisdom's high art; most of us who work at it, however, are muddlers and bunglers. We usually move toward forgiving in the cross-currents of our confusion.

The confusion is not all our fault. The material we work with is often a mess. Exactly what happened is often unclear. Who did what to whom? How badly?

True, at the kernel of every falling-out, one person hurt another person. The bad guy does a bad thing and the good guy suffers for it. But tangled around that simple core of wrongful pain, we often find a skein of hurts and hates that is nearly impossible to unravel.

We are also hampered by a bog of *emotional* slough. To expect two people caught in mutual hate to sort out their pains is like asking a child to calculate the national debt. We often have to grope into forgiving through snarls of feeling as well as clogs of misunderstanding.

Just to show how decent people can stumble their way into forgiving through the dust of their homemade confusion, let me tell you about a sorry little drama in which I played a leading, but rather ridiculous role.

I had come to a new job in a new city where I had no friends, and I felt very insecure about my prospects for doing well. I knew only two people in town, Ted and Doreen, old acquaintances whom I hoped would become instant friends. I certainly needed them to.

Ted and Doreen had a chance to be a lot of help to

Doris and me almost as soon as we arrived. Doris landed in the hospital just as I got going at my work, and the children sometimes needed a place to go after school. Doreen came through generously and warmly. We were on our way to friendship, I thought.

Then, silently but effectively, Doreen closed the door. A freeze on friendship! A foreclosure on warmth!

What had I done? How had I offended? I went to Ted.

"Tell me what I did to hurt Doreen."

"Don't ask. Let well enough alone."

I couldn't let well enough alone. I had to get it all straightened out; I became a compulsive penitent. I asked again, got the same silence.

I wrote Doreen a letter, grieving for whatever pain I caused, asking forgiveness.

No answer. I didn't exist.

Now it was my turn. I was hurt, and my hurt quickly turned to hate. I was no longer the groveling penitent who had done someone wrong. Now I was the hurting victim; Doreen was doing *me* wrong. And I admit that sour resentment tasted better in my mouth than stale penitence.

But the situation was confused.

Which one of us really had to forgive the other and which of us needed to be forgiven? And if we both needed to forgive *and* be forgiven, who needed it most? Could we ever get it straightened out?

Out of molehills like this smart people are stupid enough to make mountains that only free forgivers can climb.

Forgiveness did come. It came by fits and starts, trickles, driblets of it seeping down the drains of our mutual resentments, but it did come.

Doreen and I moved toward forgiveness *as we made three shifts in our feelings* about our falling-out.

First, *we reduced our stakes*. In the early stage of our petty falling-out, we invested massive emotional resources in trivial offenses. We put our personal self-esteem on the block. We inflated the stakes beyond anything like their real worth. But time, that unsung colleague of love, gave us a chance to reduce our investments.

After all, what had Doreen done? And what had I done? Nothing much, probably; the impact on our feelings simply did not match the weight of each other's offenses. So we let each other's faults melt down to their real size. And our pain melted with our anger as we scaled down our mutual indictments.

Second, *we reduced what we expected from forgiveness.* As a matter of fact, Doreen and I no longer really wanted to be close friends. All we wanted from each other now was good will and a little respect. Once we understood that we did not *have* to be close friends after we forgave each other, that we did not *have* to come together the way I had wanted it earlier, our worried resentments receded as a spring flood slips back into the soft earth. Forgiveness was no longer a threat; we could forgive without feeling an obligation to embrace each other as good friends do. Being comfortable with each other in the same room, at the same table, at the same party was enough.

Third, *we reduced our desire for an even score.* We gave up trying to keep score of who did what to whom and how badly it hurt. We learned to leave the loose ends dangling, the scales off balance, to accept a score that neither of us could make come out even.

Full forgiving did not come in the twinkling of an eye. It came in bits and pieces with an unexpected meeting here, a gesture there, the exchange of a greeting, and a hint that better feelings were beginning to flow. We floundered into forgiving.

Not a triumph of the forgiver's art, I agree. But healing often comes on the wings of trivia. And the end is not always an ecstasy. We go to the same receptions and feel good wishing each other a Merry Christmas. Sometimes small mercies are tender enough.

We don't have to be virtuosos at the forgiving game to make it work.

CHAPTER 14

With Anger Left Over

Is there anger after forgiving?

Yes, often. It can't be helped.

Some people believe that they should not feel anger in their hearts once they forgive.

I do not agree. I think that anger and forgiving can live together in the same heart. You are not a failure at forgiving just because you are still angry that a painful wrong was done to you.

It is terribly unrealistic to expect a single act of forgiving to get rid of all angry feelings.

Anger is the executive power of human decency. If you do not get angry and stay angry when a bad thing happens, you lose a piece of your humanity.

Remember, you cannot erase the past, you can only heal the pain it has left behind.

When you are wronged, that wrong becomes an indestructible reality of your life. When you forgive, you heal your hate for the person who created that reality. But you do not change the facts. And you do not undo all of their consequences. The dead stay dead; the wounded are often crippled still. The reality of evil and its damage to human beings is not magically undone and it can still make us very mad.

A man does not *forget* that his father abused him as a child. A woman does not *forget* that her boss lied to her about her future in the company. You do not *forget* that a person you loved has taken cheap advantage of you and dropped you when the relationship was not paying off. I dare say that Jesus has not forgotten that a man named Judas betrayed him. And survivors of the holocaust do not forget the hell of that experience.

And when you do remember what happened, how can you remember except in anger?

Can you look back on the painful moment—or painful years—without a passionate, furious, aching longing that what hurt you so much had never happened? Some people probably can. But I don't think you should expect such placid escape from terrible memories. You can be angry still, and you can have your anger without hate.

Once you start on your forgiving journey, you will begin to lose the passion of malice. Malice goes while anger lingers on. When forgiving begins its liberating work, the malice that once hissed like white flame from an acetylene torch begins to fizzle out.

A man slowly finds himself wishing his ex-wife well in her new marriage. A father is surprised at how desperately he wants his rebellious daughter to be happy. We wish a blessing on the frail humanity of the person who hurt us, even if we were hurt unfairly and deeply.

What is happening? Malice is gradually fading, just as your head gradually stops pounding after you take three aspirin. You have anger without malice—a sign that your forgiving is real.

Anger minus malice gives hope. Malice, unrelieved, will gradually choke you. But anger can goad you to prevent the wrong from happening again. Malice keeps the pain alive and raw inside your feelings, anger pushes you with hope toward a better future.

There are three things you can do to drain the poison of malice while you use the energy of anger. They may be worth trying.

First, *express your malice*. Be specific, nail the object of your fury down. It doesn't help to let malice fester as an ugly glob of undirected misery. And it doesn't help to throw it at people, either. But you need to express it to somebody who can help you get rid of it. You can express it secretly to God, or to someone who represents God to you.

Then, you can let *God handle* those people you would like to manhandle in your hate. If they need teaching, let God teach them. If they need rescuing from their own stupidity, let God rescue them. If they need saving from their own crazy wickedness, let God save them. What you need is *healing* from the infection of malice left over from the open wounds they left in your life.

Finally, you can even *try a prayer* for the peace of the person you hate.

If you do, you may discover another secret of forgiving; you don't have to choke your anger, you only have to surrender your malice. For *your* sake. Malice is misery that needs healing. Anger is energy that needs direction. After malice, let anger do its reforming work. Forgiving and anger can be partners in a good cause.

CHAPTER 15

A Little at a Time

Wholesale forgiving is too much for anybody.

Not long ago a man named Arthur Fram came to me seeking a way to forgive his daughter, Becky, a fragile twenty-one-year old who had been suffering a fairly serious depression for a couple of years.

Becky stayed in bed until noon every morning. The rest of the day she lay on the couch in front of the television set watching soap operas and reruns of sitcoms. She got up once in a while during commercials, but only to stuff herself with junk food.

But there was more. Becky was surly and spiteful toward anyone who got close enough to join her at the television set. When Arthur offered to help her, or when he gingerly suggested that she help herself, she snarled at him like a cornered leopard. If anyone tactfully suggested psychological therapy, she shrieked in defiance against a family that accused her of being crazy.

In this way, Becky wrapped a thick blanket of rage and resentment around her, enveloping her whole family within it.

She needed help—lots of it, and soon.

But so did Arthur. He was ravaged by Becky's ferocious rejection of his longsuffering love. Because she spat poison at him as thanks for his fatherly care, he coiled a serpent of resentment around his fatherly heart. He felt cheated and he couldn't even the score.

Why should *he* have a daughter who had come of

age just in time to hate him with a vicious passion? Why should *he* have to explain to his successful friends, who bragged about their successful kids, why *his* daughter did nothing creative with her life? Why should his daughter play such a dirty trick on him?

Whose fault was it? Arthur had a hunch that it was his. Somewhere, somehow, he must have failed to be the kind of father he should have been. But he suppressed his hunch; he would not accept responsibility. "I'll be damned if I'm going to bear the guilt," he growled to himself—and growled it thirty times a day.

But bear it he did. And he was doubly angry at Becky for being the reason he had to feel such guilt when in another part of his mind he knew himself to be innocent.

Then he heard me talk about forgiving as a road to healing. He wondered whether he might have stumbled onto a quick cure for his aching heart.

He wanted to know how to forgive Becky.

"What do you want to forgive her for?" I asked. "Do you want to forgive her for suffering so much? Do you want to forgive her for hating herself? For condemning herself day and night because of the pain she knows she's causing you? Do you want to forgive her for being a person subject to depression?

"Must Becky be forgiven for letting you down by not being the classy young woman you need to impress your successful friends?"

Arthur was stunned. It was as though he had gone to a doctor for help and the doctor had assaulted him. But I was on to him; I recognized too much of myself in Arthur to let him pull a fast one on me.

Arthur was trying to use forgiveness as a quick and cheap nostrum for pains that forgiveness cannot cure. It cannot heal our narcissistic resentments toward people for not being all that we expect them to be. Nobody can really forgive people for *being* what they are. Forgiveness wasn't invented for such unfair maneuvering.

Arthur may be able to forgive Becky for cursing him

when he offered to take her to a therapist. He can probably forgive her for telling him she hated him at dinner the other night. In fact, he may have the power to forgive her for any of the *specific* things she *did* to help make his life miserable.

But he cannot forgive Becky for being a depressed person.

We overload the circuits of forgiveness when we try to forgive people for being burdens to our existence, or for not being the sort of people we want them to be. There are other means for coping with the threads of tragedy that are woven into the fabric of our lives. They go by such names as courage, empathy, patience, and hope. And God knows they come hard.

But I'm sure that I wouldn't have helped Arthur at all if I had encouraged him to think that he should—or even could—forgive his daughter for being the person she is, even though she has become the sad and needy center of his real, if self-centered, tragedy.

I believe that there is a natural law of forgiveness which requires a price from us when we try to forgive people for being what they are: *Those who forgive people for being what they are only increase their own pain*.

Pain compounds itself when we indulge ourselves with grandiose forgiving. The reason is simple to see. When we try—and fail, as we are bound to—to forgive someone for being what he is, resentment is added to resentment. We blame *him* for our failure to forgive him, as well as for wronging us.

We also end up feeling sorrier for ourselves than we did before, and guiltier too, because now, besides everything else, we are ashamed of ourselves for not being able to forgive. Our pain feeds on itself. It grows like an invisible carcinoma.

The long and short of what I've been saying is that the forgiving that heals focuses on what people *do,* not on what people *are*. The healing art of forgiving has to be practiced a little at a time—for most people anyway.

Ordinary people forgive best if they go at it in bits and pieces, and for specific acts. They bog down if they try to forgive people in the grand manner, because wholesale forgiving is almost always fake. Forgiving anything at all is a minor miracle; forgiving *carte blanche* is silly. Nobody can do it. Except God.

And the first rule for mere human beings in the forgiving game is to remember that we are not God.

CHAPTER 16

Freely, or Not at All

We are never so free as when we reach back into our past and forgive a person who caused us pain.

No one can be forced to forgive. No one forgives by blind instinct. Nor can anyone truly forgive out of duty. We stretch ourselves beyond the call of duty and the push of instinct into the lively sport of personal freedom when we genuinely forgive a person who did us wrong.

How silly, then, for a parent to nag at a daughter to forgive her brother for reading her diary and tattling about the secrets he found there. How futile, too, for a preacher to wheedle his congregation into forgiving their enemies by threats of judgment against unforgiving spirits.

The parent who nags and the preacher who wheedles are using a tactic that cannot work. We forgive freely or we do not really forgive at all.

We are not forgiving freely when we are driven to forgive by some inner need to control the person we forgive. Manipulating through forgiving only makes matters worse. But a lot of people try it.

There are three kinds of manipulative forgivers.

Trigger-happy forgivers fire off forgiveness at a moment's notice. Every time someone causes them some puny inconvenience, they clobber that person with punishing magnanimity.

If you are half an hour late for an appointment with

Joe, he forgives you before you can explain that a long distance phone call came just as you were leaving home. If you do not remember Fran's birthday, she forgives you with the gravity of a judge issuing a death sentence. If Teresa's son does not have his room cleaned, she forgives him without asking for an explanation.

The trigger-happy forgiver forgives the way an old boxer shoots out a left when he sees a twitch in his opponent's eye.

Stung by such indiscriminate forgiving, you may want to say: "But I do not need to be forgiven for this; I did not do anything bad enough to deserve your guilt-loaded forgiving." But you are trapped. The trigger-happy forgiver needs to be in control, so he intimidates through forgiveness.

Then there is *the stalking forgiver*, who sniffs out guilt and tracks it down, stalking it, like a hound dog on the trail of a rabbit. These forgiving sleuths want to find the culprits, tag them as wrongdoers, and then slap them with forgiveness.

Stan Hackley is a stalking forgiver. Stan is in charge of an office where keeping accurate records is of the essence. He walks in the valley of the shadow of fear, lest someone upstairs catch his office in a computer error. But there are ten people in his office who feed the computer at least once a day. He cannot control the diet, and the law of human fallibility decrees that, now and then, one of the ten will offer the wrong menu. When that happens, Stan the manager becomes Stan the stalker. He goes on a furtive hunt, poking for clues, uncloaking the culprit.

Stan wants tension, tears, grinding teeth.

Of course he always forgives. But his forgiving leaves judgment and shame in its backwash. He forgives and runs, leaving resentment circling through the office like summer heat blown around by a ceiling fan.

We also have the *entrappers,* who set people up to do the very thing they need to be forgiven for. Entrappers trap, forgive, and then drive their victims back to do the same thing again—so that they can be forgiven again.

Irma Walcort is an entrapper. She has forgiven her husband Clint at least a thousand times. But each time she forgives, she digs Clint's hole a foot deeper, and shoves him into it again.

Clint is a drunk. He does most of his drinking in the late afternoon, out of Irma's sight. Then he comes home, grunts, flops on the sofa, and sleeps the long evening away.

But on weekends he drinks early, and, by five o'clock Saturday afternoon, at the crescendo of a yelling brawl, he takes a few swats at Irma. He never remembers on Sunday morning. But Irma always remembers.

Like a burned-out priest reciting a Sunday morning liturgy, she snarls back to him all the rotten things he had said the day before, shows him a bruise or two, assures him that, beyond all doubt, he is considerably less than a worm, and then, with the inevitability of a closing commercial, she forgives him. She always forgives. She "forgives" the way a typist slams the carriage back at the end of a line.

Each time Irma forgives him, Clint is reminded that he is the worst louse ever to crawl through the crevices of humanity. The least he can do in response is to punish himself.

How does a lush smite himself? Why he gets drunk, of course. So that he can be thumped and smitten by Irma again, just as he deserves. And be forgiven again.

Loaded with contempt, Irma's forgiving is a cage in which she keeps her tippling husband where she wants him. It is the way of the manipulating forgiver.

To set anyone free, forgiving must be freely given—an act of free love, not a devious power play. Forced forgiving makes matters worse for everybody.

A major ingredient in free forgiving is respect for the person being forgiven. This person is a magnificent creature. You do not forgive your pet dog; you do not forgive your personal computer; you forgive only a superb being called a person. In practice, respect means that you let a person do whatever he or she wants to do with your forgiving.

You forgive in freedom only when you give other people freedom—to do what you don't want them to do at all, if they so choose. Anything less than the gift of freedom is control through forgiving manipulation.

If you try to manipulate people into your contrived version of a happy ending, you are not forgiving freely. And you are not really forgiving at all.

Only if you respect them enough to let them be responsible for what they do with your forgiveness will your forgiving be genuine. It is the risk one always takes in the forgiving game.

A free act is always a risk, one way or the other. Forgiving, above all, is one of freedom's biggest risks. But there is no genuine forgiving any other way.

CHAPTER 17

With a Fundamental Feeling

Ruth has been trying to forgive her mother for years. God knows it is hard to do. She knew early on that her mother never wanted her. She cannot remember ever being held in her mother's arms; as far as she knows, she was never cuddled, never tucked in bed, never kissed. What she does remember is being handed a lot of very expensive toys at a stiff arm's length.

When she was eight, her parents' marriage fell apart; her mother wanted a divorce. But there was Ruth, what would become of little Ruth? So, for the sake of a child she did not want, she hung on with a man she did not love. But she only resented Ruth more for burdening her twice—first with herself and then with her father.

Ruth, in her turn, hates her mother, who locked her out of family love as if she were an enemy alien. She has hated her mother so terribly long. All these years—the hound of her hate always growling in the bottom of her heart! She wishes her mother would die and let her forget, but she knows that her hate will outlive her mother.

Ruth's hate for her mother doesn't stop there—it has a hook in it that catches Ruth herself. In her heart of hearts she feels as if her mother was right about her from the start, that she probably was never worth loving. So she hates herself as much as she hates her mother.

How can Ruth break through the matted tangle of

hate that both binds her to and alienates her from her mother?

I do not think that Ruth will ever forgive her mother or herself until she feels forgiven herself. Coming to terms with the pain of her mother's guilt must follow the pain of coming to terms with her own. When she finally feels forgiven, fully and unconditionally forgiven, she will be free to forgive herself. And in forgiving herself, she will find freedom to forgive her mother.

What is it like to feel forgiven?

Forgiveness is fundamental to every other good feeling.

Try other sorts of delightful feelings and compare them with the feeling of being forgiven. Think of the feeling you have when you finally manage to do what you have been trying to do forever: "I did it! I did it!" The feeling is triumphant. Think of the feeling of making love with someone you really love. Or even the feeling of relief at seeing a familiar landmark after you've been lost and almost out of gas. These are all jubilant feelings, but none of them is fundamental. They do not make or break our joy.

But the fundamental feeling makes a difference to everything.

You feel forgiven at the ground floor of your being, where everything else rests. It is a feeling of total acceptance, a feeling lodged in your deepest self, a feeling that no bad thing you do can take away. You feel totally affirmed, totally loved, totally received. Your entire being is rested because you feel that nothing can separate you from the source of love, even though you cannot do enough good things to earn your right to be there. You know that nothing can really hurt you now.

This fundamental feeling happens *to* you. It comes as you are open to it. You cannot create it; you can only be receptive to it.

But you can *close* yourself to it. How?

One sure way of missing out on the fundamental

feeling is to worry too much about being a spiritual success.

We all want badly to have a place in the sun, nestled securely alongside the lucky people who have made it and who think very well of themselves for succeeding so well. We want to walk straight, heads high, in the well-earned sense of our own conspicuous worth. Of course, why not?

But sometimes we need to look at ourselves more honestly.

We do well sometimes to follow our feelings into the darker regions of our lives where we are neither very pretty nor very pure. We are a mixed breed, shadow and light, weak and strong, foul and clean, hate and love, all at the same time. Our middle name is *ambiguity*. Admitting this fundamental ambiguity opens us to the fundamental feeling of being forgiven.

Obsession with spiritual success can take you on idiotic detours around the fundamental feeling. I know a man who needs to be good so badly that he cannot face up to the puniest fault. He often groans about being a poor, poor sinner—always in gorgeous generalities, and always as a trick to get people to reassure him of his unusual virtue. But when his wife complains that he forgot to take out the garbage, he is ready to hire a criminal lawyer to defend himself against her indictment.

Why? The reason is simple: his passion to be a spiritual success will not let him fail at anything at all. He needs to be terribly good because he is scared to death of being the least bit bad. And he loses his chances at the fundamental feeling of being forgiven.

Let me speak for myself. When I am most anxious about my personal worth I become an armed guard of my ego's imperial highness. If someone assaults my self-esteem, I call up all my reserves to defend myself. I get rigid, grim, frightened; I am poised for attack.

I cannot allow myself to accept the feeling of being forgiven.

But in some awful hours of emptiness, when I knew that I could not win my case by defending my virtue, I have emerged feeling forgiven—and free and joyful and hopeful as well. I was free to forgive. Liberated by the fundamental freedom of being forgiven.

My favorite story of the freedom to forgive is the one Corrie Ten Boom tells about herself. Corrie was liberated from a Nazi concentration camp a few days after the Allies conquered Germany. It took longer to be liberated from her simmering hate. But she set out on the forgiving journey through her remembered pain and kept traveling until she arrived at the place where she forgave even the Nazis who had dehumanized her life in the camps.

In forgiving, she believed she had discovered the only power that could heal the history of hurt and hate for the people of Europe. So she preached the possibilities of forgiveness. She preached it in Holland, in France, and then in Germany, too. In Munich one Sunday she preached forgiving, preached it to all those German people who were so eager to be forgiven.

Outside, after the service was over, a major drama of the human spirit unfolded. A man walked over to her; he reached out his hand to her, expecting her to take it. "Ja, Fraulein Ten Boom, I am so glad that Jesus forgives us all of our sin, just as you say."

Corrie knew him. She remembered how she was forced to take showers, with other women prisoners, while this beast looked on, a leering, mocking "superman," guarding helpless naked women. Corrie remembered. He put his hand close to her. Her own hand froze at her side.

She could not forgive. She was stunned and terrified by her own weakness. What could she do, she who had been so sure that she had overcome the deep hurt and the desperate hate and had arrived at forgiving, what could she do now that she was confronted by a man she could not forgive?

She prayed. "Jesus, I can't forgive this man. Forgive me." At once, in some wonderful way that she was not prepared for, she felt forgiven. Forgiven for not forgiving.

At that moment—in the power of the fundamental feeling—her hand went up, took the hand of her enemy, and released him. In her heart she freed him from his terrible past. And she freed herself from hers.

The linkage between feeling forgiven and the power to forgive is the key to everything else.

Let me get back to my friend Ruth, the gifted woman who has suffered so long because she cannot forgive her mother. Ruth cannot forgive her mother because she does not feel forgiven herself.

Her freedom to forgive must come from a fundamental feeling of personal freedom from any and all condemnation, her own or God's or anyone else's. The fundamental feeling has no soil for hate to grow in, no nourishment for hate to feed on; when we experience the fundamental feeling, hate dies a natural death, and when hate dies we are free to forgive.

Do you remember Roger Sewall? Roger was the young man who was killed so cruelly by a hit-and-run driver.

Roger's mother, Phyllis, poured some of her pain into a diary, to help herself get through her terrible tangle of anger while she awaited the trial of the man who killed her son. She let me read her diary and allowed me to share what she wrote in it.

First, she reveals her hurt, and her hate.

"I don't know how I feel. I'm still mad. I'm mad at [Charid] for being on drugs . . . I want him to hurt. I want him to suffer for his guilt and feel our pain. I want him to have years of tortured dreams and sleepless nights. . . . God, I don't want to forgive him. . . ."

But Phyllis is a deeply spiritual person, and she could not feel her hate without feeling a need within herself. Moved by her own need, she approaches the edge of the fundamental feeling.

"What foolish children we are. . . . We keep turning

away . . . yet you reach out . . . and you say—I forgive you."

Now she claims it.

"I . . . receive . . . receive the forgiveness you have held out for us since the day *your* son died."

But she struggles a while longer.

"Can I forgive like that? No. I can't. . . . Help me God. Help me . . . to say . . ."

She couldn't finish the sentence; she couldn't write, "I forgive."

A few months later. Tears and anger later. In the power that comes from life's fundamental feeling, she finished the struggle.

"I forgive Sid Charid."

And she really did.

I don't know whether Phyllis's act ever touched the life of the man she forgave. I don't know whether he will ever forgive himself. What I do know is that when she forgave the man who killed her son, Phyllis began her own journey into healing. Maybe she has had to begin again, many times, but she is on the way.

Part 4

WHY FORGIVE?

There is a lot to be said for *not* forgiving people who have done us wrong. Why should people cut and thrust their way through our lives, leaving us bleeding in their wake, and then expect us to forgive everything and act as if nothing went wrong?

Forgiving *is* an outrage against straight-line dues-paying morality. "A beggar's refuge," George Bernard Shaw called it. And anyone who preaches the beauty of forgiveness should get it through his head that what he urges us to do goes against the grain of any decent person's yen for a fair deal.

We must face up to the skeptic's suspicion that forgiving is really a religious trick to seduce hurting people into putting up with wrongs they do not deserve.

Remember that we are talking about forgiving things that we feel are insufferable. We are not talking about the petty pains in the neck that we inevitably suffer in the human crush.

We are talking about forgiving people who have wronged us, hurt us, deeply and unfairly, and left us feeling lower than any human being in God's image should ever feel.

We must listen to the voices that cry out against forgiving such people indiscriminately.

If we hear these voices clearly, we will recognize in them an echo coming from our own hearts.

For the honest heart is outraged by cheap nostrums for unfair hurts; it does not want to forgive at all, if forgiving leaves the victim exposed and encourages the wrongdoer to hurt again.

So we shall ask: Why forgive?

And we shall answer: because forgiving is the *only* way we have to a better fairness in our unfair world; it is love's unexpected revolution against unfair pain and it alone offers strong hope for healing the hurts we so unfairly feel.

Let us go on, then, so that you can test the fairness of forgiving on the touchstone of your own heart.

CHAPTER 18

Forgiving Makes Life Fairer

Did Shylock have a case? He is, as all villain haters know, the classic unforgiver. But who looks at the business from Shylock's point of view?

We find Shylock in Shakespeare's *Merchant of Venice;* he had been kicked around, badly, and for no good reason. Listen to his complaint. "Antonio," he said,

> hath disgraced me . . .
> Laughed at my losses,
> Mocked my gains,
> Scorned my nation,
> Thwarted my bargains,
> Cooled my friends,
> Heated mine enemies.

And for what? Why did Antonio rub Shylock's face in the muck? Had Shylock done him wrong? Were there scores to settle? No, Antonio was spurred only by the evil spirit of anti-Semitism. Shylock was brutalized only because he was a Jew.

Why, then, should Shylock forgive Antonio as if nothing had happened between them? He asked for no more than he had coming. Antonio had made a bargain. Let the wrongdoer pay his dues. One pound of flesh please! As promised.

Shylock's simple-minded sense of fairness dimmed his wits. It did not take a genius to turn the tables on him: let him have one pound, not an ounce more, and only flesh, not a drop of blood. The Gentiles won the game. But our question is not whether Shylock was smart; it is whether his case was just.

I bring up Shylock only to raise the question of fairness in forgiving.

Simon Wiesenthal tells another sort of story we must hear at all costs; this story of his own terrible crisis of forgiveness in a concentration camp forces us to tremble a little as he asks again whether forgiving is really fair. Wiesenthal was the very opposite of a vengeful Shylock smacking his lips over the pound of flesh that was coming to him. He was a decent person, an architect by profession, caught in the Nazi claws, hoping for no more than to survive the holocaust, and hardly daring to hope for that much.

We find him one afternoon in a Polish concentration camp. Wiesenthal had been assigned that day to clean rubbish out of a hospital that the Germans had improvised for wounded soldiers carried in from the Eastern Front. A nurse walked over to him, out of nowhere, took his arm, ordered him to come with her, and led him upstairs, along a row of stinking wounded, to the side of a bed where a young soldier, his head wrapped in yellow, pus-stained bandages, was dying. He was maybe twenty-two, an SS Trooper.

The soldier, whose name was Karl, reached out and grabbed Wiesenthal's hand, clamped it as if he feared Wiesenthal would run away. He told Wiesenthal that he had to speak to a Jew. He had to confess the terrible things he had done so that he could be forgiven. Or he could not die in peace.

What had he done? He was fighting in a Russian village where a few hundred Jewish people had been rounded up. His group was ordered to plant full cans of gasoline in a certain house. Then they marched about two hundred people into the house, crammed them in until they could hardly move. Next they threw grenades through the windows to set the house on fire. The soldiers were ordered to shoot anyone who tried to jump out of a window.

The young soldier recalled, "Behind the window of

the second floor, I saw a man with a small child in his arms. His clothing was alight. By his side stood a woman, doubtless the mother of the child. With his free hand the man covered the child's eyes—then he jumped into the street. Seconds later the mother followed. We shot . . . Oh, God . . . I shall never forget it—it haunts me."

The young man paused and then said, "I know that what I have told you is terrible. I have longed to talk about it to a Jew and beg forgiveness from him. I know that what I am asking is almost too much, but without your answer I cannot die in peace."

Silence! The sun was high in heaven. God was somewhere. But here, two strangers were all by themselves, caught in the crisis of forgiveness. A member of the super race begged to be forgiven by a member of the condemned race.

Wiesenthal tells us what he did. "I stood up and looked in his direction, at his folded hands. At last I made up my mind and without a word I left the room." The German went to God unforgiven by man.

Wiesenthal survived the concentration camp. But he could not forget the SS trooper. He wondered, troubled, for a long time whether he should have forgiven the soldier. He told the story in his book *The Sunflower,* and ended it with an awful question for every reader: "What would you have done?"

I do not know what I would have done. I can never be sure how I would act in someone else's crisis. I only want to let his story compel us to consider well the outrageous thing we do when we urge anyone, including ourselves, to forgive someone.

Would it have been right for Wiesenthal to forgive? Or would it have been wrong?

Thirty-two distinguished people wrote their answers to Wiesenthal. Most of them echoed Josek, a fellow prisoner, who said to Wiesenthal:

You would have had no right to forgive him in the name of people who had not authorized you to do so. What people have done to you, yourself, you can, if you like, forgive and forget. That is your own affair. But it would have been a terrible sin to burden your conscience with other people's suffering.

A terrible sin to forgive! Why? Because no one may free a criminal's conscience unless he has been the criminal's victim.

But we must not let Wiesenthal's fairness to other victims keep us from asking the question of fairness to the SS trooper and to Wiesenthal himself.

A few writers came out with it: the SS trooper did not deserve forgiveness. Philosopher Herbert Marcuse said what one suspects was on the minds of most people.

One cannot, and should not go around happily killing and torturing and then, when the moment has come, simply ask, and receive forgiveness.

But no one else put the case against forgiving with the passion of novelist Cynthia Ozick:

Often we are asked to think this way: vengeance brutalizes, forgiveness refines. But the opposite can be true. The rabbis said, "Whoever is merciful to the cruel will end by being indifferent to the innocent." Forgiveness can brutalize . . . The face of forgiveness is mild, but how stony to the slaughtered . . . Let the SS man die unshriven. Let him go to hell.

Why *should* he die in peace? Why *should* he be released from his sin by a Jew's word? Why should anyone anywhere forgive this murderer and thus let him go free as if he had never pulled a trigger? Did he not *deserve* to die unforgiven?

Would it have been fair to Wiesenthal himself? He, too, had been awesomely wronged. Here he was, a hugely moral person, locked in a concentration camp, doomed to die with all the others. The Nazis left him with almost nothing; eighty-nine of his relatives were killed. Now, in one unexpected moment, he had the fate of a Nazi in his hands. Why should he not slice the super-race with the cutting edge of his silent contempt? Would he not have done *himself* a terrible injustice if he had spoken gentle words of forgiveness to the German?

Some people do not need a story like Wiesenthal's to tell them forgiving is unfair. They have felt the unfairness inside themselves, in the smaller fires of their own soul's furnace.

Take Jane Graafschap, for example. Jane and her husband, Ralph, had finally brought their three children through the crazy maze of adolescence, and gently pushed them out of the house. Jane was glad they had flown the coop; finally she was going to have a life of her own, get back on her own track and make something of herself.

But a family tragedy stopped her. Ralph's younger brother and his wife were killed in a car crash, and left three children, ages eight, ten and twelve, all by themselves. Ralph had a strong sense of duty; he knew that it was his sacred calling to take his brother's orphaned children in. Jane was too compassionate or too tired to disagree, she never did know which. She took them in, not for a month, but for the duration. As for Ralph, he was gone a lot, a traveling man, on the road, making deals. Nine years groan by. Two of the kids are gone; the only one still home is seventeen, his mind bent slightly out of shape but functional. In a few years Jane and Ralph would be home free.

Not quite. Jane's body had gotten a little lumpy by this time, while Ralph's secretary, Sue, was a dazzler; besides, Sue really understood his large male needs. How could he help falling in love? He and Sue knew that their love was too true to be denied and too powerful to be resisted. So, Ralph divorced Jane and he married Sue.

Ralph and Sue were very happy, and they dunked their happiness in a warm religious froth; their convivial, accepting church celebrated their new-found joy with them. They were kept afloat in togetherness by their affirming Christian community. But Ralph needed one more stroke of acceptance. So he called Jane to ask her to forgive him, and be glad with him that he was finally a happy man. "I want you to bless me," he said.

"I want you to go to hell," she replied. What? Forgive? Throw away the only power she had—the strength of her hate, the energy of her contempt? Her contempt was her power, her dignity, her self-esteem. It was unfair to ask her to forgive. The least the louse deserved was a steady stream of her scorn.

When we urge people to forgive, are we asking them to suffer twice? First they suffer the wrong of another person's assault. They were ripped off. Betrayed. Left out in the cold. Now must they suffer a second injury and swallow an insult to boot? They are stuck with the hurt—must they also bless the person who hurt them?

We must not preach the sublime duty of forgiving to the Simon Wiesenthals or to the Jane Graafschaps until we have chewed the cud of fairness a while. We can "believe in forgiveness only if justice is maintained and guilt is confirmed." Paul Tillich was right. When we say "forgive" we may be asking someone to commit an outrage against humankind's universal instinct for fair play.

Let us see if we *can* make a case for a fair forgiving. I suggest that we look at it from two points of view.

FORGIVING OPENS THE WAY TO A BETTER FAIRNESS

Forgiving is fair to the facts, to begin with.

Forgiving does not try to change the facts in our past. Tampering with the facts of history is faker's fancy; history is implacable. We can begin to forgive only when we refuse the soft-soaped temptation of toning down the wrong of what happened to us.

Someone has been hurt. If we are too proud to admit

that a worm like our husband or our former partner could hurt us, we may avoid the crisis for a little while. If we are too afraid of our own pain to permit ourselves to feel it fully, we may skirt the issue of forgiveness. What shoves us into crisis is our respect for the fact that we have been treated unfairly by somebody who did not have to do it. Forgiving is only for people who are fair to the wretched fact of unfair pain.

Forgiving is also fair, in a paradoxical way, to the dignity of the wrongdoer. If you believe that everything we do is determined for us ahead of time by forces beyond our control, you will never enter the forgiveness circle. If you agree that the idiots who hurt you were only victims of the fates, that they were stuck in the groove their neurotic parents set them in, that they could not help themselves, you do not need to forgive them. Pity them maybe. Retune them if possible. But do not forgive them.

You will forgive only when you dare look at people eyeball to eyeball and tell them that they are responsible for what they did. Forgiving is fair to wrongdoers because it holds them to the incriminating touchstone of their own free humanity.

But back to the heart of the matter. Is forgiving an honorable way to come to terms with the pain you feel when a responsible person stings you deeply and unfairly?

Well, what is the alternative to forgiving?

Must you freeze yourself in the unfairness of a cruel moment in the past? Do you want your private world to stand still at that wretched incident in your irreversible history? Or are you ready to find a better way? Better than what? Better than the pain of a memory glued forever to the unfair past.

But suppose you do refuse to settle for the past and you also refuse to forgive. Is there another option? Maybe revenge?

Vengeance is a passion to get even. It is a hot desire to give back as much pain as someone gave you. An eye for an eye! Fairness!

167

The problem with revenge is that it never gets what it wants; it never evens the score. Fairness never comes. The chain reaction set off by every act of vengeance always takes its unhindered course. It ties both the injured and the injurer to an escalator of pain. Both are stuck on the escalator as long as parity is demanded, and the escalator never stops, never lets anyone off.

Why do family feuds go on and on until everyone is dead—or gets too old and too tired to fight?

The reason is simple: no two people, no two families, ever weigh pain on the same scale. The pain a person causes me always feels heavier to me than it feels to the person who caused it. The pain I inflict on you always feels worse to you than it seems to me. Pains given and pains received never balance out. The difference between pain given and pain suffered is like the difference between climbing a hill and scampering down, it never feels the same in both directions.

If you hurt me and I retaliate in kind, I may think that I have given you only what you deserve, no more. But you will feel it as a hurt that is too great for you to accept. Your passion for fairness will force you to retaliate against me, harder this time. Then it will be my turn. And will it ever stop?

An eye for an eye becomes a leg for a leg and, eventually, a life for a life. No matter what our weapons are—words, clubs, arrows, guns, bombs, nuclear missiles—revenge locks us into an escalation of violence. Gandhi was right: if we all live by "an eye for an eye" the whole world will be blind. The only way out is forgiveness.

Forgiveness is not the alternative to revenge because it is soft and gentle; *it is a viable alternative because it is the only creative route to less unfairness.*

Forgiveness has creative power to move us away from a past moment of pain, to unshackle us from our endless chain of reactions, and to create a new situation in which both the wrongdoer and the wronged can begin a new way.

Forgiveness offers a chance at reconciliation; it is an opportunity for a life together instead of death together. Forgiveness is a miracle of the will that moves away the heavy hindrance to fellowship, a miracle that will be fulfilled when the two estranged people come together in as fair a new relationship as is possible at that time and under those circumstances.

The alternative to reconciliation is, in the end, a ceaseless process of self-destruction. The brilliant American theologian Reinhold Niebuhr saw this after World War II and said: "We must finally be reconciled with our foe, lest we both perish in the vicious circle of hatred." There must be a release from the past or we are forever grounded on its unfair pain.

Vengeance never wholly satisfies. For one thing, we are not always able to fight back. Maybe the person who hurt us is dead. Maybe we are old and weak. What is left to us then but our private truculence? We simmer in our spite, impotent to retaliate and powerless to forgive. Frustrated! Immobilized! This is not the way to make things fairer.

Vengeance mires people in a painful and unjust past. They ought to move toward a new future of fairer relationships, but the inner lust for revenge pushes them deeper into endless repetition of the old unfairness. All in the name, mind you, of fair play.

Forgiveness begins midstream in the flow of unfairness, and starts a new movement toward another fairness, imperfect fairness, to be sure, but better at least than endless perpetuation of the old unfairness. It breaks the grip that past wrong and past pain have on our minds and frees us for whatever fairer future lies amid the unknown potentialities of our tomorrows.

There is no guarantee. But forgiving is the only open door to *possibility*.

FORGIVING IS THE ONLY WAY TO BE FAIR TO OURSELVES

When you suspect that forgiving is not fair, you worry that the people who hurt you are not getting what is coming to them. But you worry, too, that you are getting a bad deal; you get hurt and do not get even. Forgiving may not seem fair to the people who must do the forgiving.

But you are not thinking clearly when you refuse to forgive on grounds that you would not be fair to yourself. Forgiving is the *only* way to be fair to yourself. Getting even is a loser's game. It is the ultimate frustration because it leaves you with more pain than you got in the first place.

Recall the pain of being wronged, the hurt of being stung, cheated, demeaned. Doesn't the memory of it fuel the fire of fury again, reheat the pain again, make it hurt again? Suppose you never forgive, suppose you feel the hurt each time your memory lights on the people who did you wrong. And suppose you have a compulsion to think of them constantly. You have become a prisoner of your past pain; you are locked into a torture chamber of your own making. Time should have left your pain behind; but you keep it alive to let it flay you over and over.

Your own memory is a replay of your hurt—a video-tape within your soul that plays unending reruns of your old rendezvous with pain. You cannot switch it off. You are hooked into it like a pain junkie; you become addicted to your remembrance of pain past. You are lashed again each time your memory spins the tape. Is this fair to yourself—this *wretched justice of not forgiving?* You could not be more unfair to yourself.

The only way to heal the pain that will not heal itself is to forgive the person who hurt you. Forgiving stops the reruns of pain. Forgiving heals your memory as you change your memory's vision.

When you release the wrongdoer from the wrong, you cut a malignant tumor out of your inner life.

You set a prisoner free, but you discover that the real prisoner was yourself.

CHAPTER 19

Forgiving Is a Better Risk

Forgiving could be dangerous to your children's health. A little private forgiving now and then, for the small things, done discreetly and without a lot of fuss, will not threaten the future of human society. But if you forgive big wrongs, and forgive them indiscriminately and openly, you may doom the lives of tomorrow's innocent children.

Forgiving, then, is a serious risk.

Forgiveness, cheaply given, *is* dangerous, let us face it. If we forgive, we are likely to forget; and if we forget the horrors of the past we are likely to let them happen again in the future.

Every act of forgiving can be a nail in somebody else's coffin. If you forgive a man who rapes your sister, you may mute society's scream of outrage against rapists. If you forgive a pusher who sells your daughter cocaine, you may make it a little easier for him to get to your neighbor's daughter too. If you forgive too easily and forget too quickly, you may be turning innocent people over to predators who give not a damn about your forgiveness.

If you forgive the Nazi, it is argued, you will eventually forget the holocaust. If the Armenians forgive the Turks, their children will forget the massacres. If Ukrainian kulaks forgive Stalin, their children will forget how he starved their parents. If Cambodians forgive Pol Pot, their children will forget his massive atrocities against millions of innocent Cambodian people.

The risks of forgetting are both personal and global. Once we forgive and learn to swallow history's stinking garbage without throwing up, we condition ourselves to digest the worst the monsters of the future can force down our throats. When forgiving cures our nausea it encourages us to forget that the evil thing happened and can happen again. If we open the dike a crack, we may be in for a deluge.

After you have forgiven people, it is feared, you will begin to discover all sorts of good things about them. Concentration camp commanders were fine family men. They saw to the slaughter of little children from nine to five and went home to make soothing love to their wives in warm beds of teutonic fidelity. Mafia mobsters gun down their competition in cold blood at noon and by five are home with their children in their old-fashioned family ways. Look at both sides. Maybe the monsters of our history were not as bad as their victims thought.

Ordinary people, it is said, cannot be trusted with forgiveness. Maybe God can forgive sinners without losing his outrage at their sin. Maybe God does not bamboozle himself, maybe he knows that forgiven sinners still have enough rot in their guts to sin again. But most ordinary people let their forgiving wash out the memory and rinse away its bitter taste. They are like drunks who hate booze only as long as their hangover lasts.

As their memories dim, they turn soft. And they make their softness sound like sophisticated insight. They are all too ready, once they forgive, to plead extenuating circumstances—the burdens of history, the hard times, the poverty-drained culture, the pathological family life, the weak genes. They say it was destiny.

Beware the muddle-headed softness of the easy forgiver!

Could I put the case *against* forgiving any more strongly?

One way to reduce the risk is simply to determine not to let the future generations forget. We can tell our children the stories of the past's terrible wrongs. We can build museums to genocide, design artistic monuments to slaughter. We can vow that our children and our children's children will never be allowed not to know. We can tell it on the mountains in every generation.

We must know, however, that remembering has problems of its own. If forgetting invites repetition, remembering incites perpetuation. Memory can nurse a flame that brings hate to its boiling point, creating a pressure inside that only getting even can relieve. But you cannot get even, not ever, not if you try for a million years. So remembering takes its worst toll on the spirits of the people who suffered most.

Is there a narrows to be navigated between the rock of risky forgetting and the hard place of futile remembering?

There is a *redemptive remembering*. There is a healing way to remember the wrongs of our irreversible past, a way that can bring hope for the future along with our sorrow for the past. Redemptive remembering keeps a clear picture of the past, but it adds a new setting and shifts its focus.

No people can tell us about redemptive remembering the way the old Hebrews can. Remembering was their lifestyle. Their memories told them who they were, how they fit into the human picture, and what they were expected to do with themselves. Their future was born yesterday, and by remembering yesterday well they discovered the meaning of their today and the goal of their tomorrow.

Moses posted notice early on that the Hebrews' terrible yesterday had to be kept alive forever so people would know the meaning of what was, what is and what shall be. "Only take heed, and keep your soul diligently, lest you forget the things your eyes have seen and lest they depart from your heart all the days of your life; make them known to your children and your children's children."

No forgetting, ever. If you lose your memory, you lose your own identity. And you lose your personal stake in your people's future.

But take a closer look at what the Jews were supposed to remember. It was not the horror of their four hundred years of slavery. Though slavery was their past. Not the titantic injustice of the Pharaoh in Egypt. Though injustice was their past. They were not ordered to memorialize the evil. An astonishing feature of the post-slavery memorials is that the people are not urged to remember their misery.

What had to be remembered was the miracle of survival and renewal. What had to be remembered were not the days when God was on a leave of absence, but the day when God came back to bring them out of slavery and out of suffering.

The Passover feast was their memory day.

This day shall be a memorial day . . . and when your children shall say to you, "what do you mean by this sacrifice?" you shall say, "It is the sacrifice of the Lord's passover, for he passed over the houses of Israel in Egypt when he slew the Egyptians but spared our houses."

Release, liberation, redemption from the pain, were memorialized—not the bondage, not the wrong by itself. The monument was to the possibilities for the future, not to the horror of the past.

Redemptive remembering drives us to a better future, it does not nail us to a worse past.

When Israel remembered its own past bondage, the memory incited them to seek justice in the present. You were once strangers in a strange land; remember now to be hospitable to the stranger in your land. You were exploited by unjust masters; remember not to exploit your own poor people. You were slaves once; remember to set your own slaves free. Good hopes for a better life were filaments in the light ignited by the redemptive memory of Jewish suffering.

The Christian community, too, was told from the beginning not to forget the sufferings of its founder. Remember the terrible death of Jesus until he comes again at the end of time—so early believers were commanded to do. But this remembrance is not meant to stoke the fire of resentment against the unfairness of his dying; just the opposite.

The point of remembering is to be renewed again and again by the life that rises from the aftershocks of his unfair death.

Redemptive memory is focused on love emerging from ashes, light that sheds darkness, hope that survives remembered evil.

I do not mean to underrate the chance that we will forget and that people will take advantage of our forgetting. Grace is a gamble, always. God knows. He knows what it is like to forgive and have it thrown back at him as a dare to forgive again. "Sin that grace may abound!" Why not? If forgiving is your game, and you like the exercise, we'll give you double the pleasure.

But God does take the risk, and so does anyone who ever forgives another human being.

The question is not whether forgiving is dangerous, but only whether it is a safer bet. It almost always comes down to where we get the best odds.

Forgiving is risky, but there are ways to improve the odds. One of them is to turn your remembered terrors into redemptive memories.

The risk, I believe, is worth taking.

CHAPTER 20

Forgiving Is Stronger

Passionate people are often sure that power comes only from hate and violence. We must listen to what they tell us.

Nobody in modern times has persuaded more people that violent hate is the power of the future than has Franz Fanon, the fervent Algerian psychiatrist who, in the 1960s, was the inspiration of many future black leaders. He set down his passionate philosophy in a book called *The Wretched of the Earth*—meaning all the people who live in the unfair pain of oppression and poverty. Their salvation, he believed, lies in hate's violence.

"Violence," he said, "is a cleansing force. It frees [the person who suffers unfair hurt] from his inferiority complex and from his despair and inaction; it makes him fearless and restores his self-respect."

I do not think I could find a more compelling challenge to my passion for forgiving than I find in Fanon's passion for violence.

Hate does have a feel of power to it, I admit. To a person energized by hate, forgiving feels flaccid, sapless, impotent. We feel stronger when we nourish our contempt and plot to get even. We dream up brilliant schemes for putting our enemies in their place, we pin them down in public, we make them grovel—and our vengeful dreams make us feel very strong. "The hell with you" feels a lot more macho than "I forgive you."

Hate does generate real energy. People who have been hurt and hate the villain who hurt them experience a surge of power inside. American prisoners, survivers of Bataan, forced on their terrible death march, prodded by the enemies' bayonets, fed rotten food, given no reason to hope for escape or survival, tell us that it was their hate that gave them the power to make it out alive.

But we must bring the matter down to where ordinary people live. Take Marcie Rozen, for instance. Marcie was deserted by her husband, left without money, without skills for the marketplace, without self-esteem, feeling unloved and unlovable. Ask her what helped her most to get out of the sinking sand of her despair, into school to train for a job, into the marketplace to find one, and, from there, into success at the job she found. Marcie will tell you: "I wanted to show the louse he couldn't hurt me. Hate gave me strength."

What does a forgiver have to say to Marcie's testimony?

This: hate gives instant energy, but it runs dry after the suffering stops. Hate can keep us going while we feel battered, but the drive dies down as time goes on after the ordeal is over. And then hate turns its power against the hater. It saps the energy of the soul, leaving it weaker than before, too weak to create a better life beyond the pain.

Hate is for emergencies, like a fast battery charge; it is a quick fix like heroin. As a long-term energizer, it is unreliable. And in the end it kills.

Hate-power is especially superficial when it is generated by our *fear* of weakness. Let me share a typical little story to show what I mean.

Mark Zwaak thinks of his wife, Karen, as an efficient, aggressive, domineering woman, while he sees himself as an ineffective, timid, submissive man. Karen goads Mark a lot; she wants him to take charge of the children, make decisions, face up to the mechanic who rips him off, get ahead in his job, and generally stop letting people push him around. Mark is miserable; he hates himself for being the weak member of the partnership.

One night, at a party with friends, overextended on Chablis, Karen laughingly said that she despised Mark for being a mama's boy who had never grown up. The icy meanness of Karen's jibe froze Mark's feelings into a hard block of hate. His wilted shame became an erection of rage. When they got home Mark stepped on the throttle of his humiliated ego and screamed: "For this, I will never forgive you, never!"

And he did not forgive. His hate became his secret pet; he succored it, nourished it, fondled it, and let it roam the ranges of his soul. His hate felt to him like a generator of inner power.

But his hate was only surface strength. Beneath his hate, he still suspected that Karen had him sized up right; he really was weak, impotent, ineffective. His hate was a cover for the weakness he dared not face.

Karen wasn't fooled; she understood that Mark's powerful hate was only a mask for his weakness, the only disguise he could find. She knew Mark.

But she hardly knew herself at all. She closed her eyes to the fact that her own cocky toughness was a well-tuned instrument for keeping her own weakness under control. Karen was scared of a legion of secret demons flitting inside of her soul, and she needed strength from Mark so that he could be her crutch. But Mark was not strong enough, so she played the tiresome game of being stronger than he was in order to hide her weakness.

But Karen learned. It took a near nervous collapse to teach her that we never win the game of being only strong and never weak. Through counsel and through pain, she came to terms with being weak, with being afraid, with being needy. So she threw away the mark of her jaunty self-confidence.

When she finally came to terms with being needy she found a truer strength. For instance, she found the courage to tell Mark how weak and how afraid she

178

really was, and how cruel she had been when she demanded that Mark never be weak. She knew now that strength comes only in weakness. Why not be weak together?

The happy ending began when Mark agreed to join Karen in a counseling program that aimed, not at getting strong, but at helping them to accept their fragile, weak, human selves. It took tears, a river of tears, to wash away the crazy conviction that in order to be strong he was not allowed to be weak. But he shed the tears, and they washed away his illusion.

As he learned that strength is given to us only in a package of weakness, Mark became strong enough to drop his mask of manly hate. Why not? A person who is not ashamed of being weak does not need the disguise.

The notion that hate is strong and forgiving is weak is a fallacy fabricated of a phony notion of strength. It pits strength against weakness as if we have to be one or the other, either strong *or* weak. And so, like a bad movie, it presents life in blacks and whites the way life seldom is. We are never *either* strong *or* weak; we are always *both* strong *and* weak. And in that combination we find our humanness.

Forgiving is a creative way to be weak and, therewith, a most human way to be strong.

Let us go on to *name* some of its strengths.

FORGIVING IS REALISM

Forgiving comes equipped with the toughness of realism. To be able to forgive we must have the guts to look hard at the wrongness, the horridness, the sheer wickedness of what somebody did to us. We cannot camouflage; we cannot excuse; we cannot ignore. We eye the evil face to face and we call it what it is. Only realists can be forgivers.

One prime reason why some people cannot forgive is their fear of reality. Parents miss chances to forgive their children because they are afraid to face the facts. A mother has a sixth sense that her son is stealing money from her. He needs money to buy drugs for himself and gas for his van; but he has lost his job. So he pilfers at home. She misses a ten-dollar bill here, a twenty there, out of her purse and out of her dresser drawer. He leaves hints behind, clear enough to give himself away. She knows; but she refuses to acknowledge what she knows. She stuffs her knowledge safely into her subconscious bag of unpleasant facts. She closes her eyes and she avoids the crisis of forgiving.

Self-deception is a lot easier than forgiving. But it has no payoff in healing.

Forgiving begins with the power to shake off deception and deal with reality.

FORGIVING IS CONFRONTATION

The strength of forgiving is seen most clearly whenever it is born of confrontation. We cannot completely forgive anyone whom we do not—one way or the other—face up to and say: "You did me wrong and I hate you for it."

Liz Bentley is an assistant professor of biology at a university in California. She is not a scholar, but she is a good teacher. She was up for promotion and the chairman of her department promised that he would persuade the dean to promote her on the basis of her work in the classroom. Liz counted on him.

As it turned out the dean called her in and told her that she was not going to get a promotion. And he advised her to begin applying for other jobs.

She felt like a hopeless failure at first, and was just beginning to climb out of her slough when a gossipy colleague let it slip that her chairman had not recommended her at all, had in fact pooh-poohed her performance as a teacher.

Liz was betrayed by the man who promised to be

her advocate. She had been bitten from behind by an academic jackal. She hated him.

She also needed a recommendation from him. So, for a while, she played games, acting as if she believed him when he told her how sorry he was that not even his strong support for her could convince the dean. And she went home each night and vomited.

But Liz could not keep her dialogue of duplicity going for long. She had to stop lying to the chairman and force him to stop lying to her. She would confront him, and if she had to she would flush his recommendation down the toilet. She met him at the coffee urn, drew him aside, looked him in the eye, and said: "Jack, I know you threw me down the shaft and I hate you for it." The chairman lied again and walked away.

Liz now began to feel the power she needed to forgive the man. She knew it would not be easy; she was not sure whether she could do it at all. But having risen in power, she felt strong enough to be weak enough to forgive. So, in her mind, she stripped his jackal's hide and saw him as the poor, weak person he was beneath it.

And in her decision to forgive she was set free. She went to bed without vomiting; she put away the Valium. Now she knew that whatever academic road she walked, she would walk it as a free woman.

FORGIVING IS FREEDOM

Nobody can make you forgive.

Only a free person can choose to live with an uneven score. Only free people can choose to start over with someone who has hurt them. Only a free person can live with accounts unsettled. Only a free person can heal the memory of hurt and hate.

When you forgive another person you are surprised at your own freedom to do what you did. All the king's armies could not have forced you to do it. You forgive in freedom and then move on to greater freedom. Freedom is strength; you know you have it when you have the power to forgive.

FORGIVING IS LOVE'S ULTIMATE POWER

Love is the power behind forgiveness.

But it does not work the way a lot of people suppose.

Love is not a soft and fuzzy sentiment that lets people get away with almost everything, no matter what they do to us. Love does not make us pushovers for people who hurt us unfairly.

Love forgives, but only because love is powerful.

Love has two ingredients that make it strong. One ingredient is respect. The other is *commitment*.

On the one hand, these two qualities make us vulnerable enough to need to forgive. On the other hand, they give us power to do the forgiving we need to do.

First, consider love's power to give you respect for yourself.

If you love yourself truly, you will respect yourself truly. And it is precisely your self-respect that gets you into situations where you are challenged to forgive.

When you respect yourself, you set limits to the abuse that you can accept from thoughtless or cruel people, even if you love them. Some pain will be unacceptable to you for the simple reason that you have too much dignity to deserve it. You will not accept disloyalty from friends you trust, or betrayals from spouses you love, or abuse from children you care for. Such hurts go beyond the limits that a self-respecting person allows.

Love is too powerful to let you lump all the blame for your pain on yourself, as if it must always be your fault when your father deprives you of love, or your spouse has an affair, or your children throw away your values. Love does not let you blame yourself falsely for long. Sometimes it reaches down into the reservoir of your nobility and says: "No more, I have too much self-respect to put up with any more."

When love gives you back your self-respect, and you refuse to take it anymore, you will have to make a decision about forgiveness.

Will you glue yourself to the painful memory of the hurt you didn't deserve? Will you roll it around your memories, savor its bitter taste, squeeze the last ounce of crazy-making pleasure you can get out of your pain? Or will you, in self-respect, forgive and set yourself free?

The same self-respecting love that gets you into the *crisis of forgiving* has the power to move you into the *place of self-healing*.

Love will not let you lock yourself in the prison cell of your bitter memories. It will not permit you the demeaning misery of wallowing in yesterday's pain. Your love for yourself will generate enough energy, finally, to say: "I have had enough; I am not going to put myself down by letting somebody's low blow keep hurting me forever." And so you begin forgiving.

Now you can reverse your focus and point your love toward the people who hurt you. Love enables you to respect them too, no matter how mean, cruel, or terribly unfair they were.

The highest respect you can show people is to let them take responsibility for their own actions. Love has this power, the power to let people be responsible for hurting us.

Love does *not* forever cover up for people, it does *not* forever find excuses for them, or protect them. I know a man whose wife is an alcoholic, and who, when she drinks, is abusive and cutting. She hurts him very deeply. But he does not dare tell her to get help for herself, nor does he dare leave her on her own to decide whether she wants to get help, and he certainly will not get out of the house to protect himself. He says he loves her too much. But he does not love her with the powerful love of respect; he does not give her the simplest respect of letting her take responsibility for herself.

When we really love people with respect, we let them be accountable for what they do to us. And then we face the crisis of forgiving.

But now comes the marvelous turnabout. Again, just as love gets us into the crisis, love gives us the power to get out of it.

Love respects people as genuine human beings, even after they have treated you like dirt. People who hurt you so badly are not just lumps of degenerate corruption; they are complex people with more to them than meanness and craziness. They have the potential to become better people, truer people, than they were when they stung you. Respect for them will help you to see the *person* behind the rat. And this respect can stimulate you to move in the direction of forgiveness.

So much, then, for love's power to respect yourself and the person who hurt you.

Now let us go on to the second ingredient in the power of love, *love's power to risk a commitment*.

True love dares to commit itself to someone, and therein lies both its vulnerability and its power.

When you commit yourself you reach out into a future you cannot control and you make an appointment to be there with someone you love. You pledge yourself to be there with them no matter what the circumstances are. And in committing yourself to people, you expect them to commit themselves to you.

But what a risk it is to trust anyone's commitment, not least your own. I am not surprised that people break their commitments; what amazes me is that we have the courage to make them in the first place. Commitments make us very vulnerable.

If you do not dare to risk forgiving, all you have to do is avoid commitments. You can keep your options open, your bags packed, so you can slip out into greener pastures whenever you are not getting a good payoff on your relationship. You can run away from pain, run quickly and leave others to pick up the pieces for you. Or you can become an urban hermit and never allow yourself to get involved with anyone beyond what it takes to get along on the job. If you can avoid any of love's commitments, you can live a long time without ever having to forgive.

But anyone whose love dares to commit him is a candidate for forgiving. For when love commits you, it opens you up to hurts from people who go back on their commitments. And when you get hurt, as most of us do, you either walk onstage to dance to the music of forgiveness or stew backstage in your own depressing pain.

But now comes the turnabout again. The very love that dares to be vulnerable by making a commitment has power to heal you of the pain that commitments bring.

Committed love does not say "finish" before the last act is played out. It gives us the strength to tough out bad times in the hope of better times. Committed love does not throw in the towel before the fight is really over. It holds on. And while it holds, it energizes, it gives you strength to keep the door open for the day when a new beginning may be possible.

I have been saying that, over the long run, love's power to forgive is stronger than hate's power to get even. I admit that hate gives a temporary power for surviving today's brutality and it has a short-term power to move us into tough action for tomorrow. But hate lacks staying power to create a fairer future beyond revenge.

It is forgiveness that supplies the healing stream of the long-term tomorrows. For long distance, forgiving is stronger than hate.

CHAPTER 21

Forgiving Fits Faulty People

There is a good guy and a bad guy in every forgiving crisis. Someone has hurt someone else, wrongly and deeply; one person needs to forgive and another needs to be forgiven.

But when we look at the *whole* picture, we always discover that those who get hurt probably need to be forgiven, too, by somebody. And if they need forgiveness, they have extra reason to forgive those who hurt them.

We always feel like innocent lambs when someone hurts us unfairly. But we are never as pure as we feel. I may have been betrayed, cheated, maligned, and in several other ways badly abused, and feel as if I am as benign as a shorn sheep. But being abused does not make me a good person. As Reinhold Neibuhr kept telling us years ago: "There is a labyrinth of motives in every heart; and every action, both good and evil, is the consequence of a complicated debate and tension within the soul." We are all too complex to be pure.

Moreover, we are seldom *merely* sinned against. We often contribute to our own vulnerability. We set ourselves up for hurt. Sometimes we invite pain, not because we love somebody too much, but because we are too stupid. Maybe we contribute to our being ripped-off because we are too lazy to look hard before we leap into a deal. Maybe we contribute to our spouse's infidelity by our unfeeling ignorance of their needs and desires. Maybe we contribute to our children's rebellion by our cold judgments and hot tempers. Surely, we know at least this much, that even if we are the *hurt* party, we are seldom a completely *innocent* party.

Our virtue is always compromised; we are never as innocent as we feel when we taste our early hate for a person who hurt us.

Our own faults, therefore, reduce the gap between us and whoever did us wrong. We do not toss our forgiving down from the peak of a holy mountain; we are in the valley with those who hurt us.

Aleksandr Solzhenitsyn, the novelist who was kicked out of Russia because he could not keep his mouth shut about the truth, and now lives and works in the United States, tells, in *The Gulag Archipelago,* about his friendship with an army officer during World War II. He felt then that he and his friend were almost completely alike; they had the same convictions, the same hopes, and the same feelings about everything.

But after the war, their destinies took them in opposite directions.

Solzhenitsyn was thrown into prison with uncounted other innocent Russians, gobbled into the unfathomable Soviet gulag machinery. He survived on a daily regimen of courage.

But what happened to his friend? He became one of the interrogators who forced confessions out of innocent people by methods so vicious that one cringes to read of them.

So we have two friends who loved each other, who felt as if they came out of the same mold, and who were sure that they would live out their lives in the same useful way. But one becomes his generation's eloquent example of human courage. The other becomes a willing agent in an insane network of human brutality.

Solzhenitsyn wondered how he and his friend could have turned out so differently from each other. But one thing he would not believe. He would not believe that he was a totally good person and his friend was a totally evil person. Solzhenitsyn knew himself too well.

So we find him saying that, if he had been in the wrong place, under the wrong teachers, in the wrong circumstance, he could have ended up exactly as his friend did.

Consider what he says while he wonders about the difference between him and his former friend:

> If only there were vile people . . . committing evil deeds, and it were only necessary to separate them from the rest of us and destroy them. But the line dividing good and evil cuts through the heart of every human being. And who is willing to destroy a piece of his own heart?
>
> During the life of any heart this line keeps changing place; sometimes it is squeezed one way by exuberant evil and sometimes it shifts to allow enough space for good to flourish. One and the same human being is, at various ages, under various circumstances, a totally different human being. At times he is close to being a devil, at times to sainthood. But his name doesn't change, and to that name we ascribe the whole lot, good and evil.

These, mind you, are the words of a man whose own character has come, in our time, to incarnate simple human courage and uncorrupted integrity.

I have a troubling habit of putting myself in the shoes of people who do wrong. When I read a true story about a villain who does great harm to people, I wonder what I might have done had I been subject to the same influences as he was. Take slaveholders for instance, including those who were cruelest to their slaves. What if I had been a Georgia plantation owner? Would I have had the moral sense to see how evil slavery was? I don't know for sure, but I suspect I would have done what most other white people did then.

When I am counseling a man who admits to having

hurt someone he loved, I put myself in his place and wonder whether I would have done all that much better than he did. And I know in my heart that I may well have done no better.

I do not think I am being morbid. I think that I am reminding myself that much of my apparent virtue is nothing but good luck and the grace of God. Put me in other circumstances, where to be honest or courageous requires a very high price, and I could not guarantee anyone that I would be a hero.

We are all a mixed breed. We have both Jezebel and the Virgin Mary inside our souls—all of us—and they are never far apart. So who are *we* to believe that we are too innocent to forgive the person who is guilty of hurting us?

Forgiving fits faulty folk. And we are all faulty. The best of us belong to that catholic club where nobody dares throw the first stone. For us to forgive others, then, has a certain congruity about it, a kind of fittingness, for the mixed bag of vice and virtue that we all are.

All this explains why Jesus was so tough on sinners who refused to forgive other sinners. He saw the laughable incongruity of people who need to be forgiven a lot turning their backs on people who need a little forgiving from them.

He tells a story about a palace servant who was forgiven a large debt; his king forgave him a debt of ten thousand talents, a sum it would take fifteen years to pay off in labor. After he was forgiven this enormous debt, the servant met a man who owed him a mere hundred denarii, a sum that could be worked off in a day; the king's servant demanded every denarius. When the king heard, he summoned the servant, took back his forgiveness, and slapped him into servitude to work off the ten thousand talents to the last denarius.

The story is about God and us. If we act like the unforgiving servant, God will act like the king.

Jesus grabs the hardest trick in the bag—forgiving—and says we have to perform it or we are out in the cold, way out, in the boondocks of the unforgiven. He makes us feel like the miller's daughter who was told that if she didn't spin gold out of a pile of straw before morning, she would lose her head. And no Rumpelstiltskin is going to come and spin forgiving out of our straw hearts. But why is Jesus so tough on us?

He is tough because the incongruity of sinners refusing to forgive sinners boggles God's mind. He cannot cope with it; there is no honest way to put up with it.

So he says: if you want forgiving from God and you cannot forgive someone who needs a little forgiving from you, forget about the forgiveness you want. Take away the eloquence of King James English and you get Jesus saying something like this: if you refuse to forgive other people when you expect to be forgiven, you can go to hell.

The gift of being forgiven and love's power to forgive are like yin and yang. Each needs the other to exist. To receive the gift without using the power is absurd; it is like exhaling without inhaling or like walking without moving your legs.

It is really a question of style. How do you *usually* respond to people who hurt you? Do you *always* go for the jugular? Do you plan revenge *every time* someone treats you badly? Is getting even a way of life? If you *never* even *want* to forgive, *never* even *try* to remove a hateful memory and restore a loving relationship, you are in a lot of trouble.

If you are *trying* to forgive; even if you manage forgiving in fits and starts, if you forgive today, hate again tomorrow, and have to forgive again the day after, you are a forgiver. Most of us are amateurs, bungling duffers sometimes. So what? In this game nobody is an expert. We are all beginners.

Postlude

We have seen the unpredictable, outrageous, and creative thing we do when we forgive another human being.

We reverse the flow of seemingly irreversible history . . . of our own history . . . of our private painful history. We reverse the flow of pain that began in the past when someone hurt us, a flow that filters into our present to wound our memory and poison our future. We heal ourselves.

It is utterly *unpredictable;* no one could suspect, in the nature of things, in the natural cause and effect of things, that anyone should ever forgive.

We perform a miracle that hardly anyone notices.

We do it alone; other people can help us, but when we finally do it, we perform the miracle in the private place of our inner selves.

We do it silently, no one can record our miracle on tape.

We do it invisibly, no one can record our miracle on film.

We do it freely, no one can ever trick us into forgiving someone.

It is *outrageous:* when we do it we commit an outrage against the strict morality that will not rest with anything short of an even score.

It is *creative:* when we forgive we come as close as any human being can to the essentially divine act of creation. For we create a new beginning out of past

191

pain that never had a right to exist in the first place. We create healing for the future by changing a past that had no possibility in it for anything but sickness and death.

When we forgive we ride the crest of love's cosmic wave; we walk in stride with God.

And we heal the hurt we never deserved.

In memory of my parents,
Corky and Carl Coben

and in celebration of their grandchildren,
Charlotte, Aleksander, Benjamin, and Gabrielle

Acknowledgments

I wrote this book alone. Nobody helped me. But if mistakes were made, I wish to keep in the long-standing American tradition of passing the buck. So with that in mind, the author would like to thank the following wonderful people: Aaron Priest, Lisa Erbach Vance, and everyone at the Aaron Priest Literary Agency; Carole Baron, Leslie Schnur, Jacob Hoye, Heather Mongelli, and everyone at Dell Publishing; Maureen Coyle of the New York Liberty; Karen Ross, ME of the Dallas County Institute of Forensic Science; Peter Roisman of Advantage International; Sergeant Jay Vanderbeck of the Livingston Police Department; Detective Lieutenant Keith Killion of the Ridgewood Police Department; Maggie Griffin, James Bradbeer, Chip Hinshaw, and of course, Dave Bolt. Again I repeat: any errors – factual or otherwise – are totally the fault of these people. The author is not to blame.

Prologue

September 15

The cemetery overlooked a schoolyard.

Myron pushed at the loose dirt with the toe of his Rockport. There was no stone here yet, just a metal marker holding a plain index card with a name typed in capital letters. He shook his head. Why was he standing here like some cliché from a bad TV show? In his mind's eye Myron could see how the whole scene should be played out. Torrential rain should be pounding on his back, but he would be too bereaved to notice. His head should be lowered, tears glistening in his eyes, maybe one running down his cheek, blending in with the rain. Cue the stirring music. The camera should move off his face and pull back slowly, very slowly, showing his slumped shoulders, the rain driving harder, more graves, no one else present. Still pulling back, the camera eventually shows Win, Myron's loyal partner, standing in the distance, silently understanding, giving his buddy time alone to grieve. The TV image should suddenly freeze and the executive producer's name should flash across the screen in yellow caps. Slight hesitation before the viewers are urged to stay tuned for scenes from next week's episode. Cut to commercial.

But that would not happen here. The sun shone like it was the first day and the skies had the hue of the freshly painted. Win was at the office. And Myron would not cry.

So why was he here?

Because a murderer would be coming soon. He was sure of it.

Myron searched for some kind of meaning in the landscape but only came up with more clichés. It had been two weeks since the funeral. Weeds and dandelions had already begun to break through the dirt and stretch toward the heavens. Myron waited for his inner voice-over to spout the standard drivel about weeds and dandelions representing cycles and renewal and life going on, but the voice was mercifully mute. He sought irony in the radiant innocence of the schoolyard – the faded chalk on black asphalt, the multicolor three-wheelers, the slightly rusted chains for the swings – cloaked in the shadows of tombstones that watched over the children like silent sentinels, patient and almost beckoning. But the irony would not hold. Schoolyards were not about innocence. There were bullies down there too and sociopaths-in-waiting and burgeoning psychoses and young minds filled prenatally with undiluted hate.

Okay, Myron thought, *enough abstract babbling for one day*.

On some level, he recognized that this inner dialogue was merely a distraction, a philosophical sleight of hand to keep his brittle mind from snapping like a dry twig. He wanted so very much to cave in, to let his legs give way, to fall to the ground and claw at the dirt with his bare hands and beg forgiveness and plead for a higher power to give him one more chance.

But that too would not happen.

Myron heard footsteps coming up from behind him. He closed his eyes. It was as he expected. The footsteps came closer. When they stopped, Myron did not turn around.

'You killed her,' Myron said.

'Yes.'

A block of ice melted in Myron's stomach. 'Do you feel better now?'

The killer's tone caressed the back of Myron's neck with a cold, bloodless hand. 'The question is, Myron, do you?'

1

Myron hunched his shoulders and slurred his words. 'I am not a baby-sitter,' he said. 'I am a sports agent.'

Norm Zuckerman looked pained. 'Was that supposed to be Bela Lugosi?'

'The Elephant Man,' Myron said.

'Damn, that was awful. And who said anything about being a baby-sitter? Did I say the word *baby-sitter* or *baby-sitting* or for that matter any form of the verb *to baby-sit* or noun or even the word *baby* or the word *sit* or *sat* or—'

Myron held up a hand. 'I get the point, Norm.'

They sat under a basket at Madison Square Garden in those cloth-and-wood directors' chairs that have stars' names on the back. Their chairs were set high so that the net from the basket almost tickled Myron's hair. A model shoot was going on at half-court. Lots of those umbrella lights and tall, bony women-cum-children and tripods and people huffing and fluffing about. Myron waited for someone to mistake him for a model. And waited.

'A young woman may be in danger,' Norm said. 'I need your help.'

Norm Zuckerman was approaching seventy and as CEO of Zoom, a megasize sports manufacturing conglomerate, he had more money than Trump. He looked, however, like a beatnik trapped in a bad acid trip. Retro, Norm had explained earlier, was cresting, and he was catching the wave by wearing a psychedelic poncho, fatigue pants, love beads, and an earring with a dangling peace sign. Groovy, man. His black-to-gray beard was unruly enough to nest beetle larvae, his hair newly curled like something out of a bad production of *Godspell*.

Che Guevara lives and gets a perm.

'You don't need me,' Myron said. 'You need a bodyguard.'

Norm waved a dismissing hand. 'Too obvious.'

'What?'

'She'd never go for it. Look, Myron, what do you know about Brenda Slaughter?'

'Not much,' Myron said.

He looked surprised. 'What do you mean, not much?'

'What word are you having trouble with, Norm?'

'For crying out loud, you were a basketball player.'

'So?'

'So Brenda Slaughter may be the greatest female player of all time. A pioneer in her sport – not to mention the pinup girl, pardon the political insensitivity, for my new league.'

'That much I know.'

'Well, know this: I'm worried about her. If something happens to Brenda Slaughter, the whole WPBA – and my substantial investment – could go right down the toilet.'

'Well, as long as it's for humanitarian reasons.'

'Fine, I'm a greedy capitalist pig. But you, my friend, are a sports agent. There is not a greedier, sleazier, slimier, more capitalist entity in existence.'

Myron nodded. 'Suck up to me,' he said. 'That'll work.'

'You're not letting me finish. Yes, you're a sports agent. But a damn fine one. The best, really. You and the Spanish shiksa do incredible work for your clients. Get the most for them. More than they should get really. By the time you finish with me, I feel violated. Hand to God, you're that good. You come into my office, you rip off my clothes and have your way with me.'

Myron made a face. 'Please.'

'But I know your secret background with the feds.'

Some secret. Myron was still hoping to bump into someone above the equator who didn't know about it.

'Just listen to me for a second, Myron, okay? Hear me out. Brenda is a lovely girl, a wonderful basketball player – and a pain in my left *tuchis*. I don't blame her. If I grew up with a father like that, I'd be a pain in the left *tuchis* too.'

'So her father is the problem?'

Norm made a yes-and-no gesture. 'Probably.'

'So get a restraining order,' Myron said.

'Already done.'

'Then what's the problem? Hire a private eye. If he steps within a hundred yards of her, call the cops.'

'It's not that easy.' Norm looked out over the court. The workers involved in the shoot darted about like trapped particles under sudden heat. Myron sipped his coffee. Gourmet coffee. A year ago he never drank coffee. Then he started stopping into one of the new coffee bars that kept cropping up like bad movies on cable. Now Myron could not go through a morning without his gourmet coffee fix.

There is a fine line between a coffee house and a crack house.

'We don't know where he is,' Norm said.

'Excuse me?'

'Her father,' Norm said. 'He's vanished. Brenda is always looking over her shoulder. She's terrified.'

'And you think the father is a danger to her?'

'This guy is the Great Santini on steroids. He used to play ball himself. Pac Ten, I think. His name is—'

'Horace Slaughter,' Myron said.

'You know him?'

Myron nodded very slowly. 'Yeah,' he said. 'I know him.'

Norm studied his face. 'You're too young to have played with him.'

Myron said nothing. Norm did not catch the hint. He rarely did.

'So how do you know Horace Slaughter?'

'Don't worry about it,' Myron said. 'Tell me why you think Brenda Slaughter is in danger.'

'She's been getting threats.'

'What kind of threats?'

'Death.'

'Could you be a little more specific?'

The photo shoot frenzy continued to whirl. Models sporting the latest in Zoom wear and oodles of attitude cycled through poses and pouts and postures and pursed lips. Come on and vogue. Someone called out for Ted, where the hell is Ted, that prima donna, why isn't Ted dressed yet, I swear, Ted will be the death of me yet.

'She gets phone calls,' Norm said. 'A car follows her. That kind of thing.'

'And you want me to do what exactly?'

'Watch her.'

Myron shook his head. 'Even if I said yes – which I'm not – you said she won't go for a bodyguard.'

Norm smiled and patted Myron's knee. 'Here's the part where I lure you in. Like a fish on a hook.'

'Original analogy.'

'Brenda Slaughter is currently unagented.'

7

Myron said nothing.

'Cat got your tongue, handsome?'

'I thought she signed a major endorsement deal with Zoom.'

'She was on the verge when her old man disappeared. He was her manager. But she got rid of him. Now she's alone. She trusts my judgment, to a point. This girl is no fool, let me tell you. So here's my plan: Brenda will be here in a couple of minutes. I recommend you to her. She says hello. You say hello. Then you hit her with the famed Bolitar charm.'

Myron arched one eyebrow. 'Set on full blast?'

'Heavens, no. I don't want the poor girl disrobing.'

'I took an oath to only use my powers for good.'

'This is good, Myron, believe me.'

Myron remained unconvinced. 'Even if I agreed to go along with this cockamamy scheme, what about nights? You expect me to watch her twenty-four hours a day?'

'Of course not. Win will help you there.'

'Win has better things to do.'

'Tell that goy boy-toy it's for me,' Norm said. 'He loves me.'

A flustered photographer in the great Eurotrash tradition hurried over to their perch. He had a goatee and spiky blond hair like Sandy Duncan on an off day. Bathing did not appear to be a priority here. He sighed repeatedly, making sure all in the vicinity knew that he was both important and being put out. 'Where is Brenda?' he whined.

'Right here.'

Myron swiveled toward a voice like warm honey on Sunday pancakes. With her long, purposeful stride – not the shy-girl walk of the too-tall or the nasty strut of a model – Brenda Slaughter swept into the room like a radar-tracked weather system. She was very tall, over six feet for sure, with skin the color of Myron's Starbucks Mocha Java with a hefty splash of skim milk. She wore faded jeans that hugged deliciously but without obscenity and a ski sweater that made you think of cuddling inside a snow-covered log cabin.

Myron managed not to say wow out loud.

Brenda Slaughter was not so much beautiful as electric. The air around her crackled. She was far too big and broad-shouldered to be a model. Myron knew some professional models. They were always throwing themselves at him – snicker – and were ridiculously thin, built like strings with helium balloons on top. Brenda was no size six. You felt strength with this woman, substance, power, a force if you will, and yet it was all completely feminine, whatever that meant, and incredibly attractive.

Norm leaned over and whispered, 'See why she's our poster girl?'

Myron nodded.

Norm jumped down from the chair. 'Brenda, darling, come over here. I want you to meet someone.'

The big brown eyes found Myron's, and there was a hesitation. She smiled a little and strode toward them. Myron rose, ever the gentleman. Brenda headed straight for him and stuck out her hand. Myron shook it. Her grip was strong. Now that they were both standing, Myron could see he had an inch or two on her. That made her six-two, maybe six-three.

'Well, well,' Brenda said. 'Myron Bolitar.'

Norm gestured as if he were pushing them closer together. 'You two know each other?'

'Oh, I'm sure Mr. Bolitar doesn't remember me,' Brenda said. 'It was a long time ago.'

It took Myron only a few seconds. His brain immediately realized that had he met Brenda Slaughter before, he would have undoubtedly remembered. The fact that he didn't meant their previous encounter was under very different circumstances. 'You used to hang out at the courts,' Myron said. 'With your dad. You must have been five or six.'

'And you were just entering high school,' she added. 'The only white guy that showed up steadily. You made all-state out of Livingston High, became an all-American at Duke, got drafted by the Celtics in the first round—'

Her voice dovetailed. Myron was used to that. 'I'm flattered you remembered,' he said. Already wowing her with the charm.

'I grew up watching you play,' she went on. 'My father followed your career like you were his own son. When you got hurt—' She broke off again, her lips tightening.

He smiled to show he both understood and appreciated the sentiment.

Norm jumped into the silence. 'Well, Myron is a sports agent now. A damn good one. The best, in my opinion. Fair, honest, loyal as hell—' Norm stopped suddenly. 'Did I just use those words to describe a sports agent?' He shook his head.

The goateed Sandy Duncan bustled over again. He spoke with a French accent that sounded about as real as Pepe LePew's. '*Monsier Zuckermahn?*'

Norm said, '*Oui.*'

'I need your help, *s'il vous plaît.*'

'*Oui,*' Norm said.

Myron almost asked for an interpreter.

'Sit, both of you,' Norm said. 'I have to run a sec.' He patted the empty chairs to drive home the point. 'Myron is going to help me set up the league. Kinda like a consultant. So talk to him, Brenda. About your career, your future, whatever. He'd be a good agent for you.' He winked at Myron. Subtle.

When Norm left, Brenda high-stepped into the director's chair. 'So was all that true?' she asked.

'Part of it,' Myron said.

'What part?'

'I'd like to be your agent. But that's not why I'm really here.'

'Oh?'

'Norm is worried about you. He wants me to watch out for you.'

'Watch out for me?'

Myron nodded. 'He thinks you're in danger.'

She set her jaw. 'I told him I didn't want to be watched.'

'I know,' Myron said. 'I'm supposed to be under-cover. Shh.'

'So why are you telling me?'

'I'm not good with secrets.'

She nodded. 'And?'

'And if I'm going to be your agent, I'm not sure it pays to start our relationship with a lie.'

She leaned back and crossed legs longer than a DMV line at lunchtime. 'What else did Norm tell you to do?'

'To turn on my charm.'

She blinked at him.

'Don't worry,' Myron said. 'I took a solemn oath to only use it for good.'

'Lucky me.' Brenda brought a long finger up to her face and tapped it against her chin a few times. 'So,' she said at last, 'Norm thinks I need a baby-sitter.'

Myron threw up his hands and did his best Norm impression. 'Who said anything about a baby-sitter?' It was better than his Elephant Man, but nobody was speed-dialing Rich Little either.

She smiled. 'Okay,' she said with a nod. 'I'll go along with this.'

'I'm pleasantly surprised.'

'No reason to be. If you don't do it, Norm might hire someone else who might not be so forthcoming. This way I know the score.'

'Makes sense,' Myron said.

'But there are conditions.'

'I thought there might be.'

'I do what I want when I want. This isn't carte blanche to invade my privacy.'

'Of course.'

'If I tell you to get lost for a while, you ask how lost.'

'Right.'

'And no spying on me when I don't know about it,' she continued.

'Okay.'

'You keep out of my business.'

'Agreed.'

'I stay out all night, you don't say a thing.'

'Not a thing.'

'If I choose to participate in an orgy with pygmies, you don't say a thing.'

'Can I at least watch?' Myron asked.

That got a smile. 'I don't mean to sound difficult, but I have enough father figures in my life, thank you. I want to make sure you know that we're not going to be hanging out with each other twenty-four a day or anything like that. This isn't a Whitney Houston–Kevin Costner movie.'

'Some people say I look like Kevin Costner.' Myron gave her a quick flash of the cynical, rogue smile, à la Bull Durham.

She looked straight through him. 'Maybe in the hairline.'

Ouch. At half-court the goateed Sandy Duncan started calling for Ted again. His coterie followed suit. The name Ted bounced about the arena like rolled-up balls of Silly Putty.

'So do we understand each other?' she asked.

'Perfectly,' Myron said. He shifted in his seat. 'Now do you want to tell me what's going on?'

From the right, Ted – it simply had to be a guy named Ted – finally made his entrance. He wore only Zoom shorts, and his abdomen was rippled like a relief map in marble. He was probably in his early twenties, model handsome, and he squinted like a prison guard. As he sashayed toward the shoot, Ted kept running both hands through his Superman blue-black hair, the movement expanding his chest and shrinking his waist and demonstrating shaved underarms.

Brenda muttered, 'Strutting peacock.'

'That's totally unfair,' Myron said. 'Maybe he's a Fulbright scholar.'

'I've worked with him before. If God gave him a second brain, it would die of loneliness.' Her eyes veered toward Myron. 'I don't get something.'

'What?'

'Why you? You're a sports agent. Why would Norm ask you to be my bodyguard?'

'I used to work' – he stopped, waved a vague hand – 'for the government.'

'I never heard about that.'

'It's another secret. Shh.'

'Secrets don't stay secret much around you, Myron.'

'You can trust me.'

She thought about it. 'Well, you were a white man who could jump,' she said. 'Guess if you can be that, you could be a trustworthy sports agent.'

Myron laughed, and they fell into an uneasy silence.

He broke it by trying again. 'So do you want to tell me about the threats?'

'Nothing much to tell.'

'This is all in Norm's head?'

Brenda did not reply. One of the assistants applied oil to Ted's hairless chest. Ted was still giving the crowd his tough guy squint. Too many Clint Eastwood movies. Ted made two fists and continuously flexed his pecs. Myron decided that he might as well beat the rush and start hating Ted right now.

Brenda remained silent. Myron decided to try another approach. 'Where are you living now?' he asked.

'In a dorm at Reston University.'

'You're still in school?'

'Medical school. Fourth year. I just got a deferment to play pro ball.'

Myron nodded. 'Got a specialty in mind?'

'Pediatrics.'

He nodded again and decided to wade in a bit deeper. 'Your dad must be very proud of you.'

A flicker crossed her face. 'Yeah, I guess.' She started to rise. 'I better get dressed for this shoot.'

'You don't want to tell me what's going on first?'

She stayed in her seat. 'Dad is missing.'

'Since when?'

'A week ago.'

'Is that when the threats started?'

She avoided the question. 'You want to help? Find my father.'

'Is he the one threatening you?'

'Don't worry about the threats. Dad likes control, Myron. Intimidation is just another tool.'

'I don't understand.'

'You don't have to understand. He's your friend, right?'

'Your father? I haven't seen Horace in more than ten years.'

'Whose fault is that?' she asked.

The words, not to mention the bitter tone, surprised him. 'What's that supposed to mean?'

'Do you still care about him?' she asked.

Myron didn't have to think about it. 'You know I do.'

She nodded and jumped down from the chair. 'He's in trouble,' she said. 'Find him.'

2

Brenda reappeared in Lycra Zoom shorts and what was commonly called a sports bra. She was limbs and shoulders and muscles and substance, and while the professional models glared at her size (not her height – most of them were six-footers too), Myron thought that she stood out like a bursting supernova next to, well, gaseous entities.

The poses were risqué, and Brenda was clearly embarrassed by them. Not so Ted. He undulated and squinted at her in what was supposed to be a look of smoldering sexuality. Twice Brenda broke out and laughed in his face. Myron still hated Ted, but Brenda was starting to grow on him.

Myron picked up his cellular phone and dialed Win's private line. Win was a big-time financial consultant at Lock-Horne Securities, an old-money financial firm that first sold equities on the *Mayflower*. His office was in the Lock-Horne Building on Park Avenue and Forty-seventh Street in midtown Manhattan. Myron rented space there from Win. A sports agent on Park Avenue – now that was class.

After three rings the machine picked up. Win's annoyingly superior accent said, 'Hang up without leaving a message and die.' Beep. Myron shook his head, smiled, and, as always, left a message.

He hit the switch and dialed his office. Esperanza answered. 'MB SportsReps.'

The *M* was for Myron, the *B* for Bolitar, and the

SportsReps because they Represented people in the world of Sports. Myron had come up with the name with no help from professional marketing personnel. Despite the obvious accolades, Myron remained humble.

'Any messages?' he asked.

'About a million.'

'Anything crucial?'

'Greenspan wanted your take on interest rate hikes. Outside of that, no.' Esperanza, ever the wiseass. 'So what did Norm want?'

Esperanza Diaz – the 'Spanish shiksa' in Norm's words – had been at MB SportsReps since its inception. Before that, she had wrestled professionally under the moniker Little Pocahontas; put simply, she wore a bikini reminiscent of Raquel Welch in *One Million Years B.C.* and groped other women in front of a drooling horde. Esperanza considered her career shift to representing athletes as something of a step down.

'It involves Brenda Slaughter,' he began.

'The basketball player?'

'Yes.'

'I've seen her play a couple of times,' Esperanza said. 'On TV she looks hot.'

'In person too.'

There was a pause. Then Esperanza said, 'Think she participates in the love that dare not speaketh its name?'

'Huh?'

'Does she swing the way of the woman?'

'Gee,' Myron said, 'I forgot to check for the tattoo.'

Esperanza's sexual preference flip-flopped like a politician in a nonelection year. Currently she seemed to be on a man kick, but Myron guessed that was one of the advantages of bisexuality: love everyone. Myron had no problem with it. In high school he had dated almost exclusively bisexual girls – he'd mention sex, the girls would say 'bye'. Okay, old joke, but the point remained.

'Doesn't matter,' Esperanza said. 'I really like David.' Her current beau. It wouldn't last. 'But you got to admit, Brenda Slaughter is steaming.'

'So admitted.'

'It might be fun for a night or two.'

Myron nodded into the phone. A lesser man might mentally conjure up a few choice images of the lithe, petite Hispanic beauty in the throes of passion with the ravishing black Amazon in the sports bra. But not Myron. Too worldly.

'Norm wants us to watch her,' Myron said. He filled her in. When he finished, he heard her sigh.

'What?' he said.

'Jesus Christ, Myron, are we a sports agency or Pinkertons?'

'It's to get clients.'

'Keep telling yourself that.'

'What the hell does that mean?'

'Nothing. So what do you need me to do?'

'Her father is missing. His name is Horace Slaughter. See what you can dig up on him.'

'I'll need help here,' she said.

Myron rubbed his eyes. 'I thought we were going to hire someone on a permanent basis.'

'Who has the time?'

Silence.

'Fine,' Myron said. He sighed. 'Call Big Cyndi. But make sure she knows it's just on a trial basis.'

'Okey-dokey.'

'And if any client comes in, I want Cyndi to hide in my office.'

'Yeah, fine, whatever.'

She hung up the phone.

When the photo shoot ended, Brenda Slaughter approached him.

'Where does your father live now?' Myron asked.

'Same place.'

'Have you been there since he disappeared?'

'No.'

'Then let's start there,' Myron said.

3

Newark, New Jersey. The bad part. Almost a redundancy.

Decay was the first word that came to mind. The buildings were more than falling apart – they actually seemed to be breaking down, melting from some sort of acid onslaught. Here urban renewal was about as familiar a concept as time travel. The surroundings looked more like a war newsreel – Frankfurt after the Allies' bombing – than a habitable dwelling.

The neighborhood was even worse than he remembered. When Myron was a teenager, he and his dad had driven down this very street, the car doors suddenly locking as though even they sensed oncoming danger. His father's face would tighten up. 'Toilet,' he would mutter. Dad had grown up not far from here, but that had been a long time ago. His father, the man Myron loved and worshiped like no other, the most gentle soul he had ever known, would barely contain his rage. 'Look what they did to the old neighborhood,' he would say.

Look what they did.

They.

Myron's Ford Taurus slowly cruised by the old playground. Black faces glared at him. A five-on-five was going on with plenty of kids sprawled on the sidelines waiting to take on the winners. The cheap sneakers of Myron's day – Thorn McAn or Keds or Kmart – had been replaced with the hundred-dollar-plus variety these kids could ill afford. Myron felt a twinge. He would have liked to take a noble stand on the issue – the corruption of values and materialism and such – but as a sports agent who made money off sneaker deals, such perceptions paid his freight. He didn't feel good about that, but he didn't want to be a hypocrite either.

Nobody wore shorts anymore either. Every kid was dressed in blue or black jeans that journeyed far south of baggy, like something a circus clown might sport for an extra laugh. The waist drooped below the butt, revealing designer boxer shorts. Myron did not want to sound like an old man, grousing over the younger generation's fashion sense, but these made bell-bottoms and platforms seem practical. How do you play your best when you're constantly pausing to pull up your pants?

But the biggest change was in those glares. Myron had been scared when he first came down here as a fifteen-year-old high school student, but he had known that if he wanted to rise to the next level, he had to face down the best competition. That meant playing here. He had not been welcomed at first. Not even close. But the looks of curious animosity he received back then were nothing compared with the dagger-death glares of these kids. Their hatred was naked, up front, filled with cold resignation. Corny to say, but back then – less than twenty years ago – there had been something different here. More hope maybe. Hard to say.

As though reading his thoughts, Brenda said, 'I wouldn't even play down here anymore.'

Myron nodded.

'It wasn't easy on you, was it? Coming down here to play.'

'Your father made it easy,' he said.

She smiled. 'I never understood why he took such a liking to you. He usually hated white people.'

Myron feigned a gasp. 'I'm white?'

'As Pat Buchanan.'

They both forced out a laugh. Myron tried again. 'Tell me about the threats.'

Brenda stared out the window. They passed a place that sold hubcaps. Hundreds, if not thousands, of hubcaps gleamed in the sun. Weird business when you thought about it. The only time people need a new hubcap is when one of theirs is stolen. The stolen ones end up in a place like this. A mini fiscal cycle.

'I get calls,' she began. 'At night mostly. One time they said they were going to hurt me if they didn't find my father. Another time they told me I better keep Dad as my manager or else.' She stopped.

'Any idea who they are?'

'No.'

'Any idea why someone would want to find your father?'

'No.'

'Or why your father would disappear?'

She shook her head.

'Norm said something about a car following you.'

'I don't know anything about that,' she said.

'The voice on the phone,' Myron said. 'Is it the same one every time?'

'I don't think so.'

'Male, female?'

'Male. And white. Or least, he sounds white.'

Myron nodded. 'Does Horace gamble?'

'Never. My grandfather gambled. Lost everything he had, which wasn't much. Dad would never go near it.'

'Did he borrow money?'

'No.'

'Are you sure? Even with financial aid, your schooling had to cost.'

'I've been on scholarship since I was twelve.'

Myron nodded. Up ahead a man stumbled about the sidewalk. He was wearing Calvin Klein underwear, two different ski boots, and one of those big Russian hats like Dr. Zhivago. Nothing else. No shirt, no pants. His fist gripped the top of a brown paper bag like he was helping it cross the street.

'When did the calls start?' Myron asked.

'A week ago.'

'When your dad disappeared?'

Brenda nodded. She had more to say. Myron could see it in the way she stared off. He kept silent and waited her out.

'The first time,' she said quietly, 'the voice told me to call my mother.'

Myron waited for her to say more. When it was apparent she wouldn't, he said, 'Did you?'

She smiled sadly. 'No.'

'Where does your mother live?'

'I don't know. I haven't seen her since I was five years old.'

'When you say "haven't seen her"—'

'I mean just that. She abandoned us twenty years ago.' Brenda finally turned toward him. 'You look surprised.'

'I guess I am.'

'Why? You know how many of those boys back there had their fathers abandon them? You think a mother can't do the same thing?'

She had a point, but it sounded more like hollow rationalization than true conviction. 'So you haven't seen her since you were five?'

'That's right.'

23

'Do you know where she lives? A city or state or anything?'

'No idea.' She tried hard to sound indifferent.

'You've had no contact with her?'

'Just a couple of letters.'

'Any return address?'

Brenda shook her head. 'They were postmarked in New York City. That's all I know.'

'Would Horace know where she lives?'

'No. He's never so much as spoken her name in the past twenty years.'

'At least not to you.'

She nodded.

'Maybe the voice on the phone didn't mean your mother,' Myron said. 'Do you have a stepmother? Did your father remarry or live with someone—'

'No. Since my mother there has been no one.'

Silence.

'So why would someone be asking about your mother after twenty years?' Myron asked.

'I don't know.'

'Any ideas?'

'None. For twenty years she's been a ghost to me.' She pointed up ahead. 'Make a left.'

'Do you mind if I get a trace put on your phone? In case they call again?'

She shook her head.

He steered the car per her instructions. 'Tell me about your relationship with Horace,' he said.

'No.'

'I'm not asking to be nosy—'

'It's irrelevant, Myron. If I loved him or hated him, you still need to find him.'

'You got a restraining order to keep him away from you, right?'

She said nothing for a moment. Then: 'Do you remember how he was on the court?'

Myron nodded. 'A madman. And maybe the best teacher I ever had.'

'And the most intense?'

'Yes,' Myron said. 'He taught me not to play with so much finesse. That wasn't always an easy lesson.'

'Right, and you were just some kid he took a liking to. But imagine being his own child. Now imagine that on-court intensity mixed with his fear that he would lose me. That I would run away and leave him.'

'Like your mother.'

'Right.'

'It would be,' Myron said, 'stifling.'

'Try suffocating,' she corrected. 'Three weeks ago we were playing a promotional scrimmage at East Orange High School. You know it?'

'Sure.'

'A couple of guys in the crowd were getting rowdy. Two high school kids. They were on the basketball team. They were drunk or high, or maybe they were just punks. I don't know. But they started yelling things out at me.'

'What kind of things?'

'Graphic and ugly things. About what they'd like to do to me. My father stood up and went after them.'

'I can't say I blame him,' Myron said.

She shook her head. 'Then you're another Neanderthal.'

'What?'

'Why would you have gone after them? To defend my honor? I'm a twenty-five-year-old woman. I don't need any of that chivalry crap.'

'But—'

'But nothing. This whole thing, your being here – I'm

not a radical feminist or anything, but it's a load of sexist bullshit.'

'What?'

'If I had a penis between my legs, you wouldn't be here. If my name was Leroy and I got a couple of weird phone calls, you wouldn't be so hot to protect poor little me, would you?'

Myron hesitated a second too long.

'And,' she continued, 'how many times have you seen me play?'

The change of subject caught him off guard. 'What?'

'I was the number one collegiate player three years in a row. My team won two national championships. We were on ESPN all the time, and during the NCAA finals we were on CBS. I went to Reston University, which is only half an hour from where you live. How many of my games did you see?'

Myron opened his mouth, closed it, said, 'None.'

'Right. Chicks' basketball. It's not worth the time.'

'That's not it. I don't watch much sports anymore.' He realized how lame he sounded.

She shook her head and grew quiet.

'Brenda—'

'Forget I said anything. It was dumb to raise the subject.'

Her tone left little room for follow-up. Myron wanted to defend himself, but he had no idea how. He opted for silence, an option he should probably exercise more often.

'Take your next right,' she said.

'So what happened next?' he asked.

She looked at him.

'To the punks who called you names. What happened after your father went after them?'

'The security guards broke it up before anything

really happened. They threw the kids out of the gym. Dad too.'

'I'm not sure I see the point of this story.'

'It's not over yet.' Brenda stopped, looked down, summoned up a little something, raised her head again. 'Three days later the two boys – Clay Jackson and Arthur Harris – were found on the roof of a tenement building. Someone had tied them up and cut their Achilles tendon in half with pruning shears.'

Myron's face lost color. His stomach took a nosedive. 'Your father?'

Brenda nodded. 'He's been doing stuff like that my whole life. Never this bad. But he's always made people who cross me pay. When I was a little girl with no mother, I almost welcomed the protection. But I'm not a little girl anymore.'

Myron absently reached down and touched the back of his ankle. Cut the Achilles tendon in half. With pruning shears. He tried not to look too stunned. 'The police must have suspected Horace.'

'Yes.'

'So how come he wasn't arrested?'

'Not enough evidence.'

'Couldn't the victims identify him?'

She turned back to the window. 'They're too scared.' She pointed to the right. 'Park there.'

Myron pulled over. People toddled about the street. They stared at him as though they had never seen a white man; in this neighborhood that was entirely possible. Myron tried to look casual. He nodded a polite hello. Some people nodded back. Some didn't.

A yellow car – nay, a speaker on wheels – cruised by, blaring a rap tune. The bass was set so high that Myron felt the vibrations in his chest. He could not make out the lyrics, but they sounded angry. Brenda led him to a stoop. Two men were sprawled on the stairs like war wounded. Brenda stepped over them without a second glance. Myron followed. He suddenly realized that he had never been here before. His relationship with Horace Slaughter had been strictly basketball. They had always hung out on the playground or in a gym or maybe grabbing a pizza after a game. He had never been in Horace's home, and Horace had never been in his.

There was no doorman, of course, no lock or buzzers or any of that. The lighting was bad in the corridor, but not bad enough to conceal the paint flaking off like the walls had psoriasis. Most of the mailboxes were doorless. The air felt like a beaded curtain.

She climbed up the cement stairs. The railing was industrial metal. Myron could hear a man coughing as if he were trying to dislodge a lung. A baby cried. Then another joined in. Brenda stopped on the second floor and turned right. Her keys were already in her hand and at the ready. The door too was made of some sort of reinforced steel. There was a peephole and three bolt locks.

Brenda unlocked the three bolts first. They jerked back noisily, like the prison scene in a movie where the warden yells, 'Lockdown!' The door swung open. Myron was hit by two thoughts at exactly the same time. One was how nice Horace's setup was. Whatever was outside this apartment, whatever grime and rot were on the streets or even in his corridor, Horace Slaughter had not allowed to sneak past the steel door. The walls were as white as a hand cream commercial. The floors looked newly buffed. The furniture was a mix of what looked like fixed-up family pieces and newer Ikea acquisitions. It was indeed a comfortable home.

The other thing Myron noticed as soon as the door was open was that someone had trashed the room.

Brenda rushed in. 'Dad?'

Myron followed, wishing that he had his gun. This scene called for a gun. He would signal her to be quiet, take it out, have her stand behind him, creep through the apartment with her clutching on to his free arm in fear. He would do that gun swing thing into each room, his body crouched and prepared for the worst. But Myron did not regularly carry a gun. It was not that he disliked guns – when in trouble, in fact, he rather enjoyed their company – but a gun is bulky and chafes like a tweed condom. And let's face it, for most prospective clients, a sports agent packing heat does not inspire confidence, and for those it does, well, Myron would rather do without them.

Win, on the other hand, always carried a gun – at least two, actually, not to mention a prodigious pot-pourri of concealed weaponry. The man was like a walking Israel.

The apartment consisted of three rooms and a kitchen. They hurried through them. Nobody. And no body.

'Anything missing?' Myron asked.

She looked at him, annoyed. 'How the hell would I know?'

'I mean, anything noticeable. The TV is here. So is the VCR. I want to know if you think it's a robbery.'

She glanced about the living room. 'No,' she said. 'It doesn't look like a robbery.'

'Any thoughts on who did this or why?'

Brenda shook her head, her eyes still taking in the mess.

'Did Horace hide money someplace? A cookie jar or under a floorboard or something?'

'No.'

They started in Horace's room. Brenda opened up his closet. For a long moment she stood and said nothing.

'Brenda?'

'A lot of his clothes are missing,' she said softly. 'His suitcase too.'

'That's good,' Myron said. 'It means he probably ran; it makes it less likely that he met up with foul play.'

She nodded. 'But it's creepy.'

'How so?'

'It's just like my mother. I can still remember Dad just standing here, staring at the empty hangers.'

They moved back into the living room and then into a small bedroom.

'Your room?' Myron asked.

'I'm not here very much, but yeah, this is my room.'

Brenda's eyes immediately fell on a spot near her night table. She gave a little gasp and dived to the floor. Her hands began to paw through her effects.

'Brenda?'

Her pawing grew more intense, her eyes aflame. After a few minutes she got up and ran to her father's room. Then the living room. Myron kept back.

'They're gone,' she said.

'What?'

Brenda looked at him. 'The letters my mother wrote me. Someone took them.'

4

Myron parked the car in front of Brenda's dorm room. Except for monosyllabic directions, Brenda had not spoken during the drive. Myron did not push it. He stopped the car and turned toward her. She continued to stare ahead.

Reston University was a place of green grass and big oaks and brick buildings and Frisbees and bandannas. Professors still had long hair and unkempt beards and tweed jackets. There was such a feeling of innocence here, of make-believe, of youth, of startling passion. But that was the beauty of such a university: students debating over life-and-death issues in an environment as insulated as Disney World. Reality had nothing to do with the equation. And that was okay. In fact, that was how it should be.

'She just left,' Brenda said. 'I was five years old, and she just left me alone with him.'

Myron let her speak.

'I remember everything about her. The way she looked. The way she smelled. The way she'd come home from her job so tired she could barely put her feet up. I don't think I've talked about her five times in the past twenty years. But I think about her every day. I think about why she gave me up. And I think about why I still miss her.'

She put her hand to her chin then and turned away. The car stayed silent.

'You good at this, Myron?' she asked. 'At investigating?'

'I think so,' he said.

Brenda grabbed the door handle and pulled. 'Could you find my mother?'

She did not wait for a response. She hurried out of the car and up the steps. Myron watched her disappear into the colonial brick building. Then he started up the car and headed home.

Myron found a spot on Spring Street right outside Jessica's loft. He still referred to his new dwelling as Jessica's loft, even though he now lived here and paid half the rent. Weird how that worked.

Myron took the stairs to the third floor. He opened the door and immediately heard Jessica yell out, 'Working.'

He did not hear any clacking on the computer keyboard, but that didn't mean anything. He made his way into the bedroom, closed the door, and checked the answering machine. When Jessica was writing, she never answered the phone.

Myron hit the play button. 'Hello, Myron? This is your mother.' Like he wouldn't recognize the voice. 'God, I hate this machine. Why doesn't she pick up? I know she's there. Is it so hard for a human being to pick up a phone and say hello and take a message? I'm in my office, my phone rings, I pick it up. Even if I'm working. Or I have my secretary take a message. Not a machine. I don't like machines, Myron, you know that.' She continued on in a similar vein for some time. Myron longed for the old days when there was a time limit on answering machines. Progress was not always a good thing.

Finally Mom began to wind down. 'Just calling to say hello, doll face. We'll talk later.'

For the first thirty-plus years of his life, Myron had lived with his parents in the New Jersey suburb of Livingston. As an infant he'd started life in the small nursery upstairs on the left. From the age of three to sixteen, he'd lived in the bedroom upstairs on the right; from sixteen to just a few months ago, he'd lived in the basement. Not all the time, of course. He went to Duke down in North Carolina for four years, spent summers working basketball camps, stayed on occasion with Jessica or Win in Manhattan. But his true home had always been, well, with Mommy and Daddy – by choice, strangely enough, though some might suggest that serious therapy would unearth deeper motives.

That changed several months ago, when Jessica asked him to move in with her. This was a rarity in their relationship, Jessica making the first move, and Myron had been deliriously happy and heady and scared out of his mind. His trepidation had nothing to do with fear of commitment – that particular phobia plagued Jessica, not him – but there had been rough times in the past, and to put it simply, Myron never wanted to be hurt like that again.

He still saw his folks once a week or so, going out to the house for dinner or having them make the trip into the Big Apple. He also spoke to either his mom or his dad nearly every day. Funny thing is, while they were undoubtedly pests, Myron liked them. Crazy as it might sound, he actually enjoyed spending time with his parents. Uncool? Sure. Hip as a polka accordionist? Totally. But there you go.

He grabbed a Yoo-Hoo from the refrigerator, shook it, popped the top, took a big swig. Sweet nectar. Jessica yelled in, 'What are you in the mood for?'

'I don't care.'

'You want to go out?'

'Do you mind if we just order in?' he asked.

'Nope.' She appeared in the doorway. She wore his oversize Duke sweatshirt and black knit pants. Her hair was pulled back in a ponytail. Several hairs had escaped and fell in front of her face. When she smiled at him, he still felt his pulse quicken.

'Hi,' he said. Myron prided himself on his clever opening gambits.

'You want Chinese?' she asked.

'Whatever, sure. Hunan, Szechwan, Cantonese?'

'Szechwan,' she said.

'Okay. Szechwan Garden, Szechwan Dragon, or Empire Szechwan?'

She thought a moment. 'Dragon was greasy last time. Let's go with Empire.'

Jessica crossed the kitchen and kissed him lightly on the cheek. Her hair smelled like wildflowers after a summer storm. Myron gave her a quick hug and grabbed the delivery menu from the cabinet. They figured out what they'd get – the hot and sour soup, one shrimp entrée, one vegetable entrée – and Myron called it in. The usual language barriers applied – why don't they ever hire a person who speaks English at least to take the phone order? – and after repeating his telephone number six times, he hung up.

'Get much done?' he asked.

Jessica nodded. 'The first draft will be finished by Christmas.'

'I thought the deadline was August.'

'Your point being?'

They sat at the kitchen table. The kitchen, living room, dining room, TV room were all one big space. The ceiling was fifteen feet high. Airy. Brick walls with exposed metal beams gave the place a look that was both artsy and railroad station-like. The loft was, in a word, neat-o.

The food arrived. They chatted about their day. Myron told her about Brenda Slaughter. Jessica sat and listened in that way of hers. She was one of those people who had the ability to make any speaker feel like the only person alive. When he finished, she asked a few questions. Then she stood up and poured a glass of water from their Brita pitcher.

She sat back down. 'I have to fly out to L.A. on Tuesday,' Jessica said.

Myron looked up. 'Again?'

She nodded.

'For how long?'

'I don't know. A week or two.'

'Weren't you just out there?'

'Yeah, so?'

'For that movie deal, right?'

'Right.'

'So why are you going out again?' he asked.

'I got to do some research for this book.'

'Couldn't you have done both when you were there last week?'

'No.' Jessica looked at him. 'Something wrong?'

Myron fiddled with a chopstick. He looked at her, looked away, swallowed, and just said it: 'Is this working?'

'What?'

'Our living together.'

'Myron, it's just for a couple of weeks. For research.'

'And then it's a book tour. Or a writer's retreat. Or a movie deal. Or more research.'

'What, you want me to stay home and bake cookies?'

'No.'

'Then what's going on here?'

'Nothing,' Myron said. Then: 'We've been together a long time.'

'On and off for ten years,' she added. 'So?'

He was not sure how to continue. 'You like traveling.'

'Hell, yes.'

'I miss you when you're gone.'

'I miss you too,' she said. 'And I miss you when you go away on business too. But our freedom – that's part of the fun, isn't it? And besides' – she leaned forward a little – 'I give great reunion.'

He nodded. 'You do at that.'

She put her hand on his forearm. 'I don't want to do any pseudoanalysis, but this move has been a big adjustment for you. I understand that. But so far I think it's working great.'

She was, of course, right. They were a modern couple with skyrocketing careers and worlds to conquer. Separation was part of that. Whatever nagging doubts he had were a by-product of his innate pessimism. Things were indeed going so well – Jessica had come back, she had asked him to move in – that he kept waiting for something to go wrong. He had to stop obsessing. Obsession does not seek out problems and correct them; it manufactures them out of nothing, feeds them, makes them stronger.

He smiled at her. 'Maybe this is all a cry for attention,' he said.

'Oh?'

'Or maybe it's a ploy to get more sex.'

She gave him a look that curled his chopsticks. 'Maybe it's working,' she said.

'Maybe I'll slip into something more comfortable,' he said.

'Not that Batman mask again.'

'Aw, c'mon, you can wear the utility belt.'

She thought about it. 'Okay, but no stopping in the middle and shouting, "Same Bat Time, same Bat Channel." '

'Deal.'

Jessica stood, walked over to him, and sat on his lap. She hugged him and lowered her lips toward his ear. 'We've got it good, Myron. Let's not fuck it up.'

She was right.

She got off his lap. 'Come on, let's clear the table.'

'And then?'

Jessica nodded. 'To the Batpoles.'

5

As soon as Myron hit the street the next morning, a black limousine pulled in front of him. Two mammoth men – muscle-headed, neckless wonders – lumbered out of the car. They wore ill-fitted business suits, but Myron did not fault their tailor. Guys built like that always looked ill fitted. They both had Gold's Gym tans, and though he could not confirm this by sight, Myron bet that their chests were as waxed as Cher's legs.

One of the bulldozers said, 'Get in the car.'

'My mommy told me to never get in a car with strangers,' Myron said.

'Oh,' the other bulldozer said, 'we got ourselves a comedian here.'

'Yeah?' The bulldozer tilted his head at Myron. 'That right? You a comedian?'

'I'm also an exciting vocalist,' Myron said. 'Want to hear my much-loved rendition of "Volare"?'

'You'll be singing out the other end of your ass if you don't get in the car.'

'Other end of my ass,' Myron said. He looked up as though in deep thought. 'I don't get it. Out of the end of my ass, okay, that makes sense. But out of the *other* end? What does that mean exactly? I mean, technically, if we follow the intestinal tract, isn't the other end of your ass simply your mouth?'

The bulldozers looked at each other, then at Myron. Myron was not particularly scared. These thugs were delivery boys; the package was not supposed to be delivered bruised. They would take a little needling. Plus, you never show these guys fear. They smell fear, they swarm in and devour you. Of course Myron could be wrong. They might be unbalanced psychotics who'd snap at the slightest provocation. One of life's little mysteries.

'Mr. Ache wants to see you,' Bulldozer One said.

'Which one?'

'Frank.'

Silence. This was not good. The Ache brothers were leading mob figures in New York. Herman Ache, the older brother, was the leader, a man responsible for enough suffering to make a third world dictator envious. But next to his whacked-out brother Frank, Herman Ache was about as scary as Winnie-the-Pooh.

The muscleheads cracked their necks and smiled at Myron's silence. 'Not so funny now, are you, smart guy?'

'Testicles,' Myron said, stepping toward the car. 'They shrink when you use steroids.'

It was an old Bolitar rejoinder, but Myron never got tired of the classics. He had no choice really. He had to go. He slid into the backseat of the stretch limo. There was a bar and a television tuned in to Regis and Kathie Lee. Kathie Lee was regaling the audience with Cody's most recent exploits.

'No more, I beg you,' Myron said. 'I'll tell you everything.'

The bulldozers did not get it. Myron leaned forward and snapped the television off. No one protested.

'We going to Clancy's?' Myron asked.

Clancy's Tavern was the Aches' hangout. Myron had been there with Win a couple of years back. He had hoped never to return.

'Sit back and shut up, asshole.'

Myron kept still. They took the West Side Highway north – in the opposite direction of Clancy's Tavern. They turned right at Fifty-seventh Street. When they hit a Fifth Avenue parking garage, Myron realized where they were headed.

'We're going to TruPro's office,' he said out loud.

The bulldozers said nothing. Didn't matter. He had not said it for their benefit anyway.

TruPro was one of the larger sports agencies in the country. For years it'd been operated by Roy O'Connor, a snake in a suit, who had been nothing if not an expert in how to break the rules. O'Connor was the master of illegally signing athletes when they were barely out of diapers, using payoffs and subtle extortion. But like so many who flitted in and out of the world of corruption, Roy inevitably got nuked. Myron had seen it happen before. A guy figures he can be a 'little pregnant', a tad enmeshed with the underworld. But the mob does not work that way. You give them an inch, they take the whole damn yardstick. That was what had happened to TruPro. Roy owed money, and when he couldn't pay up, the appropriately named Ache brothers took control.

'Move it, asshole.'

Myron followed Bubba and Rocco – if those weren't their names, they should have been – into the elevator. They got out on the eighth floor and headed past the receptionist. She kept her head down but sneaked a glance. Myron waved to her and kept moving. They stopped in front of an office door.

'Search him.'

Bulldozer One started patting him down.

Myron closed his eyes. 'God,' he said. 'This feels good. A little left.'

Bulldozer stopped, threw him a glare. 'Go in.'

Myron opened the door and entered the office.

Frank Ache spread his arms and stepped toward him. 'Myron!'

Whatever fortune Frank Ache had amassed, the man never did spend it on clothes. He favored chintzy velour sweat suits, like something the guys on *Lost in Space* might consider casual wear. The one Frank sported today was burnt orange with yellow trim. The top was zippered lower than a *Cosmo* cover, his gray chest hair so thick it looked like a natty sweater. He had a huge head, tiny shoulders, and a spare tire that was the envy of the Michelin man – an hourglass figure with all the time run out. He was big and puffy and the kind of bald where the top of the head looks like it exploded through the hair during an earthquake.

Frank gave Myron a ferocious bear hug. Myron was taken aback. Frank was usually about as cuddly as a jackal with shingles.

He pulled Myron to arm's length. 'Sheesh, Myron, you're looking good.'

Myron tried not to wince. 'Thanks, Frank.'

Frank offered him a big smile – two rows of corn-kernel teeth jam-packed together. Myron tried not to flinch. 'How long's it been?'

'A little over a year.'

'We were at Clancy's, right?'

'No, Frank, we weren't.'

Frank looked puzzled. 'Where were we?'

'On a road in Pennsylvania. You shot out my tires, threatened to kill members of my family, and then you told me to get out of your car before you used my nuts for squirrel food.'

Frank laughed and clapped Myron on the back. 'Good times, eh?'

Myron kept very still. 'What can I do for you, Frank?'

'You in a rush?'

'Just wanted to get to the heart of it.'

'Hey, Myron.' Frank opened his arms wide. 'I'm trying to be friendly here. I'm a changed man. It's a whole new me.'

'Find religion, did you, Frank?'

'Something like that.'

'Uh-huh.'

Frank's smile slowly faded. 'You like my old ways better?'

'They're more honest.'

The smile was gone completely now. 'You're doing it again, Myron.'

'What?'

'Crawling up the crack of my ass,' he said. 'It cozy up there?'

'Cozy,' Myron said with a nod. 'Yeah, Frank, that's the word I'd use.'

The door behind them opened. Two men came in. One was Roy O'Connor, the figurative president of TruPro. He crept in silently, as though waiting for permission to exist. Probably was. When Frank was around, Roy probably raised his hand before going to the bathroom. The second guy was in his mid-twenties. He was immaculately dressed and looked like an investment banker fresh off his M.B.A.

Myron gave a big wave. 'Hi, Roy. Looking good.'

Roy nodded stiffly, sat down.

Frank said, 'This here's my kid. Frankie Junior. Call him FJ.'

'Hi,' Myron said. FJ?

The kid gave him a hard glare and sat down.

'Roy here just hired FJ,' Frank said.

Myron smiled at Roy O'Connor. 'The selection

process must have been hell, Roy. Combing through all those résumés and everything.'

Roy said nothing.

Frank waddled around the desk. 'You and FJ got something in common, Myron.'

'Oh?'

'You went to Harvard, right?'

'For law school,' Myron said.

'FJ got his M.B.A. there.'

Myron nodded. 'Like Win.'

His name quieted the room. Roy O'Connor crossed his legs. His face lost color. He had experienced Win up close, but they all knew him. Win would be pleased by the reaction.

The room started up again slowly. Everyone took seats. Frank put two hands the size of canned hams on the desk. 'We hear you're representing Brenda Slaughter,' he said.

'Where did you hear that?'

Frank shrugged as if to say, silly question.

'Is it true, Myron?'

'No.'

'You're not repping her?'

'That's right, Frank.'

Frank looked at Roy. Roy sat like hardening plaster. Then he looked at FJ, who was shaking his head.

'Is her old man still her manager?' Frank asked.

'I don't know, Frank. Why don't you ask her?'

'You were with her yesterday,' Frank said.

'So?'

'So what were you two doing?'

Myron stretched out his legs, crossing the ankles. 'Tell me something, Frank. What's your interest in all this?'

Frank's eyes widened. He looked at Roy, then at FJ;

43

then he pointed a meaty finger at Myron. 'Pardon my fucking French,' he said, 'but do I look like I'm here to answer your fucking questions?'

'The whole new you,' Myron said. 'Friendly, changed.'

FJ leaned forward and looked in Myron's eyes. Myron looked back. There was nothing there. If the eyes were indeed the window to the soul, these read NO VACANCY. 'Mr. Bolitar?' FJ's voice was soft and willowy.

'Yes?'

'Fuck you.'

He whispered the words with the strangest smile on his face. He did not lean back after he said it. Myron felt something cold scramble up his back, but he did not look away.

The phone on the desk buzzed. Frank hit a button. 'Yeah?'

'Mr. Bolitar's associate on the line,' a female voice said. 'He wanted to speak with you.'

'With me?' Frank said.

'Yes, Mr. Ache.'

Frank looked confused. He shrugged his shoulders and hit a button.

'Yeah,' he said.

'Hello, Francis.'

The room became still as a photograph.

Frank cleared his throat. 'Hello, Win.'

'I trust that I am not interrupting,' Win said.

Silence.

'How is your brother, Francis?'

'He's good, Win.'

'I must give Herman a call. We haven't hit the links together in ages.'

'Yeah,' Frank said, 'I'll tell him you asked for him.'

'Fine, Francis, fine. Well, I must be going. Please give my best to Roy and your charming son. How rude of me not to have said hello earlier.'

Silence.

'Hey, Win?'

'Yes, Francis.'

'I don't like this cryptic shit, you hear?'

'I hear everything, Francis.'

Click.

Frank Ache gave Myron a hard glare. 'Get out.'

'Why are you so interested in Brenda Slaughter?'

Frank lifted himself out of the chair. 'Win's scary,' he said. 'But he ain't bulletproof. Say one more word, and I'll tie you to a chair and set your dick on fire.'

Myron did not bother with good-byes.

Myron took the elevator down. Win – real name Windsor Horne Lockwood III – stood in the lobby. He was dressed this morning in Late American Prep. Blue blazer, light khakis, white button-down Oxford shirt, loud Lilly Pulitzer tie, the kind with more colors than a gallery at a golf course. His blond hair was parted by the gods, his jaw jutting in that way of his, his cheekbones high and pretty and porcelain, his eyes the blue of ice. To look at Win's face, Myron knew, was to hate him, was to think elitism, class-consciousness, snobbery, anti-Semitism, racism, old-world money earned from the sweat of other men's brows, all that. People who judged Windsor Horne Lockwood III solely by appearance were always mistaken. Often dangerously so.

Win did not glance in Myron's direction. He looked out as though posing for a park statue. 'I was just thinking,' Win said.

'What?'

'If you clone yourself, and then have sex with yourself, is it incest or masturbation?'

Win.

'Good to see you're not wasting your time,' Myron said.

Win looked at him. 'If we were still at Duke,' he said, 'we'd probably discuss the dilemma for hours.'

'That's because we'd be drunk.'

Win nodded. 'There's that.'

They both switched off their cellular phones and started heading down Fifth Avenue. It was a relatively new trick that Myron and Win used with great effect. As soon as the Hormonal He-Men pulled up, Myron had switched on the phone and hit the programmed button for Win's cellular. Win had thus heard every word. That was why Myron had commented out loud on where they were heading. That was how Win knew exactly where he was and exactly when to call. Win had nothing to say to Frank Ache; he just wanted to make sure that Frank knew that Win knew where Myron was.

'Tie you to a chair and set your dick on fire,' Win repeated. 'That would sting.'

Myron nodded. 'Talk about having a burning sensation when you urinate.'

'Indeed. So tell me.'

Myron started talking. Win, as always, did not appear to be listening. He never glanced in Myron's direction, his eyes searching the streets for beautiful women. Midtown Manhattan during work hours was full of them. They wore business suits and silk blouses and white Reebok sneakers. Every once in a while Win would reward one with a smile; unlike almost anybody else in New York, he was often rewarded with one in return.

When Myron told him about bodyguarding Brenda Slaughter, Win suddenly stopped and broke out in song: '*AND I-I-I-I-I WILL ALWAYS LOVE YOU-OU-OU-OU-OU-OU-OU.*'

Myron looked at him. Win stopped, put his face back in place, continued walking. 'When I sing that,' Win said, 'it's almost like Whitney Houston is in the room.'

'Yeah,' Myron said. 'Or something.'

'So what is the Aches' interest in all this?'

'I don't know.'

'Perhaps TruPro just wishes to represent her.'

'Doubtful. She'll make somebody money but not enough for pulling this.'

Win thought about it, nodded his agreement. They headed east on Fiftieth Street. 'Young FJ might pose a problem.'

'Do you know him?'

'A bit. He is something of an intriguing story. Daddy groomed him to go legit. He sent him to Lawrenceville, then to Princeton, finally Harvard. Now he's setting him up in the business of representing athletes.'

'But.'

'But he resents it. He is still Frank Ache's son and thus wants his approval. He needs to show that despite the upbringing, he's still a tough guy. Worse, he is genetically Frank Ache's son. My guess? If you trample through FJ's childhood, you'll stumble across many a legless spider and wingless fly.'

Myron shook his head. 'This is definitely not a good thing.'

Win said nothing. They hit the Lock-Horne Building on Forty-seventh Street. Myron got off the elevator on the twelfth floor. Win stayed in, his office being two flights up. When Myron looked at the reception desk – the place where Esperanza usually sat – he nearly jumped back. Big Cyndi sat silently watching him. She was far too big for the desk – far too big for the building, really – and the desk actually teetered on her knees. Her makeup would be labeled 'too garish' by members of Kiss. Her hair was short and seaweed green. The T-shirt she wore had the sleeves ripped off, revealing biceps the size of basketballs.

Myron gave her a tentative wave. 'Hello, Cyndi.'

'Hello, Mr. Bolitar.'

Big Cyndi was six-six, three hundred pounds and had been Esperanza's tag team wrestling partner, known in the ring as Big Chief Mama. For years Myron had only heard her growl, never speak. But her voice could be anything she wanted. When she worked as a bouncer at Leather-N-Lust on Tenth Street, she put on an accent that made Arnold Schwarzenegger sound like a Gabor sister. Right now, she was doing her perky Mary-Richards-off-decaf.

'Is Esperanza here?' he asked.

'Miss Diaz is in Mr. Bolitar's office.' She smiled at him. Myron tried not to cringe. Forget what he'd said about Frank Ache – this smile made his fillings hurt.

He excused himself and headed into his office. Esperanza was at his desk, talking on the phone. She wore a bright yellow blouse against the olive skin that always made him think of stars shimmering off the warm water in the Amalfi bay. She looked up at him, signaled to give her a minute with a finger, and kept on talking. Myron sat down across from her. It was an interesting perspective, seeing what clients and corporate sponsors saw when they sat in his office. The Broadway musical posters behind his chair – too desperate, he decided. Like he was trying to be irreverent for irreverence's sake.

When she finished the call, Esperanza said, 'You're late.'

'Frank Ache wanted to see me.'

She crossed her arms. 'He need a fourth for mah-jongg?'

'He wanted to know about Brenda Slaughter.'

Esperanza nodded. 'So we got trouble.'

'Maybe.'

'Dump her.'

'No.'

She looked at him with flat eyes. 'Tattoo me surprised.'

'Did you get anything on Horace Slaughter?'

She grabbed a piece of paper. 'Horace Slaughter. None of his credit cards has been used in the past week. He has one bank account at Newark Fidelity. Balance: zero dollars.'

'Zero?'

'He cleaned it out.'

'How much?'

'Eleven grand. In cash.'

Myron whistled and leaned back. 'So he was planning on running. That fits with what we saw in his apartment.'

'Uh-huh.'

'I got a harder one for you,' Myron said. 'His wife, Anita Slaughter.'

'They still married?'

'I don't know. Maybe legally. She ran away twenty years ago. I don't think they ever bothered with a divorce.'

She frowned. 'Did you say twenty years ago?'

'Yes. Apparently no one has seen her since then.'

'And what exactly are we trying to find?'

'In a word: her.'

'You don't know where she is?'

'Not a clue. Like I said, she's been missing for twenty years.'

Esperanza waited a beat. 'She could be dead.'

'I know.'

'And if she's managed to stay hidden this long, she could have changed her name. Or left the country.'

'Right.'

'And there'd be few records, if any, from twenty years ago. Certainly nothing on the computer.'

Myron smiled. 'Don't you hate it when I make it too easy?'

'I realize I'm only your lowly assistant—'

'You're not my lowly assistant.'

She gave him a look. 'I'm not your partner either.'

That quieted him.

'I realize that I'm only your lowly assistant,' she said again, 'but do we really have time for this bullshit?'

'Just do a standard check. See if we get lucky.'

'Fine.' Her tone was like a door slamming shut. 'But we got other things to discuss here.'

'Shoot.'

'Milner's contract. They won't renegotiate.'

They dissected the Milner situation, batted it around a bit, developed and fine-tuned a strategy, and then concluded that their strategy would not work. Behind them Myron could hear the construction starting. They were cutting space out of the waiting area and conference room to make a private office for Esperanza.

After a few minutes Esperanza stopped and stared at him.

'What?'

'You're going to follow through with this,' she said. 'You're going to search for her parents.'

'Her father is an old friend of mine.'

'Oh Christ, please don't say, "I owe him."'

'It's not just that. It's good business.'

'It's not good business. You're out of the office too much. Clients want to talk to you directly. So do the sponsors.'

'I have my cellular.'

Esperanza shook her head. 'We can't keep going on like this.'

'Like what?'

'Either you make me a partner or I walk.'

'Don't hit me with that now, Esperanza. Please.'

'You're doing it again.'

'What?'

'Stalling.'

'I'm not stalling.'

She gave him a look that was half harsh, half pity. 'I know how you hate change—'

'I don't hate change.'

'—but one way or the other, things are going to be different. So get over it.'

Part of him wanted to yell, Why? Things were good the way they were. Hadn't he been the one who'd encouraged her to get a law degree in the first place? A change, sure, he expected that after her graduation. He had been slowly giving her new responsibilities. But a partnership?

He pointed behind him. 'I'm building you an office,' he said.

'So?'

'So doesn't that scream commitment? You can't expect me to rush this. I'm taking baby steps here.'

'You took one baby step, and then you fell on your ass.' She stopped, shook her head. 'I haven't pushed you on this since we were down at Merion.' The golf U.S. Open in Philadelphia. Myron was in the midst of finding a kidnap victim when she hit him with her partnership demands. Since then, he had been, well, er, stalling.

Esperanza stood. 'I want to be a partner. Not full. I understand that. But I want equity.' She walked to the door. 'You have a week.'

Myron was not sure what to say. She was his best friend. He loved her. And he needed her here. She was a part of MB. A big part. But things were not that simple.

Esperanza opened the door and leaned against the frame. 'You going to see Brenda Slaughter now?'

He nodded. 'In a few minutes.'

'I'll start the search. Call me in a few hours.'

She closed the door behind her. Myron went around to his chair and picked up the phone. He dialed Win's number.

Win picked up on the first ring. 'Articulate.'

'You got plans for tonight?'

'*Moi*? But of course.'

'Typical evening of demeaning sex?'

'Demeaning sex,' Win repeated. 'I told you to stop reading Jessica's magazines.'

'Can you cancel?'

'I could,' he said, 'but the lovely lass will be very disappointed.'

'Do you even know her name?'

'What? Off the top of my head?'

One of the construction workers started hammering. Myron put a hand over his free ear. 'Could we meet at your place? I need to bounce a few things off you.'

Win did not hesitate. 'I am but a brick wall awaiting your verbal game of squash.'

Myron guessed that meant yes.

6

Brenda Slaughter's team, the New York Dolphins, practiced at Englewood High School in New Jersey. Myron felt a tightness in his chest when he entered the gym. He heard the sweet echo of dribbling basketballs; he savored the high school gym scent, that mix of strain and youth and uncertainty. Myron had played in huge venues, but whenever he walked into a new gymnasium, even as a spectator, he felt as if he'd been dropped through a time portal.

He climbed up the steps of one of those wooden space-saving pull-out stands. As always, it shook with each step. Technology may have made advancements in our daily lives, but you wouldn't know it from a high school gymnasium. Those velvet banners still hung from one wall, showing a variety of state or country or group championships. There was a list of track and field records down one corner. The electric clock was off. A tired janitor swept the hardwood floor, moving in a curling up-and-down pattern like a Zamboni on a hockey rink.

Myron spotted Brenda Slaughter shooting foul shots. Her face was lost in the simple bliss of this purest of motions. The ball backspun off her fingertips; it never touched the rim, but the net jumped a bit at the bottom. She wore a sleeveless white T-shirt over what looked like a black tube top. Sweat shimmered on her skin.

Brenda looked over at him and smiled. It was an unsure smile, like a new lover on that first morning. She dribbled the ball toward him and threw him a pass. He caught it, his fingers automatically finding the grooves.

'We need to talk,' he said.

She nodded and sat next to him on the bench. Her face was wide and sweaty and real.

'Your father cleared out his bank account before he disappeared,' Myron said.

The serenity fled from her face. Her eyes flicked away, and she shook her head. 'This is too weird.'

'What?' Myron said.

She reached toward him and took the ball from his hands. She held on to it as though it might grow wings and fly off. 'It's so like my mother,' she said. 'First the clothes gone. Now the money.'

'Your mother took money?'

'Every dime.'

Myron looked at her. She kept her eyes on the ball. Her face was suddenly so guileless, so frail, Myron felt something inside him crumble. He waited a moment before changing the subject. 'Was Horace working before he disappeared?'

One of her teammates, a white woman with a ponytail and freckles, called out to her and clapped her hands for the ball. Brenda smiled and led her with a one-armed pass. The ponytail bounced up and down as the woman speed-dribbled toward the basket.

'He was a security guard at St. Barnabas Hospital,' Brenda said. 'You know it?'

Myron nodded. St. Barnabas was in Livingston, his hometown.

'I work there too,' she said. 'In the pediatric clinic. Sort of a work-study program. I helped him get the job. That's how I first knew he was missing. His supervisor called me and asked where he was.'

'How long had Horace been working there?'

'I don't know. Four, five months.'

'What's his supervisor's name?'

'Calvin Campbell.'

Myron took out a notecard and wrote it down.

'Where else does Horace hang out?'

'Same places,' she said.

'The courts?'

Brenda nodded. 'And he still refs high school games twice a week.'

'Any close friends who might help him out?'

She shook her head. 'No one in particular.'

'How about family members?'

'My aunt Mabel. If there is anyone he'd trust, it's his sister Mabel.'

'She live near here?'

'Yeah. In West Orange.'

'Could you give her a call for me? Tell her I'd like to drop by.'

'When?'

'Now.' He looked at his watch. 'If I hurry, I can be back before practice is over.'

Brenda stood. 'There's a pay phone in the hallway. I'll call her.'

7

On the ride to Mabel Edwards's house, Myron's cellular phone rang. It was Esperanza. 'Norm Zuckerman is on the line,' she said.

'Patch it through.'

There was a click.

'Norm?' Myron said.

'Myron, sweetie, how are you?'

'Fine.'

'Good, good. You learn anything yet?'

'No.'

'Good, okay, fine.' Norm hesitated. His jocular tone was a little off, forced. 'Where are you?'

'In my car.'

'I see, I see, okay. Look, Myron, you going to go over to Brenda's practice?'

'I just came from there.'

'You left her alone?'

'She's at practice. A dozen people are there with her. She'll be fine.'

'Yeah, I guess you're right.' He didn't sound convinced. 'Look, Myron, we need to talk. When can you get back to the gym?'

'I should be back in an hour. What's this about, Norm?'

'An hour. I'll see you then.'

Aunt Mabel lived in a suburb outside Newark. West Orange was one of those 'changing' suburbs, the percentage of white families sinking bit by bit. It was the spreading effect. Minorities scratched their way out of the city and into the nearest suburbs; the whites then wanted out of said suburbs and moved still farther away from the city. In real estate terms this was known as progress.

Still, Mabel's tree-lined avenue seemed a zillion light-years from the urban blight that Horace called home. Myron knew the town of West Orange well. His own hometown of Livingston bordered it. Livingston too was starting to change. When Myron was in high school, the town had been white. Very white. Snow white. It had been so white that of the six hundred kids in Myron's graduating class, only one was black – and he was on the swim team. Can't get much whiter than that.

The house was a one-level structure – fancier folks might call it a ranch – the kind of place that probably had three bedrooms, one and a half baths, and a finished basement with a used pool table. Myron parked his Ford Taurus in the driveway.

Mabel Edwards was probably late forties, maybe younger. She was a big woman with a fleshy face, loosely curled hair, and a dress that looked like old drapes. When she opened the door, she gave Myron a smile that turned her ordinary features into something almost celestial. A pair of half-moon reading glasses hung from a chain, resting on her enormous chest. There was a puffiness in her right eye, remnants of a contusion maybe. She gripped some sort of knitting project in her hand.

'Goodness me,' she said. 'Myron Bolitar. Come in.'

Myron followed her inside. The house had the stale smell of a grandparent. When you're a kid, the smell gives you the creeps; when you're an adult, you want to bottle it and let it out with a cup of cocoa on a bad day.

'I put coffee on, Myron. Would you like some?'

'That would be nice, thank you.'

'Sit down over there. I'll be right back.'

Myron grabbed a seat on a stiff sofa with a flowered print. For some reason he put his hands in his lap. As if he were waiting for a schoolteacher. Myron glanced about. There were African sculptures made of wood on the coffee table. The fireplace mantel was lined with family photographs. Almost all of them featured a young man who looked vaguely familiar. Mabel Edwards's son, he guessed. It was the standard parental shrine – that is, you could follow the offspring's life from infancy through adulthood with the images in these frames. There was a baby photo, those school portraits with the rainbow background, a big Afro playing basketball, a tuxedo-and-date prom, a couple of graduations, blah, blah, blah. Corny, yes, but these photomontages always touched Myron, exploiting his overtuned sensitivity like a sappy Hallmark commercial.

Mabel Edwards came back into the living room with a tray. 'We met once before,' she said.

Myron nodded, trying to remember. Something played along the edges, but it wouldn't come into focus.

'You were in high school.' She handed him a cup on a saucer. Then she pushed the tray with cream and sugar toward him. 'Horace took me to one of your games. You were playing Shabazz.'

It came back to Myron. Junior year, the Essex County tournament. Shabazz was short for Malcolm X Shabazz High School of Newark. The school had no whites. Its starting five featured guys named Rhahim and Khalid. Even back then Shabazz High had been surrounded by a barbwire fence with a sign that read GUARD DOGS ON DUTY.

Guard dogs at a high school. Think about it.

'I remember,' Myron said.

Mabel burst into a short laugh. When she did, every part of her jiggled. 'Funniest thing I ever saw,' she said. 'All these pale boys walking in scared out of their wits, eyes as big as saucers. You were the only one at home, Myron.'

'That's because of your brother.'

She shook her head. 'Horace said you were the best he ever worked with. He said nothing would have stopped you from being great.' She leaned forward. 'You two had something special, didn't you?'

'Yes, ma'am.'

'Horace loved you, Myron. Talked about you all the time. When you got drafted, I tell you, it was the happiest I'd seen him in years. You called him, right?'

'As soon as I heard.'

'I remember. He came over and told me all about it.' Her voice was wistful. She paused and adjusted herself in the seat. 'And when you got hurt, well, Horace cried. Big, tough man came to this house and sat right where you are now, Myron, and he cried like a little baby.'

Myron said nothing.

'You want to know something else?' Mabel continued. She took a sip of her coffee. Myron held his cup, but he could not move. He managed a nod.

'When you tried that comeback last year, Horace was so worried. He wanted to call you, talk you out of it.'

Myron's voice was thick. 'So why didn't he?'

Mabel Edwards gave him a gentle smile. 'When was the last time you spoke to Horace?'

'That phone call,' Myron said. 'Right after the draft.'

She nodded as though that explained everything. 'I think Horace knew you were hurting,' she said. 'I think he figured you'd call when you were ready.'

Myron felt something well up in his eyes. Regrets and

could-have-beens tried to sneak in, but he shoved them away. No time for this now. He blinked a few times and put the coffee to his lips. After he had taken a sip, he asked, 'Have you seen Horace lately?'

She put her cup down slowly and studied his face. 'Why do you want to know?'

'He hasn't shown up for work. Brenda hasn't seen him.'

'I understand that,' Mabel continued, her voice set on caution now, 'but what's your interest in this?'

'I want to help.'

'Help what?'

'Find him.'

Mabel Edwards waited a beat. 'Don't take this the wrong way, Myron,' she said, 'but how does this concern you?'

'I'm trying to help Brenda.'

She stiffened slightly. 'Brenda?'

'Yes, ma'am.'

'Do you know she got a court order to keep her father away from her?'

'Yes.'

Mabel Edwards slipped on the half-moon glasses and picked up her knitting. The needles began to dance. 'I think maybe you should stay out of this, Myron.'

'Then you know where he is?'

She shook her head. 'I didn't say that.'

'Brenda is in danger, Mrs. Edwards. Horace might be connected.'

The knitting needles stopped short. 'You think Horace would hurt his own daughter?' Her voice was a little sharp now.

'No, but there might be a connection. Somebody broke into Horace's apartment. He packed a bag and cleared out his bank account. I think he may be in trouble.'

The needles started again. 'If he is in trouble,' she said, 'maybe it's best that he stay hid.'

'Tell me where he is, Mrs. Edwards. I'd like to help.'

She stayed silent for a long time. She pulled at the yarn and kept knitting. Myron looked around the room. His eyes found the photographs again. He stood and studied them.

'Is this your son?' he asked.

She looked up over her glasses. 'That's Terence. I got married when I was seventeen, and Roland and I were blessed with him a year later.' The needles picked up speed. 'Roland died when Terence was a baby. Shot on the front stoop of our home.'

'I'm sorry,' Myron said.

She shrugged, managed a sad smile. 'Terence is the first college graduate in our family. That's his wife on the right. And my two grandsons.'

Myron lifted the photograph. 'Beautiful family.'

'Terence worked his way through Yale Law School,' she continued. 'He became a town councilman when he was just twenty-five.' That was probably why he looked familiar, Myron thought. Local TV news or papers. 'If he wins in November, he'll be in the state senate before he's thirty.'

'You must be proud,' Myron said.

'I am.'

Myron turned and looked at her. She looked back.

'It's been a long time, Myron. Horace always trusted you, but this is different. We don't know you anymore. These people who are looking for Horace' – she stopped and pointed to the puffy eye – 'you see this?'

Myron nodded.

'Two men came by here last week. They wanted to know where Horace was. I told them I didn't know.'

Myron felt his face flush. 'They hit you?'

She nodded, her eyes on his.

'What did they look like?'

'White. One was a big man.'

'How big?'

'Maybe your size.'

Myron was six-four, two-twenty. 'How about the other guy?'

'Skinny. And a lot older. He had a tattoo of a snake on his arm.' She pointed to her own immense biceps, indicating the spot.

'Please tell me what happened, Mrs. Edwards.'

'It's just like I said. They came into my house and wanted to know where Horace was. When I told them I didn't know, the big one punched me in the eye. The little one, he pulled the big one away.'

'Did you call the police?'

'No. But not because I was afraid. Cowards like that don't scare me. But Horace told me not to.'

'Mrs. Edwards,' Myron said, 'where is Horace?'

'I've already said too much, Myron. I just want you to understand. These people are dangerous. For all I know, you're working for them. For all I know, your coming here is just a trick to find Horace.'

Myron was not sure what to say. To protest his innocence would do little to assuage her fears. He decided to switch tracks and head in a completely different direction. 'What can you tell me about Brenda's mother?'

Mabel Edwards stiffened. She dropped the knitting into her lap, the half-moon glasses falling back to her bosom. 'Why on earth would you ask about that?'

'A few minutes ago I told you that somebody broke into your brother's apartment.'

'I remember.'

'Brenda's letters from her mother were missing. And Brenda has been receiving threatening phone calls. One of them told her to call her mother.'

Mabel Edwards's face went slack. Her eyes began to glisten.

After some time had passed, Myron tried again. 'Do you remember when she ran away?'

Her eyes regained focus. 'You don't forget the day your brother dies.' Her voice was barely a whisper. She shook her head. 'I can't see how any of this matters. Anita's been gone for twenty years.'

'Please, Mrs. Edwards, tell me what you remember.'

'Not much to tell,' Mabel said. 'She left my brother a note and ran away.'

'Do you remember what the note said?'

'Something about how she didn't love him anymore, how she wanted a new life.' Mabel Edwards stopped, waved her hand as though making space for herself. She took a handkerchief out of her bag and just held it in a tight ball.

'Could you tell me what she was like?'

'Anita?' She smiled now, but the handkerchief remained at the ready. 'I introduced them, you know. Anita and I worked together.'

'Where?'

'The Bradford estate. We were maids. We were young girls then, barely in our twenties. I only worked there for six months. But Anita, she stayed on for six years, slaving for those people.'

'When you say the Bradford estate—'

'I mean, *the* Bradfords. Anita was a servant really. For the old lady mostly. That woman must be eighty by now. But they all lived there. Children, grandchildren, brothers, sisters. Like on *Dallas*. I don't think that's healthy, do you?'

Myron had no comment on that.

'Anyway, when I met Anita, I thought she was a fine young woman except' – she looked in the air as though searching for the right words, then shook her head because they weren't there – 'well, she was just too beautiful. I don't know how else to say it. Beauty like that warps a man's brain, Myron. Now Brenda, she's attractive, I guess. Exotic, I think they call it. But Anita . . . hold on. I'll find you a picture.'

She stood fluidly and semiglided out of the room. Despite her size, Mabel moved with the unlabored grace of a natural athlete. Horace too moved like that, blending bulk with finesse in an almost poetic way. She was gone for less than a minute, and when she returned, she handed him a photograph. Myron looked down.

A knockout. A pure, undiluted, knee-knocking, breathstealing knockout. Myron understood the power a woman like that had over a man. Jessica had that kind of beauty. It was intoxicating and more than a little scary.

He studied the photograph. A young Brenda – no more than four or five years old – held her mother's hand and smiled brightly. Myron tried to imagine Brenda smiling like that now, but the image would not form. There was a resemblance between mother and daughter, but as Mabel had pointed out, Anita Slaughter was certainly more beautiful – at least in the conventional sense – her features sharper and more defined where Brenda's seemed large and almost mismatched.

'Anita put a dagger through Horace when she ran off,' Mabel Edwards continued. 'He never recovered.

Brenda neither. She was only a little girl when her mama left. She cried every night for three years. Even when she was in high school, Horace said she'd call out for her mama in her sleep.'

Myron finally looked up from the picture. 'Maybe she didn't run away,' he said.

Mabel's eyes narrowed. 'What do you mean?'

'Maybe she met up with foul play.'

A sad smile crossed Mabel Edwards's face. 'I understand,' she said gently. 'You look at that picture and you can't accept it. You can't believe a mother would abandon that sweet little child. I know. It's hard. But she did it.'

'The note could have been a forgery,' Myron tried. 'To throw Horace off the track.'

She shook her head. 'No.'

'You can't be sure—'

'Anita calls me.'

Myron froze. 'What?'

'Not often. Maybe once every two years. She'd ask about Brenda. I'd beg her to come back. She'd hang up.'

'Do you have any idea where she was calling from?'

Mabel shook her head. 'In the beginning it sounded like long distance. There'd be static. I always figured she was overseas.'

'When was the last time she called you?'

There was no hesitation. 'Three years ago. I told her about Brenda getting accepted to medical school.'

'Nothing since?'

'Not a word.'

'And you're sure it was her?' Myron realized that he was reaching.

'Yes,' she said. 'It was Anita.'

'Did Horace know about the calls?'

'At first I told him. But it was like ripping at a wound

that wasn't closing anyhow. So I stopped. But I think maybe she called him too.'

'What makes you say that?'

'He said something about it once when he had too much to drink. When I asked him about it later, he denied it, and I didn't push him. You have to understand, Myron. We never talked about Anita. But she was always right there. In the room with us. You know what I'm saying?'

The silence moved in like a cloud covering. Myron waited for it to disperse, but it hung there, thick and heavy.

'I'm very tired, Myron. Can we talk more about this another time?'

'Of course.' He rose. 'If your brother calls again—'

'He won't. He thinks maybe they bugged the phone. I haven't heard from him in almost a week.'

'Do you know where he is, Mrs. Edwards?'

'No. Horace said it'd be safer that way.'

Myron took a business card and a pen. He jotted down the number of his cellular phone. 'I can be reached at this number twenty-four hours a day.'

She nodded, drained, the simple act of reaching for the card suddenly a chore.

8

'I wasn't totally honest with you yesterday.'

Norm Zuckerman and Myron sat alone in the top row of the stands. Below them the New York Dolphins scrimmaged five-on-five. Myron was impressed. The women moved with finesse and strength. Being something of the semisexist Brenda had described, he had expected their movements to be more awkward, more the old stereotype of 'throwing like a girl'.

'You want to hear something funny?' Norm asked. 'I hate sports. Me, owner of Zoom, the sports apparel king, detests anything to do with a ball or a bat or a hoop or any of that. Know why?'

Myron shook his head.

'I was always bad at them. A major spaz, as the kids say today. My older brother, Herschel, now he was an athlete.' He looked off. When he started speaking again, his voice was throaty. 'So gifted, sweet Heshy. You remind me of him, Myron. I'm not just saying that. I still miss him. Dead at fifteen.'

Myron did not need to ask how. Norm's entire family had been slaughtered in Auschwitz. They all went in; only Norm came out. Today was warm, and Norm was wearing short sleeves. Myron could see his concentration camp tattoo and no matter how many times he saw one, he always fell into a respectful hush.

'This league' – Norm motioned toward the court – 'it's a long shot. I understood that from the start. It's why I link so much of the league promotion with the clothing. If the WPBA goes down the tubes, well, at least Zoom athletic wear would have gotten a ton of exposure out of it. You understand what I'm saying?'

'Yes.'

'And let's face it: without Brenda Slaughter, the investment is shot. The league, the endorsements, the tie-in with the clothing, the whole thing goes kaput. If you wanted to destroy this enterprise, you would go through her.'

'And you think someone wants to do that?'

'Are you kidding? Everybody wants to do that. Nike, Converse, Reebok, whoever. It's the nature of the beast. If the sneaker were on the other foot, so to speak, I would want the same thing. It's called capitalism. It's Economics one-oh-one. But this is different, Myron. Have you heard of the PWBL?'

'No.'

'You aren't supposed to. Yet. It stands for the Professional Women's Basketball League.'

Myron sat up a bit. 'A second women's basketball league?'

Norm nodded. 'They want to start up next year.'

On the court Brenda got the ball and drove hard baseline. A player jumped up to block the shot. Brenda pump-faked, glided under the basket, and made a reverse layup. Improvised ballet.

'Let me guess,' Myron said. 'This other league. It's being set up by TruPro.'

'How did you know that?'

Myron shrugged. Things were beginning to click.

'Look, Myron, it's like I said before: women's basketball is a tough sell. I'm promoting it a ton of different ways – to sports nuts, women eighteen to thirty-five, families who want something more genteel, fans who want more access to athletes – but at the end of the day there is one problem that this league will never overcome.'

'What's that?'

Again Norm motioned to the court below them. 'They're not as good as the men. I'm not being a chauvinist here. It's a fact. The men are better. The best player on this team could never compete against the worst player in the NBA. And when people watch professional sports, they want to watch the best. I'm not saying that the problem destroys us. I think we can build a nice fan base. But we have to be realistic.'

Myron massaged his face with his hands. He felt a headache coming on. TruPro wanted to start a women's basketball league. It made sense. Sports agencies were moving in that direction, aiming to corner markets. IMG, one of the world's biggest agencies, ran entire golf events. If you can own an event or run a league, you can make money a dozen different ways – not to mention how many clients you'd pick up. If a young golfer, for example, wanted to qualify for the big moneymaking IMG events, wouldn't he naturally want to have IMG as his sports rep?

'Myron?'

'Yes, Norm.'

'Do you know this TruPro well?'

Myron nodded. 'Oh, yeah.'

'I got hemorrhoids older than this kid they're making league commissioner. You should see him. He comes up to me and shakes my hands and gives me this icy smile. Then he tells me they're going to wipe me out. Just like that. Hello, I'm going to wipe you off the face of the earth.' Norm looked at Myron. 'Are they, you know, connected?' He bent his nose with his index fingers in case Myron did not get the drift.

'Oh, yeah,' Myron said again. Then he added, 'Very.'

'Great. Just great.'

'So what do you want to do, Norm?'

'I don't know. I don't run and hide – I had enough of that in my life – but if I'm putting these girls in danger—'

'Forget they're women.'

'What?'

'Pretend it's a men's league.'

'What, you think this is about sex? I wouldn't want men in danger either, okay?'

'Okay,' Myron said. 'Has TruPro said anything else to you?'

'No.'

'No threats, nothing?'

'Just this kid and his wipeout stuff. But don't you think they're probably the ones making the threats?'

It made sense, Myron guessed. Old gangsters had indeed moved into more legitimate enterprises – why limit yourself to prostitution and drugs and loan sharking when there were so many other ways to turn a buck? – but even with the best of intentions, it never worked out. Guys like the Aches couldn't help themselves really. They'd start out legit, but once things got the slightest bit tough, once they lost out on a contract or a sale or something, they reverted back to their old ways. Couldn't help it. Corruption too was a terrible addiction, but where were the support groups?

In this case TruPro would quickly realize that it needed to get Brenda away from its competition. So it started applying pressure. It put the screws to her manager – her father – and then moved on to Brenda herself. It was a classic scare tactic. But that scenario was not without problems. The phone call that mentioned Brenda's mother, for example – how did that fit in?

The coach blew the whistle ending practice. She gathered her players around, reminded them that they needed to be back in two hours for the second session, thanked them for their hustle, dismissed them with a clap.

Myron waited for Brenda to shower and get dressed. It didn't take her long. She came out in a long red T-shirt and black jeans, her hair still wet.

'Did Mabel know anything?' she asked.

'Yes.'

'Has she heard from Dad?'

Myron nodded. 'She says he's on the run. Two men came to her house looking for him. They roughed her up a bit.'

'My God, is she okay?'

'Yes.'

She shook her head. 'What's he on the run from?'

'Mabel doesn't know.'

Brenda looked at him, waited a beat. 'What else?' she said.

Myron cleared his throat. 'Nothing that can't wait.'

She kept looking at him. Myron turned and headed for his car. Brenda followed.

'So where we going?' she asked.

'I thought we'd stop by St. Barnabas and talk to your father's supervisor.'

She caught up to him. 'You think he knows something?'

'Highly doubtful. But this is what I do. I go poking around and hope something stirs.'

They reached the car. Myron unlocked the doors, and they both got in.

'I should be paying you for your time,' she said.

'I'm not a private investigator, Brenda. I don't work by the hour.'

'Still. I should be paying you.'

'Part of client recruitment,' Myron said.

'You want to represent me?'

'Yes.'

'You haven't made much of a sales pitch or applied any pressure.'

'If I had,' he said, 'would it have worked?'

'No.'

Myron nodded and started up the car.

'Okay,' she said. 'We've got a few minutes. Tell me why I should choose you and not one of the big boys. Personal service?'

'Depends on your definition of personal services. If you mean someone always following you around with lips firmly planted on your buttocks, then no, the big boys are better at puckering. They have the staff for it.'

'So what does Myron Bolitar offer? A little tongue with those lips?'

He smiled. 'A total package designed to maximize your assets while allowing room for integrity and a personal life.'

She nodded. 'What a crock.'

'Yeah, but it sounds good. In truth, MB SportsReps is a three-prong system. Prong one is earning money. I'm in charge of negotiating all contracts. I will continually seek out new endorsement deals for you and whenever possible get a bidding war going for your services. You'll make decent money playing for the WPBA, but you'll make a hell of a lot more on endorsements. You got a lot of pluses in that department.'

'Such as?'

'Three things off the top of my head. One, you're the best female player in the country. Two, you're studying to be a doctor – a pediatrician, no less – so we can play up the whole role model thing. And three, you're not hard on the eyes.'

'You forgot one.'

'What?'

'Four, that perennial white man favorite: well spoken. You ever notice that no one ever describes a white athlete as well spoken?'

'As a matter of fact, I have. It's why I left it off the list. But the truth is, it helps. I'm not going to get into a debate on Ebonics and the like, but if you are what is commonly referred to as well spoken, it adds revenue. Simple as that.'

She nodded. 'Go on.'

'In your case we need to design a strategy. Clearly you would have tremendous appeal to clothing and sneaker companies. But food products would love you too. Restaurant chains.'

'Why?' she asked. 'Because I'm big?'

'Because you're not waiflike,' Myron corrected. 'You're real. Sponsors like real – especially when it comes in an exotic package. They want someone attractive yet accessible – a contradiction, but there you go. And you have it. Cosmetic companies will want to get in on this too. We could also pick up a lot of local deals, but I would advise against it in the beginning. Try to stick with the national markets where we can. It doesn't pay to go after every dime out there. But that will be up to you. I'll present them to you. The final decision is always yours.'

'Okay,' she said. 'Give me prong two.'

'Prong two is what you do with your money after you earn it. You've heard of Lock-Horne Securities?'

'Sure.'

'All of my clients are required to set up a long-term

financial plan with their top man, Windsor Horne Lockwood the Third.'

'Nice name.'

'Wait till you meet him. But ask around. Win is considered one of the best financial advisers in the country. I insist that every client meet with him quarterly – not by fax or phone but in person – to go over their portfolios. Too many athletes get taken advantage of. That won't happen here, not because Win or I am watching your money but because you are.'

'Impressive. Prong three?'

'Esperanza Diaz. She is my right hand and handles everything else. I mentioned before that I'm not the best with ass kissing. That's true. But the reality of this business means I have to wear a lot of hats – travel agent, marriage counselor, limo driver, whatever.'

'And this Esperanza helps out with all that?'

'She's crucial.'

Brenda nodded. 'Sounds like you give her the shit detail.'

'Esperanza just graduated law school, as a matter of fact.' He tried not to sound too defensive, but her words had struck bone. 'She takes on more responsibility every day.'

'Okay, one question.'

'What?' Myron asked.

'What aren't you telling me about your visit to Mabel?'

Myron said nothing for a moment.

'It's about my mother, isn't it?'

'Not really. It's just . . .' He let his voice drift off before starting up again. 'Are you sure you want me to find her, Brenda?'

She crossed her arms and slowly shook her head. 'Cut it out.'

'What?'

'I know you think protecting me is sweet and noble. But it's not. It's annoying and insulting. So stop it. Now. If your mother ran away when you were five, wouldn't you want to know what happened?'

Myron thought about it, nodded. 'Point taken. I won't do it again.'

'Fine. So what did Mabel say?'

He recounted his conversation with her aunt. Brenda stayed still. She reacted only when he mentioned the phone calls Mabel and perhaps her father had received from her mother.

'They never told me,' she said. 'I suspected as much, but' – she looked at Myron – 'looks like you weren't the only one who thought I couldn't handle the truth.'

They fell into silence and continued the drive. Before making the left off Northfield Avenue, Myron noticed a gray Honda Accord in the rearview mirror. At least it looked like a Honda Accord. All cars pretty much looked the same to Myron, and there was no vehicle more unassuming than a gray Honda Accord. No way to tell for sure, but Myron thought that maybe they were being followed. He slowed down, memorized the license plate. New Jersey plate. 890UB3. When he entered the St. Barnabas Medical Center lot, the car drove on. Didn't mean anything. If the guy doing the tailing was good, he'd never pull in behind him.

St. Barnabas was bigger than when he was a kid, but what hospital wasn't? His dad had taken Myron here several times when he was a kid, for sprains and stitches and X rays and even one ten-day stint for rheumatic fever when he was twelve.

'Let me talk to this guy alone,' Myron said.

'Why?'

'You're the daughter. He may speak more freely without you there.'

'Yeah, okay. I have some patients I'm following on the fourth floor anyway. I'll meet you back down in the lobby.'

Calvin Campbell was in full uniform when Myron found him in the security office. He sat behind a high counter with several dozen TV monitors running. The pictures were in black and white and, from what Myron could see, completely uneventful. Campbell's feet were up. He was downing a submarine sandwich slightly longer than a baseball bat. He took off his policelike cap to reveal tightly curled white hair.

Myron asked him about Horace Slaughter.

'He didn't show for three straight days,' Calvin said. 'No call, no nothing. So I fired his ass.'

'How?' Myron asked.

'What?'

'How did you fire him? In person? On the phone?'

'Well, I tried to call him. But nobody answered. So I wrote a letter.'

'Return receipt?'

'Yes.'

'Did he sign it?'

He shrugged. 'Haven't gotten it back yet, if that's what you mean.'

'Was Horace a good worker?'

Calvin's eyes narrowed. 'You a private eye?'

'Something like that.'

'And you're working for the daughter?'

'Yes.'

'She got juice.'

'Huh?'

'Juice,' Calvin repeated. 'I mean, I never wanted to hire the man in the first place.'

'So why did you?'

He scowled. 'Don't you listen? His daughter got juice. She's tight with some of the bigwigs here. Everybody likes her. So you start hearing things. Rumors, you know. So I figured, what the hell. Being a security guard ain't brain surgery. I hired him.'

'What kind of rumors?'

'Hey, don't get me in the middle here.' He held his palms as though pushing trouble back. 'People talk, is all I'm saying. I've been here eighteen years. I ain't one to make waves. But when a guy don't show for work, well, I have to draw the line.'

'Anything else you can tell me?'

'Nope. He came. He did his job okay, I guess. Then he didn't show and I fired him. End of story.'

Myron nodded. 'Thank you for your time.'

'Hey, man, can you do me a favor?'

'What?' Myron asked.

'See if his daughter can clear out his locker. I got a new man coming on board, and I could use the space.'

Myron took the elevator up to the pediatric floor. He circled the nurses' station and spotted Brenda through a big window. She was sitting on the bed of a little girl who could not have been more than seven. Myron stopped and watched for a moment. Brenda had put on a white coat, a stethoscope draped around her neck. The little girl said something. Brenda smiled and put the stethoscope on the little girl's ears. They both laughed. Brenda beckoned behind her, and the girl's parents joined them on the bed. The parents had gaunt faces – the sunken cheeks, hollow eyes of the terminally harrowed. Brenda said something to them. More laughter. Myron continued to watch, mesmerized.

When she finally came out, Brenda walked straight to him. 'How long have you been standing here?'

'Just a minute or two,' he said. Then he added, 'You like it here.'

She nodded. 'It's even better than being on the court.'

Enough said.

'So what's up?' she asked.

'Your father has a locker here.'

They took the elevator to the basement. Calvin Campbell was waiting for them. 'Do you know the combination?' he asked.

Brenda said no.

'No problem.' Calvin had a lead pipe in his hand. With practiced precision he belted the combination lock. It shattered like glass. 'You can use that empty carton in the corner,' he said. Then he sauntered out.

Brenda looked at Myron. He nodded. She reached out and opened the locker. An odor like oft-soiled socks popped out. Myron made a face and looked in. Using his index finger and thumb like a pair of tweezers, he lifted a shirt into view. The shirt looked like the before picture in a Tide commercial.

'Dad wasn't great with laundry,' Brenda said.

Or with throwing away garbage, from the looks of things. The entire locker resembled a condensed frat house. There were dirty clothes and empty cans of beer and old newspapers and even a pizza box. Brenda brought over the carton, and they began to load stuff in. Myron started with a pair of uniform pants. He wondered if Horace owned them or if they belonged to the hospital, and then he wondered why he was wondering about something so irrelevant. He searched through the pockets and pulled out a crumpled ball of paper.

Myron smoothed it out. An envelope. He plucked out a sheet of paper and began to read.

'What is it?' Brenda asked.

'A letter from an attorney,' Myron said.

He handed it to her:

Dear Mr. Slaughter:

We are in receipt of your letters and are aware of your constant communications with this office. As explained to you in person, the matter you are asking about is confidential. We ask you to kindly stop contacting us. Your behavior is fast approaching harassment.

Sincerely,

Thomas Kincaid

'Do you know what he's talking about?' Myron asked.

She hesitated. 'No,' she said slowly. 'But that name – Thomas Kincaid – it rings a bell. I just can't place it.'

'Maybe he did work for your dad before.'

Brenda shook her head. 'I don't think so. I can't remember my father ever hiring a lawyer. And if he had, I doubt he would have gone to Morristown.'

Myron took out his cellular phone and dialed the office. Big Cyndi answered and transferred the call to Esperanza.

'What?' Esperanza said. Always with the pleasantries.

'Did Lisa fax over Horace Slaughter's phone bill?'

'It's right in front of me,' Esperanza said. 'I was just working on it.'

Scary as it might sound, getting a list of someone's long-distance calls has always been fairly easy. Almost every private investigator has a source at the phone company. All it takes is a little grease.

Myron signaled that he wanted the letter back. Brenda handed it to him. Then she knelt and extracted a plastic bag from the back of the locker. Myron looked at the phone number for Kincaid's office on the letter.

'Is five-five-five-one-nine-zero-eight on there?' he asked.

'Yeah. Eight times. All less than five minutes.'

'Anything else?'

'I'm still tracking down all the numbers.'

'Anything stick out?'

'Maybe,' Esperanza said. 'For some reason he called Arthur Bradford's gubernatorial headquarters a couple of times.'

Myron felt a familiar, not unpleasant jolt. The Bradford name rears its ugly head yet again. Arthur Bradford, one of two prodigal sons, was running for governor in November. 'Okay, good. Anything else?'

'Not yet. And I found nothing – I mean, *nada* – on Anita Slaughter.'

No surprise there. 'Okay, thanks.'

He hung up.

'What?' Brenda asked.

'Your father has been calling this Kincaid guy a lot. He's also called Arthur Bradford's campaign headquarters.'

She looked confused. 'So what does that mean?'

'I don't know. Was your dad political at all?'

'No.'

'Did he know Arthur Bradford or anybody connected with the campaign?'

'Not that I'm aware of.' Brenda opened the garbage bag and peered inside. Her face went slack. 'Oh Christ.'

Myron dropped down next to her. Brenda spread open the top of the bag so he could see the contents. A referee's shirt, black and white striped. On the right breast pocket was a patch reading 'New Jersey Basketball Referee Association.' On the left breast was a big crimson stain.

A bloodstain.

9

'We should call the police,' Myron said.

'And tell them what?'

Myron was not sure. The bloody shirt didn't have a hole in it – there were no rips or tears visible – and the stain was a concentrated fan shape over the left breast. How had it gotten there? Good question. Not wanting to contaminate any possible clues, Myron gave the shirt a quick, gentle once-over. The stain was thick and looked a bit sticky, if not wet. Since the shirt had been wrapped in a plastic bag, it was hard to say how long the blood had been there. Probably not long, though.

Okay, good. Now what?

The position of the stain itself was puzzling. If Horace had been wearing the shirt, how could the blood have ended up on just that one spot? If, for example, he had had a bloody nose, the stain would be more widespread. If he had been shot, well, there'd be a hole in the shirt. If he had hit somebody else, again the stain would probably be more like a spray or at least more dispersed than this.

Why was the stain so concentrated in that one spot?

Myron studied the shirt again. Only one scenario fit: Horace had *not* been wearing the shirt when the injury occurred. Strange but probably true. The shirt had been used to stave off blood flow, like a bandage. That would explain both the placement and concentration. The fan shape indicated it had probably been pressed against a bleeding nose.

Okey-dokey, we're on a roll. It didn't help him in any

way, shape, or form. But rolling was good. Myron liked to roll.

Brenda interrupted his thoughts. 'What are we going to tell the police?' she asked again.

'I don't know.'

'You think he's on the run, right?'

'Yes.'

'Then maybe he doesn't want to be found.'

'Almost definitely.'

'And we know he ran away by his own volition. So what are we going to tell them? That we found some blood on a shirt in his locker? You think the police are going to give a rat's ass?'

'Not even one cheek,' Myron agreed.

They finished clearing out the locker. Then Myron drove her to the late practice. He kept his eye on the rearview mirror, looking for the gray Honda Accord. There were many, of course, but none with the same license plate.

He dropped her off at the gym, and then he took Palisades Avenue toward the Englewood Public Library. He had a couple of hours to kill, and he wanted to do some research on the Bradford family.

The Englewood Library sat on Grand Avenue off Palisades Avenue like a clunky spaceship. When it was erected in 1968, the building had probably been praised for its sleek, futuristic design; now it looked like a rejected movie prop for *Logan's Run*.

Myron quickly found a reference librarian who was straight from central casting: gray bun, glasses, pearls, boxy build. The nameplate on her desk read 'Mrs. Kay.' He approached her with his boyish grin, the one that usually made such ladies pinch his cheek and offer him hot cider.

'I hope you can help me,' he said.

Mrs. Kay looked at him in that way librarians often do, wary and tired, like cops who know you're going to lie about how fast you were driving.

'I need to look up articles from the *Jersey Ledger* from twenty years ago.'

'Microfiche,' Mrs. Kay said. She rose with a great sigh and led him to a machine. 'You're in luck.'

'Why's that?'

'They just computerized an index. Before that you were on your own.'

Mrs. Kay taught him how to use the microfilm machine and the computer indexing service. It looked pretty standard. When she left him alone, Myron first typed in the name Anita Slaughter. No hits. Not a surprise, but hey, you never know. Sometimes you get lucky. Sometimes you plug in the name, and an article comes up and says, 'I ran away to Florence, Italy. You can find me at the Plaza Lucchesi hotel on the Arno River, room 218.' Well, not often. But sometimes.

Typing in the Bradford name would produce ten zillion hits. Myron was not sure what he was looking for exactly. He knew who the Bradfords were, of course. They were New Jersey aristocracy, the closest thing the Garden State had to the Kennedys. Old Man Bradford had been the governor in the late sixties, and his older son, Arthur Bradford, was the current front-runner for the same office. Arthur's younger brother, Chance – Myron would have made fun of the name, but when your name is Myron, well, glass houses and big stones and all that – was his campaign manager and – to keep within the Kennedy metaphor – played Robert to Arthur's Jack.

The Bradfords had started modestly enough. Old Man Bradford had come from farm stock. He had owned half the town of Livingston, considered the boonies in the sixties, and sold it in small pieces over the years to developers, who built split-levels and colonials for baby boomers escaping Newark and Brooklyn and the like. Myron in fact had grown up in a split-level that had been built on what had formerly been Bradford farmland.

But Old Man Bradford had been smarter than most. For one thing, he reinvested his money in strong local businesses, mostly malls, but more important, he sold his land slowly, over time, not immediately cashing in. By holding on a bit longer, he became a true baron as the price for land increased at an alarming rate. He married a blue blood aristocrat from Connecticut. She redid the old farmhouse and made it something of a monument to excess. They stayed in Livingston, in the original spot of the old farmhouse, fencing off an enormous chunk of real estate. They were the mansion on the hill, surrounded by hundreds of middle-class cookie-cut houses: feudal lords overlooking the serf-dom. Nobody in town really knew the Bradfords. When Myron was a kid, he and his friends just referred to them as the millionaires. They were the stuff of legends. Supposedly, if you climbed their fence, armed guards shot at you. Two sixth graders gave a wide-eyed Myron this stern warning when he was seven years old. He of course believed it absolutely. Outside of the Bat Lady, who lived in a shack near the Little League field and kidnapped and then ate little boys, no one was more feared than the Bradfords.

Myron tried limiting the search on the Bradfords to 1978, the year Anita Slaughter disappeared, but there were still a ton of hits. Most, he noticed, were from March, while Anita had run off in November. A vague memory prodded him, but he couldn't conjure up more than a glimpse. He'd been just starting high school then, but there had been something in the news about the Bradfords. A scandal of some sort. He threaded microfilm into the machine. He was a tad spastic with anything mechanical – something he blamed on his ancestry – so it took him longer than it should have. After a few screeching false starts, Myron managed to look up a couple of articles. In fairly short order he stumbled across the obituary. *'Elizabeth Bradford. Age thirty. Daughter of Richard and Miriam Worth. Wife of Arthur Bradford. Mother of Stephen Bradford . . .'*

No cause of death given. But now Myron remembered the story. It had, in fact, been rehashed a bit recently, what with the press on the gubernatorial race. Arthur Bradford was now a fifty-two-year-old widower who, if the accounts were to be believed, still pined for his dead love. He dated, sure, but the spin was that he had never gotten over the devastating heartbreak of losing his young bride; it made for a nice, too-neat contrast with his thrice-married gubernatorial opponent, Jim Davison. Myron wondered if there was any truth in the spin. Arthur Bradford was perceived as a little too mean, a little Bob Dole. Sick as it sounded, what better way to offset that image than resurrecting a dead wife?

But who knew for sure? Politics and the press: two cherished institutions that spoke with tongues so forked they could double for fine dinnerware. Arthur Bradford refused to talk about his wife, and that could reflect either genuine pain or clever media manipulation. Cynical, but there you have it.

Myron continued to review the old articles. The story had made the front page on three consecutive dates in March 1978. Arthur and Elizabeth Bradford had been college sweethearts and married six years. Everyone described them as a 'loving couple', one of those media buzz phrases that meant as much as calling a dead youth an honor student. Mrs. Bradford had fallen off a third-level balcony at the Bradford mansion. The surface below was brick, and Elizabeth Bradford had landed on her head. There was not much in the way of details. A police investigation stated unequivocally that the death had been a tragic accident. The balcony was tiled and slippery. It had been raining and dark. A wall was being replaced and thus not secure in certain spots.

Awfully clean.

The press played very fair with the Bradfords. Myron now recalled the obvious rumors that had gone around the schoolyard. What the heck was she doing out on her balcony in March? Was she drunk? Probably. How else do you fall off your own deck? Naturally some of the guys speculated that she'd been pushed. It made for interesting high school cafeteria fodder for at least, oh, two days. But this was high school. Hormones inevitably recaptured the flag, and everybody returned to panicking about the opposite sex. Ah, the sweet bird of youth.

Myron leaned back and stared at the screen. He thought again about Arthur Bradford's refusal to comment. Maybe it had nothing to do with genuine grief or media manipulation; maybe Bradford refused to talk because he didn't want something brought to light after twenty years.

Hmm. Right, Myron, sure. And maybe he had kidnapped the Lindbergh baby. Stick to the facts. One, Elizabeth Bradford had been dead for twenty years. Two, there was not a scintilla of evidence that her death was anything but an accident. Three – and most important to Myron – this had all happened a full nine months before Anita Slaughter ran away.

Conclusion: there was not even the flimsy hint of a connection.

At least not right then.

Myron's throat went dry. He'd continued to read the article from the March 18, 1978, issue of the *Jersey Ledger*. The page one story finished up on page eight. Myron played with the knob on the microfiche machine. It screamed in protest but trudged forward.

There it was. Near the bottom right-hand corner. One line. That was all. Nothing that anybody would notice: '*Mrs. Bradford's body was first discovered on the brick back porch of the Bradford estate at 6:30 A.M. by a maid arriving for work.*'

A maid arriving for work. Myron wondered what the maid's name was.

10

Myron immediately called Mabel Edwards. 'Do you remember Elizabeth Bradford?' he asked.

There was a brief hesitation. 'Yes.'

'Did Anita find her body?'

A longer hesitation. 'Yes.'

'What did she tell you about it?'

'Wait a second. I thought you were trying to help Horace.'

'I am.'

'So why are you asking about that poor woman?' Mabel sounded slightly put out. 'She died more than twenty years ago.'

'It's a little complicated.'

'I bet it is.' He heard her take a deep breath. 'I want the truth now. You're looking for her too, aren't you? For Anita?'

'Yes, ma'am.'

'Why?'

Good question. But when you stripped it bare, the answer was pretty simple. 'For Brenda.'

'Finding Anita ain't gonna help that girl.'

'You tell her that.'

She chuckled without humor. 'Brenda can be head-strong,' Mabel said.

'I think it runs in the family.'

'Guess it does at that,' she said.

'Please tell me what you remember.'

'Not much to it, I guess. She came to work, and the

poor woman was lying there like a broken rag doll. That's all I know.'

'Anita never said anything else about it?'

'No.'

'Did she seem shaken up?'

'Of course. She worked for Elizabeth Bradford for almost six years.'

'No, I mean beyond the shock of finding the body.'

'I don't think so. But she never talked about it. Even when the reporters called, Anita just hung up the phone.'

Myron computed this information, sorted it through his brain cells, came up with zippo. 'Mrs. Edwards, did your brother ever mention a lawyer named Thomas Kincaid?'

She thought a moment. 'No, I don't think so.'

'Were you aware of him seeking legal advice on anything?'

'No.'

They said their good-byes, and then he hung up. The phone was barely disconnected when it rang again. 'Hello?'

'Got something strange here, Myron.'

It was Lisa from the phone company.

'What's up?'

'You asked me to put a tracer on the phone in Brenda Slaughter's dorm.'

'Right.'

'Someone beat me to it.'

Myron nearly slammed on the brake. 'What?'

'There's already a tap on her phone.'

'For how long?'

'I don't know.'

'Can you trace it back? See who put it on?'

'Nope. And the number is blocked out.'

'What does that mean?'

'I can't read anything on it. I can't get a trace or even look at old bills on the computer. My guess is, someone in law enforcement is behind it. I can poke around, but I doubt I'll come up with anything.'

'Please try, Lisa. And thanks.'

He hung up. A missing father, threatening phone calls, a possible car tail, and now a phone tap: Myron was starting to get nervous here. Why would someone – someone with authority – have a tap on Brenda's phone? Was that person part of the group making the threatening phone calls? Were they tapping her phone to track down her father or—

Hold the phone.

Hadn't one of the threatening calls told Brenda to call her mother? Why? Why would someone have said that? More important, if Brenda had obeyed the call – and if she had indeed known where her mother was hiding – the people behind the trace would have been able to find Anita too. Was that what this was really all about?

Was someone looking for Horace . . . or Anita?

'We have a problem,' Myron told her.

They sat in the car. Brenda turned toward him and waited.

'Your phone is bugged,' he said.

'What?'

'Someone has been listening in to your calls. You're also being tailed by someone.'

'But—' Brenda stopped, shrugged. 'Why? To find my father?'

'That's the best bet, yes. Someone is anxious to get to Horace. They've already attacked your aunt. You might be next on their list.'

'So you think I'm in danger.'

'Yes.'

She watched his face. 'And you have a suggested course of action.'

'I do,' he said.

'I'm listening.'

'First, I'd like to have your dorm room swept for bugs.'

'I have no problem with that.'

'Second, you have to get out of your dorm room. You're not safe there.'

She considered this for a moment. 'I can stay with a friend. Cheryl Sutton. She's the other captain of the Dolphins.'

Myron shook his head. 'These people know you. They've been following you, listening to your phone calls.'

'Meaning?'

'Meaning they probably know who your friends are.'

'Including Ms. Sutton.'

'Yes.'

'And you think they'll look for me there?'

'It's a possibility.'

Brenda shook her head and faced forward. 'This is spooky.'

'There's more.'

He told her about the Bradford family and about her mother finding the body.

'So what does that mean?' Brenda asked when he finished.

'Probably nothing,' Myron said. 'But you wanted me to tell you everything, right?'

'Right.' She leaned back and chewed at her lower lip. After some time had passed, she asked, 'So where do you think I should stay?'

'Do you remember my mentioning my friend Win?'

'The guy who owns Lock-Horne Securities?'

'His family does, right. I'm supposed to go to his place tonight to discuss a business problem. I think you should come too. You can stay at his apartment.'

'You want me to stay with him?'

'Just for tonight. Win has safe houses all over. We'll find you someplace.'

She made a face. 'A preppy Mainliner who knows about safe houses?'

'Win,' Myron said, 'is more than he appears.'

She crossed her arms under her chest. 'I don't want to act like a jackass and hand you that phony crap about how I'm not going to let this interfere with my life. I know you're helping me, and I want to cooperate.'

'Good.'

'But,' she added, 'this league means a lot to me. So does my team. I'm not going to just walk away from that.'

'I understand.'

'So whatever we do, will I be able to go to practice? Will I be able to play in the opener Sunday?'

'Yes.'

Brenda nodded. 'Okay then,' she said. 'And thank you.'

They drove to her dorm room. Myron waited downstairs while she packed a bag. She had her own room, but she wrote a note to her suite mate that she was staying with a friend for a few days. The whole enterprise took her less than ten minutes.

She came down with two bags over her shoulders. Myron relieved her of one. They were heading out the door when Myron spotted FJ standing next to his car.

'Stay here,' he told her.

Brenda ignored him and kept pace. Myron looked to

his left. Bubba and Rocco were there. They waved at him. Myron did not wave back. That'll show them.

FJ leaned against the car, completely relaxed, almost too relaxed, like an old movie drunk against a lamppost.

'Hello, Brenda,' FJ said.

'Hello, FJ.'

Then he nodded toward Myron. 'And you too, Myron.'

His smile did more than lack warmth. It was the most purely physical smile Myron had ever seen, a byproduct strictly of the brain giving specific orders to certain muscles. It touched no part of him but his lips.

Myron circled the car and feigned inspecting it. 'Not a bad job, FJ. But next time put a little muscle into the hubcaps. They're filthy.'

FJ looked at Brenda. 'This the famed Bolitar rapier wit I've heard so much about?'

She shrugged sympathetically.

Myron motioned at them with his hands. 'You two know each other?'

'But of course,' FJ said. 'We went to prep school together. At Lawrenceville.'

Bubba and Rocco lumbered a few steps closer. They looked like Luca Brasa Youth.

Myron eased between Brenda and FJ. The protective move would probably piss her off, but tough. 'So what can we do for you, FJ?'

'I just want to make sure that Ms. Slaughter is honoring her contract with me.'

'I don't have a contract with you,' Brenda said.

'Your father – one Horace Slaughter – is your agent, no?'

'No,' Brenda said. 'Myron is.'

'Oh?' FJ's eyes slithered toward Myron. Myron kept

up the eye contact, but there was still nothing there, like looking into the windows of an abandoned building. 'I'd been informed otherwise.'

Myron shrugged. 'Life is change, FJ. Gotta learn to adapt.'

'Adapt,' FJ said, 'or die.'

Myron nodded and said, 'Oooo.'

FJ kept the stare going a few more seconds. He had skin that looked like wet clay, as if it might dissolve under heavy rains. He turned back to Brenda. 'Your father used to be your agent,' he said. 'Before Myron.'

Myron handled that one. 'And what if he was?'

'He signed with us. Brenda was going to bow out of the WPBA and join the PWBL. It's all spelled out in the contract.'

Myron looked at Brenda. She shook her head. 'You have Ms. Slaughter's signature on those contracts?' he asked.

'Like I said, her father—'

'Who has no legal standing in this matter whatsoever. Do you have Brenda's signature or not?'

FJ looked rather displeased. Bubba and Rocco moved closer still. 'We do not.'

'Then you have nothing.' Myron unlocked his car door. 'But we've all enjoyed this too brief time together. I know I'm a better person for it.'

Bubba and Rocco started toward him. Myron opened the car door. His gun was under his car seat. He debated making a move. It would be dumb, of course. Someone – probably Brenda or Myron – would get hurt.

FJ lifted a hand, and the two men stopped as though they'd been sprayed by Mr. Freeze. 'We're not mobsters,' FJ said. 'We're businessmen.'

'Right,' Myron said. 'And Bubba and Rocco over there – they your CPAs?'

A tiny smile came to FJ's lips. The smile was strictly reptilian, meaning it was far warmer than his other ones. 'If you are indeed her agent,' FJ said, 'then it would behoove you to speak with me.'

Myron nodded. 'Call my office, make an appointment,' he said.

'We'll talk soon then,' FJ said.

'Looking forward to it. And keep using the word *behoove*. It really impresses people.'

Brenda opened her car door and got in. Myron did likewise. FJ came around to Myron's window and knocked on the glass. Myron lowered the window.

'Sign with us or don't sign with us,' FJ said quietly. 'That's business. But when I kill you, well, that will be for fun.'

Myron was about to crack wise again, but something – probably a fly-through of good sense – made him pause. FJ moved away then. Rocco and Bubba followed. Myron watched them disappear, his heart flapping in his chest like a caged condor.

11

They parked on a lot on Seventy-first Street and walked to the Dakota. The Dakota remains one of New York's premier buildings, though it's still best known for John Lennon's assassination. A fresh bouquet of roses marked the spot where his body had fallen. Myron always felt a little weird crossing over it, as if he were trampling on a grave or something. The Dakota doorman must have seen Myron a hundred times by now, but he always pretended otherwise and buzzed up to Win's apartment.

Introductions were brief. Win found Brenda a place to study. She broke out a medical textbook the size of a stone tablet and made herself comfortable. Win and Myron moved back into a living room semidecorated in the manner of Louis the Somethingteenth. There was a fireplace with big iron tools and a bust on the mantel. The substantial furniture looked, as always, freshly polished yet plenty old. Oil paintings of stern yet effeminate men stared down from the walls. And just to keep things in the proper decade, there were a big-screen TV and VCR front and center.

The two friends sat and put their feet up.

'So what do you think?' Myron asked.

'She's too big for my tastes,' Win said. 'But nicely toned legs.'

'I mean, about protecting her.'

'We'll find a place,' Win said. He laced his hands behind his neck. 'Talk to me.'

'Do you know Arthur Bradford?'

'The gubernatorial candidate?'

'Yes.'

Win nodded. 'We've met several times. I played golf with him and his brother once at Merion.'

'Can you set up a meet?'

'No problem. They've been hitting us up for a sizable donation.' He crossed his ankles. 'So how does Arthur Bradford fit into all this?'

Myron recapped the day's developments: the Honda Accord following them, the phone taps, the bloody clothes, Horace Slaughter's phone calls to Bradford's office, FJ's surprise visit, Elizabeth Bradford's murder, and Anita's role in finding the body.

Win looked unimpressed. 'Do you really see a link between the Bradfords' past and the Slaughters' present?'

'Yeah, maybe.'

'Then let me see if I can follow your rationale. Feel free to correct me if I'm wrong.'

'Okey-dokey.'

Win dropped his feet to the floor and steepled his fingers, resting his indexes against his chin. 'Twenty years ago Elizabeth Bradford died under somewhat murky circumstances. Her death was ruled an accident, albeit a bizarre one. You do not buy that one. The Bradfords are rich, and thus you are extra-suspicious of the official rendering—'

'It's not just that they're rich,' Myron interrupted. 'I mean, falling off her own porch? Come on.'

'Yes, fine, fair enough.' Win did the hand-steeple again. 'Let us pretend that you are correct in your suspicions. Let us assume that something unsavory did indeed occur when Elizabeth Bradford plunged to her death. And I am further going to assume – as you no doubt have – that Anita Slaughter, in her capacity as maid or servant or what have you, happened upon the scene and witnessed something incriminating.'

Myron nodded. 'Continue.'

Win spread his hands. 'Well, my friend, that is where you reach an impasse. If the dear Ms. Slaughter did indeed see something that she was not supposed to, the issue would have been resolved immediately. I know the Bradfords. They are not people who take chances. Anita Slaughter would have been killed or forced to run immediately. But instead – and here is the rub – she waited a full nine months before disappearing. I therefore conclude that the two incidents are unrelated.'

Behind them Brenda cleared her throat. They both turned to the doorway. She stared straight at Myron. She did not look happy.

'I thought you two were discussing a business problem,' she said.

'We are,' Myron said quickly. 'I, uh, mean, we're going to. That's why I came here. To discuss a business problem. But we just started talking about this first, and well, you know, one thing led to another. But it wasn't intentional or anything. I mean, I came here to discuss a business problem, right, Win?'

Win leaned forward and patted Myron's knee. 'Smooth,' he said.

She crossed her arms. Her eyes were two drill bits – say, three-sixteenths of an inch, quarter-inch tops.

'How long have you been standing there?' Myron asked.

Brenda gestured toward Win. 'Since he said I had nicely toned legs,' she said. 'I missed the part about being too big for his tastes.'

Win smiled. Brenda did not wait to be asked. She crossed the room and grabbed an open chair. She kept her eyes on Win. 'For the record, I don't buy any of this either,' Brenda said to him. 'Myron has trouble believing a mother would just abandon her little daughter. He has no trouble believing a father would do the same, just not a mother. But as I've explained to him, he's something of a sexist.'

'A snorting pig,' Win agreed.

'But,' she continued, 'if you two are going to sit here and play Holmes and Watson, I do see a way around your' – she made quote marks with her finger – 'impasse.'

'Do tell,' Win said.

'When Elizabeth Bradford fell to her death, my mother may have seen something that appeared innocuous at first. I don't know what. Something bothersome maybe but nothing to get excited about. She continues to work for these people, scrubbing their floors and toilets. And maybe one day she opens a drawer. Or a closet. And maybe she sees something that coupled with what she saw the day Elizabeth Bradford died leads her to conclude that it wasn't an accident after all.'

Win looked at Myron. Myron raised his eyebrows.

Brenda sighed. 'Before you two continue your patronizing glances – the ones that say, "Golly gee, the woman is actually capable of cogitation" – let me add that I'm just giving you a way around the impasse. I don't buy it for a second. It leaves too much unexplained.'

'Like what?' Myron asked.

She turned to him. 'Like why my mother would run away the way she did. Like why she would leave that cruel note for my father about another man. Like why she left us penniless. Like why she would leave behind a daughter she theoretically loved.'

There was no quiver in the voice. Just the opposite, in

fact. The tone was far too steady, straining too hard for normality.

'Maybe she wanted to protect her daughter from harm,' Myron said. 'Maybe she wanted to discourage her husband from looking for her.'

She frowned. 'So she took all his money and faked running away with another man?' Brenda looked at Win. 'Does he really believe this crap?'

Win held his hands palms up and nodded apologetically.

Brenda turned back to Myron. 'I appreciate what you're trying to do here, but it just doesn't add up. My mother ran away twenty years ago. Twenty years. In all that time couldn't she have done more than write a couple of letters and call my aunt? Couldn't she have figured out a way to see her own daughter? To set up a meet? At least once in twenty years? In all that time couldn't she have gotten herself settled and come back for me?'

She stopped as though out of breath. She hugged her knees to her chest and turned away. Myron looked at Win. Win kept still. The silence pressed against the windows and doors.

Win was the one who finally spoke. 'Enough speculating. Let me call Arthur Bradford. He'll see us tomorrow.'

Win left the room. With some people, you might be skeptical or at least wonder how they could be so sure a gubernatorial candidate would see them on such short notice. Not so when it came to Win.

Myron looked over at Brenda. She did not look back. A few minutes later Win returned.

'Tomorrow morning,' Win said. 'Ten o'clock.'

'Where?'

'The estate at Bradford Farms. In Livingston.'

Brenda stood. 'If we're finished with this topic, I'll leave you two alone.' She looked at Myron. 'To discuss a business problem.'

'There is one more thing,' Win said.

'What?'

'The question of a safe house.'

She stopped and waited.

Win leaned back. 'I am inviting both you and Myron to stay here if you're comfortable. As you can see, I have plenty of room. You can use the bedroom at the end of the corridor. It has its own bathroom. Myron will be across the hallway. You'll have the security of the Dakota and easy, close proximity to the two of us.'

Win glanced at Myron, who tried to hide his surprise. Myron frequently stayed overnight – he even kept clothes and a bunch of toiletries here – but Win had never made an offer like this before. He usually demanded total privacy.

Brenda nodded and said, 'Thank you.'

'The only potential problem,' Win said, 'is my private life.'

Uh-oh.

'I may bring in a dizzying array of ladies for a variety of purposes,' he went on. 'Sometimes more than one. Sometimes I film them. Does that bother you?'

'No,' she said. 'As long as I can do the same with men.'

Myron started coughing.

Win remained unfazed. 'But of course. I keep the video camera in that cabinet.'

She turned to the cabinet and nodded. 'Got a tripod?'

Win opened his mouth, closed it, shook his head. 'Too easy,' he said.

'Smart man.' Brenda smiled. 'Good night, guys.'

When she left, Win looked at Myron. 'You can close your mouth now.'

Win poured himself a cognac. 'So what business problem did you want to discuss?'

'It's Esperanza,' Myron said. 'She wants a partnership.'

'Yes, I know.'

'She told you?'

Win swirled the liquid in the snifter. 'She consulted me. On the hows mostly. The legal setup for such a change.'

'And you never told me?'

Win did not reply. The answer was obvious. Win hated stating the obvious. 'Care for a Yoo-Hoo?'

Myron shook his head. 'The truth is, I don't know what to do about it.'

'Yes, I know. You've been stalling.'

'Did she tell you that?'

Win looked at him. 'You know her better than that.'

Myron nodded. He did know better. 'Look, she's my friend—'

'Correction,' Win interrupted. 'She's your best friend. More so, perhaps, than even I. But you must forget that for now. She is just an employee – a great one perhaps – but your friendship must be meaningless in this decision. For your sake as well as hers.'

Myron nodded. 'Yeah, you're right, forget I said that. And I do understand where she's coming from. She's been with me since the beginning. She's worked hard. She's finished law school.'

'But?'

'But a partnership? I'd love to promote her, give her her own office, give her more responsibility, even work out a profit-sharing program. But she won't accept that. She wants to be a partner.'

'Has she told you why?'

'Yeah,' Myron said.

'And?'

'She doesn't want to work for anyone. It's as simple as that. Not even me. Her father worked menial jobs for scumbags his whole life. Her mother cleaned other people's houses. She swore that one day she would work for herself.'

'I see,' Win said.

'And I sympathize. Who wouldn't? But her parents probably worked for abusive ogres. Forget our friendship. Forget the fact that I love Esperanza like a sister. I'm a good boss. I'm fair. Even she'd have to admit that.'

Win took a deep sip. 'But clearly that is not enough for her.'

'So what am I supposed to do? Give in? Business partnerships between friends or family never work. Never. It's just that simple. Money screws up every relationship. You and I – we work hard to keep our businesses linked but separate. That's why we get away with it. We have similar goals, but that's it. There is no money connection. I know a lot of good relationships – and good businesses – that have been destroyed over something like this. My father and his brother still don't talk because of a business partnership. I don't want that to happen here.'

'Have you told Esperanza this?'

He shook his head. 'But she's given me a week to make a decision. Then she walks.'

'Tough spot,' Win said.

'Any suggestions?'

'Not a one.' Then Win tilted his head and smiled.

'What?'

'Your argument,' Win said. 'I find it ironic.'

'How so?'

'You believe in marriage and family and monogamy and all that nonsense, correct?'

'So?'

'You believe in raising children, the picket fences, the basketball pole in the driveway, peewee football, dance classes, the whole suburbia scene.'

'And again I say, so?'

Win spread his arms. 'So I would argue that marriages and the like never work. They inevitably lead to divorce or disillusionment or the deadening of dreams or at the very least, bitterness and resentment. I might – similar to you – point to my own family as an example.'

'It's not the same thing, Win.'

'Oh, I recognize that. But the truth is, we all take facts and compute them through our own experiences. You had a wonderful family life; thus you believe as you do. I am of course the opposite. Only a leap of faith could change our positions.'

Myron made a face. 'Is this supposed to be helping?'

'Heavens, no,' Win said. 'But I do so enjoy philosophical folly.'

Win picked up the remote and switched on the television. *Nick at Night*. *Mary Tyler Moore* was on. They grabbed fresh drinks and settled back to watch.

Win took another sip, reddening his cheeks. 'Maybe Lou Grant will have your answer.'

He didn't. Myron imagined what would happen if he treated Esperanza the same way Lou treated Mary. If Esperanza were in a good mood, she'd probably tear out his hair until he looked like Murray.

Bedtime. On his way to his room, Myron checked on

Brenda. She was sitting lotus-style on the antique Queen Something-or-other bed. The large textbook was open in front of her. Her concentration was total, and for a moment he just watched her. Her face displayed the same serenity he'd seen on the court. She wore flannel pajamas, her skin still a little wet from a recent shower, a towel wrapped around her hair.

Brenda sensed him and looked up. When she smiled at him, he felt something tighten in his stomach.

'You need anything?' he asked.

'I'm fine,' she said. 'You solve your business problem?'

'No.'

'I didn't mean to eavesdrop before.'

'Don't worry about it.'

'I meant what I said earlier. I'd like you to be my agent.'

'I'm glad.'

'You'll draw up the papers?'

Myron nodded.

'Good night, Myron.'

'Good night, Brenda.'

She looked down and turned a page. Myron watched her for another second. Then he went to bed.

12

They took Win's Jaguar to the Bradford estate because, as Win explained, people like the Bradfords 'don't do Taurus'. Neither did Win.

Win dropped Brenda off at practice and headed down Route 80 to Passaic Avenue, which had finally completed a widening program that began when Myron was in high school. They finished up on Eisenhower Parkway, a beautiful four-lane highway that ran for maybe five miles. Ah, New Jersey.

A guard with enormous ears greeted them at the gate of, as the sign said, Bradford Farms. Right. Most farms are known for their electronic fences and security guards. Wouldn't want anyone getting into the carrots and corn. Win leaned out the window, gave the guy the snooty smile, and was quickly waved through. A strange pang struck Myron as they drove through. How many times had he gone past the gate as a kid, trying to peer through the thick shrubs for a glance at the proverbial greener grass, dreaming up scenarios for the lush, adventure-filled life that lay within these manicured grounds?

He knew better now, of course. Win's familial estate, Lockwood Manor, made this place look like a railroad shanty, so Myron had seen up close how the superrich lived. It was indeed pretty, but pretty doesn't mean happy. Wow. That was deep. Maybe next time Myron would conclude that money can't buy happiness. Stay tuned.

Scattered cows and sheep helped keep the farm illusion – for the purpose of nostalgia or a tax write-off, Myron could not say, though he had his suspicions. They pulled up to a white farmhouse that had undergone more renovations than an aging movie queen.

An old black man wearing gray butler's tails answered the door. He gave them a slight bow and asked them to follow him. In the corridor were two goons dressed like Secret Service men. Myron glanced at Win. Win nodded. Not Secret Service guys. Goons. The bigger of the two smiled at them like they were cocktail franks heading back to the kitchen. One big. One skinny. Myron remembered Mabel Edwards's descriptions of her attackers. Not much to go on if he couldn't check for a tattoo, but worth keeping in mind.

The butler or manservant or whatever led them into the library. Rounded walls of books climbed three stories high, topped by a glass cupola that let in the proper amount of fresh light. The room might have been a converted silo, or maybe it just looked that way. Hard to tell. The books were leather and in series and untouched. Cherry mahogany dominated the scene. Paintings of old sailing vessels were framed under portrait lamps. There was a huge antique globe in the center of the room, not unlike the one Win had in his own office. Rich people like old globes, Myron surmised. Maybe it has something to do with the fact that they are both expensive and utterly useless.

The chairs and couches were leather with gold buttons. The lamps were Tiffany. A book lay strategically open on a coffee table next to a bust of Shakespeare. Rex Harrison was not sitting in the corner wearing a smoking jacket, but he should have been.

As though on cue, a door on the other side of the room – a bookshelf actually – swung open. Myron half expected Bruce Wayne and Dick Grayson to storm into the room calling for Alfred, maybe tilt back the head of Shakespeare, and turn a hidden knob. Instead it was Arthur Bradford, followed by his brother, Chance. Arthur was very tall, probably six-six, thin, and stooped a bit the way tall people over the age of fifty are. He was bald, his fringe hair trimmed short. Chance was under six feet with wavy brown hair and the kind of boyish good looks that made it impossible to tell his age, though Myron knew from the press clippings that he was forty-nine, three years younger than Arthur.

Playing the part of the perfect politician, Arthur beelined toward them, a fake smile at the ready, hand extended in such a way as either to shake hands or to imply that the extended hand hoped to touch more than just flesh.

'Windsor!' Arthur Bradford exclaimed, grasping Win's hand as if he'd been searching for it all his life. 'How wonderful to see you.'

Chance headed toward Myron like it was a double date and he had gotten stuck with the ugly girl and was used to it.

Win flashed the vague smile. 'Do you know Myron Bolitar?'

The brothers switched handshaking partners with the practiced proficiency of experienced square dancers. Shaking Arthur Bradford's hand was like shaking hands with an old, unoiled baseball glove. Up close, Myron could see that Arthur Bradford was big-boned and rough-hewn and large-featured and red-faced. Still the farm boy under the suit and manicure.

'We've never met,' Arthur said through the big smile, 'but everyone in Livingston – heck, all of New Jersey – knows Myron Bolitar.'

Myron made his aw-shucks face but refrained from batting his eyes.

'I've been watching you play ball since you were in high school,' Arthur continued with great earnestness. 'I'm a big fan.'

Myron nodded, knowing that no Bradford had ever set foot in Livingston High School's gymnasium. A politician who stretched the truth. What a shock.

'Please, gentlemen, sit down.'

Everyone grabbed smooth leather. Arthur Bradford offered coffee. Everyone accepted. A Latina woman opened the door. Arthur Bradford said to her, '*Café, por favor.*' Another linguist.

Win and Myron were on a couch. The brothers sat across from them in matching wingback chairs. Coffee was wheeled in on something that could have doubled as a coach for a palace ball. The coffee was poured and milked and sugared. Then Arthur Bradford, the candidate himself, took over and actually handed Myron and Win their beverages. Regular guy. Man of the people.

Everyone settled back. The servant faded away. Myron raised the cup to his lips. The problem with his new coffee addiction was that he drank only coffee-bar coffee, the potent 'gourmet' stuff that could eat through driveway sealant. The at-home brews tasted to his suddenly picky palate like something sucked through a sewer grate on a hot afternoon – this coming from a man who could not tell the difference between a perfectly aged Merlot and a recently stomped Manischewitz. But when Myron took a sip from the Bradfords' fine china, well, the rich have their ways. The stuff was ambrosia.

Arthur Bradford put down his Wedgwood cup and saucer. He leaned forward, his forearms resting on his knees, his hands in a quiet clasp. 'First, let me tell you how thrilled I am to have you both here. Your support means a great deal to me.'

Bradford turned toward Win. Win's face was totally neutral, patient.

'I understand Lock-Horne Securities wants to expand its Florham Park office and open a new one in Bergen County,' Bradford went on. 'If I can be of any help at all, Windsor, please let me know.'

Win gave a noncommittal nod.

'And if there are any state bonds Lock-Horne has any interest in underwriting, well, again I would be at your disposal.'

Arthur Bradford sat up on his haunches now, as though waiting for a scratch behind the ears. Win rewarded him with another noncommittal nod. Good doggie. Hadn't taken Bradford long to start with the graft, had it? Bradford cleared his throat and turned his attention to Myron.

'I understand, Myron, that you own a sports representation company.'

He tried to imitate the Win nod, but he went too far. Not subtle enough. Must be something in the genes.

'If there is anything I can do to help, please do not hesitate to ask.'

'Can I sleep in the Lincoln bedroom?' Myron asked.

The brothers froze for a moment, looked at each other, then exploded into laughter. The laughs were about as genuine as a televangelist's hair. Win looked over at Myron. The look said, go ahead.

'Actually, Mr. Bradford—'

Through his laugh he stuck up a hand the size of a throw pillow and said, 'Please, Myron, call me Arthur.'

'Arthur, right. There is something you can do for us.'

Arthur and Chance's laughter segued into chuckles before fading away like a song on the radio. Their faces grew harder now. Game time. They both leaned into the strike zone a bit, signaling to one and all that they were going to listen to Myron's problem with four of the most sympathetic ears in existence.

'Do you remember a woman named Anita Slaughter?' Myron asked.

They were good, both of them thoroughbred politicians, but their bodies still jolted as if they'd been zapped with a stun gun. They recovered fast enough, busying themselves with the pretense of scouring for a recollection, but there was no doubt. A nerve had been jangled big time.

'I can't place the name,' Arthur said, his face twisted as though he'd given this thought process an effort equal to childbirth. 'Chance?'

'The name is not unfamiliar,' Chance said, 'but . . .' He shook his head.

Not unfamiliar. You gotta love it when they speak politicianese.

'Anita Slaughter worked here,' Myron said. 'Twenty years ago. She was a maid or house servant of some kind.'

Again the deep, probing thought. If Rodin were here, he'd break out the good bronze for these guys. Chance kept his eyes on his brother, waiting for his stage cue. Arthur Bradford held the pose for a few more seconds before he suddenly snapped his fingers.

'Of course,' he said. 'Anita. Chance, you remember Anita.'

'Yes, of course,' Chance chimed in. 'I guess I never knew her last name.'

They were both smiling now like morning anchors during a sweeps week.

'How long did she work for you?' Myron asked.

'Oh, I don't know,' Arthur said. 'A year or two, I

guess. I really don't remember. Chance and I weren't responsible for household help, of course. That was more Mother's doing.'

Already with the 'plausible deniability'. Interesting. 'Do you remember why she left your family's employ?'

Arthur Bradford's smile stayed frozen, but something was happening to his eyes. His pupils were expanding, and for a moment it looked like he was having trouble focusing. He turned to Chance. They both looked uncertain now, not sure how to handle this sudden frontal assault, not wanting to answer but not wanting to lose the potentially massive Lock-Horne Securities support either.

Arthur took the lead. 'No, I don't remember.' When in doubt, evade. 'Do you, Chance?'

Chance spread his hands and gave them the boyish smile. 'So many people in and out.' He looked to Win as if to say, You know how it is. But Win's eyes, as usual, offered no solace.

'Did she quit or was she fired?'

'Oh, I doubt she was fired,' Arthur said quickly. 'My mother was very good to the help. She rarely, if ever, fired anyone. Not in her nature.'

The man was pure politician. The answer might be true or not – that was pretty much irrelevant to Arthur Bradford – but under any circumstances, a poor black woman fired as a servant by a wealthy family would not play well in the press. A politician innately sees this and calculates his response in a matter of seconds; reality and truth must always take a backseat to the gods of sound bite and perception.

Myron pressed on. 'According to her family, Anita Slaughter worked here until the day she disappeared.'

They were both too smart to bite and say, 'Disappeared?' but Myron decided to wait them out anyway.

People hate silence and often jump in just to break it. This was an old cop trick: say nothing and let them dig their own graves with explanations. With politicians the results were always interesting: they were smart enough to know they should keep their mouths shut, yet genetically incapable of doing so.

'I'm sorry,' Arthur Bradford said at last. 'As I explained earlier, Mother handled these matters.'

'Then maybe I should talk to her,' Myron said.

'Mother is not well, I'm afraid. She's in her eighties, poor dear.'

'I'd still like to try.'

'I'm afraid that won't be possible.'

There was just a hint of steel in his voice now.

'I see,' Myron said. 'Do you know who Horace Slaughter is?'

'No,' Arthur said. 'I assume he's a relative of Anita's?'

'Her husband.' Myron looked over at Chance. 'You know him?'

'Not that I recall,' Chance said. Not that I recall. Like he was on a witness stand, needing to leave himself the out.

'According to his phone records, he's been calling your campaign headquarters a lot lately.'

'Many people call our campaign headquarters,' Arthur said. Then he added with a small chuckle, 'At least I hope they do.'

Chance chuckled too. Real yucksters, these Bradford boys.

'Yeah, I guess.' Myron looked at Win. Win nodded. Both men stood up.

'Thank you for your time,' Win said. 'We'll show ourselves out.'

The two politicians tried not to look too stunned. Chance finally cracked a bit. 'What the hell is this?'

Arthur silenced him with a look. He rose to shake hands, but Myron and Win were already at the door.

Myron turned and did his best Columbo. 'Funny.'

'What?' Arthur Bradford said.

'That you don't remember Anita Slaughter better. I thought you would.'

Arthur turned his palms upward. 'We've had lots of people work here over the years.'

'True,' Myron said, stepping through the portal. 'But how many of them found your wife's dead body?'

The two men turned to marble – still and smooth and cool. Myron did not wait for more. He released the door and followed Win out.

13

As they drove through the gate, Win said, 'What exactly did we just accomplish?'

'Two things. One, I wanted to find out if they had something to hide. Now I know they do.'

'Based on?'

'Their outright lies and evasiveness.'

'They're politicians,' Win said. 'They'd lie and evade if you asked them what they had for breakfast.'

'You don't think there's something there?'

'Actually,' Win said, 'I do. And thing two?'

'I wanted to stir them up.'

Win smiled. He liked that idea. 'So what next, Kemo Sabe?'

'We need to investigate Elizabeth Bradford's premature demise,' Myron said.

'How?'

'Hop onto South Livingston Avenue. I'll tell you where to make the turn.'

The Livingston Police Station sat next to the Livingston Town Hall and across the street from the Livingston Public Library and Livingston High School. A true town center. Myron entered and asked for Officer Francine Neagly. Francine had graduated from the high school across the street the same year as Myron. He'd hoped to get lucky and catch her at the station.

A stern-looking desk sergeant informed Myron that Officer Neagly was 'not present at this particular time' –

that's how cops talk – but that she had just radioed in for her lunch break and would be at the Ritz Diner.

The Ritz Diner was truly ugly. The formerly work-manlike brick structure had been spray-painted seaweed green with a salmon pink door – a color scheme too gaudy for a Carnival Cruise ship. Myron hated it. In its heyday, when Myron was in high school, the diner had been a run-of-the-mill, unpretentious eatery called the Heritage. It'd been a twenty-four-hour spot back then, owned by Greeks naturally – this seemed to be a state law – and frequented by high school kids grabbing burgers and fries after a Friday or Saturday night of doing nothing. Myron and his friends would don their varsity jackets, go out to a variety of house parties, and end up here. He tried now to remember what he did at those parties, but nothing specific came to mind. He didn't imbibe in high school – alcohol made him sick – and was prudish to the point of Pollyanna when it came to the drug scene. So what did he do at these things? He remembered the music, of course, blaring the Doobie Brothers and Steely Dan and Supertramp, gleaning deep meaning from the lyrics of Blue Oyster Cult songs ('Yo, man, what do you think Eric *really* means when he says, "I want to do it to your daughter on a dirt road?"'). He remembered occasionally making out with a girl, rarely more, and then their avoiding each other at all costs for the rest of their scholastic lives. But that was pretty much it. You went to the parties because you were afraid you'd miss something. But nothing ever happened. They were all an indistinguishable, monotonous blur now.

What he did remember – what, he guessed, would always remain vivid in the old memory banks – was coming home late and finding his dad feigning sleep in the recliner. It didn't matter what time it was. Two, three in the morning. Myron did not have a curfew. His parents trusted him. But Dad still stayed up every Friday and Saturday night and waited in that recliner and worried, and when Myron put his key in the lock, he faked being asleep. Myron knew he was faking. His dad knew Myron knew. But Dad still tried to pull it off every time.

Win elbowed him back to reality. 'Are you going to go in, or are we just going to marvel at this monument to *nouveau* tackiness?'

'My friends and I used to hang out here,' Myron said. 'When I was in high school.'

Win looked at the diner, then at Myron. 'You guys were the balls.'

Win waited in the car. Myron found Francine Neagly at the counter. He sat on the stool next to her and fought off the desire to spin it.

'That police uniform,' Myron said, and gave a little whistle. 'It's quite the turn-on.'

Francine Neagly barely looked up from her burger. 'Best part is, I also use it to strip at bachelor parties.'

'Saves on the overhead.'

'Right-o.' Francine took a bite out of a burger so rare it screamed ouch. 'As I live and breathe,' she said, 'the local hero appears in public.'

'Please don't make a fuss.'

'Good thing I'm here, though. If the women get out of control, I can shoot them for you.' She wiped very greasy hands. 'I heard you moved out of town,' she said.

'I did.'

'Been the opposite around here lately.' She grabbed another napkin out of the dispenser. 'Most towns, all you hear about is how people want to grow up and move away. But here, well, everyone's coming back to Livingston and raising their own families. Remember

Santola? He's back. Three kids. And Friedy? He lives in the Weinbergs' old house. Two kids. Jordan lives by St. Phil's. Fixed up some old piece of shit. Three kids, all girls. I swear, half our class got married and moved back to town.'

'How about you and Gene Duluca?' Myron asked with a little smile.

She laughed. 'Dumped him my freshman year of college. Christ, we were gross, huh?'

Gene and Francine had been the class couple. They spent lunch hours sitting at a table, French-kissing while eating cafeteria food, both wearing debris-enmeshed braces.

'Gross City,' Myron agreed.

She took another bite. 'Wanna order something gooey and suck face? See what it was like?'

'If only I had more time.'

'That's what they all say. So what can I do for you, Myron?'

'Remember that death at the Bradford place when we were in high school?'

She stopped mid-bite. 'A little,' she said.

'Who would've handled it for the department?'

She swallowed. 'Detective Wickner.'

Myron remembered him. Ever-present reflector sunglasses. Very active in Little League. Cared about winning waaaaay too much. Hated the kids once they got into high school and stopped worshiping him. Big on speeding tickets for young drivers. But Myron had always liked the man. Old Americana. As dependable as a good tool set.

'He still on the force?'

Francine shook her head. 'Retired. Moved to a lake cabin upstate. But he still comes to town a lot. Hangs out at the fields and shakes hands. They named a

backstop after him. Had a big ceremony and everything.'

'Sorry I missed that,' Myron said. 'Would the case file
still be at the station?'

'How long ago this happen?'

'Twenty years.'

Francine looked at him. Her hair was shorter than in
high school, and the braces were gone, but other than
that, she looked exactly the same. 'In the basement
maybe. Why?'

'I need it.'

'Just like that.'

He nodded.

'You're serious?'

'Yep.'

'And you want me to get it for you.'

'Yep.'

She wiped her hands with a napkin. 'The Bradfords
are powerful folks.'

'Don't I know it.'

'You looking to embarrass him or something? He
running for governor and all.'

'No.'

'And I guess you have a good reason for needing it?'

'Yep.'

'You want to tell me what it is, Myron?'

'Not if I don't have to.'

'How about a teensy-weensy hint?'

'I want to verify that it was an accident.'

She looked at him. 'You have anything that says
otherwise?'

He shook his head. 'I barely have a suspicion.'

Francine Neagly picked up a fry and examined it.
'And if you do find something, Myron, you'll come to
me, right? Not the press. Not the bureau boys. Me.'

'Deal,' Myron said.

She shrugged. 'Okay. I'll take a look for it.'

Myron handed her his card. 'Good seeing you again, Francine.'

'Likewise,' she said, swallowing another bite. 'Hey, you involved with anyone?'

'Yeah,' Myron said. 'You?'

'No,' she said. 'But now that you mention it, I think I kinda miss Gene.'

14

Myron hopped back into the Jaguar. Win started it up and pulled out.

'Your Bradford plan,' Win said. 'It involved prodding him into action, did it not?'

'It did.'

'Then congratulations are in order. The two gentlemen from the Bradfords' foyer did a pass by while you were inside.'

'Any sign of them now?'

Win shook his head. 'They're probably covering the ends of the road. Someone will pick us up. How would you like to play it?'

Myron thought a moment. 'I don't want to tip them off yet. Let them follow us.'

'Where to, O wise one?'

Myron checked his watch. 'What's your schedule look like?'

'I need to get back to the office by two.'

'Can you drop me off at Brenda's practice? I'll get a ride back.'

Win nodded. 'I live to chauffeur.'

They took Route 280 to the New Jersey Turnpike. Win turned on the radio. A commercial voice-over sternly warned people not to buy a mattress over the phone but, rather, to go to Sleepy's and 'consult your mattress professional.' Mattress professional. Myron wondered if that was a master's program or what.

'Are you armed?' Win asked.

'I left my gun in my car.'

'Open the glove compartment.'

Myron did. There were three guns and several boxes of ammunition. He frowned. 'Expecting an armed invasion?'

'My, what a clever quip,' Win said. He gestured to a weapon. 'Take the thirty-eight. It's loaded. There's a holster under the car seat.'

Myron feigned reluctance, but the truth was, he should have been carrying all along.

Win said, 'You realize, of course, that young FJ will not back down.'

'Yeah, I know.'

'We have to kill him. There is no choice.'

'Kill Frank Ache's son? Not even you could survive that.'

Win sort of smiled. 'Is that a challenge?'

'No,' Myron said quickly. 'Just don't do anything yet. Please. I'll come up with something.'

Win shrugged.

They paid a toll and drove past the Vince Lombardi rest stop. In the distance Myron could still see the Meadowlands Sports Complex. Giant Stadium and the Continental Arena floated above the vast swampland that was East Rutherford, New Jersey. Myron stared off at the arena for a moment, silent, remembering his recent shot at playing pro basketball again. It hadn't worked out, but Myron was over that now. He had been robbed of playing the game he loved, but he'd accepted it, come to terms with reality. He'd put it behind him, had moved on, had let go of his anger.

So what if he still thought about it every day?

'I've done a bit of digging,' Win said. 'When young FJ was at Princeton, a geology professor accused him of cheating on an exam.'

'And?'

'Na, na, na. Na, na, na. Hey, hey, hey. Good-bye.'

Myron looked at him. 'You're kidding, right?'

'Never found the body,' Win said. 'The tongue, yes. It was sent to another professor, who'd been considering leveling the same charges.'

Myron felt something flitter in his throat. 'Might have been Frank, not FJ.'

Win shook his head. 'Frank is psychotic but not wasteful. If Frank had handled it, he would have used a few colorful threats perhaps punctuated by a few well-placed blows. But this kind of overkill – it's not his style.'

Myron thought about it. 'Maybe we can talk to Herman or Frank,' he said. 'Get him off our back.'

Win shrugged. 'Easier to kill him.'

'Please don't.'

Another shrug. They kept driving. Win took the Grand Avenue exit. On the right was an enormous complex of town houses. During the mid-eighties, approximately two zillion such complexes had mushroomed across New Jersey. This particular one looked like a staid amusement park or the housing development in *Poltergeist*.

'I don't want to sound maudlin,' Myron said, 'but if FJ does manage to kill me—'

'I'll spend several fun-filled weeks spreading slivers of his genitalia throughout New England,' Win said. 'After that, I'll probably kill him.'

Myron actually smiled. 'Why New England?'

'I like New England,' Win said. Then he added, 'And I would be lonely in New York without you.'

Win pushed the MODE button, and the CD player spun to life. The music from *Rent*. The lovely Mimi was asking Roger to light her candle. Great stuff. Myron looked at his friend. Win said nothing more. To most people, Win seemed about as sentimental as a meat locker. But the fact was, Win just cared for very few people. With those select few, he was surprisingly open; much like his lethal hands, Win struck deep and hard and then backed off, ready to elude.

'Horace Slaughter only had two credit cards,' Myron said. 'Could you check them out?'

'No ATM?'

'Only off his Visa.'

Win nodded, took the card numbers. He dropped Myron off at Englewood High School. The Dolphins were running through a one-on-one defensive drill. One player dribbled in a zigzag formation up the court while the defender bent low and worked on containment. Good drill. Tiring as all hell, but it worked the quads like no other.

There were about a half dozen people in the stands now. Myron took a seat in the front row. Within seconds the coach bee-lined toward him. She was husky with neatly trimmed black hair, a knit shirt with the New York Dolphins logo on the breast, gray sweatpants, a whistle, and Nike high-tops.

'You Bolitar?' the coach barked.

Her spine was a titanium bar, her face as unyielding as a meter maid's.

'Yes.'

'Name's Podich. Jean Podich.' She spoke like a drill sergeant. She put her hands behind her back and rocked on her heels a bit. 'Used to watch you play, Bolitar. Friggin' awesome.'

'Thank you.' He almost added *sir*.

'Still play at all?'

'Just pickup games.'

'Good. Had a player go down with a twisted ankle. Need someone to fill in for the scrimmage.'

'Pardon me?' Coach Podich was not big on using pronouns.

'Got nine players here, Bolitar. Nine. Need a tenth. Plenty of gym clothes in the equipment room. Sneakers too. Go suit up.'

This was not a request.

'I need my knee brace,' Myron said.

'Got that too, Bolitar. Got it all. The trainer will wrap you up good and tight. Now hustle, man.'

She clapped her hands at him, turned, walked away. Myron stayed still for a second. Great. This was just what he needed.

Podich blew her whistle hard enough to squeeze out an internal organ. The players stopped. 'Shoot foul shots, take ten,' she said. 'Then scrimmage.'

The players drifted off. Brenda jogged toward him.

'Where you going?' she asked.

'I have to suit up.'

Brenda stifled a smile.

'What?' he said.

'The equipment room,' Brenda said. 'All they have is yellow Lycra shorts.'

Myron shook his head. 'Then somebody should warn her.'

'Who?'

'Your coach. I put on tight yellow shorts, no way anybody's going to concentrate on basketball.'

Brenda laughed. 'I'll try to maintain a professional demeanor. But if you post me down low, I may be forced to pinch your butt.'

'I'm not just a plaything,' Myron said, 'here for your amusement.'

'Too bad.' She followed him into the equipment

room. 'Oh, that lawyer who wrote to my dad,' she said. 'Thomas Kincaid.'

'Yes.'

'I remember where I heard his name before. My first scholarship. When I was twelve years old. He was the lawyer in charge.'

'What do you mean, in charge?'

'He signed my checks.'

Myron stopped. 'You received checks from a scholarship?'

'Sure. The scholarship covered everything. Tuition, board, schoolbooks. I wrote out my expenses, and Kincaid signed the checks.'

'What was the name of the scholarship?'

'That one? I don't remember. Outreach Education or something like that.'

'How long did Kincaid administer the scholarship?'

'It covered through my high school years. I got an athletic scholarship to college, so basketball paid the freight.'

'What about medical school?'

'I got another scholarship.'

'Same deal?'

'It's a different scholarship, if that's what you mean.'

'Does it pay for the same stuff? Tuition, board, the works?'

'Yep.'

'Handled by a lawyer again?'

She nodded.

'Do you remember his name?'

'Yeah,' she said. 'Rick Peterson. He works out of Roseland.'

Myron thought about this. Something clicked.

'What?' she asked.

'Do me a favor,' he said. 'I got to make a couple of calls. Can you stall Frau Brucha for me?'

She shrugged. 'I can try.'

Brenda left him alone. The equipment room was enormous. An eighty-year-old guy worked the desk. He asked Myron for his sizes. Myron told him. Two minutes later the old man handed Myron a pile of clothes. Purple T-shirt, black socks with blue stripes, white jockstrap, green sneakers, and, of course, yellow Lycra shorts.

Myron frowned. 'I think you missed a color,' he said.

The old man gave him the eye. 'I got a red sports bra, if you're interested.'

Myron thought about it but ultimately declined.

He slipped on his shirt and jock. Pulling on the shorts was like pulling on a wet suit. Everything felt compressed – not a bad feeling, actually. He grabbed his cellular phone and hurried to the trainer's room. On the way he passed a mirror. He looked like a box of Crayolas left too long on a windowsill. He lay on a bench and dialed the office. Esperanza answered.

'MB SportsReps.'

'Where's Cyndi?' Myron asked.

'At lunch.'

A mental image of Godzilla snacking on Tokyo's citizenry flashed in front of his eyes.

'And she doesn't like to be called just Cyndi,' Esperanza added. 'It's Big Cyndi.'

'Pardon my overabundance of political sensitivity. Do you have the list of Horace Slaughter's phone calls?'

'Yes.'

'Any to a lawyer named Rick Peterson?'

The pause was brief. 'You're a regular Mannix,' she said. 'Five of them.'

Wheels were beginning to churn in Myron's head. Never a good thing. 'Any other messages?'

'Two calls from the Witch.'

'Please don't call her that,' Myron said.

Witch was actually an improvement over what Esperanza usually called Jessica (hint: rhymes with *Witch* but starts with the letter *B*). Myron had recently hoped for a thawing between the two – Jessica had invited Esperanza to lunch – but he now recognized that nothing short of a thermonuclear meltdown would soften that particular spread of earth. Some mistook this for jealousy. Not so. Five years ago Jessica had hurt Myron. Esperanza had watched it happen. She had seen up close the devastation.

Some people held grudges; Esperanza clutched them and tied them around her waist and used cement and Krazy glue to hold them steady.

'Why does she call here anyway?' Esperanza half snapped. 'Doesn't she know your cellular number?'

'She only uses it for emergencies.'

Esperanza made a noise like she was gagging on a soup ladle. 'You two have such a mature relationship.'

'Can I just have the message, please?'

'She wants you to call her. At the Beverly Wilshire. Room six-one-eight. Must be the Bitch Suite.'

So much for improvement. Esperanza read off the number. Myron jotted it down.

'Anything else?'

'Your mom called. Don't forget dinner tonight. Your dad is barbecuing. A potpourri of aunts and uncles will be in attendance.'

'Okay, thanks. I'll see you this afternoon.'

'Can't wait,' she said. Then she hung up.

Myron sat back. Jessica had called twice. Hmm.

The trainer tossed Myron a leg brace. Myron strapped it on, fastening it with Velcro. The trainer silently worked on the knee, starting with stretch wrap. Myron debated calling Jessica back right now and decided he still had time. Lying back with his head on a sponge pillow of some sort, he dialed the Beverly Wilshire and asked for Jessica's room. She picked up as though she'd had her hand on the receiver.

'Hello?' Jessica said.

'Hello there, gorgeous,' he said. Charm. 'What are you doing?'

'I just spread out a dozen snapshots of you on the floor,' she said. 'I was about to strip naked, coat my entire body with some type of oil, and then undulate on them.'

Myron looked up at the trainer. 'Er, can I have an ice pack?'

The trainer looked puzzled. Jessica laughed.

'Undulate,' Myron said. 'That's a good word.'

'Me a writer,' Jessica said.

'So how's the left coast?' Left coast. Hip lingo.

'Sunny,' she said. 'There's too much damn sun here.'

'So come home.'

There was a pause. Then Jessica said, 'I have some good news.'

'Oh?'

'Remember that production company that optioned *Control Room*?'

'Sure.'

'They want me to produce it and cowrite the screenplay. Isn't that cool?'

Myron said nothing. A steel band wrapped around his chest.

'It'll be great,' she continued, forcing pseudojocularity into the cautious tone. 'I'll fly home on weekends. Or you can fly out here sometimes. Say, you can do some recruiting out here, nab some West Coast clients. It'll be great.'

Silence. The trainer finished up and left the room. Myron was afraid to speak. Seconds passed.

'Don't be like that,' Jessica said. 'I know you're not happy about this. But it'll work out. I'll miss you like mad – you know that – but Hollywood always screws up my books. It's too big an opportunity.'

Myron opened his mouth, closed it, started again. 'Please come home.'

'Myron . . .'

He closed his eyes. 'Don't do this.'

'I'm not doing anything.'

'You're running away, Jess. It's what you do best.'

Silence.

'That's not fair,' she said.

'Screw fair. I love you.'

'I love you too.'

'Then come home,' he said.

Myron's grip on the phone was tight. His muscles were tensing. In the background he heard Coach Podich blow that damn whistle.

'You still don't trust me,' Jessica said softly. 'You're still afraid.'

'And you've done so much to assuage my fears, right?' He was surprised by the edge in his voice.

The old image jarred him anew. Doug. A guy named Doug. Five years ago. Or was he a Dougie? Myron bet he was. He bet his friends called him Dougie. Yo, Dougie, wanna party, man. Probably called her Jessie. Dougie and Jessie. Five years ago. Myron had walked in on them, and his heart had crumbled as though it'd been molded in ash.

'I can't change what happened,' Jessica said.

'I know that.'

'So what do you want from me?'

'I want you to come home. I want us to be together.'

More cellular static. Coach Podich called out his name. Myron could feel something vibrating in his chest like a tuning fork.

'You're making a mistake,' Jessica said. 'I know I've had some trouble with commitment before—'

'*Some* trouble?'

'—but this isn't like that. I'm not running away. You're pushing on the wrong issue.'

'Maybe I am,' he said. He closed his eyes. It was hard for him to breathe. He should hang up now. He should be tougher, show some pride, stop wearing his heart on his sleeve, hang up. 'Just come home,' he said. 'Please.'

He could feel their distance, a continent separating them, their voices bypassing millions of people.

'Let's both take a deep breath,' she said. 'Maybe this isn't for the phone anyway.'

More silence.

'Look, I got a meeting,' she said. 'Let's talk later, okay?'

She hung up then. Myron held the empty receiver. He was alone. He stood. His legs were shaky.

Brenda met him at the doorway. A towel was draped around her neck. Her face was shiny from sweat. She took one look at him and said, 'What's wrong?'

'Nothing.'

She kept her eyes on him. She didn't believe him, but she wouldn't push either.

'Nice outfit,' she said.

Myron looked down at his clothing. 'I was going to wear a red sports bra,' he said. 'It throws the whole look together.'

'Yummy,' she said.

He managed a smile. 'Let's go.'

They started heading down the corridor.

'Myron?'

'Yeah?'

'We talk a lot about me.' She continued walking, not looking at him. 'Wouldn't kill either of us to switch roles now and again. Might even be nice.'

Myron nodded, said nothing. Much as he might wish to be more like Clint Eastwood or John Wayne, Myron was not the silent type, not a macho tough guy who kept all his problems inside him. He confided to Win and Esperanza all the time. But neither one of them was helpful when it came to Jessica. Esperanza hated her so much that she could never think rationally on the subject. And in Win's case, well, Win was simply not the man to discuss matters of the heart. His views on the subject could conservatively be called 'scary'.

When they reached the edge of the court, Myron pulled up short. Brenda looked at him questioningly. Two men stood on the sidelines. Ragged brown suits, totally devoid of any sense of style of fashion. Weary faces, short hair, big guts. No doubt in Myron's mind.

Cops.

Somebody pointed at Myron and Brenda. The two men sauntered over with a sigh. Brenda looked puzzled. Myron moved a little closer to her. The two men stopped directly in front of them.

'Are you Brenda Slaughter?' one asked.

'Yes.'

'I am Detective David Pepe of the Mahwah Police Department. This is Detective Mike Rinsky. We'd like you to come with us, please.'

15

Myron stepped forward. 'What's this about?'

The two cops looked at him with flat eyes. 'And you are?'

'Myron Bolitar.'

The two cops blinked. 'And Myron Bolitar is?'

'Miss Slaughter's attorney,' Myron said.

One cop looked at the other. 'That was fast.'

Second cop: 'Wonder why she called her attorney already.'

'Weird, huh?'

'I'd say.' He looked the multicolored Myron up and down. Smirked. 'You don't dress like an attorney, Mr. Bolitar.'

'I left my gray vest at home,' Myron said. 'What do you guys want?'

'We would like to bring Miss Slaughter to the station,' the first cop said.

'Is she under arrest?'

First Cop looked at Second Cop. 'Don't lawyers know that when we arrest people, we read them their rights?'

'Probably got his degree at home. Maybe from that Sally Struthers school.'

'Got his law degree and VCR repairman certificate in one.'

'Right. Like that.'

'Or maybe he went to that American Bartenders Institute. They got a competitive program, I hear.'

Myron crossed his arms. 'Whenever you guys are through. But please keep going. You're both extremely amusing.'

First Cop sighed. 'We'd like to bring Miss Slaughter to the station,' he said again.

'Why?'

'To talk.'

Boy, this was moving along nicely. 'Why do you want to talk to her?' Myron tried.

'Not us,' Second Cop said.

'Right, not us.'

'We're just supposed to pick her up.'

'Like escorts.'

Myron was about to make a comment on their being male escorts, but Brenda put her hand on his forearm. 'Let's just go,' she said.

'Smart lady,' First Cop said.

'Needs a new lawyer,' Second Cop added.

Myron and Brenda sat in the back of an unmarked police car that a blind man could tell was an unmarked police car. It was a brown sedan, the same brown as the cops' suits, a Chevrolet Caprice with simply too much antenna.

For the first ten minutes of the ride nobody spoke. Brenda's face was set. She moved her hand along the seat closer until it touched his. Then she left it there. She looked at him. The hand felt warm and nice. He tried to look confident, but he had a terrible sinking feeling in the pit of his stomach.

They drove down Route 4 and up Route 17. Mahwah. Nice suburb, almost on the New York border. They parked behind the Mahwah municipal building. The entrance to the station was in the back. The two cops led them into an interrogation room. There was a metal table bolted to the floor and four chairs. No hot lamp. A mirror took up half a wall. Only a moron who never, ever watched television didn't know that it was a one-way mirror. Myron often wondered if anybody was fooled by that anymore. Even if you never watched TV, why would the police need a giant mirror in an interrogation room? Vanity?

They were left alone.

'What do you think this is about?' Brenda asked.

Myron shrugged. He had a pretty good idea. But speculating at this stage was worthless. They would find out soon enough. Ten minutes passed. Not a good sign. Another five. Myron decided to call their bluff.

'Let's go,' he said.

'What?'

'We don't have to wait around here. Let's go.'

As if on cue, the door opened. A man and a woman entered. The man was big and barrel-like with explosions of hair every place. He had a mustache so thick it made Teddy Roosevelt's look like a limp eyelash. His hairline was low, the kind of low where you can't tell where the eyebrow ends and the actual hairline begins. He looked like a member of the Politburo. His pants were stretched tautly in the front, creasing obscenely, yet his lack of an ass made them too big in the back. His shirt was also too tight. The collar strangled him. The rolled-up sleeves worked the forearms like tourniquets. He was red-faced and angry.

For those with a scorecard, this would be your Bad Cop.

The woman wore a gray skirt with her detective shield on the waistband and a high-neck white blouse. She was early thirties, blonde with freckles and pink cheeks. Healthy-looking. If she were a veal entree, the menu would describe her as 'milk-fed'.

She smiled at them warmly. 'Sorry to keep you

waiting.' Nice, even teeth. 'My name is Detective Maureen McLaughlin. I'm with the Bergen County Prosecutor's Office. This is Detective Dan Tiles. He works for the Mahwah Police Department.'

Tiles did not say anything. He folded his arms and glowered at Myron like he was a vagrant urinating in his garden. Myron looked up at him.

'Tiles,' Myron repeated. 'As in the porcelain things in my bathroom?'

McLaughlin kept up the smile. 'Miss Slaughter – may I call you Brenda?'

Already with the friendly.

Brenda said, 'Yes, Maureen.'

'Brenda, I'd like to ask you a few questions, if that's okay.'

Myron said, 'What's this all about?'

Maureen McLaughlin flashed him the smile now. With the freckles it made for a very pert look. 'Can I get either of you something? A coffee maybe? A cold beverage?'

Myron stood. 'Let's go, Brenda.'

'Whoa,' McLaughlin said. 'Settle down a second, okay? What's the problem?'

'The problem is you won't tell us why we're here,' Myron said. 'Plus you used the word *beverage* in casual conversation.'

Tiles spoke for the first time. 'Tell them,' he said. His mouth never moved. But the shrub below his nose bounced up and down. Kinda like Yosemite Sam.

McLaughlin suddenly looked distraught. 'I can't just blurt it out, Dan. That wouldn't—'

'Tell them,' Tiles said again.

Myron motioned at them. 'You guys rehearse this?' But he was flailing now. He knew what was coming. He just did not want to hear it.

'Please,' McLaughlin said. The smile was gone. 'Please sit down.'

They both slid slowly back into their seats. Myron folded his hands and put them on the table.

McLaughlin seemed to be considering her words. 'Do you have a boyfriend, Brenda?'

'You running a dating service?' Myron said.

Tiles stepped away from the wall. He reached out and picked up Myron's right hand for a moment. He dropped it and picked up his left. He studied it, looked disgusted, put it back down.

Myron tried not to look confused. 'Palmolive,' he said. 'More than just mild.'

Tiles moved away, recrossed his arms. 'Tell them,' he said again.

McLaughlin's eyes were only on Brenda now. She leaned forward a little and lowered her voice. 'Your father is dead, Brenda. We found his body three hours ago. I'm sorry.'

Myron had steeled himself, but the words still hit like a meteorite. He gripped the table and felt his head spin. Brenda said nothing. Her face didn't change, but her breathing became shallow gulps.

McLaughlin did not leave much time for condolences. 'I realize that this is a very tough time, but we really need to ask you a few questions.'

'Get out,' Myron said.

'What?'

'I want you and Stalin to get the hell out of here right now. This interview is over.'

Tiles said, 'You got something to hide, Bolitar?'

'Yeah, that's it, wolf boy. Now get out.'

Brenda still had not moved. She looked at McLaughlin and uttered one word. 'How?'

'How what?'

Brenda swallowed. 'How was he murdered?'

Tiles almost leaped across the room. 'How did you know he was murdered?'

'What?'

'We didn't say anything about murder,' Tiles said. He looked very pleased with himself. 'Just that your father was dead.'

Myron rolled his eyes. 'You got us, Tiles. Two cops drag us in here, play Sipowicz and Simone, and somehow we figure that her father didn't die of natural causes. Either we're psychic or we did it.'

'Shut up, asshole.'

Myron stood up quickly, knocking over his chair. He went eyeball to eyeball with Tiles. 'Get out.'

'Or?'

'You want a piece of me, Tiles?'

'Love it, hotshot.'

McLaughlin stepped between them. 'You boys sprinkle on a little extra testosterone this morning? Back off, both of you.'

Myron kept his eyes on Tiles's. He took several deep breaths. He was acting irrationally. He knew that. Stupid to lose control. He had to get his act together. Horace was dead. Brenda was in trouble. He had to keep calm.

Myron picked up his chair and sat back down. 'My client will not talk to you until we confer.'

'Why?' Brenda said to him. 'What's the big deal?'

'They think you did it,' Myron said.

That surprised her. Brenda turned to McLaughlin. 'Am I a suspect?'

McLaughlin gave a friendly, on-your-side shrug. 'Hey, it's too early to rule anybody in or out.'

'That's cop-speak for yes,' Myron said.

'Shut up, asshole.' Tiles again.

Myron ignored him. 'Answer her question, McLaughlin. How was her father killed?'

McLaughlin leaned back, weighing her options. 'Horace Slaughter was shot in the head.'

Brenda closed her eyes.

Dan Tiles moved in again. 'At close range,' he added.

'Right, close range. Back of the head.'

'Close range,' Tiles repeated. He put his fists on the table. Then he leaned in closer. 'Like maybe he knew the killer. Like maybe it was somebody he trusted.'

Myron pointed at him. 'You got some food stuck in your mustache. Looks like scrambled eggs.'

Tiles leaned in closer until their noses almost touched. He had big pores. Really big pores. Myron almost feared he'd fall into one. 'I don't like your attitude, asshole.'

Myron leaned in a bit too. Then he gently shook his head from side to side, nose tip making contact with nose tip. 'If we were Eskimos,' Myron said, 'we'd be engaged right now.'

That backed Tiles up. When he recovered, he said, 'Your acting like an ass doesn't change the facts: Horace Slaughter was shot at close range.'

'Which means squat, Tiles. If you were part of a real force, you'd know that most assassins for hire shoot their victims at close range. Most family members don't.' Myron had no idea if that was true, but it sounded good.

Brenda cleared her throat. 'Where was he shot?'

'Excuse me?' McLaughlin said.

'Where was he shot?'

'I just told you. In the head.'

'No, I mean where. What city?'

But of course they had known that she meant that. They did not want to tell her, hoping to trip her up.

Myron answered the question. 'He was found here in Mah-wah.' Then he looked at Tiles. 'And before Magnum PI pounces again, I know that because we're in the Mahwah police station. The only reason for that is that the body was found here.'

McLaughlin did not respond directly. She folded her hands in front of her. 'Brenda, when was the last time you saw your father?'

'Don't answer,' Myron said.

'Brenda?'

Brenda looked at Myron. Her eyes were wide and unfocused. She was fighting to hold it all back, and the strain was starting to show. Her voice was almost a plea. 'Let's just get through this, okay?'

'I'm advising you against it.'

'Good advice,' Tiles said. 'If you got something to hide.'

Myron looked at Tiles. 'I can't tell. Is that a mustache or really long nostril hair?'

McLaughlin remained overly earnest, a perp's dearest chum. 'It's like this, Brenda. If you can answer our questions now, we can end this. If you clam up, well, we'll have to wonder why. It won't look good, Brenda. It'll look like you've got something to hide. And then there's the media.'

Myron put his hand out. 'What?'

Tiles handled this one. 'Simple, asshole. You lawyer her up, we tell the media she's a suspect and that she wouldn't cooperate.' He smiled. 'Miss Slaughter here will be lucky to endorse condoms.'

Momentary silence. Striking an agent where he lives.

'When did you last see your father, Brenda?'

Myron was about to interrupt, but Brenda silenced him by putting her hand on his forearm. 'Nine days ago.'

'Under what circumstances?'

'We were in his apartment.'

'Please continue.'

'Continue with what?' Myron interrupted. Rule twenty-six of lawyering: never let the interrogator – cop or fellow attorney – get a rhythm. 'You asked her when she last saw her father. She told you.'

'I asked under what circumstances,' McLaughlin replied. 'Brenda, please tell me what occurred during your visit.'

'You know what occurred,' Brenda said.

That put her a step ahead of Myron.

Maureen McLaughlin nodded. 'I have in my possession a sworn complaint.' She slid a piece of paper across the metal table. 'Is that your signature, Brenda?'

'Yes.'

Myron took the sheet and began to skim it.

'Does that accurately describe your last meeting with your father?'

Brenda's eyes were hard now. 'Yes.'

'So on this occasion at your father's apartment – the last time you saw him – your father assaulted you both physically and verbally. Is that correct?'

Myron kept still.

'He shoved me,' Brenda said.

'Hard enough for you to want a restraining order, isn't that correct?'

Myron tried to keep pace, but he was starting to feel like a buoy in rough waters. Horace had assaulted his own daughter and was now dead. Myron had to get a handle on this, get back into the fray.

'Stop badgering,' he said, his voice sounding weak and forced. 'You have the documentation, so let's get on with it.'

'Brenda, please tell me about your father's assault.'

'He pushed me,' she said.

'Can you tell me why?'

'No.'

'No, you won't tell me. Or no, you don't know.'

'No, I don't know.'

'He just shoved you?'

'Yes.'

'You walked into his apartment. You said, "Hi, Dad." Then he cursed at you and assaulted you. Is that what you're telling us?'

Brenda was trying to keep her face steady, but there was shaking near the fault lines. The facade was about to crack.

'That's enough,' Myron said.

But McLaughlin moved in. 'Is that what you're trying to tell us, Brenda? Your father's attack was completely unprovoked?'

'She's not telling you anything, McLaughlin. Back off.'

'Brenda—'

'We're out of here.' Myron took hold of Brenda's arm and half dragged her to a standing position. Tiles moved to block the door.

McLaughlin kept talking. 'We can help you, Brenda. But this is your last chance. You walk out of here, you're talking a murder indictment.'

Brenda seemed to snap out of whatever trance she'd been in. 'What are you talking about?'

'They're bluffing,' Myron said.

'You know how this looks, don't you?' McLaughlin continued. 'Your father has been dead awhile. We haven't done an autopsy yet, but I'd bet he's been dead for close to a week. You're a smart girl, Brenda. You put it together. The two of you had problems. We have your own list of serious grievances right here. Nine days ago he assaulted you. You went to court to get him to keep away from you. Our theory is that your father did not obey that order. He was clearly a violent man, probably angered beyond control by what he perceived as your disloyalty. Is that what happened, Brenda?'

Myron said, 'Don't answer.'

'Let me help you, Brenda. Your father didn't listen to the court order, right? He came after you, didn't he?'

Brenda said nothing.

'You were his daughter. You disobeyed him. You publicly humiliated him, so much so that he decided to teach you a lesson. And when he came after you – when that big, scary man was going to attack you again – you had no choice. You shot him. It was self-defense, Brenda. I understand that. I would have done the same thing. But if you walk out that door, Brenda, I can't help you. It moves from something justifiable to cold-blooded murder. Plain and simple.'

McLaughlin took her hand. 'Let me help you, Brenda.'

The room went still. McLaughlin's freckled face was totally earnest, the perfect mask of concern and trust and openness. Myron glanced over at Tiles. Tiles quickly diverted his gaze.

Myron didn't like that.

McLaughlin had laid out a neat little theory. It made sense. Myron could see why they would believe it. There was bad blood between father and daughter. A well-documented history of abuse. A court order . . .

Hold the phone.

Myron looked back over at Tiles. Tiles would still not meet his eyes.

Then Myron remembered the blood on the shirt in the locker. The cops didn't know about that, couldn't know about it . . .

'She wants to see her father,' Myron blurted out.

Everybody looked at him. 'Excuse me?'

'His body. We want to see Horace Slaughter's body.'

'That won't be necessary,' McLaughlin said. 'We've positively identified him through fingerprints. There's no reason to put—'

'Are you denying Miss Slaughter the opportunity to view her father's body?'

McLaughlin backpedaled a bit. 'Of course not. If that's what you really want, Brenda—'

'That's what we want.'

'I'm speaking to Brenda—'

'I'm her attorney, Detective. You speak to me.'

McLaughlin stopped. Then she shook her head and turned to Tiles. Tiles shrugged.

'Okay then,' McLaughlin said. 'We'll drive you over.'

16

The Bergen County Medical Examiner's Office looked like a small elementary school. It was one level, red brick, right angles, and as unassuming a building as one could construct, but then again, what did you want in a morgue? The waiting room chairs were molded plastic and about as comfortable as a pinched nerve. Myron had been here once before, not long after Jessica's father had been murdered. The memory was not a pleasant one.

'We can go in now,' McLaughlin said.

Brenda stayed close to Myron as they all walked down a short corridor. He put his arm around her waist. She moved in a touch. He was comforting her. He knew that. He also knew that it shouldn't have felt so right.

They entered a room of gleaming metal and tile. No big storage drawers or anything like that. Clothes – a security guard's uniform – were in a plastic bag in one corner. All the instruments and utensils and what-have-you's were in another corner, covered by a sheet. So was the table in the center. Myron could see right away that the body underneath it belonged to a big man.

They paused at the door before gathering around the gurney. With minimum fanfare, a man – Myron assumed he was the medical examiner – pulled the sheet back. For the briefest of moments, Myron thought that maybe the cops had screwed up the ID. It was a whimsical hope, he realized, not anything based on fact.

He was sure it ran through every person's mind who came here to identify someone, even when he knew the truth, a last gasp, a fantasy that a wonderful, beautiful mistake had been made. It was only natural.

But there was no mistake here.

Brenda's eyes filled. She tilted her head and screwed up her mouth. Her hand reached out and brushed the still cheek.

'That's enough,' McLaughlin said.

The medical examiner started pulling the sheet back. But Myron reached his hand out and stopped him. He looked down at the remains of his old friend. He felt tears sting his own eyes, but he forced them back. Now was not the time. He had come here for a purpose.

'The bullet wound,' Myron said, his voice thick. 'It's in the back of the head?'

The medical examiner glanced at McLaughlin. McLaughlin nodded. 'Yes,' the medical examiner said. 'I cleaned him up when I heard you were coming.'

Myron pointed to Horace's right cheek. 'What's that?'

The medical examiner looked nervous. 'I have not yet had the time to properly analyze the body.'

'I didn't ask you for an analysis, Doctor. I asked you about this.'

'Yes, I understand that. But I do not wish to make any suppositions until I perform a complete autopsy.'

'Well, Doctor, it's a bruise,' Myron said. 'And it happened premortem. You can tell by the lividity and coloring.' Myron had no idea if that was true, but he ran with it. 'His nose also appears to be broken, does it not, Doctor?'

'Don't answer that,' McLaughlin said.

'He doesn't have to.' Myron started leading Brenda away from the shell that was once her father. 'Nice try,

McLaughlin. Call us a taxi. We're not saying another word to you.'

When they were alone outside, Brenda said, 'Do you want to tell me what that was all about?'

'They were trying to con you.'

'How?'

'For the sake of argument, let's say you did murder your father. The police are questioning you. You're nervous. Suddenly they give you the perfect out.'

'That self-defense stuff.'

'Right. Justifiable homicide. They pretend they're on your side, that they understand. You as the killer would jump at the chance, right?'

'If I were the killer, yeah, I guess I would.'

'But you see, McLaughlin and Tiles knew about those bruises.'

'So?'

'So if you shot your father in self-defense, why was he beaten beforehand?'

'I don't understand.'

'Here's how it works. They get you to confess. You follow their lead, come up with a story about how he attacked you and how you had to shoot him. But the problem is, if that's the case, where did the facial bruises come from? All of a sudden, McLaughlin and Tiles produce this new physical evidence that contradicts your version of the events. So what are you left with? A confession you can't retract. With that in hand, they use the bruises to show it wasn't self-defense. You've screwed yourself.'

Brenda chewed that over. 'So they figure someone beat him right before he was killed?'

'Right.'

She frowned. 'But do they really believe I could have beaten him up like that?'

'Probably not.'

'So how are they figuring?'

'Maybe you surprised him with a baseball bat or something. But more likely – and this is the tricky part – they think you had an accomplice. You remember how Tiles checked my hands?'

She nodded.

'He was looking for bruised knuckles or some other telltale sign of trauma. When you punch somebody, your hand usually shows it.'

'And that's also why she asked me about a boyfriend?'

'Right.'

The sun was starting to weaken a bit. Traffic whizzed by. There was a parking lot across the street. A sprinkling of men and women in business suits trudged to their cars after a day of unnatural office light, their faces pale, their eyes blinking.

'So they believe that Dad was beaten right before he was shot,' she said.

'Yes.'

'But we know that it probably isn't true.'

Myron nodded. 'The blood in the locker. My guess is, your father was beaten a day or two before. Either he got away or the beating was just a warning. He went to his locker at St. Barnabas to clean up. He used a shirt to stop the blood flowing out of his nose. Then he ran away.'

'And someone found him and shot him.'

'Yes.'

'Shouldn't we tell the police about the bloody shirt?'

'I'm not sure. Think about it a second. The cops firmly believe you did it. Now you produce a shirt with your dad's blood on it. Is that going to help us or hurt us?'

Brenda nodded and suddenly turned away. Her breathing became funny again. Too much too fast, Myron thought. He stayed back and gave her a little space. His heart started swelling up. Mother and father both gone, no sisters or brothers. What must that feel like?

A taxi pulled up a few minutes later. Brenda faced him again.

'Where do you want to be dropped off?' Myron asked. 'A friend's house? Your aunt's?'

She thought about it. Then she shook her head and met his gaze. 'Actually,' she said, 'I'd like to stay with you.'

17

The taxi pulled up to the Bolitar house in Livingston.

'We can go somewhere else,' he tried again.

She shook her head. 'Just do me one favor.'

'What?'

'Don't tell them about my father. Not tonight.'

He sighed. 'Yeah, okay.'

Uncle Sidney and Aunt Selma were already there. So were Uncle Bernie and Aunt Sophie and their boys. Other cars pulled up as he paid the taxi driver. Mom sprinted down the driveway and hugged Myron as though he'd just been released by Hamas terrorists. She also hugged Brenda. So did everyone else. Dad was in the back at the barbecue. A gas grill now, thank goodness, so Dad could stop loading on the lighter fluid with a hose. He wore a chef's hat somewhat taller than a control tower and an apron that read REFORMED VEGETARIAN. Brenda was introduced as a client. Mom quickly grabbed her away from Myron, threading her arm through Brenda's, and led her into the house for a tour. More people came. The neighbors. Each with a pasta salad or fruit salad or something. The Dempseys and the Cohens and the Daleys and the Weinsteins. The Brauns had finally surrendered to the warm allure of Florida, and a couple younger than Myron with two kids had moved in. They came over too.

The festivities began. A Wiffle ball and bat were produced. Teams were chosen. When Myron swung and missed, everyone fell down as though from the breeze. Funny. Everyone talked with Brenda. They wanted to hear about the new women's league, but they were far more impressed when they heard Brenda was going to be a doctor. Dad even let Brenda take over the grill for a while, a move for Dad tantamount to donating a kidney. The smell of charred foods filled the air. Chicken and burgers and hot dogs from Don's deli (Mom bought her hot dogs only from Don) and shish kebabs and even a few salmon steaks for the health-conscious.

Myron kept meeting Brenda's eye. Brenda kept smiling.

Kids, all dutifully wearing helmets, parked their bikes at the end of the driveway. The Cohens' kid had gotten an earring. Everyone ribbed him about it. He slumped his head and smiled. Vic Ruskin gave Myron a stock tip. Myron nodded and promptly forgot it. Fred Dempsey grabbed a basketball from the garage. The Daley girl picked teams. Myron had to play. So did Brenda. Everyone laughed. Myron downed a cheeseburger between points. Delicious. Timmy Ruskin fell down and cut his knee. He cried. Brenda bent down and examined the cut. She put on a Band-Aid and smiled at Timmy. Timmy beamed.

Hours passed. Darkness crept in slowly as it does in suburban summer skies. People began to drift home. Cars and bikes faded away. Fathers threw their arms around sons. Little girls rode home on shoulders. Everyone kissed Mom and Dad good-bye. Myron looked at his parents. They were the only original family left in the neighborhood now, the surrogate grandparents of the block. They suddenly looked old to Myron. That scared him.

Brenda came up behind him. 'This is wonderful,' she said to him.

And it was. Win might poke fun at it. Jessica did not care for scenes like these – her own family had created the perfect Rockwellian facade to hide the rot below – and rushed back to the city as though it held an antidote. Myron and Jess often drove back from such events in total silence. Myron thought about that. And he thought again what Win had said about taking leaps of faith.

'I miss your father,' Myron said. 'I haven't talked to him in ten years. But I still miss him.'

She nodded. 'I know.'

They helped clean up. Not much to it. They'd used only paper plates and cups and plastic utensils. Brenda and Mom laughed the whole time. Mom kept sneaking glances at Myron. The looks were a little too knowing.

'I always wanted Myron to be a doctor,' Mom said. 'Isn't that a shock? A Jewish mother who wants her son to be a doctor?'

Both women laughed.

'But he faints at the sight of blood,' Mom continued. 'Can't stand it. Myron wouldn't even go to an R-rated movie until he was in college. Slept with a night-light until he was—'

'Mom.'

'Oh, I'm embarrassing him. I'm your mother, Myron. I'm supposed to embarrass you. Isn't that right, Brenda?'

'Definitely, Mrs. Bolitar.'

'For the tenth time, it's Ellen. And Myron's father is Al. Everyone calls us El Al. Get it? Like the Israeli airline.'

'Mom.'

'Shush, you, I'm going. Brenda, you'll stay tonight? The guest room is all ready for you.'

'Thank you, Ellen. That would be very nice.'

Mom turned. 'I'll leave you kids alone.' Her smile was too happy.

The backyard fell silent. A full moon was the only source of illumination. Crickets hummed. A dog barked. They started walking. They talked about Horace. Not about the murder. Not about why he vanished or about Anita Slaughter or FJ or the league or the Bradfords or any of that. Just about Horace.

They reached Burnet Hill, Myron's elementary school. A few years ago the town had closed down half the building because of its proximity to high-tension electromagnetic wires. Myron had spent three years under those wires. Might explain a few things.

Brenda sat on a swing. Her skin glistened in the moonlight. She started swinging, kicking her legs high. He sat on the swing next to her and joined her in the air. The metal apparatus was strong, but it still started swaying a bit under their onslaught.

They slowed.

'You haven't asked about the assault,' she said.

'There will be time.'

'It's a pretty simple story,' she said.

Myron said nothing, waited.

'I came to Dad's apartment. He was drunk. Dad didn't drink much. When he did, it really hit him. He was barely coherent when I opened the door. He started cursing me. He called me a little bitch. Then he pushed me.'

Myron shook his head, not sure what to say.

Brenda stopped the swing. 'He also called me Anita,' she said.

Myron's throat went dry. 'He thought you were your mother?'

Brenda nodded. 'He had such hate in his eyes,' she said. 'I've never seen him look like that.'

Myron stayed still. A theory had been slowly taking shape in his mind. The blood in the locker at St. Barnabas. The call to the lawyers and to the Bradfords. Horace's running away. His being murdered. It all sort of fit. But right now, it was just a theory based on the purest of speculation. He needed to sleep on it, marinate the whole thing in the brain fridge for a while, before he dared articulate it.

'How far is it to the Bradfords' place?' Brenda asked.

'Half a mile maybe.'

She looked away from him. 'Do you still think my mom ran away because of something that happened in that house?'

'Yes.'

She stood. 'Let's walk over there.'

'There's nothing to see. A big gate and some shrubs.'

'My mother walked through those gates for six years. That'll be enough. For now.'

They took the path between Ridge Drive and Coddington Terrace – Myron could not believe it was still here after all these years – and made a right. The lights on the hill were visible from here. Not much else. Brenda approached the gate. The security guard squinted at her. She stopped in front of the iron bars. She stared for several seconds.

The guard leaned out. 'Can I help you, ma'am?'

Brenda shook her head and moved away.

They got back to the house late. Myron's father was feigning sleep in the recliner. Some habits die hard. Myron 'woke' him up. He startled to consciousness. Pacino never overacted this much. He smiled good night at Brenda. Myron kissed his father on the cheek. The cheek felt rough and smelled faintly of Old Spice. As it should.

The bed was made in the downstairs guest room. The

maid must have been in that day because Mom stayed away from domestic chores as though they were radioactive. She had been a working mother, one of the most feared defense attorneys in the state, since the days before Gloria Steinem.

His parents saved toiletry bags from first-class flights. He gave one to Brenda. He also found her a T-shirt and pajama bottoms.

When she kissed him hard on the mouth, he felt every part of him stir. The excitement of a first kiss, the brand-newness of it, the wondrous taste and smell of her. Her body, substantial and hard and young, pressed against his. Myron had never felt so lost, so heady, so weightless. When their tongues met, Myron felt a jolt and heard himself groan.

He pulled back. 'We shouldn't. Your father just died. You—'

She shut him up with another kiss. Myron cupped the back of her head with his palm. He felt tears come to his eyes as he held on.

When the kiss ended, they held each other tightly, gasping.

'If you tell me I'm doing this because I'm vulnerable,' she said, 'you're wrong. And you know you're wrong.'

He swallowed. 'Jessica and I are going through a rough patch right now.'

'This isn't about that either,' she said.

He nodded. He did know that. And after a decade of loving the same woman, maybe that was what scared him most of all. He stepped back.

'Good night,' he managed.

Myron rushed downstairs to his old room in the basement. He crawled under the sheets and pulled them up to his neck. He stared up at the frayed posters of John Havlicek and Larry Bird. Havlicek, the old Celtic great, had been on his wall since he was six years old. Bird had joined him in 1979. Myron sought comfort and maybe escape in his old room, in surrounding himself with familiar images.

He found none.

18

The ring of the phone and the muffled voices invaded his sleep, becoming part of his dream. When Myron opened his eyes, he remembered little. He'd been younger in the dream, and he felt a deep sadness as he'd floated up toward consciousness. He closed his eyes again, trying to claw back into that warm, nocturnal realm. The second ring blew away the fading images like so much cloud dust.

He reached for his cell phone. As it had for the past three years, the bedside clock blinked 12:00 A.M. Myron checked his watch. Almost seven in the morning.

'Hello?'

'Where are you?'

It took Myron a moment to place the voice. Officer Francine Neagly, his old high school buddy.

'Home,' he croaked.

'Remember the Halloween scare?'

'Yeah.'

'Meet me there in a half hour,' she said.

'Did you get the file?'

Click.

Myron hung up the phone. He took a few deep breaths. Great. Now what?

Through the vents he heard the muffled voices again. They were coming from the kitchen. Years down here had given him the ability to tell by the echo in what room of the house a certain sound originated – not unlike the Indian brave in an old western who puts his ear to the ground to calculate the distance of incoming hoofbeats.

Myron swung his legs out of the bed. He massaged his face with his palms. He threw on a velour bathrobe circa 1978, gave the teeth a quick brush, the hair a quick pat, and headed to the kitchen.

Brenda and Mom sipped coffee at the kitchen table. Instant coffee, Myron knew. *Muy* watery. Mom wasn't big on better coffees. The wondrous smell of fresh bagels, however, jump-started his stomach. A bowlful of them along with an assortment of spreads and several newspapers adorned the tabletop. A typical Sunday morning at the Bolitar homestead.

'Good morning,' Mom said.

'Morning.'

'Want a cup of coffee?'

'No, thanks.' New Starbucks in Livingston. He'd check it out on the way to Francine.

Myron looked at Brenda. She looked back steadily. No embarrassment. He was glad.

'Good morning,' he said to her. Sparkling morning-after repartee was Myron's forte.

She nodded a good morning back.

'There are bagels,' Mom said, in case both his eyes and olfactory nerves had shorted out. 'Your father picked them up this morning. From Livingston Bagels, Myron. Remember? The one on Northfield Avenue? Near Two Gondoliers Pizzeria?'

Myron nodded. His dad had bought bagels from the same store for thirty years, yet his mother still felt a constant need to entice him with this tidbit. He joined them at the table.

Mom folded her hands in front of her. 'Brenda was filling me in on her situation,' she said. Her voice was different now, more lawyerly, less maternal. She pushed a newspaper in front of Myron. The murder of Horace Slaughter had made page one, left-hand column, the spot usually reserved for whatever teen had thrown her newborn out with the morning trash.

'I'd represent her myself,' Mom continued, 'but with your involvement, it might look like a conflict of interest. I was thinking of Aunt Clara.'

Clara was not really his aunt, just an old friend of the family and, like Mom, an awesome attorney.

'Good idea,' Myron said.

He picked up the paper and scanned the article. Nothing surprising. The article mentioned the fact that Brenda had recently gotten a restraining order against her father, that she had accused him of assaulting her, and that she was wanted for further questioning but could not be reached. Detective Maureen McLaughlin gave the standard spiel about its being 'too early to rule anybody in or out'. Right. The police were controlling the story, leaking just enough to incriminate and put pressure on one person: Brenda Slaughter.

There was a photograph of Horace and Brenda. She was wearing her college basketball uniform, and he had his arm around her. Both were smiling, but the smiles looked more of the 'say cheese' variety than anything approaching genuine joy. The caption read something about the father and daughter during 'a happier time'. Media melodrama.

Myron turned to page A-9. There was a smaller photograph of Brenda and then, more interestingly, a photograph of Horace Slaughter's nephew, Terence Edwards, candidate for state senate. According to the caption, the photograph had been taken at 'a recent campaign stop.' Hmm. Terence Edwards looked pretty much as he had in the photographs at his mother's house. With one important difference: in this picture Terence was standing next to Arthur Bradford.

Hello.

Myron showed Brenda the photograph. She looked at it a moment. 'Arthur Bradford seems to pop up frequently,' she said.

'Yes.'

'But how does Terence fit into this? He was a kid when my mother ran off.'

Myron shrugged. He checked the kitchen clock. Time to meet Francine. 'I have to run a quick errand,' he said vaguely. 'I shouldn't be long.'

'An errand?' Mom frowned. 'What kind of errand?'

'I'll be back soon.'

Mom magnified the frown, getting her eyebrows into the act. 'But you don't even live here anymore, Myron,' she went on. 'And it's only seven in the morning.' In the morning. In case he mistook it for being seven at night. 'Nothing's even open at seven in the morning.'

Mother Bolitar, Mossad Interrogation.

Myron stood through the grilling. Brenda and Mom weighed him with their eyes. He shrugged and said, 'I'll tell you about it when I come back.' He hurried off, showered, dressed in record time, and jumped into his car.

Francine Neagly had mentioned the Halloween scare. He surmised that this was a kind of code. When they were in high school, about a hundred of their classmates had gone to see the movie *Halloween*. It was a new movie then, just out, and it scared the piss out of everyone. The next day Myron and his friend Eric had dressed up like the murderous Michael Myers – i.e., in black and wearing a goalie mask – and hidden in the woods during the girls' gym class. They never approached, just popping into sight every once in a while. A few of the kids freaked out and started screaming.

Hey, it was high school. Cut him some slack, okay?

Myron parked the Taurus near the Livingston football field. AstroTurf had replaced grass almost a decade earlier. AstroTurf at a high school. Was that necessary? He climbed through the woods. Sticky dew. His sneakers got wet. He quickly found the old path. Not far from this very spot Myron had made out – necked, to use his parents' terminology – with Nancy Pettino. Sophomore year. Neither one of them liked the other very much, but all their friends had paired up, and they'd both been bored and figured what the hell.

Ah, young love.

Francine sat in full uniform on the same big rock the two fake Michael Myers had stood upon nearly two decades ago. Her back was to him. She did not bother to turn around when he approached. He stopped a few feet from her.

'Francine?'

She let out a deep breath and said, 'What the hell is going on, Myron?'

In their high school days Francine had been something of a tomboy, the kind of fierce, spunky competitor you could not help envying. She tackled everything with energy and relish, her voice daunting and confident. Right now she was balled up on the rock, hugging her knees to her chest and rocking back and forth.

'Why don't you tell me?' Myron said.

'Don't play games with me.'

'I'm not playing games.'

'Why did you want to see that file?'

'I told you. I'm not sure it was an accident.'

'What makes you unsure?'

'Nothing concrete. Why? What happened?'

Francine shook her head. 'I want to know what's going on,' she said. 'The whole story.'

'Nothing to tell.'

'Right. Yesterday you woke up and you said to yourself, "Hey, that accidental death that occurred twenty years ago, I bet it wasn't an accident at all. So I'll go ask my old buddy Francine to get the police file for me." That what happened, Myron?'

'No.'

'So start talking.'

Myron hesitated a moment. 'Let's say that I'm right, that Elizabeth Bradford's death was not an accident. And let's say there is something in those files that proves it. That would mean the police covered it up, right?'

She shrugged, still not looking at him. 'Maybe.'

'And maybe they would want it to stay buried.'

'Maybe.'

'So maybe they would want to know what I know. Maybe they would even send an old friend to make me talk.'

Francine's head snapped around as if someone had pulled a string. 'You accusing me of something, Myron?'

'No,' he said. 'But if there's a cover-up going on, how do I know I can trust you?'

She rehugged her knees. 'Because there is no cover-up,' she said. 'I saw the file. A little thin, but nothing unusual. Elizabeth Bradford fell. There were no signs of a struggle.'

'They did an autopsy?'

'Yep. She landed on her head. The impact crushed her skull.'

'Tox screen?'

'They didn't run one.'

'Why not?'

'She died from a fall, not an overdose.'

'But a tox screen would have shown if she'd been drugged,' Myron said.

'So?'

'There were no signs of a struggle, okay, but what would have prevented someone from drugging her and then dumping her over the side?'

Francine made a face. 'And maybe little green men pushed her.'

'Hey, if this was a poor couple and the wife had accidentally fallen off her fire escape—'

'But this wasn't a poor couple, Myron. It was the Bradfords. Did they get preferential treatment? Probably. But even if Elizabeth Bradford had been drugged, it still doesn't add up to murder. Quite the opposite, in fact.'

Now it was Myron's turn to look confused. 'How do you figure?'

'The fall was only three stories,' Francine said. 'A short three stories.'

'So?'

'So a murderer who pushed her off that terrace could not have counted on that low a fall killing her. More likely she would have just broken a leg or something.'

Myron stopped. He had not thought of that. But it made sense. Pushing someone off a third-floor balcony with the hopes that she would land on her head and die was risky at best. Arthur Bradford did not strike Myron as a man who took risks.

So what did that mean?

'Maybe she was hit over the head beforehand,' Myron tried.

Francine shook her head. 'The autopsy didn't show any signs of an earlier blow. And they also checked the rest of the house. There was no blood anywhere. They might have cleaned it up, of course, but I doubt we'll ever know.'

'So there's absolutely nothing suspicious in the report?'

'Nothing,' she said.

Myron raised his hands. 'So why are we out here? Trying to recapture our lost youth?'

Francine looked at him. 'Somebody broke into my house.'

'What?'

'After I read the file. It was supposed to look like a burglary, but it was a search. A thorough one. The place is trashed. Then right after that Roy Pomeranz calls me. Remember him?'

'No.'

'He was Wickner's old partner.'

'Oh, right,' Myron said, 'an early musclehead?'

'That's him. He's chief of detectives now. So yesterday he calls me into his office, something he's never done before. He wants to know why I was looking at the old Bradford file.'

'What did you tell him?'

'I made up some bullshit story about studying old police techniques.'

Myron made a face. 'And Pomeranz bought that?'

'No, he didn't buy it,' Francine snapped. 'He wanted to slam me against a wall and shake the truth out of me. But he was afraid. He was pretending like his questions were just routine, no big deal, but you should have seen his face. He looked maybe half an egg sandwich away from a coronary. He claimed that he was worried about the implications of what I was doing because it was an election year. I nodded a lot and apologized and bought his story about as much as he bought mine. When I drove home, I spotted a tail. I shook it this morning, and here we are.'

'And they trashed your place?'

'Yup. The work of professionals.' Francine stood now and moved closer to him. 'So now that I've stepped into a pail of snakes for you, you want to tell me why I'm taking all these bites?'

Myron considered his options, but there weren't any. He had indeed gotten her into this mess. She had a right to know.

'You read this morning's paper?' he asked.

'Yes.'

'You see the story on the murder of Horace Slaughter?'

'Yes.' Then she held a hand out as though to silence him. 'There was a Slaughter in the file. But it was a woman. A maid or something. She found the body.'

'Anita Slaughter. The victim's wife.'

Her face lost a little color. 'Oh, Christ, I don't like the sound of this. Go on.'

So he did. He told her the whole story. When he finished, Francine looked down below them at the patch of grass where she had captained the field hockey team. She chewed on her lower lip.

'One thing,' she said. 'I don't know if it's important or not. But Anita Slaughter had been assaulted before Elizabeth Bradford's death.'

Myron took a step back. 'What do you mean, assaulted?'

'In the report. Wickner wrote that the witness, Anita Slaughter, still displayed abrasions from the earlier assault.'

'What assault? When?'

'I don't know. That's all it said.'

'So how do we find out?'

'There might be a police report on it in the basement,' she said. 'But—'

'Right, you can't risk it.'

Francine checked her watch. She moved toward him. 'I got some errands to run before I start my shift.'

'Be careful,' he said. 'Assume your phone is tapped and your house bugged. Assume at all times you're being followed. If you spot a tail, call me on the cell phone.'

Francine Neagly nodded. Then she looked down at the field again. 'High school,' she said softly. 'Ever miss it?'

Myron looked at her.

She smiled. 'Yeah, me neither.'

19

On the ride back to his house the cell phone rang. Myron picked it up.

'I got the information on Slaughter's credit card.' Win. Another one who loved to exchange pleasantries. It was still before eight in the morning.

Myron said, 'You're awake?'

'My God, man.' Win waited a beat. 'What gave it away?'

'No, I mean, you usually sleep late.'

'I haven't gone to bed yet.'

'Oh.' Myron almost asked what he'd been doing, but he knew better. When it came to Win and the night, ignorance was quite often bliss.

'Only one charge in the past two weeks,' Win said. 'A week ago Thursday Horace used his Discover card at the Holiday Inn in Livingston.'

Myron shook his head. Livingston. Again. The day before Horace vanished. 'How much?'

'Twenty-six dollars even.'

Curious amount. 'Thanks.'

Click.

Livingston. Horace Slaughter had been in Livingston. Myron replayed the theory that had been rumbling in his head since last night. It was looking better and better.

By the time he got back to his house, Brenda was showered and dressed. The cornrows in her hair cascaded down her shoulders in a wondrous dark wave.

The *café con leche* skin was luminous. She gave him a smile that corkscrewed right through his heart.

He wanted very much to hold her.

'I called Aunt Mabel,' Brenda said. 'People are gathering at her house.'

'I'll drop you off.'

They said good-bye to Mom. Mom warned them sternly not to talk to the police without an attorney present. And to wear seat belts.

When they got in the car, Brenda said, 'Your parents are great.'

'Yeah, I guess they are.'

'You're lucky.'

He nodded.

Silence. Then Brenda said, 'I keep waiting for one of us to say, "About last night."'

Myron smiled. 'Me too.'

'I don't want to forget it.'

Myron swallowed. 'Neither do I.'

'So what do we do?'

'I don't know.'

'Decisiveness,' she said. 'I love that in a man.'

He smiled again and turned right on Hobart Gap Road.

Brenda said, 'I thought West Orange was the other way.'

'I want to make a quick stop, if you don't mind.'

'Where?'

'The Holiday Inn. According to your father's charge cards, he was there a week ago Thursday. It was the last time he used any of his cards. I think he met someone for a meal or drinks.'

'How do you know he didn't stay overnight?'

'The charge was for twenty-six dollars even. That's too low for a room yet too high for a meal for one. It's also a straight twenty-six dollars. No cents. When people tip, they often round off. Best guess is that he met someone there for lunch.'

'So what are you going to do?'

Myron gave a half shrug. 'I have the photograph of Horace from the paper. I'm going to show it around and see what happens.'

On Route 10 he made a left and pulled into the Holiday Inn lot. They were less than two miles from Myron's house. The Holiday Inn was a typical two-level highway motel. Myron had last been here four years ago. An old high school buddy's bachelor party. Someone had hired a black hooker aptly named Danger. Danger put on a supposed 'sex show' far closer to freaky than erotic. She also handed out business cards. They read: 'FOR A GOOD TIME, CALL DANGER.' Original. And now that Myron thought about it, he bet that Danger was not even her real name.

'You want to wait in the car?' he asked.

Brenda shook her head. 'I'll walk around a little.'

The lobby had prints of flowers on the wall. The carpet was pale green. The reception desk was on the right. A plastic sculpture that looked like two fish tails stuck together was on the left. Serious ugly.

Breakfast was still being served. Buffet-style. Dozens of people jockeyed about the spread, moving as though choreographed – step forward, spoon food onto plate, step back, step right, step forward again. Nobody bumped into anyone else. Hands and mouths were a blur. The whole thing looked a bit like a Discovery Channel special on the anthill.

A perky hostess stepped up to him. 'How many?'

Myron put on his best cop face, adding just a hint of a smile. From his Peter Jennings line – professional yet accessible. He cleared his throat and asked, 'Have you seen this man?' Just like that. No preamble.

He held up the photograph from the newspaper. The perky hostess studied it. She did not ask who he was; as he had hoped, his demeanor made her assume that he was someone official.

'I'm not the one to ask,' the hostess said. 'You should speak to Caroline.'

'Caroline?' Myron Bolitar, Parrot Investigator.

'Caroline Gundeck. She was the one who had lunch with him.'

Every once in a while you just get lucky.

'Would that have been last Thursday?' he asked.

The hostess thought about it a moment. 'I think so, yeah.'

'Where can I find Miss Gundeck?'

'Her office is on level B. Down at the end of the corridor.'

'Caroline Gundeck works here?' He'd been told that Caroline Gundeck has an office on level B, and just like that he'd deduced that she worked here. Sherlock reincarnated.

'Caroline's worked here forever,' the hostess said with a friendly eye roll.

'What's her title?'

'Food and beverage manager.'

Hmm. Her occupation was not enlightening – unless Horace had been planning to throw a party before his murder. Doubtful. Nonetheless, this was a solid clue. He took the steps down to the basement and quickly found her office. But his luck did not hold. A secretary informed him that Miss Gundeck was not in today. Was she expected? The secretary would not say. Could he get her home number? The secretary frowned. Myron did not push it. Caroline Gundeck had to live in the area.

Getting her phone number and address would be no problem.

Back in the corridor Myron dialed information. He asked for Gundeck in Livingston. Nothing. He asked for Gundeck in East Hanover or the area. Bingo. There was a C Gundeck in Whippany. Myron dialed the number. After four rings a machine picked up. Myron left a message.

When he came back up to the lobby, he found Brenda standing alone in a corner. Her face looked drained, her eyes wide as though someone had just poked her hard in the solar plexus. She did not move or even glance his way as he approached.

'What is it?' he asked.

Brenda gulped some air and turned to him. 'I think I've been here before,' she said.

'When?'

'A long time ago. I don't remember really. It's just a feeling . . . or maybe I'm just imagining. But I think I was here as a little kid. With my mother.'

Silence.

'Do you remember—'

'Nothing,' Brenda interrupted him. 'I'm not even sure it was here. Maybe it was another motel. It's not like this one is special. But I think it was here. That weird sculpture. It's familiar.'

'What were you wearing?' he tried.

She shook her head. 'I don't know.'

'What about your mother? What was she wearing?'

'What are you, a fashion consultant?'

'I'm just trying to jar something loose.'

'I don't remember anything. She vanished when I was five. How much do you remember from back then?'

Point taken. 'Let's walk around a little,' he suggested. 'See if something comes back to you.'

But nothing surfaced, if indeed there was anything there to surface. Myron had not expected anything anyway. He was not big on repressed memory or any of that stuff. Still the whole episode was curious, and once again it fit into this scenario. As they made their way back to Myron's car, he decided that it was time to voice his theory.

'I think I know what your father was doing.'

Brenda stopped and looked at him. Myron kept moving. He got into the car. Brenda followed. The car doors closed.

Myron said, 'I think Horace was looking for your mother.'

The words took a moment to sink in. Then Brenda leaned back and said, 'Tell me why.'

He started up the car. 'Okay, but remember I used the word *think*. I *think* that's what he was doing. I don't have any real proof.'

'Okay, go ahead.'

He took a deep breath. 'Let's start with your father's phone records. One, he calls Arthur Bradford's campaign headquarters several times. Why? As far as we know, there is only one connection between your father and Bradford.'

'The fact that my mother worked in his house.'

'Right. Twenty years ago. But here's something else to consider. When I started searching for your mother, I stumbled upon the Bradfords. I thought they might somehow be connected. Your father might have come to the same conclusion.'

She looked less than impressed. 'What else?'

'The phone records again. Horace called the two attorneys who handled your scholarships.'

'So?'

'So why would he call them?'

'I don't know.'

'Your scholarships are strange, Brenda. Especially the first one. You weren't even a basketball player yet and you get a vague academic scholarship to a ritzy private school plus expenses? It doesn't make sense. Scholarships just don't work that way. And I checked. You are the only recipient of the Outreach Education scholarship. They only awarded it that one year.'

'So what are you getting at?'

'Somebody set up those scholarships with the sole intent of helping you, with the sole intent of funneling you money.' He made the U-turn by Daffy Dan's, a discount clothing store, and started heading back down Route 10 toward the circle. 'In other words, somebody was trying to help you out. Your father may have been trying to find out who that was.'

He glanced over at her, but she would not face him now. Her voice, when she finally spoke, was throaty. 'And you think it was my mother?'

Myron tried to tread gently. 'I don't know. But why else would your father call Thomas Kincaid so many times? The man had not handled your scholarship money since you left high school. You read that letter. Why would Horace pester him to the point of near harassment? The only thing I can think of is that Kincaid had information that your father wanted.'

'Where the scholarship money originated from?'

'Right. My guess is, if we can trace that back' – again, tread gently – 'we would find something very interesting.'

'Can we do that?'

'I'm not sure. The attorneys will undoubtedly claim privilege. But I'm going to put Win on it. If it involves money, he'll have the connections to track it down.'

Brenda sat back and tried to digest all this. 'Do you think my father traced it back?'

'I doubt it, but I don't know. Either way your father was starting to make some noise. He hit up the lawyers, and he even went so far as to start questioning Arthur Bradford. That was where he probably went too far. Even if there'd been no wrongdoing, Bradford would not be happy with someone poking into his past, raising old ghosts, especially during an election year.'

'So he killed my father?'

Myron was not sure how to answer that one. 'It's too early to say for sure. But let's assume for a second that your father did a little too much poking. And let's also assume the Bradfords scared him off with a beating.'

Brenda nodded. 'The blood in the locker.'

'Right. I keep wondering why we found the blood there, why Horace didn't go home to change or recuperate. My guess is he was beaten near the hospital. In Livingston, at the very least.'

'Where the Bradfords live.'

Myron nodded. 'And if Horace escaped from the beating or if he was just afraid they'd come after him again, he wouldn't go home. He'd probably change at the hospital and run. In the morgue I noticed clothes in the corner – a security guard uniform. It was probably what he changed into when he got to the locker. Then he hit the road and—'

Myron stopped.

'And what?' she asked.

'Damn,' Myron said.

'What?'

'What's Mabel's phone number?'

Brenda gave it to him. 'Why?'

Myron switched on the cell phone and dialed Lisa at

Bell Atlantic. He asked her to check the number. It took Lisa about two minutes.

'Nothing official on it,' Lisa said. 'But I checked the line. There's a noise there.'

'Meaning?'

'Someone's probably got a tap on it. Internal. You'd have to send someone by there to be sure.'

Myron thanked her and hung up. 'They have Mabel's phone tapped too. That's probably how they found your father. He called your aunt, and they traced it.'

'So who's behind the tap?'

'I don't know,' Myron said.

Silence. They passed the Star-Bright Pizzeria. In Myron's youth it was rumored that a whorehouse operated out of the back. Myron had gone several times there with his family. When his dad went to the bathroom, Myron followed. Nothing.

'There's something else that doesn't make sense,' Brenda said.

'What?'

'Even if you're right about the scholarships, where would my mother get that kind of money?'

Good question. 'How much did she take from your dad?'

'Fourteen thousand, I think.'

'If she invested well, that might be enough. There were seven years between the time she disappeared and the first scholarship payment, so . . .' Myron calculated the figures in his head. Fourteen grand to start. Hmm. Anita Slaughter would have had to score big to make the money last this long. Possible, sure, but even in the Reagan years, not likely.

Hold the phone.

'She may have found another way to get money,' he said slowly.

'How?'

Myron stayed quiet for a moment. The head gears were churning again. He checked his rearview mirror. If there was a tail, he didn't spot it. But that did not mean much. A casual glance rarely gave it away. You had to watch the cars, memorize them, study their movements. But he could not concentrate on that. Not right now.

'Myron?'

'I'm thinking.'

She looked like she was about to say something but then thought better of it.

'Suppose,' Myron continued, 'your mother did learn something about the death of Elizabeth Bradford.'

'Didn't we already try this?'

'Just stay with me a second, okay? Before, we came up with two possibilities. One, she was scared and ran. Two, they tried to hurt her and she ran.'

'And now you have a third?'

'Sort of.' He drove past the new Starbucks on the corner of Mount Pleasant Avenue. He wanted to stop – his caffeine craving worked like a magnetic pull – but he pushed on. 'Suppose your mother did run away. And suppose once she was safe, she demanded money to keep quiet.'

'You think she blackmailed the Bradfords?'

'More like compensation.' He spoke even as the ideas were still forming. Always a dangerous thing. 'Your mother sees something. She realizes that the only way to guarantee her safety, and her family's safety, is to run away and hide. If the Bradfords find her, they'll kill her. Plain and simple. If she tries to do something cute – like hide evidence in a safety-deposit box in the event she disappears or something like that – they'll torture her until she tells them where it is. Your mother has no choice. She has to run. But she wants to take care of her daughter too. So she makes sure that her daughter gets all the things she herself could never have provided for her. A top-quality education. A chance to live on a pristine campus instead of the bowels of Newark. Stuff like that.'

More silence.

Myron waited. He was voicing theories too fast now, not giving his brain a chance to process or even to inspect his words. He stopped now, letting everything settle.

'Your scenarios,' Brenda said. 'You're always looking to put my mother in the best light. It blinds you, I think.'

'How so?'

'I'll ask you again: If all that is true, why didn't she take me with her?'

'She was on the run from killers. What kind of mother would want to put her child in that kind of danger?'

'And she was so paranoid that she could never call me? Or see me?'

'Paranoid?' Myron repeated. 'These guys have a tap on your phone. They have people tailing you. Your father is dead.'

Brenda shook her head. 'You don't get it.'

'Get what?'

Her eyes were watery now, but she kept her tone a little too even. 'You can make all the excuses you want, but you can't get around the fact that she abandoned her child. Even if she had good reason, even if she was this wonderful self-sacrificing mother who did all this to protect me, why would she let her daughter go on believing that her own mother would abandon her? Didn't she realize how this would devastate a five-year-old girl? Couldn't she have found some way to tell her the truth – even after all these years?'

Her child. *Her* daughter. Tell *her* the truth. Never *I* or *me*. Interesting. But Myron kept silent. He had no answer to that one.

They drove past the Kessler Institute and hit a traffic light. After some time had passed, Brenda said, 'I still want to go to practice this afternoon.'

Myron nodded. He understood. The court was comfort.

'And I want to play in the opener.'

Again Myron nodded. It was probably what Horace would have wanted too.

They made the turn near Mountain High School and arrived at Mabel Edwards's house. There were at least a dozen cars parked on the road, most American-made, most older and beaten up. A formally dressed black couple stood by the door. The man pressed the bell. The woman held a platter of food. When they spotted Brenda, they glared at her and then turned their backs.

'They've read the papers, I see,' Brenda said.

'No one thinks you did it.'

Her look told him to stop with the patronizing.

They walked her to the front door and stood behind the couple. The couple huffed and looked away. The man tapped his foot. The woman made a production out of sighing. Myron opened his mouth, but Brenda closed it with a firm shake of her head. Already she was reading him.

Someone opened the door. There were lots of people already inside. All nicely dressed. All black. Funny how Myron kept noticing that. A black couple. Black people inside. Last night at the barbecue he had not found it strange that everyone except Brenda was white. In fact, Myron could not recall a black person ever attending one of the neighborhood barbecues. So why should he be surprised to be the only white person here? And why should it make him feel funny?

The couple disappeared inside as though sucked up by a vortex. Brenda hesitated. When they finally stepped through the doorway, it was like something out of a saloon scene in a John Wayne film. The low murmurs ceased as if somebody had snapped off a radio. Everyone turned and glowered. For a half a second Myron thought it was a racial thing – he being the only white guy – but then he saw the animosity was aimed directly at the grieving daughter.

Brenda was right. They thought she did it.

The room was crowded and sweltering. Fans whirred impotently. Men were hooking fingers into collars to let in air. Sweat coated faces. Myron looked at Brenda. She looked small and alone and scared, but she would not look away. He felt her take his hand. He gripped back. She stood ramrod straight now, her head high.

The crowd parted a bit, and Mabel Edwards stepped into view. Her eyes were red and swollen. A handkerchief was balled up in her fist. They all swung their gazes toward Mabel now, awaiting her reaction. When Mabel saw her niece, she spread her hands and beckoned Brenda forward. Brenda did not hesitate. She sprinted into the thick, soft arms, lowered her head onto Mabel's shoulder, and for the first time truly sobbed. Not cried. These were gut-wrenching sobs.

Mabel rocked her niece back and forth and patted her back and cooed comfort. At the same time, Mabel's eyes scanned the room, mother wolf-protective, challenging and then extinguishing any glare that might be aimed in the direction of her niece.

The crowd turned away, and the murmur returned to normal. Myron felt the stomach knots begin to loosen.

He scanned the room for familiar faces. He recognized a couple of the ballplayers from his past, guys he had played against on the playground or in high school. A couple nodded hellos. Myron nodded back. A little boy just past the toddler stage sprinted through the room imitating a siren. Myron recognized him from the pictures on the mantel. Mabel Edwards's grandson. Terence Edwards's son.

Speaking of whom, where was candidate Edwards?

Myron scanned the room again. No sign of him. In front of him Mabel and Brenda finally broke their hold. Brenda wiped her eyes. Mabel pointed her toward a bathroom. Brenda managed a nod and hurried off.

Mabel approached him, her gaze on him and unwavering. Without preamble she asked, 'Do you know who killed my brother?'

'No.'

'But you're going to find out.'

'Yes.'

'Do you have a thought?'

'A thought,' Myron said. 'Nothing more.'

She nodded again. 'You're a good man, Myron.'

There was a shrine of some sort on the fireplace. A photograph of a smiling Horace was surrounded by flowers and candles. Myron looked at the smile he had not seen in ten years and would never see again.

He did not feel like a good man.

'I'll need to ask you some more questions,' Myron said.

'Whatever it takes.'

'About Anita too.'

Mabel's eyes stayed on him. 'You still think she's connected with all this?'

'Yes. I'd also like to send a man around to check your phone.'

'Why?'

'I think it's tapped.'

Mabel looked confused. 'But who would tap my phone?'

Better not to speculate right now. 'I don't know,' Myron said. 'But when your brother called, did he mention the Holiday Inn in Livingston?'

Something happened to her eyes. 'Why do you want to know that?'

'Evidently Horace had lunch with a manager there the day before he disappeared. It was the last charge on his credit card. And when we stopped by, Brenda thought she recognized it. That she may have been there with Anita.'

Mabel closed her eyes.

'What?' Myron asked.

More mourners entered the house, all carrying platters of food. Mabel accepted their words of sympathy with a kind smile and a firm hand grasp. Myron waited.

When there was a free second, Mabel said, 'Horace never mentioned the Holiday Inn on the phone.'

'But there's something else,' Myron said.

'Yes.'

'Did Anita ever take Brenda to the Holiday Inn?'

Brenda stepped back into the room and looked at them. Mabel put her hand on Myron's arm. 'Now is not the time for this,' Mabel said to him.

He nodded.

'Tonight maybe. Do you think you can come alone?'

'Yes.'

Mabel Edwards left him then to attend to Horace's family and friends. Myron felt like an outsider again, but this time it had nothing to do with skin color.

He left quickly.

20

Once on the road Myron switched his cellular phone back on. Two incoming calls. One was from Esperanza at the office, the other from Jessica in Los Angeles. He briefly debated what to do. No question really. He dialed Jessica's hotel suite. Was it wimpy to call her right back? Maybe. But Myron looked at it as one of his more mature moments. Call him whipped, but engaging in head games had never been his style.

The hotel operator connected him, but there was no answer. He left a message. Then he dialed the office.

'We got a big problem,' Esperanza said.

'On Sunday?' Myron said.

'The Lord may take it off, but not team owners.'

'Did you hear about Horace Slaughter?' he asked.

'Yes,' she said. 'I'm sorry about your friend, but we still got a business to run. And a problem.'

'What?'

'The Yankees are going to trade Lester Ellis. To Seattle. They've scheduled a news conference first thing tomorrow morning.'

Myron rubbed the bridge of his nose with his pointer and thumb. 'How did you hear?'

'Devon Richards.'

Reliable source. Damn. 'Does Lester know?'

'Nope.'

'He'll have a fit.'

'Don't I know it.'

'Suggestions?'

'Not a one,' Esperanza said. 'A fringe benefit of being the underling.'

The call waiting clicked. 'I'll call you back.' He switched lines and said hello.

Francine Neagly said, 'I'm being tailed.'

'Where are you?'

'The A and P off the circle.'

'What kind of car?'

'Blue Buick Skylark. Few years old. White top.'

'Got a plate?'

'New Jersey, four-seven-six-four-five T.'

Myron thought a moment. 'When do you start your shift?'

'Half an hour.'

'You working the car or the desk?'

'Desk.'

'Good, I'll pick him up there.'

'Pick him up?'

'If you're staying in the station, he's not going to waste a beautiful Sunday hanging outside it. I'm going to follow him.'

'Tail the tailer?'

'Right. Take Mount Pleasant to Livingston Avenue. I'll pick him up there.'

'Hey, Myron?'

'Yeah.'

'If something big goes down, I want in.'

'Sure.'

They hung up. Myron backtracked to Livingston. He parked along Memorial Circle near the turnoff to Livingston Avenue. Good view of the police station and easy access to all routes. Myron kept the car running and watched the townsfolk handle Memorial Circle's half-mile perimeter. A tremendous variety of Livingstonites frequented 'the circle'. There were old ladies pacing slowly, usually in twos, some of the more adventurous swinging tiny barbells. There were couples in their fifties and sixties, many in matching sweat suits. Cute, sort of. Teenagers ambled, their mouths getting a far better workout than any extremity or cardiovascular muscle. Hard-core joggers raced past them all with nary a glance. They wore sleek sunglasses and firm faces and sported bare midriffs. Bare midriffs. Even the men. What was up with that?

He forced himself not to think about kissing Brenda. Or how it felt when she smiled at him across the picnic table. Or how her face flushed when she got excited. Or how animated she'd gotten when talking to people at the barbecue. Or how tender she'd been with Timmy when she put on that bandage.

Good thing he wasn't thinking about her.

For a brief moment he wondered if Horace would approve. Strange thought, really. But there it was. Would his old mentor approve? He wondered. He wondered what it would be like to date a black woman. Was there attraction in the taboo? Repulsion? Concern for the future? He pictured the two of them living in the suburbs, the pediatrician and the sports agent, a mixed couple with similar dreams, and then he realized how dumb it was for a man in love with a woman in Los Angeles to think such nonsense about a woman he'd only known for two days.

Dumb. Yup.

A blonde hard-core jogger dressed in tight magenta shorts and a much-tested white sports bra jogged by his car. She looked inside and smiled at him. Myron smiled back. The bare midriff. You take the good with the bad.

Across the street Francine Neagly pulled into the police station driveway. Myron shifted into drive and kept his foot on the brake. The Buick Skylark passed the station without slowing down. Myron had tried to trace the license plate from his source at the Department of Motor Vehicles, but hey, it was Sunday, it was the DMV, you put it together.

He pulled onto Livingston Avenue and followed the Buick south. He kept four cars back and craned his neck. Nobody was pushing hard on the accelerator. Livingston took its time on Sunday. But that was okay. The Buick came to a stop at a traffic light at Northfield Avenue. On the right was a brick minimall of some sort. When Myron had been growing up, the same building had been Roosevelt Elementary School; twenty-some-odd years ago someone decided what New Jersey really needed were fewer schools and more malls. Foresight.

The Skylark turned right. Myron kept back and did likewise. They were heading toward Route 10 again, but before they had gone even half a mile, the Skylark made a left onto Crescent Road. Myron frowned. Small suburban street, mostly used to cut through to Hobart Gap Road. Hmm. It probably meant that Mr. Skylark knew the town fairly well and was not an outsider.

A quick right followed the left. Myron knew now where the Skylark was headed. There was only one thing nestled into this suburban landscape besides the split-level homes and a barely flowing brook. A Little League field.

Meadowbrook Little League field. Two fields actually. Sunday and sun meant the road and parking lot were packed with vehicles. So-called utility trucks and minivans had replaced the wood-paneled station wagons of Myron's youth, but little else had changed. The lot was still unpaved gravel. The concession booth was still white cement with green trim and run by volunteer moms. The stands were still metal and rickety and filled with parents cheering a tad too loudly.

The Buick Skylark grabbed an illegal space near the backstop. Myron slowed the car and waited. When the door of the Skylark opened and Detective Wickner, the lead officer in the Elizabeth Bradford 'accident', swept out of the car in grand style, Myron was not really surprised. The retired officer took off his sunglasses with a snap and tossed them back into the car. He put on a baseball cap, green with the letter S on it. You could almost see Wickner's lined face slacken as though the field's sunlight were the most gentle masseur. Wickner waved to some guys standing behind the backstop – the Eli Wickner Backstop, according to the sign. The guys waved back. Wickner bounded toward them.

Myron stayed where he was for a moment. Detective Eli Wickner had hung out in the same spot since before the days Myron had frequented this field. Wickner's Throne. People greeted him here. They came up and slapped his back and shook his hand; Myron half expected them to kiss his ring. Wickner was beaming now. At home. In paradise. In the place where he was still a big man.

Time to change that.

Myron found a parking spot a block away. He hopped out of the car and approached. His feet crunched the gravel. He traveled back to a time when he walked upon this same surface with soft kid cleats. Myron had been a good Little League player – no, he'd been a *great* player – until the age of eleven. It'd been right here, on Field Two. He'd led the league in home runs and seemed on the verge of breaking the all-time Livingston American League Little League record. He needed to hit two more homers with four games left. Twelve-year-old Joey Davito was pitching. Davito threw hard and with no control. The first pitch hit

Myron square on the forehead, right under the brim of the helmet. Myron went down. He remembered blinking when he landed on his back. He remembered looking up into the glare of the sun. He remembered seeing the face of his coach, Mr. Farley. And then his father was there. Dad blinked back tears and scooped him up in his strong arms, gently cradling Myron's head with his large hand. He'd gone to the hospital, but there was no lasting damage. At least not physical. But after that Myron had never been able to stop from bailing out on an inside pitch. Baseball was never the same to him. The game had hurt him, had lost its innocence.

He stopped playing for good a year later.

There were half a dozen guys with Wickner. They all wore baseball caps sitting high and straight, no breaks in the brims, like you see with the kids. White T-shirts were stretched across bellies that resembled swallowed bowling balls. Bodies by Budweiser. They leaned against the fence, elbows draped over the top like they were taking a Sunday ride in a car. They commented on the kids, inspecting them, dissecting their games, predicting their futures – as though their opinions mattered a rat's ass.

There is a lot of pain in Little League. Much has been written in recent years criticizing the pushy Little League parents – deservedly so – but the namby-pamby, politically correct, everybody equal, semi-New Age alternative was not much better. A kid hits a weak grounder. Disappointed, he sighs and walks toward first. He is thrown out by a mile and sulks straight to the dugout. The New Age coach yells, 'Good hustle!' But of course it wasn't good hustle. So what message are you sending? The parents pretend that winning is irrelevant, that the best player on the team should not get more playing time or a better batting position than the worst. But the problem with all this – besides the obvious fact that it's a lie – is that the kids are not fooled. Kids aren't dumb. They know that they are being patronized with all this 'as long as he's having fun' talk. And they resent it.

So the pain remains. It probably would always be there.

Several people recognized Myron. They tapped their neighbors' shoulders and pointed. There he is. Myron Bolitar. The greatest basketball player this town ever produced. Would have been a top pro if . . . If. Fate. The knee. Myron Bolitar. Half legend, half a warning to today's youth. The athletic equivalent to the smashed-up car they used to demonstrate the dangers of drunk driving.

Myron headed straight for the men along the back-stop. Livingston fans. The same guys went to all the football games and basketball games and baseball games. Some were nice. Some were blowhards. All of them recognized Myron. They greeted him warmly. Detective Wickner stayed silent, his eyes glued to the field, studying the play with a little too much intensity, especially since it was between innings.

Myron tapped Wickner on the shoulder.

'Hello, Detective.'

Wickner turned slowly. He'd always had these piercing gray eyes, but right now they were heavily tinged with red. Conjunctivitis maybe. Or allergies. Or booze. Your choice. His skin was tan to the point of rawhide. He wore a yellow collared shirt with a little zipper in the front. The zipper was down. He had on a thick gold chain. New probably. Something to jazz up retirement. It didn't work on him.

Wickner mustered up a smile. 'You're old enough to call me Eli now, Myron.'

Myron tried it. 'How are you, Eli?'

'Not bad, Myron. Retirement's treating me good. I fish a lot. How about yourself? Saw you try that comeback. Sorry it didn't work out.'

'Thanks,' Myron said.

'You still living at your folks'?'

'No, I'm in the city now.'

'So what brings you out this way? Visiting the family?'

Myron shook his head. 'I wanted to talk to you.'

They drifted about ten feet from the entourage. No one followed, their body language working as a force field.

'What about?' Wickner asked.

'An old case.'

'A police case?'

Myron looked at him steadily. 'Yes.'

'And what case would that be?'

'The death of Elizabeth Bradford.'

To Wickner's credit, he skipped the surprise act. He took the baseball cap off his head and smoothed down the gray flyaways. Then he put the cap back on. 'What do you want to know?'

'The bribe,' Myron said. 'Did the Bradfords pay you off in a lump sum, or did they set up a more long-term payout with interest and stuff?'

Wickner took the blow but stayed upright. There was a quiver on the right side of his mouth like he was fighting back tears. 'I don't much like your attitude, son.'

'Tough.' Myron knew that his only chance here was a direct, no-barred frontal assault; dancing around or subtle interrogation would get him squat. 'You've got two choices, Eli. Choice one, you tell me what really happened to Elizabeth Bradford and I try to keep your name out of it. Choice two, I start screaming to the papers about a police cover-up and destroy your reputation.' Myron gestured to the field. 'By the time I'm done with you, you'll be lucky to hang out in the Eli Wickner Urinal.'

Wickner turned away. Myron could see his shoulders rising and falling with the labored breaths. 'I don't know what you're talking about.'

Myron hesitated a beat. Then he kept his voice soft. 'What happened to you, Eli?'

'What?'

'I used to look up to you,' Myron said. 'I used to care what you thought.'

The words struck home. Wickner's shoulders began to hitch a bit. He kept his face low. Myron waited. Wickner finally turned to face him. The rawhide skin looked drier now, sapped, more brittle. He was working up to saying something. Myron gave him space and waited.

From behind him Myron felt a large hand squeeze his shoulder.

'There a problem here?'

Myron spun around. The hand belonged to Chief of Detectives Roy Pomeranz, the musclehead who used to be Wickner's partner. Pomeranz wore a white T-shirt and white shorts that rode so high it looked like someone was giving him a power wedgie. He still had the he-man physique, but he was totally bald now, his head completely smooth as though waxed.

'Get your hand off my shoulder,' Myron said.

Pomeranz ignored the request. 'Everything okay here?'

Wickner spoke up. 'We were just talking, Roy.'

'Talking about what?'

Myron handled that one. 'About you.'

Big smile. 'Oh?'

Myron pointed. 'We were just saying that if you got a hoop earring, you'd be the spitting image of Mr. Clean.'

Pomeranz's smile vanished.

Myron lowered his voice. 'I'll tell you one more time. Move your hand, or I'll break it in three places.' Note the three-places reference. Specific threats were always the best. He'd learned that from Win.

Pomeranz kept the hand there a second or two longer – to keep face – and then he slid it off.

'You're still on the force, Roy,' Myron said. 'So you got the most to lose. But I'll make you the same offer. Tell me what you know about the Bradford case, and I'll try to keep your name out of it.'

Pomeranz smirked at him. 'Funny thing, Bolitar.'

'What?'

'You digging into all this in an election year.'

'Your point being?'

'You're working for Davison,' he said. 'You're just trying to drag down a good man like Arthur Bradford for that scum sucker.'

Davison was Bradford's opponent for governor. 'Sorry, Roy, that's incorrect.'

'Yeah? Well, either way, Elizabeth Bradford died from a fall.'

'Who pushed her?'

'It was an accident.'

'Someone accidentally pushed her?'

'Nobody pushed her, wise guy. It was late at night. The terrace was slippery. She fell. It was an accident. Happens all the time.'

'Really? How many deaths has Livingston had in the past twenty years where a woman accidentally fell to her death from her own balcony?'

Pomeranz crossed his arms over his chest. His biceps

bulged like baseballs. The guy was doing one of those subtle flexes, where you're trying to look like you're not flexing. 'Accidents in the home. You know how many people die in home accidents every year?'

'No, Roy, how many?'

Pomeranz didn't answer. Big surprise. He met Wickner's eye. Wickner remained silent. He looked vaguely ashamed.

Myron decided to go for the whammy. 'And what about the assault on Anita Slaughter? Was that an accident too?'

Stunned silence. Wickner involuntarily groaned a little. Pomeranz's thigh-thick arms dropped back to his sides.

Pomeranz said, 'I don't know what you're talking about.'

'Sure you do, Roy. Eli even alluded to it in the police file.'

Angry smirk. 'You mean the file that Francine Neagly stole from the records room?'

'She didn't steal it, Roy. She looked at it.'

Pomeranz smiled slowly. 'Well, it's missing now. She had it last. We firmly believe that Officer Neagly stole it.'

Myron shook his head. 'Not that easy, Roy. You can hide that file. You can even hide the file on the Anita Slaughter assault. But I already got my hand on the hospital file. From St. Barnabas. They keep records, Roy.'

More stunned looks. It was a bluff. But it was a good one. And it drew blood.

Pomeranz leaned very close to Myron, his breath reeking of a poorly digested meal. He kept his voice low. 'You're poking your nose where it don't belong.'

Myron nodded. 'And you're not brushing after every meal.'

'I'm not going to let you drag down a good man with false innuendos.'

'Innuendos,' Myron repeated. 'You been listening to vocabulary tapes in the squad car, Roy? Do the taxpayers know about this?'

'You're playing a dangerous game, funny man.'

'Oooo, I'm so scared.' When short a comeback, fall back on the classics.

'I don't have to start with you,' Pomeranz said. He leaned back a bit, the smile returning. 'I got Francine Neagly.'

'What about her?'

'She had no business with that file. We believe that someone in Davison's campaign – probably you, Bolitar – paid her to steal it. To gather any information that can be used in a distorted fashion to hurt Arthur Bradford.'

Myron frowned. 'Distorted fashion?'

'You think I won't do it?'

'I don't even know what that means. Distorted fashion? Was that on one of your tapes?'

Pomeranz stuck a finger in Myron's face. 'You think I won't suspend her sorry ass and ruin her career?'

'Pomeranz, not even you can be that dumb. You ever heard of Jessica Culver?'

The finger came down. 'She's your girlfriend, right?' Pomeranz said. 'She's a writer or something.'

'A big writer,' Myron said. 'Very well respected. And you know what she would love to do? A big exposé on sexism in police departments. You do anything to Francine Neagly, you so much as demote her or give her one shit detail or breathe on her between meals, and I promise you that when Jessica gets done, you'll make Bob Packwood look like Betty Friedan.'

Pomeranz looked confused. Probably didn't know who Betty Friedan was. Maybe he should have said Gloria Steinem. To his credit, Pomeranz took his time. He fought for recovery, offering up an almost sweet smile.

'Okay,' he said, 'so it's the cold war all over again. I can nuke you, you can nuke me. It's a stalemate.'

'Wrong, Roy. You're the one with the job, the family, the rep, and maybe a looming jail term. Me, I got nothing to lose.'

'You can't be serious. You're dealing with the most powerful family in New Jersey. Do you really think you've got nothing to lose?'

Myron shrugged. 'I'm also crazy,' he said. 'Or to put it another way, my mind works in a distorted fashion.'

Pomeranz looked over at Wickner. Wickner looked back. There was a crack of the bat. The crowd got to its feet. The ball hit the fence. 'Go, Billy!' Billy rounded second and slid into third.

Pomeranz walked away without another word.

Myron looked at Wickner for a long time. 'Are you a total sham, Detective?'

Wickner said nothing.

'When I was eleven, you spoke to my fifth-grade class and we all thought you were the coolest guy we'd ever seen. I used to look for you at games. I used to want your approval. But you're just a lie.'

Wickner kept his eyes on the field. 'Let it go, Myron.'

'I can't.'

'Davison is a scum. He's not worth it.'

'I'm not working for Davison. I'm working for Anita Slaughter's daughter.'

Wickner kept his eyes on the field. His mouth was set, but Myron could see the tremor starting back up in the corner of his mouth. 'All you're going to do is hurt a lot of people.'

'What happened to Elizabeth Bradford?'

'She fell,' he said. 'That's all.'

'I'm not going to stop digging,' Myron said.

Wickner adjusted his cap again and began to walk away. 'Then more people are going to die.'

There was no threat in his tone, just the stilted, pained timber of inevitability.

21

When Myron headed back to his car, the two goons from Bradford Farms were waiting for him. The big one and the skinny, older guy. The skinny guy wore long sleeves so Myron could not see if there was a snake tattoo, but the two looked right from Mabel Edwards's description.

Myron felt something inside him start to simmer.

The big guy was show. Probably a wrestler in high school. Maybe a bouncer at a local bar. He thought he was tough; Myron knew that he would be no problem. The skinny, older guy was hardly a formidable physical specimen. He looked like an aged version of the puny guy who gets the sand kicked on him in the old Charles Atlas cartoon. But the face was so ferretlike, the eyes so beady that he made you pause. Myron knew better than to judge on appearance, but this guy's face was simply too thin and too pointed and too cruel.

Myron spoke to the Skinny Ferret. 'Can I see your tattoo?' Direct approach.

The big guy looked confused, but Skinny Ferret took it all in stride.

'I'm not used to guys using that line on me,' Skinny said.

'Guys,' Myron repeated. 'But with your looks, the chicks must be asking all the time.'

If Skinny was offended by the crack, he was laughing his way through it. 'So you really want to see the snake?'

Myron shook his head. The snake. The question had been answered. These were the right guys. The big one had punched Mabel Edwards in the eye.

The simmer flicked up a notch.

'So what can I do for you fellas?' Myron said. 'You collecting donations for the Kiwanis Club?'

'Yeah,' the big guy said. 'Blood donations.'

Myron looked at him. 'I'm not a grandmother, tough guy.'

Big said, 'Huh?'

Skinny cleared his throat. 'Governor-to-be Bradford would like to see you.'

'Governor-to-be?'

The Skinny Ferret shrugged. 'Confidence.'

'Nice to see. So why doesn't he call me?'

'The next governor thought it would be best if we accompanied you.'

'I think I can manage to drive the mile by myself.' Myron looked at the big guy again and spoke slowly. 'After all, I'm not a grandmother.'

The big guy sniffed and rolled his neck. 'I can still beat you like one.'

'Beat me as you would a grandmother,' Myron said. 'Gee, what a guy.'

Myron had read recently about self-help gurus who taught their students to picture themselves successful. Visualize it, and it will happen or some such credo. Myron was not sure, but he knew that it worked in combat. If the chance presents itself, picture how you will attack. Imagine what countermoves your opponent might make and prepare yourself for them. That was what Myron had been doing since Skinny had admitted to the tattoo. Now that he saw that no one was in sight, he struck.

Myron's knee landed squarely in the big guy's groin.

The big guy made a noise like he was sucking through a straw that still had drops of liquid in it. He folded like an old wallet. Myron pulled out his gun and pointed it at the Skinny Ferret. The big guy's body melted to the pavement and formed a puddle.

The Skinny Ferret had not moved. He looked slightly amused.

'Wasteful,' Skinny said.

'Yeah,' Myron agreed. 'But I feel much better.' He looked at the big guy. 'That was for Mabel Edwards.'

Skinny shrugged. Not a care in the world. 'So now what?'

'Where's your car?' Myron asked.

'We were dropped off. We're supposed to go back to the house with you.'

'I don't think so.'

The big guy writhed and tried to suck in a breath. Neither standing man cared. Myron put away his gun.

'I'll drive myself over, if you don't mind.'

The skinny guy spread his arms. 'Suit yourself.'

Myron started to get into his Taurus.

'You don't know what you're up against,' Skinny said.

'I keep hearing that.'

'Maybe,' he said. 'But now you've heard it from me.'

Myron nodded. 'Consider me scared.'

'Ask your father, Myron.'

That made him pull up. 'What about my father?'

'Ask him about Arthur Bradford.' The smile of a mongoose gnawing on a neck. 'Ask him about me.'

Icy water flooded Myron's chest. 'What does my father have to do with any of this?'

But Skinny was not about to answer. 'Hurry now,' he said. 'The next governor of New Jersey is waiting for you.'

22

Myron put a call into Win. He quickly told him what'd happened.

'Wasteful,' Win agreed.

'He hit a woman.'

'Then shoot him in the knee. Permanently injure him. A kick in the scrotum is wasteful.'

Proper Payback Etiquette by Windsor Horne Lockwood III. 'I'm going to leave the cellular on. Can you get down here?'

'But of course. Please refrain from further violence until I am present.'

In other words: Save some for me.

The guard at Bradford Farms was surprised to see Myron alone. The gate was open, probably in expectation of a threesome. Myron did not hesitate. He drove through without stopping. The guard panicked. He jumped out of his booth. Myron gave him a little finger wave, like Oliver Hardy used to do. He even scrunched up his face into that same Hardy smile. Heck, if he had a bowler, he would have gotten that into the act too.

By the time Myron parked at the front entrance, the old butler was already standing in the doorway. He bowed slightly.

'Please follow me, Mr. Bolitar.'

They headed down a long corridor. Lots of oils on the walls, mostly of men on horses. There was one nude. A woman, of course. No horse in this one. Catherine the Great was truly dead. The butler made a right at the hallway. They entered a glass corridor that resembled a passageway in the Biosphere or maybe Epcot Center. Myron figured that they must have traveled close to fifty yards already.

The manservant stopped and opened a door. His face was perfect butler deadpan.

'Please enter, sir.'

Myron smelled the chlorine before he heard the tiny splashes.

The manservant waited.

'I didn't bring my bathing suit,' Myron said.

The manservant looked at him blankly.

'I usually wear a thong,' Myron said. 'Though I can make do with bikini mesh.'

The manservant blinked.

'I can borrow yours,' Myron continued, 'if you have an extra.'

'Please enter, sir.'

'Right, well, let's stay in touch.'

The butler or whatever left. Myron went inside. The room had that indoor-pool mustiness. Everything was done in marble. Lots of plant life. There were statues of some goddess at each corner of the pool. What goddess, Myron did not know. The goddess of indoor pools, he surmised. The pool's sole occupant sliced through the water with nary a ripple. Arthur Bradford swam with easy, almost lazy movements. He reached the edge of the pool near Myron and stopped. He was wearing swimming goggles with dark blue lenses. He took them off and ran his hand across his scalp.

'What happened to Sam and Mario?' Bradford asked.

'Mario.' Myron nodded. 'That has to be the big guy, right?'

'Sam and Mario were supposed to escort you here.'

'I'm a big boy, Artie. I don't need an escort.' Bradford

had of course sent them to intimidate; Myron needed to show him that the move had not produced the desired effect.

'Fine then,' Bradford replied, his voice crisp. 'I have six more laps to go. Do you mind?'

Myron waved a dismissal. 'Hey,' he said. 'Please go ahead. I can think of nothing that would give me greater pleasure than watching another man swim. Hey, here's an idea. Why not film a commercial here? Slogan: Vote for Art, He's Got an Indoor Pool.'

Bradford almost smiled. 'Fair enough.' He pushed himself out of the pool in one lax motion. His body was long and lean and looked sleek when wet. He grabbed a towel and signaled to two chaise longues. Myron sat in one but did not lean back. Arthur Bradford did likewise.

'It's been a long day,' Arthur said. 'I've already made four campaign stops, and I have three more this afternoon.'

Myron nodded through the small talk, encouraging Bradford to move on. Bradford picked up the hint. He slapped his thighs with his palms. 'Well, then, you're a busy man. I'm a busy man. Shall we get to it?'

'Sure.'

Bradford leaned in a bit. 'I wanted to talk to you about your previous visit here.'

Myron tried to keep his face blank.

'You'll agree, will you not, that it was all rather bizarre?'

Myron made a noise. Sort of like 'Uh-huh' but more neutral.

'Put simply, I'd like to know what you and Win were up to.'

'I wanted the answers to some questions,' Myron said.

'Yes, I realize that. My question is, why?'

'Why what?'

'Why were you asking about a woman who hasn't been in my employ for twenty years?'

'What's the difference? You barely remember her, right?'

Arthur Bradford smiled. The smile said that they both knew better. 'I would like to help you,' Bradford said. 'But I must first question your motives.' He opened his arms. 'This is, after all, a major election.'

'You think I'm working for Davison?'

'You and Windsor come to my home under false pretenses. You start asking bizarre questions about my past. You pay off a police officer to steal a file on my wife's death. You are connected with a man who recently tried to blackmail me. And you've been seen conversing with known criminal associates of Davison's.' He gave the political smile, the one that couldn't help being a touch condescending. 'If you were I, what would you think?'

'Back up,' Myron said. 'One, I didn't pay off anybody to steal a file.'

'Officer Francine Neagly. Do you deny meeting with her at the Ritz Diner?'

'No.' Too long to explain the truth, and what was the point? 'Okay, forget that one for now. Who tried to blackmail you?'

The manservant entered the room. 'Iced tea, sir?'

Bradford thought it over. 'Lemonade, Mattius. Some lemonade would be divine.'

'Very well, sir. Mr. Bolitar?'

Myron doubted that Bradford stocked much Yoo-Hoo. 'Same here, Mattius. But make mine *extra* divine.'

Mattius the Manservant nodded. 'Very well, sir.' He slid back out the door.

Arthur Bradford wrapped a towel around his shoulders. Then he lay back on the chaise. They were long so that his legs would not hang over the ends. He closed his eyes. 'We both know that I remember Anita Slaughter. As you implied, a man does not forget the name of the person who found his wife's body.'

'That the only reason?'

Bradford opened one eye. 'Excuse me?'

'I've seen pictures of her,' Myron said simply. 'Hard to forget a woman who looked like that.'

Bradford reclosed the eye. For a moment he did not speak. 'There are plenty of attractive women in the world.'

'Uh-huh.'

'You think I had a relationship with her?'

'I didn't say that. I just said she was attractive. Men remember attractive women.'

'True,' Bradford agreed. 'But you see, that is the sort of false rumor Davison would love to get his hands on. Do you understand my concern? This is politics, and politics is spin. You wrongly think that my concerns for this matter prove that I have something to hide. But that's not the case. The truth is, I am worried about perception. Just because I didn't do anything does not mean my opponent won't try to make it look like I did. Do you follow?'

Myron nodded. 'Like a politician after graft.' But Bradford had a point. He was running for governor. Even if there were nothing there, he would snap into a defensive stance. 'So who tried to blackmail you?'

Bradford waited a second, internally calculating, adding up the pros and cons of telling Myron. The internal computer worked down the scenarios. The pros won.

'Horace Slaughter,' he said.

'With what?' Myron asked.

Bradford didn't answer the question directly. 'He called my campaign headquarters.'

'And he got through to you?'

'He said he had incriminating information about Anita Slaughter. I figured it was probably a crackpot, but the fact that he knew Anita's name bothered me.'

I bet, Myron thought. 'So what did he say?'

'He wanted to know what I'd done with his wife. He accused me of helping her run away.'

'Helping her how?'

He waved his hands. 'Supporting her, helping her, chasing her away. I don't know. He was rambling.'

'But what did he say?'

Bradford sat up. He swung his legs across the side of the chaise. For several seconds he looked at Myron as if he were a hamburger he wasn't sure it was time to flip. 'I want to know your interest in this.'

Give a little, get a little. Part of the game. 'The daughter.'

'Excuse me?'

'Anita Slaughter's daughter.'

Bradford nodded very slowly. 'Isn't she a basketball player?'

'Yes.'

'Do you represent her?'

'Yes. I was also friendly with her father. You heard he was murdered?'

'It was in the newspaper,' Bradford said. In the newspaper. Never a straight yes or no with this guy. Then he added, 'So what is your connection with the Ache family?'

Something in the back of Myron's head clicked. 'Are they Davison's "criminal associates"?' Myron asked.

'Yes.'

'So the Aches have an interest in his winning the election?'

'Of course. That's why I'd like to know how you're connected to them.'

'No connection,' Myron said. 'They're setting up a rival women's basketball league. They want to sign Brenda.' But now Myron was wondering. The Aches had been meeting with Horace Slaughter. According to FJ, he had even signed his daughter to play with them. Next thing you know, Horace was pestering Bradford about his deceased wife. Could Horace have been working with the Aches? Fodder for thought.

Mattius returned with the lemonades. Fresh squeezed. Cold. Delicious, if not divine. Again the rich. When Mattius left the room, Bradford fell into the feigning-deep-thought look he'd displayed so often at their previous meeting. Myron waited.

'Being a politician,' Bradford began, 'it's a strange thing. All creatures fight to survive. It's instinctive, of course. But the truth is, a politician is colder about it than most. He can't help it. A man has been murdered here, and all I see is the potential for political embarrassment. That's the plain truth. My goal is simply to keep my name out of it.'

'That's not going to happen,' Myron said. 'No matter what you or I might want.'

'What makes you say that?'

'The police are going to link you into this the same way I did.'

'I'm not following you.'

'I came to you because Horace Slaughter called you. The police will see those same phone records. They'll have to follow up.'

Arthur Bradford smiled. 'Don't worry about the police.'

Myron remembered Wickner and Pomeranz and the power of this family. Bradford might be right. Myron thought about this. And decided to turn it to his advantage.

'So you're asking me to keep quiet?' Myron said.

Bradford hesitated. Chess time. Watching the board and trying to figure out Myron's next move. 'I am asking you,' he said, 'to be fair.'

'Meaning?'

'Meaning you have no real evidence that I am involved in anything illicit.'

Myron tilted his head back and forth. Maybe yes, maybe no.

'And if you are telling the truth, if you do not work for Davison, then you would have no reason to damage my campaign.'

'I'm not sure that's true,' Myron said.

'I see.' Again Bradford tried to read the tea leaves. 'I assume then that you want something in exchange for your silence.'

'Perhaps. But it's not what you think.'

'What is it then?'

'Two things. First, I want the answer to some questions. The real answers. If I suspect you are lying or worried about how it will look, I'll hang you out to dry. I'm not out to embarrass you. I don't care about this election. I just want the truth.'

'And the second thing?'

Myron smiled. 'We'll get to that. First I need the answers.'

Bradford waited a beat. 'But how can you expect me to agree to a condition I don't even know?'

'Answer my questions first. If I am convinced that you are telling the truth, then I'll give you the second condition. But if you're evasive, the second condition becomes irrelevant.'

Bradford didn't like it. 'I don't think I can agree to that.'

'Fine.' Myron rose. 'Have a nice day, Arthur.'

His voice was sharp. 'Sit down.'

'Will you answer my questions?'

Arthur Bradford looked at him. 'Congressman Davison is not the only one who has unsavory friends.'

Myron let the words hang in the air.

'If you are to survive in politics,' Bradford continued, 'you must align yourself with some of the state's more sordid elements. That's the ugly truth, Myron. Am I making myself clear?'

'Yes,' Myron said. 'For the third time in the past hour someone is threatening me.'

'You don't appear too frightened.'

'I don't scare easily.' Half truth. Showing fear was unhealthy; you show fear, you're dead. 'So let's cut the crap. There are questions here. I can ask them. Or the press can.'

Bradford took his time again. The man was nothing if not careful. 'I still don't understand,' he said. 'What's your interest in this?'

Still stalling with questions. 'I told you. The daughter.'

'And when you came here the first time, you were looking for her father?'

'Yes.'

'And you came to me because this Horace Slaughter had called my office?'

Myron nodded. Slowly.

Bradford threw on the baffled face again. 'Then why on God's green earth did you ask about my wife? If indeed you were solely interested in Horace Slaughter, why were you so preoccupied with Anita Slaughter and what happened twenty years ago?'

The room fell silent, save for the gentle whisper of the pool waves. Light reflected off the water, bouncing to and fro like an erratic screen saver. They were at the crux of it now, and both men knew it. Myron thought about it a moment. He kept his eyes on Bradford's and wondered how much to say and how he could use it. Negotiating. Life was like being a sports agent, a series of negotiations.

'Because I wasn't just looking for Horace Slaughter,' Myron said slowly. 'I was looking for Anita Slaughter.'

Bradford wrestled to maintain control over his facial expressions and body language. But Myron's words still caused a sharp intake of air. His complexion lost a bit of color. He was good, no doubt about it, but there was something there.

Bradford spoke slowly. 'Anita Slaughter disappeared twenty years ago, did she not?'

'Yes.'

'And you think she's still alive?'

'Yes.'

'Why?'

To get information, you had to give it. Myron knew that. You had to prime the pump. But Myron was flooding it now. Time to stop and reverse the flow. 'Why would you care?'

'I don't.' Bradford hardly sounded convincing. 'But I assumed that she was dead.'

'Why?'

'She seemed like a decent woman. Why would she have run off and abandoned her child like that?'

'Maybe she was afraid,' Myron said.

'Of her husband?'

'Of you.'

That froze him. 'Why would she be afraid of me?'

'You tell me, Arthur.'

'I have no idea.'

Myron nodded. 'And your wife accidentally slipped off that terrace twenty years ago, right?'

Bradford did not reply.

'Anita Slaughter just came to work one morning and found your wife dead from a fall,' Myron continued. 'She'd slipped off her own balcony in the rainy dark and no one noticed. Not you. Not your brother. No one. Anita just happened by her dead body. Isn't that what happened?'

Bradford wasn't cracking, but Myron could sense some fault lines starting to open a touch. 'You don't know anything.'

'Then tell me.'

'I loved my wife. I loved her with everything I had.'

'So what happened to her?'

Bradford took a few breaths, tried to regain control. 'She fell,' he said. Then, thinking further, he asked, 'Why would you think that my wife's death has anything to do with Anita's disappearance?' His voice was stronger now, the timbre coming back. 'In fact, if I recall correctly, Anita stayed on after the accident. She left our employ well after Elizabeth's tragedy.'

True enough. And a point that kept irritating Myron like a grain of sand in the retina.

'So why do you keep harping on my wife's death?' Bradford pressed.

Myron had no answer, so he parried with a couple of questions. 'Why is everyone so concerned about that police file? Why are the cops so worried?'

'The same reason I am,' he said. 'It's an election year. Looking into old files is suspicious behavior. That's all there is to it. My wife died in an accident. End of story.'

His voice was growing stronger still. Negotiation can have more momentum shifts than a basketball game. If so, the Big Mo' was back on Bradford's side. 'Now you answer a question for me: why do you think Anita Slaughter is still alive? I mean, if the family hasn't heard from her in twenty years?'

'Who says they haven't heard from her?'

He arched an eyebrow. 'Are you saying they have?'

Myron shrugged. He had to be oh-so-careful here. If Anita Slaughter were indeed hiding from this guy – and if Bradford did indeed believe she was dead – how would he react to evidence that she was still alive? Wouldn't he logically try to find her and silence her? Interesting thought. But at the same time, if Bradford had been secretly paying her off, as Myron had earlier theorized, he would know she was alive. At the very least he would know that she had run away instead of having met up with foul play.

So what was going on here?

'I think I've said enough,' Myron said.

Bradford took a long pull on his lemonade glass, draining it. He stirred the pitcher and poured himself another. He gestured toward Myron's glass. Myron shook him off. Both men settled back.

'I would like to hire you,' Bradford said.

Myron tried a smile. 'As?'

'An adviser of sorts. Security, perhaps. I want to hire you to keep me up to date on your investigation. Hell, I have enough morons on the payroll in charge of damage control. Who better than the inside man? You'll be able to prepare me for a potential scandal. What do you say?'

'I think I'll pass.'

'Don't be so hasty,' Bradford said. 'I will pledge my cooperation as well as that of my staff.'

'Right. And if something bad turns up, you squash it.'

'I won't deny that I'll be interested in making sure the facts are put in the proper light.'

'Or shade.'

He smiled. 'You're not keeping your eyes on the prize, Myron. Your client is not interested in me or my political career. She is interested in finding her mother. I'd like to help.'

'Sure you would. After all, helping people is why you got into politics in the first place.'

Bradford shook his head. 'I'm making you a serious offer, and you choose to be glib.'

'It's not that.' Time to shift the momentum again. Myron chose his words carefully. 'Even if I wanted to,' he said, 'I can't.'

'Why not?'

'I mentioned a second condition before.'

Bradford put a finger to his lips. 'So you did.'

'I already work for Brenda Slaughter. She must remain my primary concern in this matter.'

Bradford put his hand behind his neck. Relaxed. 'Yes, of course.'

'You read the papers. The police think she did it.'

'Well, you'll have to admit,' Bradford said, 'she makes a good suspect.'

'Maybe. But if they arrest her, I'll have to act in her best interest.' Myron looked straight at him. 'That means I'll have to toss out any information that will lead the police to look at other potential suspects.'

Bradford smiled. He saw where this was going. 'Including me.'

Myron turned both palms up and shrugged. 'What choice would I have? My client must come first.' Slight hesitation. 'But of course none of that will occur if Brenda Slaughter remains free.'

Still the smile. 'Ah,' Bradford said.

Myron kept still.

Bradford sat up and put up both hands in stop position. 'Say no more.'

Myron didn't.

'It'll be dealt with.' Bradford checked his watch. 'Now I must get dressed. Campaign obligations.'

They both rose. Bradford stuck out his hand. Myron shook it. Bradford had not come clean, but Myron had not expected him to. They'd both learned a bit here. Myron was not sure who had gotten the better of the deal. But the first rule of any negotiation is not to be a pig. If you just keep taking, it will backfire in the long run.

Still he wondered.

'Good-bye,' Bradford said, still shaking the hand. 'I do hope you'll keep me up to date on your progress.'

The two men released their grips. Myron looked at Bradford. He didn't want to, but he couldn't stop himself from asking:

'Do you know my father?'

Bradford angled his head and smiled. 'Did he tell you that?'

'No. Your friend Sam mentioned it.'

'Sam has worked for me a long time.'

'I didn't ask about Sam. I asked about my father.'

Mattius opened the door. Bradford motioned to it.

'Why don't you ask your father, Myron? Maybe it will help clarify the situation.'

23

As Mattius the Manservant led Myron back down the long corridor, the same two words kept rocking through Myron's bone-dry skull:

My father?

Myron searched for a memory, a casual mention of the Bradford name in the house, a political tête-à-tête surrounding Livingston's most prominent resident. Nothing came to him.

So how did Bradford know his father?

Big Guy Mario and Skinny Sam were in the foyer. Mario stamped back and forth as though the very floor had pissed him off. His arms and hands gestured with the subtlety of a Jerry Lewis flick. If he had been a cartoon character, smoke would have been power-shooting out of both ears.

Skinny Sam pulled on a Marlboro, leaning against the banister like Sinatra waiting for Dino. Sam had that ease. Like Win. Myron could engage in violence, and he was good at it, but there were adrenal spikes and tingling legs and postcombat cold sweats when he did so. That was normal, of course. Only a rare few had the ability to disconnect, to remain calm in the eye, to view the outbursts in slow motion.

Big Guy Mario stormed toward Myron. His fists were clenched at his sides. His face was contorted like it'd been pressed up against a glass door. 'You're dead, asshole. You hear me? Dead. Dead and buried. I'm gonna take you outside and—'

Myron snapped up the knee again. And again it found its target. Big Dope Mario landed hard on the cool marble and thrashed around like a dying fish.

'Today's friendly tip,' Myron said. 'A protective cup is a worthwhile investment, though not as a drinking receptacle.'

Myron looked over at Sam. Sam still rested on the banister. He took another drag of the cigarette and let the smoke ease out of his nostrils.

'New guy,' Sam said in way of explanation.

Myron nodded.

'Sometimes you just want to scare stupid people,' Sam said. 'Stupid people are scared by big muscles.' Another drag. 'But don't let his incompetence get you cocky.'

Myron looked down. He was about to crack wise, but he stopped himself and shook his head. Cocky, a knee in the balls.

Too easy.

Win waited by Myron's car. He was bent slightly at the waist, practicing his golf swing. He did not have a club or a ball, of course. Remember blasting rock music and jumping on your bed and playing air guitar? Golfers do the same thing. They hear some internal sounds of nature, step on imaginary first tees, and swing air clubs. Air woods usually. Sometimes, when they want more control, they take air irons out of their air bags. And like teens with air guitars, golfers like to watch themselves in mirrors. Win, for example, often checks out his reflection in store windows. He stops on the sidewalk, makes sure his grip is right, checks his backswing, recocks his wrists, whatever.

'Win?'

'A moment.'

Win had repositioned Myron's passenger side mirror for a better full-body view. He stopped mid-swing, spotted something in the reflection, frowned.

'Remember,' Myron said. 'Objects in the mirror may appear smaller than they are.'

Win ignored him. He readdressed the, uh, ball, selected an air sand wedge, and tried a little air chip. From the look on Win's face the, uh, ball landed on the green and rolled within three feet of the cup. Win smiled and put up a hand to acknowledge the, uh, appreciative crowd.

Golfers.

'How did you get here so fast?' Myron asked.

'Batcopter.'

Lock-Horne Securities had a helicopter and a landing pad on the roof. Win had probably flown to a nearby field and jogged over.

'So you heard everything?'

Win nodded.

'What do you think?'

'Wasteful,' Win said.

'Right, I should have shot him in the knee.'

'Well, yes, there is that. But in this instance I am referring to the entire matter.'

'Meaning?'

'Meaning that Arthur Bradford may be on to something. You are not keeping your eyes on the prize.'

'And what is the prize?'

Win smiled. 'Exactly.'

Myron nodded. 'Yet again, I have no idea what you're talking about.'

He unlocked the car doors, and the two men slid into their seats. The leatherette was hot from the sun. The air conditioner sputtered out something close to warm spit.

'On occasion,' Win said, 'we have performed extra-curricular duties for one reason or another. But there was, for the most part, a purpose. A goal, if you will. We knew what we were trying to accomplish.'

'And you don't think that's the case here?'

'Correct.'

'I'll give you three goals then,' Myron said. 'One, I'm trying to find Anita Slaughter. Two, I'm trying to find Horace Slaughter's killer. Three, I'm trying to protect Brenda.'

'Protect her from what?'

'I don't know yet.'

'Ah,' Win said. 'And – let me make sure I understand you here – you feel that the best way to protect Ms. Slaughter is to agitate police officers, the most powerful family in the state, and known mobsters?'

'That can't be helped.'

'Well, yes, of course you're right about that. And we also have your other two goals to consider.' Win lowered the visor and checked his hair in the mirror. Not a blond hair out of place. He still patted about, frowning. When he finished, he snapped the visor back into place. 'Let's start with finding Anita Slaughter, shall we?'

Myron nodded, but he knew that he was not going to like where this was going.

'That is the core of the matter, is it not? Finding Brenda's mother?'

'Right,' Myron said.

'So – and again let me make sure I comprehend completely – you are taking on police officers, the most powerful family in the state, and known mobsters to find a woman who ran off twenty years ago?'

'Yes.'

'And the reason for this search?'

'Brenda. She wants to know where her mother is. She has the right—'

'Bah,' Win interrupted.

'Bah?'

'What are you, the ACLU? What right? Brenda has no right here. Do you believe Anita Slaughter is being held against her will?'

'No.'

'Then what, pray tell, are you trying to accomplish here? If Anita Slaughter craved a reconciliation with her daughter, she would seek it. Clearly she has opted not to do that. We know that she ran away twenty years ago. We know that she has worked hard to stay hidden. What we don't know, of course, is why. And instead of respecting her decision, you choose to ignore it.'

Myron said nothing.

'Under normal circumstances,' Win continued, 'this search would be a close call. But when you add in the mitigating factors – the obvious danger upsetting these particular adversaries – the call is an easy one. Simply put, we are taking a tremendous risk for very little reason.'

Myron shook his head, but he saw the logic. Had he not wondered about these same issues himself? He was doing his tightrope act again, this time over a raging inferno, and he was dragging others, including Francine Neagly, with him. And for what? Win was right. He was pissing off powerful people. He might even be inadvertently helping those who wished Anita Slaughter great harm, flushing her out into the open where they could set their sights with greater ease. He knew that he had to step carefully here. One false move and ka-pow.

'There's more to it,' Myron tried. 'A crime may have been covered up.'

'Are you speaking now of Elizabeth Bradford?'

'Yes.'

Win frowned. 'So is that what you're after, Myron? You're risking lives in order to give her justice after twenty years? Elizabeth Bradford is calling out to you from the grave or some such thing?'

'There's also Horace to think about.'

'What about him?'

'He was my friend.'

'And you believe that finding his killer will ease your guilt over not talking to him in ten years?'

Myron swallowed at that one. 'Low blow, Win.'

'No, my friend, I am merely trying to pull you back from the abyss. I am not saying that there is no value in what you are doing here. We have worked for questionable profit before. But you have to calculate some sort of cost-benefit analysis. You are trying to find a woman who does not want to be found. You are pushing against forces more powerful than you and me combined.'

'You almost sound afraid, Win.'

Win looked at him. 'You know better.'

Myron looked at the blue eyes with the flecks of silver. He nodded. He did know better.

'I'm talking about pragmatism,' Win continued, 'not fear. Pushing is fine. Forcing confrontation is fine. We've done that plenty of times before. We both know that I rarely back away from such instances, that I perhaps enjoy them too much. But there was always a goal. We were looking for Kathy to help clear a client. We were looking for Valerie's killer for the same reason. We searched for Greg because you were well compensated monetarily. The same could be said about the Coldren boy. But the goal here is too hazy.'

The volume switch on the car radio was set low, but

Myron could still hear Seal 'compare' his love to 'a kiss from the rose on the grave'. Romance.

'I have to stick with this,' Myron said. 'For a little while longer anyway.'

Win said nothing.

'And I'd like your help.'

Still nothing.

'There were scholarships set up to help Brenda,' Myron said. 'I think her mother may have been funneling money to her through them. Anonymously. I want you to try to track the money trail.'

Win reached forward and turned off the radio. Traffic was almost nonexistent. The air conditioner hummed, but otherwise the silence was heavy. After a couple of minutes, Win broke it.

'You're in love with her, aren't you?'

The question hit him by surprise. Myron opened his mouth, closed it. Win had never asked a question like this before; he did, in fact, all he could do to avoid the subject. Explaining love relationships to Win had always seemed akin to explaining jazz music to a lawn chair.

'I think I might be,' Myron said.

'It's affecting your judgment,' Win said. 'Emotion may be ruling over pragmatism.'

'I won't let it.'

'Pretend you are not in love with her. Would you still pursue this?'

'Does it matter?'

Win nodded. He understood better than most. Hypotheticals had nothing to do with reality. 'Fine then,' he said. 'Give me the information on the scholarships. I'll see what I can find.'

They both settled into silence. Win as always looked

perfectly relaxed and in a state of total readiness.

'There is a very fine line between relentless and stupid,' Win said. 'Try to stay on the right side of it.'

24

The Sunday afternoon traffic remained light. The Lincoln Tunnel was a breeze. Win fiddled with the buttons on Myron's new CD player, settling on a recently purchased compilation CD of AM seventies classics. They listened to the 'The Night Chicago Died'. Then 'The Night the Lights Went Out in Georgia'. Nights, Myron surmised, were a dangerous time in the seventies. Then the theme song to the movie *Billy Jack* blasted its peace on earth message. Remember the Billy Jack movies? Win did. A little too well, in fact.

The final song was a classic seventies tearjerker called 'Shannon'. Shannon dies pretty early in the song. In a very high pitch, we are told that Shannon is gone, that she drifted out to sea. Sad. The song always moved Myron. Mother is heartbroken at the loss. Dad always seems tired now. Nothing is the same without Shannon.

'Did you know,' Win said, 'that Shannon was a dog?'

'You're kidding.'

Win shook his head. 'If you listen closely to the chorus, you can tell.'

'I can only make out the part about Shannon being gone and drifting out to sea.'

'That is followed by the hopes that Shannon will find an island with a shady tree.'

'A shady tree?'

Win sang, 'Just like the one in our backyard.'

'That doesn't mean it's a dog, Win. Maybe Shannon liked sitting under a tree. Maybe they had a hammock.'

'Perhaps,' Win said. 'But there is one other subtle giveaway.'

'What's that?'

'The CD liner notes say the song is about a dog.'

Win.

'Do you want me to drop you off at home?' Myron asked.

Win shook his head. 'I have paperwork,' he said. 'And I think it best if I stay close.'

Myron did not argue.

'You have the weapon?' Win asked.

'Yes.'

'Do you want another?'

'No.'

They parked at the Kinney lot and took the elevator up together. The high-rise was silent today, the ants all away from the hill. The effect was sort of eerie, like one of those end-of-the-earth apocalypse movies where everything is abandoned and ghostlike. The dinging of the elevator echoed in the still air like a thunderclap.

Myron got off at the twelfth floor. Despite its being Sunday, Big Cyndi was at her desk. As always, everything around Big Cyndi looked tiny, like that episode of *The Twilight Zone* where the house starts shrinking or like someone had jammed a large stuffed animal into Barbie's pink Corvette. Big Cyndi was wearing a wig today that looked like something stolen from Carol Channing's closet. Bad hair day, Myron supposed. She stood and smiled at him. Myron kept his eyes open and was surprised when he didn't turn to stone.

Big Cyndi was normally six-six, but she was wearing high heels today. Pumps. The heels cried out in agony as she stood. She was dressed into what some might consider a business suit. The shirt was French-Revolution frilly, the jacket solid gray with a fresh tear along the shoulder stitch.

She raised her hands and twirled for Myron. Picture Godzilla rearing back after getting nailed by a Taser gun.

'Like it?' she asked.

'Very much,' Myron said. *Jurassic Park III: The Fashion Show*.

'I bought it at Benny's.'

'Benny's?'

'Down in the Village,' Big Cyndi explained. 'It's a clothing store for transvestites. But lots of us big girls shop there too.'

Myron nodded. 'Practical,' he said.

Big Cyndi sniffled once, then suddenly began to cry. She still had on waaaay too much makeup, none of it waterproof, and she quickly started to look like a lava lamp left in the microwave.

'Oh, Mr. Bolitar!'

She ran toward him, her arms spread, the floor creaking from the thumping. An image of one of those cartoon scenes where characters keep falling through floors, forming cutout silhouettes in each floor as they pass through it, came to him.

Myron put up his hands. *No! Myron good! Myron like Cyndi! Cyndi no hurt Myron!* But the gesture was useless.

She embraced him, wrapping both arms around him and lifting him off his feet. It felt as though a water bed had come to life and attacked him. He closed his eyes and tried to ride it out.

'Thank you,' she whispered through her tears.

Out of the corner of his eye he spotted Esperanza. She watched the scene with crossed arms, smiling slightly.

The new job, Myron suddenly remembered. Rehiring her full-time.

'You're welcome,' he managed.

'I won't let you down.'

'Could you at least put me down?'

Big Cyndi made a noise that might have been a giggle. Children in the tristate area screamed and reached for Mommy's hand.

She lowered him gently back to the floor like a child placing a block on the top of a pyramid. 'You won't be sorry. I'll work night and day. I'll work weekends. I'll pick up your laundry. I'll make coffee. I'll fetch Yoo-Hoos. I'll even give you backrubs.'

The image of a steamroller approaching a bruised peach flashed through his mind.

'Er, a Yoo-Hoo would be great.'

'Right away.' Big Cyndi bounced toward the refrigerator. Myron moved toward Esperanza.

'She does give a great backrub,' Esperanza said.

'I'll take your word for it.'

'I told Big Cyndi you were the one who wanted to hire her full-time.'

Myron nodded. 'Next time,' he said, 'just let me pull a thorn out of her paw, okay?'

Big Cyndi held up the can of Yoo-Hoo. 'Do you want me to shake it for you, Mr. Bolitar?'

'I'll handle that, Cyndi, thanks.'

'Yes, Mr. Bolitar.' She hopped back over, and Myron was reminded of the scene where the boat flips over in the *Poseidon Adventure*. She handed him the Yoo-Hoo. Then she smiled again. And the gods shielded their eyes.

Myron spoke to Esperanza. 'Any more word on Lester's trade?'

'No.'

'Get me Ron Dixon on the phone. Try his home number.'

Big Cyndi took that one. 'Right away, Mr. Bolitar.' Esperanza shrugged. Big Cyndi dialed and used her English accent. She sounded like Maggie Smith in a Noël Coward play. Myron and Esperanza went into his office. The call was transferred.

'Ron? It's Myron Bolitar, how are you?'

'I know who the hell this is, moron. Your receptionist told me. It's Sunday, Myron. Sunday is my day off. Sunday is my family day. My quality time. My chance to get to know the kids better. So why are you calling me on a Sunday?'

'Are you trading Lester Ellis?'

'That's why you're calling me at home on a Sunday?'

'Is it true?'

'No comment.'

'You told me you wouldn't trade him.'

'Wrong. I told you I wouldn't actively put him on the block. If you recall, Mr. Super Agent, you wanted to put in a trade approval clause in his contract. I said, no, unless you wanted to shave fifty grand off his salary. You refused. Now it's coming back and biting your ass cheek, ain't it, hotshot?'

Myron shifted in his seat. Sore ass cheek and all. 'Who are you getting for him?'

'No comment.'

'Don't do this, Ron. He's a great talent.'

'Yeah. Too bad he's not a great baseball player.'

'You're going to look foolish. Remember Nolan Ryan for Jim Fregosi? Remember Babe Ruth, uh' – Myron forgot who they got in the trade – 'being traded by the Red Sox?'

'Now Lester Ellis is Babe Ruth?'

'Let's talk about this.'

'Nothing to talk about, Myron. And now, if you'll excuse me, the wife is calling me. It's strange.'

'What's that?'

'This quality time stuff. This getting to know my children better. You know what I've learned, Myron?'

'What?'

'I hate my kids.'

Click.

Myron looked up at Esperanza.

'Get me Al Toney at the *Chicago Tribune*.'

'He's being traded to Seattle.'

'Trust me here.'

Esperanza gestured to the phone. 'Don't ask me. Ask Big Cyndi.'

Myron hit the intercom. 'Big Cyndi, could you please get me Al Toney? He should be at his office.'

'Yes, Mr. Bolitar.'

A minute later Big Cyndi beeped in. 'Al Toney on line one.'

'Al? Myron Bolitar here.'

'Hey, Myron, what's up?'

'I owe you one, right?'

'At least, one.'

'Well, I got a scoop for you.'

'My nipples are hardening as we speak. Talk dirty to me, baby.'

'You know Lester Ellis? He's being traded tomorrow to Seattle. Lester is thrilled. He's been bugging the Yankees to trade him all year. We couldn't be happier.'

'That's your big scoop?'

'Hey, this is an important story.'

'In New York or Seattle maybe. But I'm in Chicago, Myron.'

'Still. I thought you might want to know.'

'No good. You still owe me.'

Myron said, 'You don't want to check with your nipples first?'

'Hold on.' Pause. 'Soft as overripe grapes already. But I could check again in a few minutes, if you'd like.'

'Pass, Al, thanks. Frankly I didn't think it would fly with you, but it was worth a try. Between you and me, the Yankees are pushing hard on this trade. They want me to put on the best spin. I thought you could help.'

'Why? Who they getting?'

'I don't know.'

'Lester's a pretty good player. Raw but good. Why the Yankees so interested in getting rid of him?'

'You won't print this?'

Pause. Myron could almost hear Al's brain awhirring. 'Not if you tell me not to.'

'He's hurt. Home accident. Damaged the knee. They're keeping it quiet, but Lester will need surgery after the season.'

Silence.

'You can't print it, Al.'

'No problem. Hey, I gotta go.'

Myron smiled. 'Later, Al.'

He hung up.

Esperanza looked at him. 'Are you doing what I think you're doing?'

'Al Toney is the master of the loophole,' Myron explained. 'He promised *he* wouldn't print it. He won't. But he works by trading favors. He's the best barterer in the business.'

'So?'

'So now he'll call a friend at the *Seattle Times* and barter. The injury rumor will spread. If it gets public before the trade is announced, well, it's doomed.'

Esperanza smiled. 'Highly unethical.'

Myron shrugged. 'Let's just say it's fuzzy.'

'I still like it.'

'Always remember the MB SportsReps credo: the client comes first.'

She nodded and added, 'Even in sexual liaisons.'

'Hey, we're a full-service agency.' Myron looked at her for a long moment. Then he said, 'Can I ask you something?'

She tilted her head. 'I don't know. Can you?'

'Why do you hate Jessica?'

Esperanza's face clouded over. She shrugged. 'Habit, I guess.'

'I'm serious.'

She crossed her legs, uncrossed them. 'Let me just stick to taking cheap potshots, okay?'

'You're my best friend,' he said. 'I want to know why you don't like her.'

Esperanza sighed, crossed the legs again, tucked a loose strand behind her ear. 'Jessica is bright, smart, funny, a great writer, and I wouldn't throw her out of bed for eating crackers.'

Bisexuals.

'But she hurt you.'

'So? She's not the first woman to commit an indiscretion.'

'True enough,' Esperanza agreed. She slapped her knees and stood. 'Guess I'm wrong. Can I go now?'

'So why do you still hold a grudge?'

'I like grudges,' Esperanza said. 'They're easier than forgiveness.'

Myron shook his head, signaled her to sit.

'What do you want me to say, Myron?'

'I want you to tell me why you don't like her.'

'I'm just being a pain in the ass. Don't take it seriously.'

Myron shook his head again.

Esperanza put her hand to her face. She looked away for a moment. 'You're not tough enough, okay?'

'What do you mean?'

'For that kind of hurt. Most people can take it. I can. Jessica can. Win certainly can. But you can't. You're not tough enough. You're just not built that way.'

'Then maybe that's my fault.'

'It is your fault,' Esperanza said. 'At least in part. You idealize relationships too much, for one thing. And you're too sensitive. You used to expose yourself too much. You used to leave yourself too open.'

'Is that such a bad thing?'

She hesitated. 'No. In fact, it's a good thing, I guess. A bit naive, but it's a lot better than those assholes who hold everything back. Can we stop talking about this now?'

'I still don't think you've answered my question.'

Esperanza raised her palms. 'That's as good as I can do.'

Myron flashed back to Little League again, to being hit by Joey Davito's pitch, to never planting his feet in the batter's box the same again. He nodded. Used to expose, Esperanza had said. 'Used to.' A curious use of words.

Esperanza took advantage of the silence and changed subjects. 'I checked into Elizabeth Bradford for you.'

'And?'

'There's nothing there that would suggest her death was anything other than an accident. You can take a run at her brother, if you want. He lives in Westport. He's also closely aligned to his old brother-in-law, so I doubt you'll get anywhere.'

Waste of time. 'Any other family?'

'A sister who also lives in Westport. But she's spending the summer on the Côte d'Azur.'

Strike two.

'Anything else?'

'One thing bothered me a little,' Esperanza said. 'Elizabeth Bradford was clearly a social animal, a society dame of the first order. Barely a week went by when her name wasn't in the paper for some function or other. But about six months before she fell off the balcony, mentions of her stopped.'

'When you say "stopped"—'

'I mean, completely. Her name was nowhere, not even in the town paper.'

Myron thought about this. 'Maybe she was on the Côte d'Azur.'

'Maybe. But her husband wasn't there with her. Arthur was still getting plenty of coverage.'

Myron leaned back and spun his chair around. He checked out the Broadway posters behind his desk again. Yep, they definitely had to go. 'You said there were a lot of stories on Elizabeth Bradford before that?'

'Not stories,' Esperanza corrected. 'Mentions. Her name was almost always preceded by "Hosting the event was" or "Attendees included" or "Pictured from right to left are." '

Myron nodded. 'Were these in some kind of column or general articles or what?'

'The *Jersey Ledger* used to have a social column. It was called "Social Soirées".'

'Catchy.' But Myron remembered the column vaguely from his childhood. His mother used to skim it, checking out the boldface names for a familiar one. Mom had even been listed once, referred to as 'prominent local attorney Ellen Bolitar.' That was how she wanted to be addressed for the next week. Myron would yell down, 'Hey, Mom!' and she would reply,

'That's Prominent Local Attorney Ellen Bolitar to you, Mr. Smarty Pants.'

'Who wrote the column?' Myron asked.

Esperanza handed him a sheet of paper. There was a head shot of a pretty woman with an overstylized helmet of hair, à la Lady Bird Johnson. Her name was Deborah Whittaker.

'Think we can get an address on her?'

Esperanza nodded. 'Shouldn't take long.'

They looked at each other for a long moment. Esperanza's deadline hung over them like a reaper's scythe.

Myron said, 'I can't imagine you not in my life.'

'Won't happen,' Esperanza replied. 'No matter what you decide, you'll still be my best friend.'

'Partnerships ruin friendships.'

'So you tell me.'

'So I know.' He had avoided this conversation long enough. To use basketball vernacular, he had gone into four corners, but the twenty-four-second clock had run down. He could no longer delay the inevitable in the hope that the inevitable would somehow turn to smoke and vanish in the air. 'My father and my uncle tried it. They ended up not talking to each other for four years.'

She nodded. 'I know.'

'Even now their relationship is not what it was. It never will be. I know literally dozens of families and friends – good people, Esperanza – who tried partnerships like this. I don't know one case where it worked in the long run. Not one. Brother against brother. Daughter against father. Best friend against best friend. Money does funny things to people.'

Esperanza nodded again.

'Our friendship could survive anything,' Myron said, 'but I'm not sure it can survive a partnership.'

Esperanza stood again. 'I'll get you an address on Deborah Whittaker,' she said. 'It shouldn't take long.'

'Thanks.'

'And I'll give you three weeks for the transition. Will that be long enough?'

Myron nodded, his throat dry. He wanted to say something more, but whatever came to mind was even more inane than what preceded it.

The intercom buzzed. Esperanza left the room. Myron hit the button.

'Yes?'

Big Cyndi said, 'The *Seattle Times* on line one.'

25

The Inglemoore Convalescent Home was painted bright yellow and cheerfully maintained and colorfully landscaped and still looked like a place you went to die.

The inner lobby had a rainbow on one wall. The furniture was happy and functional. Nothing too plush. Didn't want the patrons having trouble getting out of chairs. A table in the room's center had a huge arrangement of freshly cut roses. The roses were bright red and strikingly beautiful and would die in a day or two.

Myron took a deep breath. *Settle, boy, settle.*

The place had a heavy cherry smell like one of those dangling tree-shaped car fresheners. A woman dressed in slacks and a blouse – what you'd call 'nice casual' – greeted him. She was in her early thirties and smiled with the genuine warmth of a Stepford Wife.

'I'm here to see Deborah Whittaker.'

'Of course,' she said. 'I think Deborah is in the rec room. I'm Gayle. I'll take you.'

Deborah. Gayle. Everyone was a first name. There was probably a Dr. Bob on the premises. They headed down a corridor lined with festive murals. The floors sparkled, but Myron could still make out fresh wheelchair streaks. Everyone on staff had the same fake smile. Part of the training, Myron supposed. All of them – orderlies, nurses, whatever – were dressed in civilian clothes. No one wore a stethoscope or beeper or name

tag or anything that implied anything medical. All buddies here at Inglemoore.

Gayle and Myron entered the rec room. Unused Ping-Pong tables. Unused pool tables. Unused card tables. Oft-used television.

'Please sit down,' Gayle said. 'Becky and Deborah will be with you momentarily.'

'Becky?' Myron asked.

Again the smile. 'Becky is Deborah's friend.'

'I see.'

Myron was left alone with six old people, five of whom were women. No sexism in longevity. They were neatly attired, the sole man in a tie even, and all were in wheelchairs. Two of them had the shakes. Two were mumbling to themselves. They all had skin a color closer to washed-out gray than any flesh tone. One woman waved at Myron with a bony, blue-lined hand. Myron smiled and waved back.

Several signs on the wall had the Inglemoore slogan:

INGLEMOORE – NO DAY LIKE TODAY.

Nice, Myron guessed, but he couldn't help but think up a more appropriate one:

INGLEMOORE – BETTER THAN THE ALTERNATIVE.

Hmm. He'd drop it in the suggestion box on the way out.

'Mr. Bolitar?'

Deborah Whittaker shuffled into the room. She still had Le Helmet de Hair from the newspaper portrait – black as shoe polish and shellacked on until it resembled fiberglass – but the overall effect was still like something out of Dorian Gray, as though she had aged a zillion years in one fell swoop. Her eyes had that soldier's thousand-yard stare. She had a bit of a shake in her face that reminded him of Katharine Hepburn. Parkinson's maybe, but he was no expert.

Her 'friend' Becky had been the one who called his name. Becky was maybe thirty years old. She too was dressed in civilian clothes rather than whites, and while nothing about her appearance suggested nursing, Myron still thought of Louise Fletcher in *One Flew over the Cuckoo's Nest*.

He stood.

'I'm Becky,' the nurse said.

'Myron Bolitar.'

Becky shook his hand and offered him a patronizing smile. Probably couldn't help it. Probably couldn't smile genuinely until she was out of here for at least an hour. 'Do you mind if I join you two?'

Deborah Whittaker spoke for the first time. 'Go away,' she rasped. Her voice sounded like a worn tire on a gravel road.

'Now, Deborah—'

'Don't "now Deborah" me. I got myself a handsome gentleman caller, and I'm not sharing him. So buzz off.'

Becky's patronizing smile turned a bit uncertain. 'Deborah,' she said in a tone that aimed for amiable but landed smack on, well, patronizing, 'do you know where we are?'

'Of course,' Deborah snapped. 'The Allies just bombed Munich. The Axis has surrendered. I'm a USO girl standing by the south pier in Manhattan. The ocean breeze hits my face. I wait for the sailors to arrive so I can lay a big, wet kiss on the first guy off the boat.'

Deborah Whittaker winked at Myron.

Becky said, 'Deborah, it's not 1945. It's—'

'I know, dammit. For crying out loud, Becky, don't be so damn gullible.' She sat down and leaned toward Myron. 'Truth is, I go in and out. Sometimes I'm here. Sometimes I time travel. When my grandpa had it, they called it hardening of the arteries. When my mother had

236

it, they called it senility. With me, it's Parkinson's and Alzheimer's.' She looked at her nurse, her facial muscles still doing the quivers. 'Please, Becky, while I'm still lucid, get the hell out of my face.'

Becky waited a second, holding the uncertain smile as best she could. Myron nodded at her, and she moved away.

Deborah Whittaker leaned a little closer. 'I love getting ornery with her,' she whispered. 'It's the only fringe benefit of old age.' She put her hands on her lap and managed a shaky smile. 'Now I know you just told me, but I forgot your name.'

'Myron.'

She looked puzzled. 'No, that's not it. André maybe? You look like André. He used to do my hair.'

Becky kept a watchful eye on the corner. At the ready.

Myron decided to dive right in. 'Mrs. Whittaker, I wanted to ask you about Elizabeth Bradford.'

'Lizzy?' The eyes flared up and settled into a glisten. 'Is she here?'

'No, ma'am.'

'I thought she died.'

'She did.'

'Poor thing. She threw such wonderful parties. At Bradford Farm. They'd string lights across the porch. They'd have hundreds of people. Lizzy always had the best band, the best caterer. I had such fun at her parties. I used to dress up and ...' A flicker hit Deborah Whittaker's eyes, a realization perhaps that the parties and invitations would never come again, and she stopped speaking.

'In your column,' Myron said, 'you used to write about Elizabeth Bradford.'

'Oh, of course.' She waved a hand. 'Lizzy made good

copy. She was a social force. But—' She stopped again and looked off.

'But what?'

'Well, I haven't written about Lizzy in months. Strange really. Last week Constance Lawrence had a charity ball for the St. Sebastian's Children's Care, and Lizzy wasn't there again. And that used to be Lizzy's favorite event. She ran it the past four years, you know.'

Myron nodded, trying to keep up with the changing eras. 'But Lizzy doesn't go to parties anymore, does she?'

'No, she doesn't.'

'Why not?'

Deborah Whittaker sort of half startled. She eyed him suspiciously. 'What's your name again?'

'Myron.'

'I know that. You just told me. I mean, your last name.'

'Bolitar.'

Another spark. 'Ellen's boy?'

'Yes, that's right.'

'Ellen Bolitar,' she said with a spreading smile. 'How's she doing?'

'She's doing well.'

'Such a shrewd woman. Tell me, Myron. Is she still ripping apart opposing witnesses?'

'Yes, ma'am.'

'So shrewd.'

'She loved your column,' Myron said.

Her face beamed. 'Ellen Bolitar, the attorney, reads my column?'

'Every week. It was the first thing she read.'

Deborah Whittaker settled back, shaking her head. 'How do you like that? Ellen Bolitar reads my column.' She smiled at Myron. Myron was getting confused by the verb tenses. Bouncing in time. He'd just have to try to stay with her. 'We're having such a nice visit, aren't we, Myron?'

'Yes, ma'am, we are.'

Her smile quivered and faded. 'Nobody in here remembers my column,' she said. 'They're all very nice and sweet. They treat me well. But I'm just another old lady to them. You reach an age, and suddenly you become invisible. They only see this rotting shell. They don't realize that this mind inside used to be sharp, that this body used to go to the fanciest parties and dance with the handsomest men. They don't see that. I can't remember what I had for breakfast, but I remember those parties. Do you think that's strange?'

Myron shook his head. 'No, ma'am, I don't.'

'I remember Lizzy's final soiree like it was last night. She wore a black, strapless Halston with white pearls. She was tan and lovely. I wore a bright pink summer dress. A Lilly Pulitzer, as a matter of fact, and let me tell you, I was still turning heads.'

'What happened to Lizzy, Mrs. Whittaker? Why did she stop going to parties?'

Deborah Whittaker stiffened suddenly. 'I'm a social columnist,' she said, 'not a gossip.'

'I understand that. I'm not asking to be nosy. It may be important.'

'Lizzy is my friend.'

'Did you see her after that party?'

Her eyes had the faraway look again. 'I thought she drank too much. I even wondered if maybe she had a problem.'

'A drinking problem?'

'I don't like to gossip. It's not my way. I write a social column. I don't believe in hurting people.'

'I appreciate that, Mrs. Whittaker.'

'But I was wrong anyway.'

'Wrong?'

'Lizzy doesn't have a drinking problem. Oh, sure, she might have a social drink, but she's too proper a hostess to go beyond her limit.'

Again with the verb tenses. 'Did you see her after that party?'

'No,' she said softly. 'Never.'

'Did you talk to her on the phone maybe?'

'I called her twice. After she missed the Woodmeres' party and then Constance's affair, well, I knew something had to be very wrong. But I never spoke to her. She was either out or couldn't come to the phone.' She looked up at Myron. 'Do you know where she is? Do you think she'll be all right?'

Myron was not sure how to respond. Or in what tense. 'Are you worried about her?'

'Of course I am. It's as though Lizzy just vanished. I've asked all her close friends from the club, but none of them has seen her either.' She frowned. 'Not friends really. Friends don't gossip like that.'

'Gossip about what?'

'About Lizzy.'

'What about her?'

Her voice was a conspiratorial whisper. 'I thought she was acting strange because she drank too much. But that wasn't it.'

Myron leaned in and matched her tone. 'What was it then?'

Deborah Whittaker gazed at Myron. The eyes were milky and cloudy, and Myron wondered what reality they were seeing. 'A breakdown,' she said at last. 'The ladies at the club were whispering that Lizzy had a breakdown. That Arthur had sent her away. To an institution with padded walls.'

Myron felt his body go cold.

'Gossip,' Deborah Whittaker spit. 'Ugly rumors.'

'You didn't believe it?'

'Tell me something.' Deborah Whittaker licked lips so dry they looked like they might flake off. She sat up a bit. 'If Elizabeth Bradford had been locked away in an institution,' she said, 'how come she fell at her own home?'

Myron nodded. Food for thought.

26

He stayed for a while and talked with Deborah Whittaker about people and a time period he never knew. Becky finally called a halt to the visit. Myron promised that he would visit again. He said that he'd try to bring his mother. And he would. Deborah Whittaker shuffled off, and Myron wondered if she would still remember his visit by the time she got to her room. Then he wondered if it mattered.

Myron headed back to his car and called Arthur Bradford's office. His 'executive secretary' told him that the 'next governor' would be in Belleville. Myron thanked her and hung up. He checked his watch and started on his way. If he didn't hit any traffic, he'd make it in time.

When he hit the Garden State Parkway, Myron called his father's office. Eloise, Dad's longtime secretary, said the same thing she'd said every time he'd called for the past twenty-five years: 'I'll patch you through immediately, Myron.' It didn't matter if Dad was busy. It didn't matter if he was on the phone or if someone was in the office with him. Dad had left instructions long ago: when his son called, he was always to be disturbed.

'No need,' Myron said. 'Just tell him I'll be dropping by in a couple of hours.'

'Here? My God, Myron, you haven't been here in years.'

'Yeah, I know.'

'Is anything wrong?'

'Nothing, Eloise. I just want to talk to him. Tell him it's nothing to worry about.'

'Oh, your father will be so pleased.'

Myron was not so sure.

Arthur Bradford's tour bus had red and blue stripes and big white stars. 'BRADFORD FOR GOVERNOR' was painted in a hip, slanted font with 3-D letters. The windows were tinted black so none of the great unwashed could look in on their leader. Quite the homespun touch.

Arthur Bradford stood by the bus door, microphone in hand. Brother Chance was behind him, smiling in that the-camera-might-be-on-me, gee-isn't-the-candi-date-brilliant mode of the political underling. On his right was Terence Edwards, Brenda's cousin. He too beamed with a smile about as natural as Joe Biden's hairline. Both of them were wearing those goofy political Styrofoam hats that looked like something a barbershop's quartet might sport.

The crowd was sparse and mostly old. Very old. They looked distracted, glancing about as if someone had enticed them here with the promise of free food. Other people slowed and meandered over to take a look, not unlike pedestrians who stumbled across a fender bender and were now hoping a fight would break out. Bradford's handlers blended into the crowd and passed out big signs and buttons and even those goofy Styrofoam hats, all with the same hip 'BRADFORD FOR GOVERNOR' lettering. Every once in a while the inter-spersed handlers would break into applause, and the rest of the crowd would lazily follow suit. There was also a sprinkling of media and cable stations, local political correspondents who looked visibly pained by what they were doing, wondering what was worse:

covering yet another canned political speech or losing a limb in a machinery mishap. Their expressions indicated a toss-up.

Myron eased into the crowd and slid up toward the front.

'What we need in New Jersey is a change,' Arthur Bradford bellowed. 'What we need in New Jersey is daring and brave leadership. What we need in New Jersey is a governor who will not cave in to special interests.'

Oh, boy.

The handlers loved that line. They burst into applause like a porno starlet faking an orgasm (er, or so Myron imagined). The crowd was more tepid. The handlers started a chant: 'Bradford . . . Bradford . . . Bradford.' Original. Another voice came over the loudspeaker. 'Once again, ladies and gentlemen, the next governor of New Jersey, Arthur Bradford! What we need in New Jersey!'

Applause. Arthur waved at the common folk. Then he stepped down from his perch and actually touched a chosen few.

'I'm counting on your support,' he said after each handshake.

Myron felt a tap on his shoulder. He turned around. Chance was there. He was still smiling and wearing the goofy Styrofoam hat. 'What the hell do you want?'

Myron pointed at his head. 'Can I have your hat?'

Still smiling. 'I don't like you, Bolitar.'

Myron mirrored the smile. 'Ouch, that hurt.'

They both stayed with the frozen smiles. If one of them were female, they could have hosted one of those *Hard Copy* rip-offs.

'I need to talk to Art,' Myron said.

Still smiling. Best buddies. 'Get on the bus.'

'Sure thing,' Myron said. 'But once inside, can I stop smiling? My cheeks are starting to hurt.'

But Chance was already moving away. Myron shrugged and hopped on board. The carpet on the bus floor was thick and maroon. The regular seats had been ripped out and replaced with what looked like lounge chairs. There were several overhead televisions, a bar with a minifridge, telephones, computer terminals.

Skinny Sam was the sole occupant. He sat up front and read a copy of *People* magazine. He looked at Myron, then back at his magazine.

'Top fifty most intriguing people,' Sam said. 'And I'm not one of them.'

Myron nodded sympathetically. 'It's based on connections, not merit.'

'Politics,' Sam agreed. He flipped the page. 'Head to the back, bucko.'

'On my way.'

Myron settled into a pseudofuturistic swivel chair that looked like something from the set of *Battlestar Galactica*. He didn't have to wait long. Chance hopped on first. He was still smiling and waving. Terence Edwards came in next. Then Arthur. The driver pressed a button, and the door slid closed. So did all three faces, their smiles thrown aside like itchy masks.

Arthur signaled for Terence Edwards to sit in the front. He obeyed like, well, a political underling. Arthur and Chance moved to the back of the bus. Arthur looked relaxed. Chance looked constipated.

'Nice to see you,' Arthur said.

'Yeah,' Myron said, 'always a pleasure.'

'Would you care for a drink?'

'Sure.'

The bus pulled out. The crowd gathered around the bus and waved into the one-way glass. Arthur Bradford looked at them with utter disdain. Man of the people. He tossed Myron a Snapple and popped one open for himself. Myron looked at the bottle. Diet Peach Iced Tea. Not bad. Arthur sat down, and Chance sat next to him.

'What did you think of my speech?' Arthur asked.

'What we need in New Jersey,' Myron said, 'is more political clichés.'

Arthur smiled. 'You'd prefer a more detailed discussion on the issues, is that it? In this heat? With that crowd?'

'What can I say? I still like "Vote for Art, He's Got an Indoor Pool."'

Bradford waved the comment away. 'Have you learned something new about Anita Slaughter?'

'No,' Myron said. 'But I've learned something new about your late wife.'

Arthur frowned. Chance's face reddened. Arthur said, 'You're supposed to be trying to find Anita Slaughter.'

'Funny thing that,' Myron said. 'When I look into her disappearance, your wife's death keeps popping up. Why do you think that is?'

Chance piped up. 'Because you're a goddamn idiot.'

Myron looked at Chance. Then he put his finger to his lips. 'Shhh.'

'Useless,' Arthur said. 'Utterly useless. I have told you repeatedly that Elizabeth's death has nothing to do with Anita Slaughter.'

'Then humor me,' Myron said. 'Why did your wife stop going to parties?'

'Pardon me?'

'During the last six months of her life none of your wife's friends saw her. She never went to parties anymore. She never even went to her club.' Whatever club that might have been.

'Who told you that?'

'I've spoken to several of her friends.'

Arthur smiled. 'You've spoken,' he said, 'to one senile old goat.'

'Careful, Artie. Senile goats have the right to vote.' Myron paused. 'Hey, that rhymes. You may have another campaign slogan on your hands: "Senile Goats, We Need Your Votes."'

No one reached for a pen.

'You're wasting my time and I'm through with trying to cooperate,' Arthur said. 'I'll have the driver drop you off.'

'I can still go to the press,' Myron said.

Chance jumped on that one. 'And I can put a bullet through your heart.'

Myron put his finger to his lips again. 'Shhh.'

Chance was about to add something, but Arthur took the helm. 'We had a deal,' he said. 'I help keep Brenda Slaughter out of jail. You search for Anita Slaughter and keep my name out of the papers. But you insist on delving into peripheries. That's a mistake. Your point-less digging will eventually draw my opponent's atten-tion and give him fresh fodder to use against me.'

He waited for Myron to say something. Myron didn't.

'You leave me no choice,' Arthur continued. 'I will tell you what you want to know. You will then see that it is irrelevant to the issues at hand. And then we will move on.'

Chance did not like that. 'Arthur, you can't be serious—'

'Sit up front, Chance.'

'But—'

Chance was sputtering now. 'He could be working for Davison.'

Arthur shook his head. 'He's not.'

'But you can't know—'

'If he was working for Davison, they'd have ten guys following up on this by now. And if he continues to dig into this, he will most certainly be noticed by Davison's people.'

Chance looked at Myron. Myron winked.

'I don't like it,' Chance said.

'Sit up front, Chance.'

Chance rose with as much dignity as he could muster, which was absolutely none, and skulked to the front of the bus.

Arthur turned to Myron. 'It goes without saying that what I'm about to tell you is strictly confidential. If it's repeated . . .' He decided not to finish the sentence. 'Have you spoken to your father yet?'

'No.'

'It will help.'

'Help with what?'

But Arthur did not reply. He sat in silence and looked out the window. The bus stopped at a traffic light. A group of people waved at the bus. Arthur looked right through them.

'I loved my wife,' he began. 'I want you to understand that. We met in college. I saw her walking across the commons one day and . . .' The light turned green. The bus started up again. 'And nothing in my life was ever the same.' Arthur glanced at Myron and smiled. 'Corny, isn't it?'

Myron shrugged. 'Sounds nice.'

'Oh, it was.' He tilted his head at a memory, and for a moment the politician was replaced with a real human being. 'Elizabeth and I got married a week after graduation. We had a huge wedding at Bradford Farms. You should have seen it. Six hundred people. Our families were both thrilled, though that didn't matter a hoot to us. We were in love. And we had the certainty of the young that nothing would ever change.'

He looked off again. The bus whirred. Someone flipped on a television and then muted the sound.

'The first blow came a year after we wed. Elizabeth learned that she could not have children. Some sort of weakness in her uterine walls. She could get pregnant, but she couldn't carry past the first trimester. It's strange when I think about it now. You see, from the beginning Elizabeth had what I thought of as quiet moments – bouts of melancholy, some might call them. But they didn't seem like melancholy to me. They seemed more like moments of reflection. I found them oddly appealing. Does that make any sense to you?'

Myron nodded, but Arthur was still looking out the window.

'But now the bouts came more often. And they were deeper. Natural, I suppose. Who wouldn't be sad under our circumstances? Today, of course, Elizabeth would have been labeled a manic depressive.' He smiled. 'They say it's all physiological. That there is simply a chemical imbalance in the brain or some such thing. Some even claim that outside stimuli are irrelevant, that even without the uterine problem Elizabeth would have been equally ill in the long run.' He looked at Myron. 'Do you believe that?'

'I don't know.'

He didn't seem to hear. 'I guess it's possible. Mental illnesses are so strange. A physical problem we can understand. But when the mind works irrationally, well, by its very definition, the rational mind cannot truly relate. We can pity. But we cannot fully grasp. So I watched as her sanity began to peel away. She grew worse. Friends who had thought Elizabeth eccentric began to wonder. At times she got so bad that we would feign a vacation and keep her in the house. This went on for years. Slowly the woman I had fallen in love with was eaten away. Well before her death – five, six years before – she was already a different person. We tried our best, of course. We gave her the best medical care and propped her up and sent her back out. But nothing stopped the slide. Eventually Elizabeth could not go out at all.'

Silence.

'Did you institutionalize her?' Myron asked.

Arthur took a swig of his Snapple. His fingers started playing with the bottle's label, pulling up the corners. 'No,' he said at last. 'My family urged me to have her committed. But I couldn't do it. Elizabeth was no longer the woman I loved. I knew that. And maybe I could go on without her. But I could not abandon her. I still owed her that much, no matter what she'd become.'

Myron nodded, said nothing. The TV was off now, but a radio up front blasted an all-news station: you give them twenty-two minutes, they'll give you the world. Sam read his *People*. Chance kept glancing over his shoulder, his eyes thin slits.

'I hired full-time nurses and kept Elizabeth at home. I continued to live my life while she continued to slide toward oblivion. In hindsight, of course, my family was right. I should have had her committed.'

The bus lurched to a stop. Myron and Arthur lurched a bit too.

'You can probably guess what happened next. Elizabeth grew worse. She was nearly catatonic by the end. Whatever evil had entered her brain now moved in and laid total claim. You were right, of course. Her fall was not accidental. Elizabeth jumped. It was not bad luck that she landed on her head. It was intentional on her part. My wife committed suicide.'

He put his hand to his face and leaned back. Myron watched him. It might be an acting job – politicians make awfully good thespians – but Myron thought that he spotted genuine guilt here, that something had indeed fled from this man's eyes and left nothing in their wake. But you never know for sure. Those who claim they can spot a lie are usually just fooled with greater conviction.

'Anita Slaughter found her body?' Myron asked.

He nodded. 'And the rest is classic Bradford. The cover-up began immediately. Bribes were made. You see, a suicide – a wife so crazy that a Bradford man had driven her to kill herself – would simply not do. We would have kept Anita's name out of it too, but her name went over the radio dispatch. The media picked it up.'

That part certainly made sense. 'You mentioned bribes.'

'Yes.'

'How much did Anita get?'

He closed his eyes. 'Anita wouldn't take any money.'

'What did she want?'

'Nothing. She wasn't like that.'

'And you trusted her to keep quiet.'

Arthur nodded. 'Yes,' he said. 'I trusted her.'

'You never threatened her or—'

'Never.'

'I find that hard to believe.'

Arthur shrugged. 'She stayed on for nine more months. That should tell you something.'

That same point again. Myron mulled it over a bit.

He heard a noise at the front of the bus. Chance had stood up. He stormed to the back and stood over them. Both men ignored him.

After several moments Chance said, 'You told him?'

'Yes,' Arthur said.

Chance spun toward Myron. 'If you breathe a word of this to anyone, I'll kill—'

'Shhh.'

Then Myron saw it.

Hanging there. Just out of sight. The story was partially true – the best lies always are – but something was missing. He looked at Arthur. 'You forgot one thing,' Myron said.

Arthur's brow lines deepened. 'What's that?'

Myron pointed to Chance, then back at Arthur. 'Which one of you beat up Anita Slaughter?'

Stone silence.

Myron kept going. 'Just a few weeks before Elizabeth's suicide, someone assaulted Anita Slaughter. She was taken to St. Barnabas Hospital and still had abrasions when your wife jumped. You want to tell me about it?'

Lots of things started happening seemingly all at once. Arthur Bradford gave a small head nod. Sam put down his copy of *People* and stood. Chance turned apoplectic.

'He knows too much!' Chance shouted.

Arthur paused, considering.

'We have to take him out!'

Arthur was still thinking. Sam started moving toward them.

Myron kept his voice low. 'Chance?'

'What?'

'Your fly's undone.'

Chance looked down. Myron already had the thirty-eight out. Now he pressed it firmly against Chance's groin. Chance jumped back a bit, but Myron kept the muzzle in place. Sam took out his gun and pointed it at Myron.

'Tell Sam to sit down,' Myron said, 'or you'll never have trouble fitting a catheter again.'

Everybody froze. Sam kept the gun on Myron. Myron kept his gun against Chance's groin. Arthur still seemed lost in thought. Chance started shaking.

'Don't pee on my gun, Chance.' Tough guy talk. But Myron did not like this. He knew Sam's type. And he knew Sam might very well take the risk and shoot.

'There's no need for the gun,' Arthur said. 'No one is going to harm you.'

'I feel better already.'

'To put it simply, you are worth more to me alive than dead. Otherwise Sam would have blown your head off by now. Do you understand?'

Myron said nothing.

'Our deal remains unchanged: you find Anita, Myron, I'll keep Brenda out of jail. And both of us will leave my wife out of this. Do I make myself clear?'

Sam kept the gun at eye level and smiled a little.

Myron gestured with his head. 'How about a show of good faith?'

Arthur nodded. 'Sam.'

Sam put away the gun. He walked back to his seat and picked up his *People*.

Myron pressed the gun a little harder. Chance yelped. Then Myron pocketed his weapon.

The bus dropped him off back by his car. Sam gave Myron a little salute as he stepped off. Myron nodded in return. The bus continued down the street and disappeared around the corner. Myron realized that he had been holding his breath. He tried to relax and think straight.

'Fitting a catheter,' he said out loud. 'Awful.'

27

Dad's office was still a warehouse in Newark. Years ago they had actually made undergarments here. Not anymore. Now they shipped in finished products from Indonesia or Malaysia or someplace else that employed child labor. Everybody knew that abuses occurred and everybody still used them and every customer still bought the goods because it saved a couple of bucks, and to be fair, the whole issue was morally hazy. Easy to be against children working in factories; easy to be against paying a twelve-year-old twelve cents an hour or whatever; easy to condemn the parents and be against such exploitation. Harder when the choice is twelve cents or starvation, exploitation or death.

Easiest still not to think too much about it.

Thirty years ago, when they actually made the undergarments in Newark, Dad had lots of inner-city blacks working for him. He thought that he was good to his workers. He thought that they viewed him as a benevolent leader. When the riots broke out in 1968, these same workers burned down four of his factory buildings. Dad had never looked at them the same again.

Eloise Williams had been with Dad since before the riots. 'As long as I breathe,' Dad often said, 'Eloise will have a job.' She was like a second wife to him. She took care of him during his workday. They argued and fought and got grumpy with each other. There was genuine affection. Mom knew all this. 'Thank God

Eloise is uglier than a cow living near Chernobyl,' Mom liked to say. 'Or I might wonder.'

Dad's plant used to consist of five buildings. Only this warehouse still stood. Dad used it as a storage facility for the incoming shipments from overseas. His office was smack in the middle and raised to almost the ceiling. All four walls were made of glass, giving Dad the chance to watch over his stock like a prison guard in the main tower.

Myron trotted up the metal stairs. When he reached the top, Eloise greeted him with a big hug and a cheek pinch. He half expected her to take out a little toy from her desk drawer. When he'd visit as a child, she would always be ready for him with a popgun or one of those snap-together gliders or a comic book. But Eloise just gave him a hug this time, and Myron was only mildly disappointed.

'Go right in,' Eloise said. No buzzing in. No checking with Dad first.

Through the glass Myron could see that his father was on the phone. Animated. As always. Myron stepped in. His father held up a finger to him. 'Irv, I said, tomorrow. No excuses. Tomorrow, do you hear?'

Sunday and everyone was still doing business. The shrinking leisure time of the late twentieth century.

Dad hung up the phone. He looked at Myron, and his whole being just beamed. Myron came around the desk and kissed his father's cheek. As always, his skin felt a little like sandpaper and smelled faintly like Old Spice. Just as it should.

His father was dressed like a member of the Israeli Knesset: charcoal slacks with a white dress shirt opened at the neck and a T-shirt underneath. White chest hair popped out of the space between neck and T-shirt front collar. Dad was clearly a Semite – thick dark olive skin and a nose that polite people called prominent.

'Remember Don Rico's?' Dad asked.

'That Portuguese place we used to go?'

Dad nodded. 'Gone. As of last month. Manuel ran the place beautifully for thirty-six years. He finally had to give it up.'

'Sorry to hear that.'

Dad made a scoffing noise and waved him off. 'Who the hell cares? I'm just making silly small talk because I'm a little worried here. Eloise said you sounded funny on the phone.' His voice went soft. 'Everything okay?'

'I'm fine.'

'You need money or something?'

'No, Dad, I don't need money.'

'But something is wrong, no?'

Myron took the plunge. 'Do you know Arthur Bradford?'

Dad's face lost color – not slowly but all at once. He started fiddling with things on his desk. He readjusted the family photographs, taking a little extra time with the one of Myron holding aloft the NCAA trophy after leading Duke to the title. There was an empty box of Dunkin' Donuts. He picked it up and dropped it into a wastepaper basket.

Finally Dad said, 'Why would you ask that?'

'I'm tangled up in something.'

'And it involves Arthur Bradford?'

'Yes,' Myron said.

'Then get untangled. Fast.'

Dad lifted one of those traveling coffee cups to his lips and craned his neck. The cup was empty.

'Bradford told me to ask you about him,' Myron said. 'He and this guy who works for him.'

Dad's neck snapped back into place. 'Sam Richards?' His tone was quiet, awe-filled. 'He's still alive?'

'Yes.'

'Jesus Christ.'

Silence. Then Myron asked, 'How do you know them?'

Dad opened his drawer and fumbled about for something. Then he yelled for Eloise. She came to the door. 'Where's the Tylenol?' he asked her.

'Bottom right-hand drawer. Left side toward the back. Under the box of rubber bands.' Eloise turned to Myron. 'Would you like a Yoo-Hoo?' she asked.

'Yes, please.' Stocking Yoo-Hoos. He had not been to his father's office in almost a decade, but they still stocked his favorite drink. Dad found the bottle and played with the cap. Eloise closed the door on her way out.

'I've never lied to you,' Dad said.

'I know.'

'I've tried to protect you. That's what parents do. They shelter their children. When they see danger coming, they try to step in the way and take the hit.'

'You can't take this hit for me,' Myron said.

Dad nodded slowly. 'Doesn't make it any easier.'

'I'll be okay,' Myron said. 'I just need to know what I'm up against.'

'You're up against pure evil.' Dad shook out two tablets and swallowed them without water. 'You're up against naked cruelty, against men with no conscience.'

Eloise came back in with the Yoo-Hoo. Reading their faces, she silently handed Myron the drink and slipped back out. In the distance a forklift started beeping out the backup warning.

'It was a year or so after the riots,' Dad began. 'You're probably too young to remember them, but the riots ripped this city apart. To this day the rip has never healed. Just the opposite, in fact. It's like one of my garments.' He gestured to the boxes below. 'The garment rips near the seam, and then nobody does anything so it just keeps ripping until the whole thing falls apart. That's Newark. A shredded garment.

'Anyway, my workers finally came back, but they weren't the same people. They were angry now. I wasn't their employer anymore. I was their oppressor. They looked at me like I was the one who dragged their ancestors across the ocean in chains. Then trouble-makers started prodding them. The writing was already on the wall, Myron. The manufacturing end of this business was going to hell. Labor costs were too high. The city was just imploding on itself. And then the hoodlums began to lead the workers. They wanted to form a union. Demanded it, actually. I was against the idea, of course.'

Dad looked out his glass wall at the endless rows of boxes. Myron wondered how many times his father had looked out at this same view. He wondered what his father had thought about when looking out, what he dreamed about over the years in this dusty warehouse. Myron shook the can and popped the top. The sound startled Dad a bit. He looked back at his son and managed a smile.

'Old Man Bradford was hooked in to the mobsters who wanted to set up the union. That's who was involved in this: mobsters, hoodlums, punks who ran everything from prostitutes to numbers; all of a sudden they're labor experts. But I still fought them. And I was winning. So one day Old Man Bradford sends his son Arthur to this very building. To have a chat with me. Sam Richards is with him – the son of a bitch just leans against the wall and says nothing. Arthur sits down and puts his feet on my desk. I'm going to agree to this union, he says. I'm going to support it, in fact. Financially. With generous contributions. I tell the little snotnose there's a word for this. It's called extortion. I tell him to get the hell out of my office.'

Beads of sweat popped up on Dad's forehead. He took a hankie and blotted them a few times. There was a fan in the corner of the office. It oscillated back and forth, teasing you with moments of comfort followed by stifling heat. Myron glanced at the family photos, focusing in on one of his parents on a Caribbean cruise. Maybe ten years ago. Mom and Dad were both wearing loud shirts and looked healthy and tan and much younger. It scared him.

'So what happened then?' Myron asked.

Dad swallowed away something and started speaking again. 'Sam finally spoke. He came over to my desk and looked over the family photos. He smiled, like he was an old friend of the family. Then he tossed these pruning shears on my desk.'

Myron started to feel cold.

His father kept talking, his eyes wide and unfocused. '"Imagine what they could do to a human being," Sam says to me. "Imagine snipping away a piece at a time. Imagine not how long it would take to die but how long you could keep someone alive." That's it. That's all he said. Then Arthur Bradford started laughing, and they both left my office.'

Dad tried the cup of coffee again, but it was still empty. Myron held up the Yoo-Hoo, but Dad shook his head.

'So I go home and try to pretend that everything is hunky-dory. I try to eat. I try to smile. I play with you in the yard. But I can't stop thinking about what Sam said. Your mother knew something was wrong, but for once even she didn't push it. Later I go to bed. I can't sleep at first. It was like Sam said: I kept imagining. About cutting off little pieces of a human being. Slowly. Each cut causing a new scream. And then the phone rang. I jumped up and looked at my watch. It was three in the morning. I picked up the phone, and no one spoke. They were there. I could hear them breathing. But nobody spoke. So I hung up the phone and got out of bed.'

Dad's breathing was shallow now. His eyes were welling up. Myron rose toward him, but Dad held up a hand to stop him.

'Let me just get through this, okay?'

Myron nodded, sat back down.

'I went into your room.' His voice was more monotone now, lifeless and flat. 'You probably know that I used to do that a lot. Sometimes I would just sit in awe and watch you sleep.'

Tears started racing down his face. 'So I stepped in the room. I could hear your deep breathing. The sound comforted me immediately. I smiled. And then I walked over to tuck you in a little better. And that's when I saw it.'

Dad put a fist to his mouth as though stifling a cough. His chest started hitching. His words came in a sputter.

'On your bed. On top of the cover. Pruning shears. Someone had broken into your room and left pruning shears on your bed.'

A steel hand started squeezing Myron's insides.

Dad looked at him with reddening eyes. 'You don't fight men like that, Myron. Because you can't win. It's not a question of bravery. It's a question of caring. You have people you care about, that are connected to you. These men don't even understand that. They don't feel. How do you hurt a person who can't feel?'

Myron had no answer.

'Just walk away,' Dad said. 'There's no shame in that.'

Myron stood up then. So did Dad. They hugged, gripping each other fiercely. Myron closed his eyes. His father cupped the back of his head and then smoothed his hair. Myron snuggled in and stayed there. He inhaled the Old Spice. He traveled back, remembering how this same hand had cradled his head after Joey Davito had hit him with a pitch.

Still comforting, he thought. After all these years, this was still the safest place to be.

28

Pruning shears.

It couldn't be a coincidence. He grabbed his cellular and called the Dragons' practice site. After a few minutes Brenda came on the line.

'Hey,' Brenda said.

'Hey.'

They both fell silent.

'I love a smooth-talking man,' she said.

'Uh-huh,' Myron said.

Brenda laughed. The sound was melodious, plucking at his heart.

'How are you doing?' he asked.

'Good,' she said. 'Playing helps. I've also been thinking about you a lot. That helps too.'

'Mutual,' Myron said. Killer lines, one after another.

'Are you coming to the opener tonight?' Brenda asked.

'Sure. You want me to pick you up?'

'No, I'll take the team bus.'

'Got a question for you,' Myron said.

'Shoot.'

'What are the names of the two boys who had their Achilles tendons sliced in half?'

'Clay Jackson and Arthur Harris.'

'They were cut with pruning shears, right?'

'Right.'

'And they live in East Orange?'

'Yeah, why?'

'I don't think Horace was the one who hurt them.'

'Then who?'

'Long story. I'll tell you about it later.'

'After the game,' Brenda suggested. 'I'll have some media stuff to do, but maybe we can grab a bite and go back to Win's.'

'I'd like that,' Myron said.

Silence.

Brenda said, 'I sound too eager, don't I?'

'Not at all.'

'I should be playing harder to get.'

'No.'

'It's just that' – she stopped, started again – 'it feels right, you know?'

He nodded into the phone. He knew. He thought about what Esperanza had said, about how he 'used to' leave himself totally exposed, keeping his feet planted with nary a worry of getting beaned on the head.

'I'll see you at the game,' he said.

Then he hung up.

He sat and closed his eyes and thought about Brenda. For a moment he didn't push the thoughts away. He let them cascade over him. His body tingled. He started smiling.

Brenda.

He opened his eyes and came out of it. He switched on the car phone again and dialed Win's number.

'Articulate.'

'I need some backup,' Myron said.

'Bitching,' Win said.

They met up at the Essex Green Mall in West Orange.

'How far is the ride?' Win asked.

'Ten minutes.'

'Bad area?'

'Yes.'

Win looked at his precious Jag. 'We'll take your car.'

They got into the Ford Taurus. The late-summer sun still cast long, thin shadows. Heat rose from the sidewalk in lazy tendrils, dark and smoky. The air was so thick that an apple falling from a tree would take several minutes to hit the ground.

'I looked into the Outreach Education scholarship,' Win said. 'Whoever set up the fund had a great deal of financial acumen. The money was dumped in from a foreign source, more specifically the Cayman Islands.'

'So it's untraceable?'

'Almost untraceable,' Win corrected. 'But even in places like the Caymans a greased palm is a greased palm.'

'So who do we grease?'

'Already done. Unfortunately the account was in a dummy name and closed four years ago.'

'Four years ago,' Myron repeated. 'That would be right after Brenda received her last scholarship. Before she started medical school.'

Win nodded. 'Logical,' he said. Like he was Spock.

'So it's a dead end.'

'Temporarily, yes. Someone could prowl through old records, but it will take a few days.'

'Anything else?'

'The scholarship recipient was to be chosen by certain attorneys rather than any educational institution. The criteria were vague: academic potential, good citizenship, that type of thing.'

'In other words, it was fixed so the attorneys would select Brenda. Like we said before, it was a way of funneling her money.'

Another nod. 'Logical,' he repeated.

They started moving from West Orange into East

Orange. The transformation was gradual. The fine suburban homes turned into gated condo developments. Then the houses came back – smaller now, less land, more worn and crowded together. Abandoned factories started popping up. Subsidy housing too. It was a butterfly in reverse, turning back into a caterpillar.

'I also received a call from Hal,' Win said. Hal was an electronics expert they had worked with during their days working for the government. He'd been the one Myron had sent to check for phone taps.

'And?'

'All the residences contained telephone listening devices and traces – Mabel Edwards's, Horace Slaughter's, and Brenda's dorm room.'

'No surprise,' Myron said.

'Except for one thing,' Win corrected. 'The devices in the two households – that is, Mabel's and Horace's homes – were old. Hal estimated that they had been present for at least three years.'

Myron's head started spinning again. 'Three years?'

'Yes. It's an estimate, of course. But the pieces were old and in some cases crusted over from dirt.'

'What about the tap on Brenda's phone?'

'More recent. But she's only lived there a few months. And Hal also found listening devices in Brenda's room. One under her desk in her bedroom. Another behind a sofa in the common room.'

'Microphones?'

Win nodded. 'Someone was interested in more than Brenda's telephone calls.'

'Jesus Christ.'

Win almost smiled. 'Yes, I thought you might find it odd.'

Myron tried to enter the new data into his brain.

'Someone has obviously been spying on the family for a long time.'

'Obviously.'

'That means that it has to be somebody with resources.'

'Indeed.'

'Then it has to be the Bradfords,' Myron said. 'They're looking for Anita Slaughter. For all we know, they've been looking for twenty years. It's the only thing that makes sense. And you know what else this means?'

'Do tell,' Win said.

'Arthur Bradford has been conning me.'

Win gasped. 'A less than truthful politician? Next you'll tell me there's no Easter Bunny.'

'It's like we thought from the start,' Myron said. 'Anita Slaughter ran because she was scared. And that's why Arthur Bradford is being so cooperative. He wants me to find Anita Slaughter for him. So he can kill her.'

'And then he'll try to kill you,' Win added. He studied his hair in the visor mirror. 'Being this handsome. It is not easy, you realize.'

'And yet you suffer without complaint.'

'That is my way.' Win took one last look before snapping the visor back in place.

Clay Jackson lived in a row of houses whose backyards sat above Route 280. The neighborhood looked like working poor. The homes were all two-family, except for several corner residences that doubled as taverns. Tired neon Budweiser signs flickered through murky windows. Fences were all chain-link. So many overgrown weeds had popped through the sidewalk cracks that it was impossible to tell where pavement ended and lawn began.

Again all the inhabitants appeared to be black. Again

Myron felt his customary and seemingly inexplicable discomfort.

There was a park across the street from Clay Jackson's house. People were setting up for a barbecue. A softball game was going on. Loud laughter exploded everywhere. So did a boom box. When Myron and Win got out of the car, all eyes swerved in their direction. The boom box went suddenly silent. Myron forced up a smile. Win remained completely unbothered by the scrutiny.

'They're staring,' Myron said.

'If two black men pulled up to your house in Livingston,' Win said, 'what sort of reception would they receive?'

Myron nodded. 'So you figure the neighbors are calling the cops and describing two "suspicious youths" prowling the streets?'

Win raised an eyebrow. 'Youths?'

'Wishful thinking.'

'Yes, I'd say.'

They headed up a stoop that looked like the one on Sesame Street. A man poked through a nearby garbage can, but he looked nothing like Oscar the Grouch. Myron knocked on the door. Win started with the eyes, the gliding movement, taking it all in. The softballers and barbecuers across the street were still staring. They did not seem pleased with what they saw.

Myron knocked again.

'Who is it?' a woman's voice called.

'My name is Myron Bolitar. This is Win Lockwood. We'd like to see Clay Jackson if he's available.'

'Could you hold on a second?'

They held on for at least a full minute. Then they heard a chain rattle. The knob turned, and a woman appeared in the doorway. She was black and maybe forty years old. Her smile kept flickering like one of those neon Budweiser signs in the tavern windows. 'I'm Clay's mother,' she said. 'Please come in.'

They followed her inside. Something good was cooking on the stove. An old air-conditioning unit roared like a DC-10, but it worked. The coolness was most welcome, though short-lived. Clay's mother quickly hustled them through a narrow corridor and back out the kitchen door. They were outside again, in the backyard now.

'Can I get you a drink?' she asked. She had to yell over the sounds of traffic.

Myron looked at Win. Win was frowning. Myron said, 'No, thank you.'

'Okay.' The smile flickered faster now, almost like a disco strobe light. 'Let me just go get Clay. I'll be right back.' The screen door slammed shut.

They were alone outside. The yard was tiny. There were flower boxes bursting with colors and two large bushes that were dying. Myron moved to the fence and looked down at Route 280. The four-lane highway was moving briskly. Car fumes drifted slowly in this humidity, hanging there, not dissipating; when Myron swallowed, he could actually taste them.

'This isn't good,' Win said.

Myron nodded. Two white men show up at your house. You don't know either one. You don't ask for ID. You just show them in and leave them out back. Something was definitely not right here.

'Let's just see how it plays out,' Myron said.

It did not take long. Eight large men came from three different directions. Two burst through the back door. Three circled in from the right side of the house. Three more from the left. They all carried aluminum baseball bats and let's-kick-some-ass scowls. They fanned out, encircling the yard. Myron felt his pulse race. Win folded his arms; only his eyes moved.

These were not street punks or members of a gang. They were the softball players from across the street, grown men with bodies hardened by daily labor – dockworkers and truck loaders and the like. Some held their bats in a ready-to-swing position. Others rested them on their shoulders. Still others bounced them gently against their legs, like Joe Don Baker in *Walking Tall*.

Myron squinted into the sun. 'You guys finish your game?' he asked.

The biggest man stepped forward. He had an enormous iron-cauldron gut, calloused hands, and the muscular yet unchiseled arms of someone who could crush Nautilus equipment like so many Styrofoam cups. His Nike baseball cap was set on the largest size, but it still fitted him like a yarmulke. His T-shirt had a Reebok logo. Nike cap, Reebok T-shirt. Confusing brand loyalties.

'Game is just beginning, fool.'

Myron looked at Win. Win said, 'Decent delivery, but the line lacked originality. Plus, tagging the word *fool* on the end – that seemed forced. I'll have to give him a thumbs-down, but I look forward to his next work.'

The eight men looped around Myron and Win. Nike/Reebok, the obvious leader, gestured with the baseball bat. 'Hey, Wonder bread, get your ass over here.'

Win looked at Myron. Myron said, 'I think he means you.'

'Must be because I help build strong bodies in twelve ways.' Then Win smiled, and Myron felt his heart stutter. People always did that. They always homed in on Win. At five-ten Win was a half foot shorter than Myron. But it was more than that. The blond, pale-faced, blue-veined, china-boned exterior brought out the worst in people. Win appeared soft, unlabored, sheltered – the kind of guy you hit and he shatters like cheap porcelain. Easy prey. Everyone likes easy prey.

Win stepped toward Nike/Reebok. He arched an eyebrow and gave him his best Lurch. 'You rang?'

'What's your name, Wonder bread?'

'Thurgood Marshall,' Win said.

That reply didn't sit well with the crowd. Murmurs began. 'You making a racist crack?'

'As opposed to, say, calling someone Wonder bread?'

Win glanced at Myron and gave him a thumbs-up. Myron returned the gesture. If this were a school debate, Win would be up a point.

'You a cop, Thurgood?'

Win frowned. 'In *this* suit?' He pulled at his own lapels. 'Puleeze.'

'So what do you want here?'

'We wish to speak with one Clay Jackson.'

'What about?'

'Solar energy and its role in the twenty-first century.'

Nike/Reebok checked his troops. The troops tightened the noose. Myron felt a rushing in his ears. He kept his eyes on Win and waited.

'Seems to me,' the leader continued, 'that you white boys are here to hurt Clay again.' Moving closer. Eye to eye. 'Seems to me that we have the right to use lethal force to protect him. That right, fellas?'

The troops grunted their agreement, raising their bats.

Win's move was sudden and unexpected. He simply reached out and snatched the bat away from Nike/Reebok. The big man's mouth formed an O of surprise. He stared at his hands as though he expected the bat to rematerialize at any moment. It wouldn't. Win chucked the bat into the corner of the yard.

Then Win beckoned the big man forward. 'Care to tango, pumpernickel bread?'

Myron said, 'Win.'

But Win kept his eyes on his opponent. 'I'm waiting.'

Nike/Reebok grinned. Then he rubbed his hands together and wet his lips. 'He's all mine, fellas.'

Yep, easy prey.

The big man lunged forward like a Frankenstein monster, his thick fingers reaching for Win's neck. Win remained motionless until the last possible moment. Then he darted inside, his fingertips pressed together, transforming his hand into something of a spear. The fingertips struck deep and quick at the big man's larynx, the movement like a bird doing a fast peck. A gagging sound not unlike a dental sucking machine forced its way out the big man's mouth; his hands instinctively flew up to his throat. Win ducked low and whipped his foot around. The heel swept Nike/Reebok's legs. The big man flipped midair and landed on the back of his head.

Win jammed his .44 into the man's face. He was still smiling.

'Seems to me,' Win said, 'that you just attacked me with a baseball bat. Seems to me that shooting you in the right eye would be viewed as perfectly justifiable.'

Myron had his gun out too. He ordered everyone to drop his bat. They did so. Then he had them lie on their stomachs, hands behind their heads, fingers locked. It took a minute or two, but everyone obeyed.

Nike/Reebok was now on his stomach too. He craned his neck and croaked, 'Not again.'

Win cupped his ear with his free hand. 'Pardon *moi*?'

'We ain't gonna let you hurt that boy again.'

Win burst out laughing and nudged the man's head with his toe. Myron caught Win's eye and shook his head. Win shrugged and stopped.

'We don't want to hurt anyone,' Myron said. 'We're just trying to find out who attacked Clay on that rooftop.'

'Why?' a voice asked. Myron turned to the screen door. A young man hobbled out on crutches. The cast protecting the tendon looked like some puffy sea creature in the process of swallowing his entire foot.

'Because everyone thinks Horace Slaughter did it,' Myron said.

Clay Jackson balanced himself on one leg. 'So?'

'So did he?'

'Why do you care?'

'Because he's been murdered.'

Clay shrugged. 'So?'

Myron opened his mouth, closed it, sighed. 'It's a long story, Clay. I just want to know who cut your tendon.'

The kid shook his head. 'I ain't talking about it.'

'Why not?'

'They told me not to.'

Win spoke to the boy for the first time. 'And you have chosen to obey them?'

The boy faced Win now. 'Yeah.'

'The man who did this,' Win continued. 'You find him scary?'

Clay's Adam's apple danced. 'Shit, yeah.'

Win grinned. 'I'm scarier.'

No one moved.

'Would you care for a demonstration?'

Myron said, 'Win.'

Nike/Reebok decided to take a chance. He started to scramble up on his elbows. Win raised his foot and slammed an ax kick into the spot where the spine met the neck. Nike/Reebok slumped back to the ground like wet sand, his arms splayed. He did not move at all. Win rested his foot on the back of the man's skull. The Nike hat slipped off. Win pushed the still face into the muddy ground as though he were grinding out a cigarette.

Myron said, 'Win.'

'Stop it!' Clay Jackson cried. He looked to Myron for help, his eyes wide and desperate. 'He's my uncle, man. He's just looking out for me.'

'And doing a wonderful job,' Win added. He stepped up, gaining leverage. The uncle's face sank deeper into the soft earth. His features were fully embedded in the mud now, his mouth and nose clogged.

The big man could no longer breathe.

One of the other men started to rise. Win leveled his gun at the man's head. 'Important note,' Win said. 'I'm not big on warning shots.'

The man slinked back down.

With his foot still firmly planted on the man's head, Win turned his attention to Clay Jackson. The boy was trying to look tough, but he was visibly quaking. So, quite frankly, was Myron.

'You fear a possibility,' Win said to the boy, 'when you should fear a certainty.'

Win raised his foot, bending his knee. He angled himself for the proper heel strike.

Myron started to move toward him, but Win froze him with a glance. Then Win gave that smile again, the little one. It was casual, slightly amused. The smile said that he would do it. The smile hinted that he might even enjoy it. Myron had seen the smile many times, yet it never failed to chill his blood.

'I'll count to five,' Win told the boy. 'But I'll probably crush his skull before I reach three.'

'Two white guys,' Clay Jackson said quickly. 'With guns. A big guy tied us up. He was young and looked like he worked out. The little old guy – he was the leader. He was the one who cut us.'

Win turned to Myron. He spread his hands. 'Can we go now?'

29

Back in the car, Myron said, 'You went too far.'

'Uh-hmm.'

'I mean it, Win.'

'You wanted the information. I got it.'

'Not like that I didn't.'

'Oh, please. The man came at me with a baseball bat.'

'He was scared. He thought we were trying to hurt his nephew.'

Win played the air violin.

Myron shook his head. 'The kid would have told us eventually.'

'Doubtful. This Sam character had the boy scared.'

'So you had to scare him more?'

'That would be a yes,' Win said.

'You can't do that again, Win. You can't hurt innocent people.'

'Uh-hmm,' Win said again. He checked his watch. 'Are you through now? Is your need to feel morally superior satiated?'

'What the hell does that mean?'

Win looked at him. 'You know what I do,' he said slowly. 'Yet you always call on me.'

Silence. The echo of Win's words hung in the air, caught in the humidity like the car fumes. Myron gripped the steering wheel. His knuckles turned white.

They did not speak again until they reached Mabel Edwards's house.

'I know you're violent,' Myron said. He put the car in

park and looked at his friend. 'But for the most part you only hurt people who deserve it.'

Win said nothing.

'If the boy hadn't talked, would you have gone through with your threat?'

'Not an issue,' Win said. 'I knew the boy would talk.'

'But suppose he hadn't.'

Win shook his head. 'You are dealing with something out of the realm of possibility.'

'Humor me then.'

Win thought about it for a moment. 'I never intentionally hurt innocent people,' he said. 'But I never threaten idly either.'

'That's not an answer, Win.'

Win looked at Mabel's house. 'Go inside, Myron. Time's awasting.'

Mabel Edwards sat across from him in a small den. 'So Brenda remembers the Holiday Inn,' she said.

A small yellowish trace of the bruise remained around her eye, but hey, it would go away before the soreness in Big Mario's groin did. Mourners were still milling about, but the house was hushed now; reality set in with the darkness. Win was outside, keeping watch.

'Very vaguely,' Myron replied. 'It was more like déjà vu than anything concrete.'

Mabel nodded as though this made sense. 'It was a long time ago.'

'Then Brenda was at the hotel?'

Mabel looked down, smoothed the bottom of her dress, reached for her cup of tea. 'Brenda was there,' she said, 'with her mother.'

'When?'

Mabel held the cup in front of her lips. 'The night Anita disappeared.'

Myron tried not to look too confused. 'She took Brenda with her?'

'At first, yes.'

'I don't understand. Brenda never said anything—'

'Brenda was five years old. She doesn't remember. Or at least that's what Horace thought.'

'But you didn't say anything before.'

'Horace didn't want her knowing about it,' Mabel said. 'He thought it would hurt her.'

'But I still don't get it. Why did Anita take Brenda to a hotel?'

Mabel Edwards finally took a sip of the tea. Then she set it back down gently. She smoothed the dress again and fiddled with the chain around her neck. 'It's like I told you before. Anita wrote Horace a note saying she was running away. She cleared out all his money and took off.'

Myron saw it now. 'But she planned on taking Brenda with her.'

'Yes.'

The money, Myron thought. Anita's taking all of it had always bothered him. Running away from danger is one thing. But leaving your daughter penniless – that seemed unusually cruel. But now there was an explanation: Anita had intended to take Brenda.

'So what happened?' Myron asked.

'Anita changed her mind.'

'Why?'

A woman poked her head through the doorway. Mabel fired a glare, and the head disappeared like something in a shooting gallery. Myron could hear kitchen noises, family and friends cleaning up to prepare for another day of mourning. Mabel looked like she'd aged since this morning. Fatigue emanated from her like a fever.

'Anita packed them both up,' she managed. 'She ran away and checked them into that hotel. I don't know what happened then. Maybe Anita got scared. Maybe she realized how impossible it would be to run away with a five-year-old. No matter. Anita called Horace. She was crying and all hysterical. It was all too much for her, she said. She told Horace to come pick up Brenda.'

Silence.

'So Horace went to the Holiday Inn?' Myron asked.

'Yes.'

'Where was Anita?'

Mabel shrugged. 'She'd run off already, I guess.'

'And this all happened the first night she ran away?'

'Yes.'

'So Anita could not have been gone for more than a few hours, right?'

'That's right.'

'So what made Anita change her mind so fast?' Myron asked. 'What could possibly have made her decide to give up her daughter that quickly?'

Mabel Edwards rose with a great sigh and made her way to the television set. Her normally supple, fluid movements had been stiffened by her grief. She reached out with a tentative hand and plucked a photograph off the top. Then she showed it to Myron.

'This is Terence's father, Roland,' she said. 'My husband.'

Myron looked at the black-and-white photograph.

'Roland was shot coming home from work. For twelve dollars. Right on our front stoop. Two shots in the head. For twelve dollars.' Her voice was a monotone now, dispassionate. 'I didn't handle it well. Roland was the only man I ever loved. I started drinking. Terence was only a little boy, but he looked so much like his father I could barely stand to look at his face. So

I drank some more. And then I took some drugs. I stopped taking care of my son. The state came and put him in a foster home.'

Mabel looked at Myron for a reaction. He tried to keep his face neutral.

'Anita was the one who saved me. She and Horace sent me away to get clean. It took me a while, but I straightened myself out. Anita took care of Terence in the meantime, so the state wouldn't take him away from me.' Mabel lifted the reading glasses off her chest and put them on her nose. Then she stared at the image of her dead husband. The longing in her face was so raw, so naked, that Myron felt a tear push into his own eye.

'When I needed her most,' Mabel said, 'Anita was there for me. Always.'

She looked at Myron again.

'Do you understand what I'm telling you?'

'No, ma'am, I don't.'

'Anita was there for me,' Mabel repeated. 'But when she was in trouble, where was I? I knew she and Horace were having problems. And I ignored it. She disappeared, and what did I do? I tried to forget her. She ran off, and I bought this nice house away from the slums and tried to put it all behind me. If Anita had just left my brother, well, that would have been awful. But something scared Anita so bad she abandoned her own child. Just like that. And I keep asking myself what that something was. What could have scared her so bad that twenty years later she still won't come back?'

Myron shifted in the chair. 'Have you come up with any answers?'

'Not on my own,' she said. 'But I asked Anita once.'

'When?'

'Fifteen years ago, I guess. When she called to check

up on Brenda. I asked why she wouldn't come back and see her own daughter.'

'What did she say?'

Mabel looked him straight in the eye. 'She said, "If I come back, Brenda dies." '

Myron felt a cold gust chill his heart. 'What did she mean by that?'

'Like it was just a given. Like one and one equals two.' She put the photograph back on top of the television. 'I never asked Anita again,' she said. 'The way I see it, there are some things you're just better off never knowing.'

30

Myron and Win took separate cars back to New York City. Brenda's game started in forty-five minutes. Just enough time to run into the loft and change clothes.

He double-parked on Spring Street and left his key in the ignition. The car was safe: Win was waiting in the Jag for him. Myron took the elevator up. He opened the door. And Jessica was standing there.

He froze.

Jessica looked at him. 'I'm not running away,' she said. 'Not ever again.'

Myron swallowed, nodded. He tried to step forward, but his legs had other ideas.

'What's wrong?' she asked.

'A lot,' he said.

'I'm listening.'

'My friend Horace was murdered.'

Jessica closed her eyes. 'I'm sorry.'

'And Esperanza's leaving MB.'

'You couldn't work something out?'

'No.'

Myron's cellular phone rang. He snapped the power off. They stood there, neither of them moving.

Then Jessica said, 'What else?'

'That's it.'

She shook her head. 'You can't even look at me.'

So he did. Myron lifted his head and stared right at her for the first time since entering the loft. Jessica was, as always, achingly beautiful. He felt something inside him start to rip.

'I almost slept with someone else,' he said.

Jessica did not move. 'Almost?'

'Yes.'

'I see,' she said. Then: 'So why almost?'

'Pardon?'

'Did she stop it? Or did you?'

'I did.'

'Why?' she asked.

'Why?'

'Yes, Myron, why didn't you consummate the act?'

'Jesus, that's a hell of a question.'

'No, not really. You were tempted, right?'

'Yes.'

'More than tempted even,' she added. 'You wanted to go through with it.'

'I don't know.'

Jessica made a buzzing noise. 'Liar.'

'Fine, I wanted to go through with it.'

'Why didn't you?'

'Because I'm involved with another woman,' he said. 'In fact, I'm in love with another woman.'

'How chivalrous. So you held back for me?'

'I held back for us.'

'Another lie. You held back for you. Myron Bolitar, the perfect guy, the one-woman wonder.'

She made a fist and put it to her mouth. Myron stepped toward her, but she backed away.

'I've been dumb,' Jessica said. 'I admit that. I've done so many dumb things it's a wonder you haven't dumped me. Maybe I did all those dumb things because I knew I could. You'd always love me. No matter how dumb I acted, you'd always love me. So maybe I'm owed a little payback.'

'This isn't about payback,' Myron said.

'I know, goddamn it.' She wrapped her arms around herself. As though the room had suddenly gone very cold. As though she needed a hug. 'That's what terrifies me.'

He kept still and waited.

'You don't cheat, Myron. You don't fool around. You don't have flings. Hell, you don't even get tempted much. So the question is, how much do you love her?'

Myron held up his hands. 'I barely know her.'

'You think that matters?'

'I don't want to lose you, Jess.'

'And I'm not about to give you up without a fight. But I want to know what I'm up against.'

'It's not like that.'

'So what's it like?'

Myron opened his mouth, closed it. Then he said, 'Do you want to get married?'

Jessica blinked, but she didn't step back. 'Is this a proposal?'

'I'm asking you a question. Do you want to get married?'

'If that's what it takes, yeah, I want to get married.'

Myron smiled. 'My, what enthusiasm.'

'What do you want me to say, Myron? Whatever you want me to say, I'll say. Yes, no, whatever will keep you here with me.'

'This isn't a test, Jess.'

'Then why are you raising marriage all of a sudden?'

'Because I want to be with you forever,' he said. 'And I want to buy a house. And I want to have kids.'

'So do I,' she said. 'But life is so good right now. We've got our careers, our freedom. Why spoil it? There'll be time for all that later.'

Myron shook his head.

'What?' she said.

'You're stalling.'

'No, I'm not.'

'Having a family is not something I want to fit into a convenient time block.'

'But now?' Jessica put up her hands. 'Right now? This is what you really want? A house in the suburbs like your parents? The Saturday night barbecues? The backyard hoop? The PTA meetings? The back-to-school shopping at the mall? That's what you really want?'

Myron looked at her, and he felt something deep within him crumble. 'Yes,' he said. 'That's exactly what I want.'

They both stood and stared at each other. There was a knock on the door. Neither one of them moved. Another knock. Then Win's voice: 'Open it.'

Win was not one for casual interruptions. Myron did as he asked. Win glanced at Jessica and gave her a slight nod. He handed Myron his cellular. 'It's Norm Zuckerman,' Win said. 'He's been trying to reach you.'

Jessica turned and left the room. Quickly. Win watched her, but he kept his expression even. Myron took the phone. 'Yeah, Norm.'

Norm's voice was pure panic. 'It's almost game time.'

'So?'

'So where the hell is Brenda?'

Myron felt his heart leap into his throat. 'She told me she was riding on the team bus.'

'She never got on it, Myron.'

Myron flashed back to Horace on the morgue slab. His knees almost buckled. Myron looked at Win.

'I'll drive,' Win said.

31

They took the Jag. Win did not slow for red lights. He did not slow for pedestrians. Twice Win veered up on sidewalks to bypass heavy traffic.

Myron looked straight ahead. 'What I said before. About your going too far.'

Win waited.

'Forget it,' Myron said.

For the rest of the ride, neither man spoke.

Win screeched the car into an illegal spot on the southeast corner of Thirty-third Street and Eighth Avenue. Myron sprinted toward the Madison Square Garden employee entrance. A police officer sauntered toward Win with major attitude. Win ripped a hundred-dollar bill and handed one half to the officer. The officer nodded and tipped his cap. No words needed to be exchanged.

The guard at the employee entrance recognized Myron and waved him through.

'Where's Norm Zuckerman?' Myron asked.

'Press room. Other side of the—'

Myron knew where it was. As he bounded up the stairs, he could hear the pregame hum of the crowd. The sound was oddly soothing. When he reached court level, he veered to his right. The press room was on the other side of the floor. He ran out onto the playing surface. The crowd, he was surprised to see, was enormous. Norm had told him how he planned to darken and close off the top sections – that is, drape a black curtain over the unused seats so as to give the arena a more crowded yet intimate feel. But sales had far surpassed expectations. A sellout crowd was finding its seats. Many fans held up banners: DAWN OF AN ERA, BRENDA RULES, WELCOME TO THE HOUSE OF BRENDA, NOW IT'S OUR TURN, SISTERS ARE DOING IT FOR THEMSELVES, YOU GO, GIRLS! Stuff like that. Sponsors' logos dominated the landscape like the work of a mad graffiti artist. Giant images of a stunning Brenda flashed across the overhead scoreboard. A highlight reel of some kind. Brenda in her college uniform. Loud music started up. Hip music. That was what Norm wanted. Hip. He'd been generous with the comp tickets too. Spike Lee was courtside. So were Jimmy Smits and Rosie O'Donnell and Sam Waterston and Woody Allen and Rudy Giuliani. Several ex-MTV hosts, the biggest sort of has-beens, mugged for cameras, desperate to be seen. Supermodels wore wire-rimmed glasses, trying a little too hard to look both beautiful and studious.

They were all here to toast New York's latest phenom: Brenda Slaughter.

This was supposed to be her night, her chance to shine in the pro arena. Myron had thought that he understood Brenda's insistence on playing the opener. But he hadn't. This was more than a game. More than her love for basketball. More than a personal tribute. This was history. Brenda had seen that. In this era of jaded superstars she relished the chance to be a role model and shape impressionable kids. Corny, but there you have it. Myron paused for a moment and looked at the Jumbo-tron screen above his head. The digitally enlarged Brenda was driving hard to the hoop, her face a mask of determination, her body and movements fiercely splendid and graceful and purposeful.

Brenda would not be denied.

Myron picked up the sprint again. He left the court and dipped down the ramp and back into a corridor. In a matter of moments he reached the press room. Win was coming up behind him. Myron opened the door. Norm Zuckerman was there. So were Detectives Maureen McLaughlin and Dan Tiles.

Tiles made a point of checking his watch. 'That was fast,' he said. He may have been smirking under the hinterlands that doubled as his mustache.

'Is she here?' Myron asked.

Maureen McLaughlin gave him the on-your-side smile. 'Why don't you sit down, Myron?'

Myron ignored her. He turned to Norm. 'Has Brenda shown up?'

Norm Zuckerman was dressed like Janis Joplin guest-starring on *Miami Vice*. 'No,' he said.

Win trotted in behind Myron. Tiles didn't like the intrusion. He crossed the room and gave Win the tough guy scrutiny. Win let him. 'And who might this be?' Tiles asked.

Win pointed at Tiles's face. 'You got some food stuck in your mustache. Looks like scrambled eggs.'

Myron kept his eyes on Norm. 'What are they doing here?'

'Sit down, Myron.' It was McLaughlin again. 'We need to chat.'

Myron glanced over at Win. Win nodded. He moved toward Norm Zuckerman and put his arm around his shoulders. The two of them headed for a corner.

'Sit,' McLaughlin said again. There was just a hint of steel this time.

Myron slid into a chair. McLaughlin did likewise, maintaining oodles of eye contact along the way. Tiles stayed standing and glared down at Myron. He was one of those idiots who believed that head level equaled intimidation.

'What happened?' Myron asked.

Maureen McLaughlin folded her hands. 'Why don't you tell us, Myron?'

He shook his head. 'I don't have time for this, Maureen. Why are you here?'

'We're looking for Brenda Slaughter,' McLaughlin said. 'Do you know where she is?'

'No. Why are you looking for her?'

'We'd like to ask her some questions.'

Myron looked around the room. 'And you figured the best time to ask them would be right before the biggest game of her life?'

McLaughlin and Tiles sneaked an obvious glance. Myron checked out Win. He was still whispering with Norm.

Tiles stepped up to the plate. 'When did you last see Brenda Slaughter?'

'Today,' Myron said.

'Where?'

This was going to take too long. 'I don't have to answer your questions, Tiles. And neither does Brenda. I'm her attorney, remember? You got something, let me know. If not, stop wasting my time.'

Tiles's mustache seemed to curl up in a grin. 'Oh, we got something, smart guy.'

Myron did not like the way he said that. 'I'm listening.'

McLaughlin leaned forward, again with the earnest eyes. 'We got a search warrant this morning for the college dormitory of Brenda Slaughter.' Her tone was all police official now. 'We found on the premises one weapon, a Smith and Wesson thirty-eight, the same caliber that killed Horace Slaughter. We're waiting for a ballistics test to see if it's the murder weapon.'

'Fingerprints?' Myron asked.

McLaughlin shook her head. 'Wiped clean.'

'Even if it is the murder weapon,' Myron said, 'it was obviously planted.'

McLaughlin looked puzzled. 'How do you know that, Myron?'

'Come on, Maureen. Why would she wipe the weapon clean and then leave it where you could find it?'

'It was hidden under her mattress,' McLaughlin countered.

Win stepped away from Norm Zuckerman. He started dialing on his cell phone. Someone answered. Win kept his voice low.

Myron shrugged, feigning nonchalance. 'Is that all you got?'

'Don't try to snow us, asshole.' Tiles again. 'We have a motive: she feared her father enough to get a restraining order. We found the murder weapon hidden under her own mattress. And now we have the fact that she's clearly on the lam. That's a shitload more than enough to make an arrest.'

'So that's why you're here?' Myron countered. 'To arrest her?'

Again McLaughlin and Tiles exchanged a glance. 'No,' McLaughlin said as though pronouncing the word took great effort. 'But we would very much like to speak with her again.'

Win disconnected the call. Then he beckoned Myron with a nod.

Myron rose. 'Excuse me.'

Tiles said, 'What the hell!'

'I need to converse with my associate for a moment. I'll be right back.'

Myron and Win ducked into a corner. Tiles lowered his eyebrows to half-mast and put his fists on his hips. Win stared back for a moment. Tiles kept up the scowl. Win put his thumbs in his ears, stuck out his tongue, wiggled his fingers. Tiles did not follow suit.

Win spoke softly and quickly. 'According to Norm, Brenda received a call at practice. She took the call and ran out. The team bus waited awhile, but Brenda ended up being a no-show. When the bus left, an assistant coach waited with her car. The coach is still at the practice site. That's all Norm knew. I then called Arthur Bradford. He knew about the search warrant. He claimed that by the time you two made your arrangement vis-à-vis protecting Brenda, the warrant had been acted upon and the gun had been found. He has since contacted some friends in high places, and they have agreed to move very slowly on Ms. Slaughter.'

Myron nodded. That explained the semidiplomacy going on here. McLaughlin and Tiles clearly wanted to arrest her, but the higher-ups were holding them back. 'Anything else?'

'Arthur was very concerned about Brenda's disappearance.'

'I bet.'

'He wants you to call him immediately.'

'Well, we don't always get what we want,' Myron said. He glanced back at the two detectives. 'Okay, I got to clear out of here.'

'You have a thought?'

'The detective from Livingston. A guy named Wickner. He almost cracked at the Little League field.'

'And you think perhaps he'll crack this time?'

Myron nodded. 'He'll crack.'

'Would you like me to come along?'

'No, I'll handle it. I need you to stay here. McLaughlin and Tiles can't legally hold me, but they might try. Stall them for me.'

Win almost smiled. 'No problem.'

'See also if you can find the guy who answered the phone at the practice. Whoever called Brenda might have identified themselves. Maybe one of her teammates or coaches saw something.'

'I'll look into it.' Win handed Myron the ripped hundred and his car keys. He motioned toward his cell phone. 'Keep the line open.'

Myron did not bother with good-byes. He suddenly bounded out of the room. He heard Tiles call after him. 'Stop! Son of a—' Tiles started running after him. Win stepped in front of him, blocking his path. 'What the f—' Tiles never finished the expletive. Myron continued to run. Win closed the door. Tiles would not get out.

Once out on the street, Myron tossed the bill to the waiting cop and hopped into the Jag. Eli Wickner's lake house was listed in directory assistance. Myron dialed the number. Wickner answered on the first ring.

'Brenda Slaughter is missing,' Myron told him.

Silence.

'We need to talk, Eli.'

'Yes,' the retired detective said. 'I think we do.'

32

The ride took an hour. Night had firmly set in by now, and the lake area seemed extra dark, the way lake areas often do. There were no streetlights. Myron slowed the car. Old Lake Drive was narrow and only partially paved. At the end of the road his headlights crossed a wooden sign shaped like a fish. The sign said THE WICKNERS. Wickners. Myron remembered Mrs. Wickner. She had overseen the food stand at the Little League field. Her semiblonde hair had been overtreated to the point where it resembled hay, her laugh a constant, deep throttle. Lung cancer had claimed her ten years ago. Eli Wickner had retired to this cabin alone.

Myron pulled into the driveway. His tires chewed the gravel. Lights came on, probably by motion detector. Myron stopped the car and stepped into the still night. The cabin was what was often called saltbox. Nice. And right on the water. There were boats in the dock. Myron listened for the sound of the lapping water, but there was none. The lake was incredibly calm, as if someone had put a glass top on it for night protection. Scattered lights shone off the glacial surface, still and without deviation. The moon dangled like a loose earring. Bats stood along a tree branch like the Queen's Guards in miniature.

Myron hurried to the front door. Lamps were on inside, but Myron saw no movement. He knocked on the door. No answer. He knocked again. Then he felt the shotgun barrel against the back of his skull.

'Don't turn around,' Eli said.

Myron didn't.

'You armed?'

'Yes.'

'Assume the position. And don't make me shoot you, Myron. You've always been a good kid.'

'There's no need for the gun, Eli.' It was a dumb thing to say, of course, but he had not said it for Wickner's benefit. Win was listening in on the other end. Myron did some quick calculating. It had taken him an hour to get here. It would take Win maybe half that.

He needed to stall.

As Wickner patted him down, Myron smelled alcohol. Not a good sign. He debated making a move, but this was an experienced cop, and he was, per Wickner's request, in the position. Hard to do much from there.

Wickner found Myron's gun immediately. He emptied the bullets onto the ground and pocketed the gun.

'Open the door,' Wickner said.

Myron turned the knob. Wickner gave him a little nudge. Myron stepped inside. And his heart dropped to his knees. Fear constricted his throat, making it very hard to breathe. The room was decorated as one might expect a fishing cabin to be decorated: taxidermy catches above a fireplace, wood-paneled walls, a wet bar, cozy chairs, firewood piled high, a worn semishag carpet of beige. What wasn't expected, of course, were the dark red boot prints slashing a path through the beige.

Blood. Fresh blood that filled the room with a smell like wet rust.

Myron turned to look at Eli Wickner. Wickner kept his distance. The shotgun was leveled at Myron's chest. Easiest target. Wickner's eyes were open a bit too wide and even more red-rimmed than at the Little League field. His skin was like parchment paper. Spider veins had nestled into his right cheek. There may have been spider veins on his left cheek too, but it was hard to tell with the spray of blood on it.

'You?'

Wickner remained silent.

'What's going on, Eli?'

'Walk into the back room,' Wickner said.

'You don't want to do this.'

'I know that, Myron. Now just turn around and start walking.'

Myron followed the bloody prints as though they'd been painted there for this reason – a macabre Freedom Trail or something. The wall was lined with Little League team photographs, the early ones dating back some thirty-odd years. In each picture Wickner stood proudly with his young charges, smiling into the powerful sun on a clear day. A sign held by two boys in the front row read FRIENDLY'S ICE CREAM SENATORS or BURRELLES PRESS CLIPPING TIGERS or SEYMOUR'S LUNCHEONETTE INDIANS. Always sponsors. The children squinted and shifted and smiled toothlessly. But they all basically looked the same. Over the past thirty years the kids had changed shockingly little. But Eli had aged, of course. Year by year the photographs on the wall checked off his life. The effect was more than a little eerie.

They headed into the back room. An office of some kind. There were more photos on the wall. Wickner receiving Livingston's Big L Award. The ribbon cutting when the backstop was named after him. Wickner in his police uniform with ex-Governor Brendan Byrne. Wickner winning the Raymond J. Clarke Policeman of the Year award. A smattering of plaques and trophies and mounted baseballs. A framed document entitled 'What

Coach Means to Me' given to him by one of his teams. And more blood.

Cold fear wrapped around Myron and drew tight.

In the corner, lying on his back, his arms extended as though readying himself for crucifixion, was Chief of Detectives Roy Pomeranz. His shirt looked like someone had squeezed out a bucket of syrup over it. His dead eyes were frozen open and sucked dry.

'You killed your own partner,' Myron said. Again for Win. In case he arrived too late. For posterity or to incriminate or some such nonsense.

'Not more than ten minutes ago,' Wickner said.

'Why?'

'Sit down, Myron. Right there, if you don't mind.'

Myron sat in an oversize chair with wooden slats.

Keeping the gun at chest level, Wickner moved to the other side of a desk. He opened a drawer, dropped Myron's gun in it, then tossed Myron a set of handcuffs. 'Cuff yourself to the side arm. I don't want to have to concentrate so hard on watching you.'

Myron looked at his surroundings. It was pretty much now or never. Once the cuffs were in place, there would not be another chance. He looked for a way. Nothing. Wickner was too far away, and a desk separated them. Myron spotted a letter opener on the desk. Oh, right, like maybe he would just reach out and throw it like some martial arts death star and hit the jugular. Bruce Lee would be so proud.

As though reading his mind, Wickner raised the gun a bit.

'Put them on now, Myron.'

No chance. He would just have to stall. And hope Win arrived in time. Myron clicked the cuff on his left wrist. Then he closed the other end around the heavy chair arm.

Wickner's shoulders slumped, relaxing a bit. 'I should have guessed they'd have a tap on the phone,' he said.

'Who?'

Wickner seemed not to hear him. 'Thing is, you can't approach this house without my knowing. Forget the gravel out there. I got motion sensors all over the place. House lights up like a Christmas tree if you approach from any direction. Use it to scare away the animals – otherwise they get in the garbage. But you see, they knew that. So they sent someone I would trust. My old partner.'

Myron was trying to keep up. 'Are you saying Pomeranz came here to kill you?'

'No time for your questions, Myron. You wanted to know what happened. Now you will. And then . . .' He looked away, the rest of the sentence vaporizing before reaching his lips.

'The first time I encountered Anita Slaughter was at the bus stop on the corner of Northfield Avenue, where Roosevelt School used to be.' His voice had fallen into a cop monotone, almost as though he were reading back a report. 'We'd gotten an anonymous call from someone using the phone booth at Sam's across the street. They said a woman was cut up bad and bleeding. Check that. They said a *black* woman was bleeding. Only place you saw black women in Livingston was by the bus stop. They came in to clean houses, or they didn't come here at all. Just that simple. If they were there for other reasons in those days, well, we politely pointed out the errors in their ways and escorted them back on the bus.

'Anyway, I was in the squad car. So I took the call. Sure enough, she was bleeding pretty good. Someone had given her a hell of a beating. But I tell you what struck me right away. The woman was gorgeous. Dark as coal, but even with all those scratches on her face, she was simply stunning. I asked her what happened, but she wouldn't tell me. I figured it was a domestic dispute. A spat with the husband. I didn't like it, but back in those days you didn't do anything about it. Hell, not much different today. Anyway I insisted on taking her to St. Barnabas. They patched her up. She was pretty shook up, but she was basically okay. The scratches were pretty deep, like she'd been attacked by a cat. But hey, I did my bit and forgot all about it – until three weeks later, when I got the call about Elizabeth Bradford.'

A clock chimed and echoed. Eli lowered the shotgun and looked off. Myron checked his cuffed wrist. It was secure. The chair was heavy. Still no chance.

'Her death wasn't an accident, was it, Eli?'

'No,' Wickner said. 'Elizabeth Bradford committed suicide.' He reached out on his desk and picked up an old baseball. He stared at it like a Gypsy reading fortunes. A Little League ball, the awkward signature of twelve-year-olds scrawled over the surface.

'Nineteen seventy-three,' the old coach said with a pained smile. 'The year we won the state championship. Hell of a team.' He put down the ball. 'I love Livingston. I dedicated my life to that town. But every good place has a Bradford family in it. To add temptation, I guess. Like the serpent in the Garden of Eden. It starts small, you know? You let a parking ticket go. Then you see one of them speeding and you turn the other way. Like I said, small. They don't openly bribe you, but they have ways of taking care of people. They start at the top. You drag a Bradford in for drunk driving, someone above you just springs them anyway, and you get unofficially sanctioned. And other cops get pissed off because the Bradfords gave all of us tickets to a Giants game. Or they paid for a weekend retreat. Stuff like that. But underneath we all know it's wrong. We justify it away, but the truth is, we did wrong. I did wrong.' He motioned to the mass of flesh on the ground. 'And Roy did wrong. I always knew it would come back and get us one day. Just didn't know when. Then you tapped me on the shoulder at the ball field, and well, I knew.'

Wickner stopped, smiled. 'Getting off the subject a bit, aren't I?'

Myron shrugged. 'I'm not in any hurry.'

'Unfortunately I am.' Another smile that twisted Myron's heart. 'I was telling you about the second time I encountered Anita Slaughter. Like I said, it was the day Elizabeth Bradford committed suicide. A woman identifying herself as a maid called the station at six in the morning. I didn't realize it was Anita until I arrived. Roy and I were in the midst of the investigation when the old man called us into that fancy library. You ever seen it? The library in the silo?'

Myron nodded.

'The three of them were there – the old man, Arthur, and Chance. Still in these fancy silk pajamas and bathrobes, for chrissake. The old man asked us for a little favor. That's what he called it. A little favor. Like he was asking us to help him move a piano. He wanted us to report the death as an accident. For the family reputation. Old Man Bradford wasn't crass enough to put a dollar amount on doing this, but he made it clear we would be well compensated. Roy and I figured, what's the harm? Accident or suicide – in the long run, who really cares? That kind of stuff is changed all the time. No big deal, right?'

'Then you believed them?' Myron said.

The question nudged Wickner out of his daze. 'What do you mean?'

'That it was a suicide. You took their word?'

'It was a suicide, Myron. Your Anita Slaughter confirmed it.'

'How?'

'She saw it happen.'

'You mean she found the body.'

'No, I mean, she saw Elizabeth Bradford leap.'

That surprised him.

'According to Anita's statement, she arrived at work, walked up the driveway, spotted Elizabeth Bradford standing alone on the ledge, and watched her dive on her head.'

'Anita could have been coached,' Myron said.

Wickner shook his head. 'Nope.'

'How can you be so sure?'

'Because Anita Slaughter made this statement *before* the Bradfords got to her – both on the phone and when we first got there. Hell, most of the Bradfords were still getting out of bed. Once the spin control began, Anita changed her story. That's when she came up with that stuff about finding the body when she arrived.'

Myron frowned. 'I don't get it. Why change the time of the jump? What difference could it make?'

'I guess they wanted it to be at night so it would look more like an accident. A woman inadvertently slipping off a wet balcony late at night is an easier sell than at six in the morning.'

Myron thought about this. And didn't like it.

'There was no sign of a struggle,' Wickner continued. 'There was even a note.'

'What did it say?'

'Mostly gibberish. I don't really remember. The Bradfords kept it. Claimed it was private thoughts. We were able to confirm it was her handwriting. That's all I cared about.'

'You mentioned in the police report that Anita still showed signs of the earlier assault.'

Wickner nodded.

'So you must have been suspicious.'

'Suspicious of what? Sure, I wondered. But I didn't see any connection. A maid suffers a beating three weeks before the suicide of her employer. What's one thing got to do with the other?'

Myron nodded slowly. It made sense, he guessed. He checked the clock behind Wickner's head. Fifteen minutes more, he estimated. And then Win would have to approach carefully. Making his way around the motion detectors would take time. Myron took a deep breath. Win would make it. He always did.

'There's more,' Wickner said.

Myron looked at him and waited.

'I saw Anita Slaughter one last time,' Wickner said. 'Nine months later. At the Holiday Inn.'

Myron realized that he was holding his breath. Wickner put down the weapon on the desk – well out of Myron's reach – and grabbed hold of a whiskey bottle. He took a swig and then picked up the shotgun again.

He aimed it at Myron.

'You're wondering why I'm telling you all this.' Wickner's words came out a bit more slurred now. The barrel was still pointed at Myron, growing larger, an angry dark mouth trying to swallow him whole.

'The thought crossed my mind,' Myron said.

Wickner smiled. Then he let loose a deep breath, lowered his aim a bit, and started in again. 'I wasn't on duty that night. Neither was Roy. He called me at home and said the Bradfords needed a favor. I told him the Bradfords could go to hell, I wasn't their personal security service. But it was all bluster.

'Anyway, Roy told me to put on a uniform and meet

him at the Holiday Inn. I went, of course. We hooked up in the parking lot. I asked Roy what was up. He said that one of the Bradford kids had screwed up again. I said, screwed up how? Roy said he didn't know the details. It was girl trouble. He had gotten fresh, or they had taken too many drugs. Something like that. Understand now that this was twenty years ago. Terms like date rape didn't exist back then. You go back to a hotel room with a guy, well, let's just say you got what you got. I'm not defending it. I'm just saying it was the way that it was.

'So I asked him what we were supposed to do. Roy said that we just had to seal off the floor. See, there was a wedding going on and a big convention. The place was mobbed, and the room was in a fairly public spot. So they needed us to keep people away so they could clean up whatever mess there was. Roy and I positioned ourselves at either end of the corridor. I didn't like it, but I didn't really think I had much of a choice. What was I going to do, report them? The Bradfords already had their hooks into me. The payoff for fixing the suicide would come out. So would all the rest. And not just about me but about my buddies on the force. Cops react funny when they're threatened.' He pointed to the floor. 'Look what Roy was willing to do to his own partner.'

Myron nodded.

'So we cleared the floor. And then I saw Old Man Bradford's so-called security expert. Creepy little guy. Scared the piss out of me. Sam something.'

'Sam Richards,' Myron said.

'Yeah, right, Richards. That's the guy. He spewed out the same dribble I'd already heard. Girl trouble. Nothing to worry about. He'd clean it up. The girl was a little shaky, but they'd get her patched up and pay her off. It would all go away. That's how it is with the rich. Money cleans all spills. So the first thing this Sam guy does is carry the girl out. I wasn't supposed to see it. I was supposed to stay down at the end of the corridor. But I looked anyway. Sam had her wrapped in a sheet and carried her over his shoulder like a fireman. But for a split second I saw her face. And I knew who it was. Anita Slaughter. Her eyes were closed. She hung over his shoulder like a bag of oats.'

Wickner took a plaid handkerchief out of his pocket. He unfolded it slowly and wiped his nose as if he were buffing a fender. Then he folded it up again and put it back in his pocket. 'I didn't like what I saw,' he said. 'So I ran over to Roy and told him we had to stop it. Roy said, how would we explain even being here? What would we say, that we were helping Bradford cover up a smaller crime? He was right, of course. There was nothing we could do. So I went back to the end of the corridor. Sam was back in the room by now. I heard him using a vacuum. He took his time and cleaned the entire room. I kept telling myself it was no big deal. She was just a black woman from Newark. Hell, they all did drugs, right? And she was gorgeous. Probably partying with one of the Bradford boys and it got out of hand. Maybe she OD'd. Maybe Sam was going to take her someplace and get her some help and give her money. Just like he said. So I watched Sam finish cleaning up. I saw him get in the car. And I saw him drive away with Chance Bradford.'

'Chance?' Myron repeated. 'Chance Bradford was there?'

'Yes. Chance was the boy in trouble.' Wickner sat back. He stared at the gun. 'And that's the end of my tale, Myron.'

'Wait a second. Anita Slaughter checked into that hotel with her daughter. Did you see her there?'

'No.'

'Do you have any idea where Brenda is now?'

'She probably got tangled up with the Bradfords. Like her mother.'

'Help me save her, Eli.'

Wickner shook his head. 'I'm tired, Myron. And I got nothing more to say.'

Eli Wickner lifted the shotgun.

'It's going to come out,' Myron said. 'Even if you kill me, you can't cover it all up.'

Wickner nodded. 'I know.' He didn't lower the weapon.

'My telephone is on,' Myron continued quickly. 'My friend has heard every word. Even if you kill me—'

'I know that too, Myron.' A tear slid out of Eli's eye. He tossed Myron a small key. For the handcuffs. 'Tell everyone I'm sorry.'

Then he put the shotgun in his mouth.

Myron tried to bolt from the chair, the cuff holding him back. He yelled, 'No!' But the sound was drowned out by the blast of the shotgun. Bats squealed and flew away. Then all was silent again.

33

Win arrived a few minutes later. He looked down at the two bodies and said, 'Tidy.'

Myron did not reply.

'Did you touch anything?'

'I already wiped the place down,' Myron said.

'A request,' Win said.

Myron looked at him.

'Next time a gun is fired under similar circumstances, say something immediately. A good example might be "I'm not dead."'

'Next time,' Myron said.

They left the cabin. They drove to a nearby twenty-four-hour supermarket. Myron parked the Taurus and got in the Jag with Win.

'Where to?' Win asked.

'You heard what Wickner said?'

'Yes.'

'What do you make of it?'

'I'm still processing,' Win said. 'But clearly the answer lies within Bradford Farms.'

'So most likely does Brenda.'

Win nodded. 'If she's still alive.'

'So that's where we should go.'

'Rescuing the fair maiden from the tower?'

'If she's even there, which is a big if. And we can't go in with guns blazing. Someone might panic and kill her.' Myron reached for his phone. 'Arthur Bradford wants an update. I think I'll give him one. Now. In person.'

'They may very well try to kill you.'

'That's where you come in,' Myron said.

Win smiled. 'Bitching.' His word of the week.

They turned onto Route 80 and headed east.

'Let me bounce a few thoughts off you,' Myron said.

Win nodded. He was used to this game.

'Here's what we know,' Myron said. 'Anita Slaughter is assaulted. Three weeks later she witnesses Elizabeth Bradford's suicide. Nine months pass. Then she runs away from Horace. She empties out the bank account, grabs her daughter, and hides out at the Holiday Inn. Now here is where things get murky. We know that Chance Bradford and Sam end up there. We know they end up taking an injured Anita off the premises. We also know that sometime before that Anita calls Horace and tells him to pick up Brenda—'

Myron broke off and looked at Win. 'What time would that have been?'

'Pardon?'

'Anita called Horace to pick up Brenda. That had to be before Sam arrived on the scene, right?'

'Yes.'

'But here's the thing. Horace told Mabel that Anita called him. But maybe Horace was lying. I mean, why would Anita call Horace? It makes no sense. She's running away from the man. She's taken all his money. Why would she then call Horace and give away her location? She might call Mabel, for example, but never Horace.'

Win nodded. 'Go on.'

'Suppose . . . suppose we're looking at this all wrong. Forget the Bradfords for the moment. Take it from Horace's viewpoint. He gets home. He finds the note. Maybe he even learns that his money is gone. He'd be furious. So suppose Horace tracked Anita down at the

Holiday Inn. Suppose he went there to take back his child and his money.'

'By force,' Win added.

'Yes.'

'Then he killed Anita?'

'Not killed. But maybe he beat the hell out of her. Maybe he even left her for dead. Either way, he takes Brenda and the money back. Horace calls his sister. He tells her that Anita called him to pick up Brenda.'

Win frowned. 'And then what? Anita hides from Horace for twenty years – lets him raise her daughter by himself – because she was scared of him?'

Myron didn't like that. 'Maybe,' he said.

'And then, if I follow your logic, twenty years later Anita becomes aware that Horace is looking for her. So is she the one who killed him? A final showdown? But then who grabbed Brenda? And why? Or is Brenda in cahoots with her mother? And while we've dismissed the Bradfords for the sake of hypothesizing, how do they factor into all this? Why would they be concerned enough to cover up Horace Slaughter's crime? Why was Chance Bradford at the hotel that night in the first place?'

'There are holes,' Myron admitted.

'There are chasms of leviathan proportions,' Win corrected.

'There's another thing I don't get. If the Bradfords have had a tap on Mabel's phone this whole time, wouldn't they have been able to trace Anita's calls?'

Win mulled that one over. 'Maybe,' he said, 'they did.'

Silence. Myron flipped on the radio. The game was in the second half. The New York Dolphins were getting crushed. The announcers were speculating on the whereabouts of Brenda Slaughter. Myron turned the volume down.

'We're still missing something,' Myron said.

'Yes, but we're getting close.'

'So we still try the Bradfords.'

Win nodded. 'Open the glove compartment. Arm yourself like a paranoid despot. This may get ugly.'

Myron did not argue. He dialed Arthur's private line. Arthur answered midway through the first ring. 'Have you found Brenda?' Arthur asked.

'I'm on my way to your house,' Myron said.

'Then you've found her?'

'I'll be there in fifteen minutes,' Myron said. 'Tell your guards.'

Myron hung up. 'Curious,' he said to Win.

'What?'

And then it hit Myron. Not slowly. But all at once. A tremendous avalanche buried him in one fell swoop. With a trembling hand Myron dialed another number into the cell phone.

'Norm Zuckerman, please. Yes, I know he's watching the game. Tell him it's Myron Bolitar. Tell him it's urgent. And tell him I want to talk with McLaughlin and Tiles too.'

34

The guard at Bradford Farms shone a flashlight into the car. 'You alone, Mr. Bolitar?'

'Yes,' Myron said.

The gate went up. 'Please proceed to the main house.'

Myron drove in slowly. Per their plan, he slowed on the next curve. Silence. Then Win's voice came through the phone: 'I'm out.'

Out of the trunk. So smooth Myron had not even heard him.

'I'm going on mute,' Win said. 'Let me know where you are at all times.'

The plan was simple: Win would search the property for Brenda while Myron tried not to get himself killed.

He continued up the drive, both hands on the wheel. Part of him wanted to stall; most of him wanted to get at Arthur Bradford immediately. He knew the truth now. Some of it anyway. Enough to save Brenda.

Maybe.

The grounds were silk black, the farm animals silent. The mansion loomed above him, floating almost, only tenuously connected with the world beneath it. Myron parked and got out of the car. Before he reached the door, Mattius the Manservant was there. It was ten o'clock at night, but Mattius still displayed full butler garb and rigid spine. He said nothing, waiting with almost inhuman patience.

When Myron reached him, Mattius said, 'Mr. Bradford will see you in the library.'

Myron nodded. And that was when someone hit him in the head. There was a thud, and then a thick, blackening numbness swam through him. His skull tingled. Still reeling, Myron felt a bat smash the back of his lower thighs. His legs buckled, and he dropped to his knees.

'Win,' he managed.

A boot stomped him hard between the shoulder blades. Myron crashed facefirst into the ground. He felt the air whoosh out of him. There were hands on him now. Searching. Grabbing out the weapons.

'Win,' he said again.

'Nice try.' Sam stood over him. He was holding Myron's phone. 'But I hung it up, I Spy.'

Two other men lifted Myron by the armpits and quickly dragged him into the foyer and down the corridor. Myron tried to blink out the fuzzies. His entire body felt like a thumb hit with a hammer. Sam walked in front of him. He opened a door, and the two men tossed Myron in like a sack of peat moss. He started to roll down steps, but he managed to stop his descent before he hit bottom.

Sam stepped inside. The door closed behind him.

'Come on,' Sam said. 'Let's get this done.' Myron managed to sit up. A basement, Myron realized. He was on the steps of a basement.

Sam walked toward him. He reached out a hand. Myron took it and pulled himself to his feet. The two men walked down the steps.

'This section of the basement is windowless and cement-lined,' Sam said. Like he was giving a house tour. 'So the only way in or out is through that door. Understand?'

Myron nodded.

'I got two men at the top of the steps. They're going

to spread out now. And they're pros, not like that Mario asswipe. So no one is getting through that door. Understand?'

Another nod.

Sam took out a cigarette and put it between his lips. 'Lastly, we saw your buddy jump out of the trunk. I got two marine sharpshooters hidden out there. Persian Gulf War vets. Your friend comes anywhere near the house, he's toast. The windows are all alarmed. The motion detectors are set. I'm in radio contact with all four of my men under four different frequencies.' He showed Myron a walkie-talkie of some kind with a digital readout.

'Different frequencies,' Myron repeated. 'Wow.'

'I say all this not to impress you but to stress how dumb a flight attempt would be. Do you understand?'

One more nod.

They were in a wine cellar now. It smelled as robust and oaky as, well, a perfectly aged chardonnay. Arthur was there. His face was skull-like, his skin drawn up tautly against his cheekbones. Chance was there too. He was sipping red wine, studying the color, trying very hard to look casual.

Myron glanced about the wine cellar. Lots of bottles in criss-crossed shelves, all tilted slightly forward so the corks would remain properly moist. A giant thermometer. A few wooden barrels, mostly for show. There were no windows. No doors. No other visible entranceways. In the center of the room was a hefty mahogany table.

The table was bare except for a gleaming set of pruning shears.

Myron looked back at Sam. Sam smiled, still holding a gun.

'Label me intimidated,' Myron said.

Sam shrugged.

'Where is Brenda?' Arthur demanded.

'I don't know,' Myron said.

'And Anita? Where is she?'

'Why don't you ask Chance?' Myron said.

'What?'

Chance sat up. 'He's crazy.'

Arthur stood. 'You're not leaving here until I'm satisfied that you're not holding out on me.'

'Fine,' Myron said. 'Then let's get to it, Arthur. You see, I've been dumb about this whole thing. I mean, the clues were all there. The old phone taps. Your keen interest in all this. The earlier assault on Anita. Ransacking Horace's apartment and taking Anita's letters. The cryptic calls telling Brenda to contact her mother. Sam cutting those kids' Achilles tendons. The scholarship money. But you know what finally gave it away?'

Chance was about to say something, but Arthur waved him into silence. He strummed his chin with his index finger. 'What?' he asked.

'The timing of Elizabeth's suicide,' Myron said.

'I don't understand.'

'The timing of the suicide,' Myron repeated, 'and more important, your family's attempt to alter it. Why would Elizabeth kill herself at six in the morning – at the exact moment Anita Slaughter was coming to work? Coincidence? Possibly. But then why did you all work so hard to change the time? Elizabeth could have just as easily had her accident at six A.M. as midnight. So why the change?'

Arthur kept his back straight. 'You tell me.'

'Because the timing was not incidental,' Myron said. 'Your wife committed suicide when she did and how she did for a reason. She wanted Anita Slaughter to see her jump.'

Chance made a noise. 'That's ridiculous.'

'Elizabeth was depressed,' Myron continued, looking straight at Arthur. 'I don't doubt that. And I don't doubt that you once loved her. But that was a long time ago. You said she hadn't been herself for years. I don't doubt that either. But three weeks before her suicide Anita was assaulted. I thought one of you beat her. Then I thought that maybe Horace did it. But the most noticeable injuries were scratches. Deep scratches. Like a cat, Wickner said.' Myron looked at Arthur. Arthur seemed to be shrinking in front of him, being sucked dry by his own memories.

'Your wife was the one who attacked Anita,' Myron said. 'First she attacked her, and then three weeks later, still despondent, she committed suicide in front of her – because Anita was having an affair with her husband. It was the final mental straw that broke her, wasn't it, Arthur? So how did it happen? Did Elizabeth walk in on you two? Did she seem so far gone that you got careless?'

Arthur cleared his throat. 'As a matter of fact, yes. That's pretty much how it happened. But so what? What does that have to do with the present?'

'Your affair with Anita. How long did it last?'

'I don't see the relevance of that.'

Myron looked at him for a long moment. 'You're an evil man,' he said. 'You were raised by an evil man, and you have much of him in you. You've caused great suffering. You've even had people killed. But this wasn't a fling, was it? You loved her, didn't you, Arthur?'

He said nothing. But something behind the facade began to cave in.

'I don't know how it happened,' Myron continued. 'Maybe Anita wanted to leave Horace. Or maybe you encouraged her. It doesn't matter. Anita decided to run away and start new. Tell me what the plan was, Arthur. Were you going to set her up in an apartment? A house out of town? Surely no Bradford was going to marry a black maid from Newark.'

Arthur made a noise. Half scoff. Half groan. 'Surely,' he said.

'So what happened?'

Sam kept several steps back, his gaze moving from the basement door to Myron. He whispered into his walkie-talkie every once in a while. Chance sat frozen, both nervous and comforted; nervous about what was being unearthed; comforted because he believed it would never leave this cellar. Perhaps he was right.

'Anita was my last hope,' Arthur said. He bounced two fingers off his lips and forced up a smile. 'It's ironic, don't you think? If you come from a disadvantaged home, you can blame the environment for your sinful ways. But what about an omnipotent household? What about those who are raised to dominate others, to take what they want? What about those who are raised to believe that they are special and that other people are little more than window dressing? What about those children?'

Myron nodded. 'Next time I'm alone,' he said, 'I'll weep for them.'

Arthur chuckled. 'Fair enough,' he said. 'But you have it wrong. I was the one who wanted to run away. Not Anita. Yes, I loved her. When I was with her, every part of me soared. I can't explain it any other way.'

He didn't have to. Myron thought of Brenda. And he understood.

'I was going to leave Bradford Farms,' he continued. 'Anita and I were going to run away together. Start on our own. Escape this prison.' He smiled again. 'Naive, wouldn't you say?'

'So what happened?' Myron asked.

'Anita changed her mind.'

'Why?'

'There was someone else.'

'Who?'

'I don't know. We were supposed to meet up in the morning, but Anita never showed. I thought maybe her husband had done something to her. I kept an eye on him. And then I got a note from her. She said she needed to start new. Without me. And she sent back the ring.'

'What ring?'

'The one I gave her. An unofficial engagement ring.'

Myron looked over at Chance. Chance said nothing. Myron kept his eyes on him for a few more seconds. Then he turned back to Arthur.

'But you didn't give up, did you?'

'No.'

'You searched for her. The phone taps. You've had the taps in place all these years. You figured Anita would call her family one day. You wanted to be able to trace the call when she did.'

'Yes.'

Myron swallowed hard and hoped he would be able to keep his voice from cracking. 'And then there were the microphones in Brenda's room,' he said. 'And the scholarship money. And the severed Achilles tendons.'

Silence.

Tears welled up in Myron's eyes. Same with Arthur's. Both men knew what was coming. Myron pressed on, struggling to maintain an even and steady tone.

'The microphones were there so that you could keep an eye on Brenda. The scholarships were set up by someone with a great deal of money and financial expertise. Even if Anita had gotten her hands on cash, she wouldn't have known how to funnel it through the Cayman Islands. You, on the other hand, would. And lastly the Achilles tendons. Brenda thought it was her father who did it. She thought her father was being overprotective. And she was right.'

More silence.

'I just called Norm Zuckerman and got Brenda's blood type from the team medical records. The police had Horace's blood type from the autopsy report. They weren't related, Arthur.' Myron thought of Brenda's light coffee skin next to the far darker tones of her parents. 'That's why you've been so interested in Brenda. That's why you were so quick to help keep her out of prison. That's why you're so worried about her right now. Brenda Slaughter is your daughter.'

Tears were streaming down Arthur's face now. He did nothing to stop it.

Myron went on. 'Horace never knew, did he?'

Arthur shook his head. 'Anita got pregnant early in our relationship. But Brenda still ended up dark enough to pass. Anita insisted we keep it a secret. She didn't want our child stigmatized. She also – she also didn't want our daughter raised in this house. I understood.'

'So what happened to Horace? Why did he call you after twenty years?'

'It was the Aches, trying to help Davison. Somehow they found out about the scholarship money. From one of the lawyers, I think. They wanted to cause mischief for me in the governor's race. So they told Slaughter about it. They thought he'd be greedy and follow the money line.'

'But he didn't care about the money,' Myron said. 'He wanted to find Anita.'

'Yes. He called me repeatedly. He came to my

campaign headquarters. He wouldn't let go. So I had Sam discourage him.'

The blood in the locker. 'He was beaten?'

Arthur nodded. 'But not badly. I wanted to scare him off, not hurt him. A long time ago Anita made me promise never to harm him. I tried my best to keep that promise.'

'Sam was supposed to keep an eye on him?'

'Yes. To make sure he didn't cause any trouble. And, I don't know, maybe I had hopes he would find Anita.'

'But he ran.'

'Yes.'

It made sense, Myron thought. Horace had gotten a bloody nose. He had gone to nearby St. Barnabas after the beating. He cleaned himself up. Sam had scared him, yes, but only enough to convince Horace that he had to go into hiding. So he cleared out his bank account and disappeared. Sam and Mario searched. They followed Brenda. They visited Mabel Edwards and threatened her. They checked the tap on her phone. Eventually Horace called her.

And then?

'You killed Horace.'

'No. We never found him.'

A hole, Myron thought. There were still a few of them he hadn't plugged. 'But you did have your people make cryptic calls to Brenda.'

'Just to see if she knew where Anita was. The other calls – the threatening ones – came from the Aches. They wanted to find Horace and finalize the contract before the opener.'

Myron nodded. Again it made sense. He turned and stared down Chance. Chance met the gaze and held it. He had a small smile on his face.

'Are you going to tell him, Chance?'

Chance rose and went face-to-face with Myron. 'You're a dead man,' he said, almost leering. 'All you've done here is dig your own grave.'

'Are you going to tell him, Chance?'

'No, Myron.' He gestured to the pruning shears and leaned closer. 'I'm going to watch you suffer and then die.'

Myron reared back and head-butted Chance square on the nose. He held back at the last moment. If you head-butt at full strength, you could literally kill a person. The head is both heavy and hard; the face being hit is neither. Picture a wrecking ball heading for a bird's nest.

Still, the blow was effective. Chance's nose did the equivalent of a gymnastic split. Myron felt something warm and sticky on his hair. Chance fell back. His nose gushed. His eyes were wide and shocked. No one rushed to his aid. Sam in fact seemed to be smiling.

Myron turned to Arthur. 'Chance knew about your affair, didn't he?'

'Yes, of course.'

'And he knew about your plans to run away?'

This time the answer came slower. 'Yes. But what of it?'

'Chance has been lying to you for twenty years. So has Sam.'

'What?'

'I just spoke to Detective Wickner. He was there that night too. I don't know what happened exactly. Neither did he. But he saw Sam carry Anita out of the Holiday Inn. And he saw Chance in the car.'

Arthur glared at his brother. 'Chance?'

'He's lying.'

Arthur took out a gun and pointed it at his brother. 'Tell me.'

Chance was still trying to stem the blood flow. 'Who are you going to believe? Me or—'

Arthur pulled the trigger. The bullet smashed Chance's knee, splintering the joint. Blood spurted. Chance howled in agony. Arthur aimed the gun at the other knee.

'Tell me,' he said.

'You were insane!' Chance shouted. Then he gritted his teeth. His eyes grew small yet strangely clear, as though the pain were sweeping the debris away. 'Did you really think Father was going to let you just run off like that? You were going to destroy everything. I tried to make you see that. I talked to you. Like a brother. But you didn't want to listen. So I went to see Anita. Just to talk. I wanted her to see how destructive this whole idea was. I meant her no harm. I was just trying to help.'

Chance's face was a bloody mess, but Arthur's was a far more horrid sight. The tears were still there, still flowing freely. But he was not crying. His skin was gray-white, his features contorted like a death mask. Something behind his eyes had been short-circuited by his rage. 'What happened?'

'I found her room number. And when I got there, the door was ajar. I swear, Anita was like that when I arrived. I swear it, Arthur. I didn't touch her. At first I thought maybe you had done it. That maybe you two had a fight. But either way, I knew it would be a mess if it leaked out. There were too many questions, too many loose ends. So I called Father. He arranged the rest. Sam came over. He cleaned the place up. We took the ring and forged that note. So you'd stop looking.'

'Where is she now?' Myron asked.

Chance looked at him, puzzled. 'What the hell are you talking about?'

'Did you take her to a doctor? Give her money? Did you—'

'Anita was dead,' Chance said.

Silence.

Arthur let out a harrowing, primitive wail. He collapsed to the floor.

'She was dead when I got there, Arthur. I swear it.'

Myron felt his heart sink into deep mud. He tried to speak, but no words came out. He looked over at Sam. Sam nodded. Myron met his eye. 'Her body?' he managed.

'I get rid of something,' Sam said, 'it's gone for good.'

Dead. Anita Slaughter was dead. Myron tried to take it in. All these years Brenda had felt unworthy for nothing.

'So where is Brenda?' Myron asked.

The adrenaline was starting to wear off, but Chance still managed to shake his head. 'I don't know.'

Myron looked over at Sam. Sam shrugged.

Arthur sat up. He hugged his knees and lowered his head. He began to cry.

'My leg,' Chance said. 'I need a doctor.'

Arthur did not move.

'We also need to kill him,' Chance said through a clenched jaw. 'He knows too much, Arthur. I know you're grief-stricken, but we can't let him ruin everything.'

Sam nodded at that. 'He's right, Mr. Bradford.'

Myron said, 'Arthur.'

Arthur looked up.

'I'm your daughter's best hope.'

'I don't think so,' Sam said. He aimed the gun. 'Chance is right, Mr. Bradford. It's too risky. We just admitted covering up a murder. He has to die.'

Sam's walkie-talkie suddenly squeaked. Then a voice

came through the tinny speaker: 'I wouldn't do that if I were you.'

Win.

Sam frowned at the walkie-talkie. He turned a knob, changed frequency. The red digital readout changed numbers. Then he pressed the talk button. 'Someone got to Forster,' Sam said. 'Move in and take him out.'

The response was Win's best *Star Trek* Scotty: 'But I can't hold her, Captain. She's breaking up!'

Sam remained calm. 'How many radios you got, buddy?'

'Collect all four, now in specially marked packages.'

Sam whistled his appreciation. 'Fine,' he said. 'So we got ourselves a stalemate. Let's talk it through.'

'No.' This time it wasn't Win speaking. It was Arthur Bradford. He fired twice. Both bullets hit Sam in the chest. Sam slumped to the floor, twitched, and then lay still.

Arthur looked at Myron. 'Find my daughter,' he said. 'Please.'

35

Win and Myron rushed back to the Jag. Win drove. Myron did not ask about the fate of the men who once possessed those four walkie-talkies. He didn't much care.

'I searched the entire grounds,' Win said. 'She's not here.'

Myron sat and thought. He remembered telling Detective Wickner at the Little League field that he would not stop digging. And he remembered Wickner's response: *'Then more people are going to die.'*

'You were right,' Myron said.

Win kept driving.

'I didn't keep my eye on the prize. I pushed too hard.'

Win said nothing.

When Myron heard the first ring, he reached for his cellular. Then he remembered that Sam had taken it from him back at the estate. The ringing was coming from Win's car phone. Win answered it. He said, 'Hello.' He listened for a full minute without nodding or speaking or making any noise whatsoever. Then he said, 'Thank you,' and hung up. He slowed the car's speed and pulled over to the side of the road. The car glided to a stop. He shifted into park and snapped off the ignition.

Win turned toward Myron, his gaze as heavy as the ages.

For a fleeting moment Myron was puzzled. But only

for a moment. Then his head fell to one side, and he let out a small groan. Win nodded. And something inside Myron's chest dried up and blew away.

36

Peter Frankel, a six-year-old boy from Cedar Grove, New Jersey, had been missing for eight hours. Frantic, Paul and Missy Frankel, the boy's parents, called the police. The Frankels' backyard was up against a wooded water reservation area. The police and neighbors formed search parties. Police dogs were brought in. Neighbors even brought their own dogs along. Everyone wanted to help.

It did not take long to find Peter. Apparently the boy had crawled into a neighbor's toolshed and fallen asleep. When he woke up, he pushed at the door, but it was stuck. Peter was scared, of course, but no worse for wear. Everyone was relieved. The town fire whistle blew, signaling that all searchers should return.

One dog didn't heed the whistle. A German shepherd named Wally ran deeper into the woods and barked steadily until Officer Craig Reed, new with the canine corps, came to see what had upset Wally so.

When Reed arrived, he found Wally barking over a dead body.

The medical examiner was called in. His conclusion: the victim, a female in her twenties, had been dead less than twenty-four hours. Cause of death: two contact gunshot wounds to the back of the head.

An hour later Cheryl Sutton, cocaptain of the New York Dolphins, positively identified the body as belonging to her friend and teammate Brenda Slaughter.

The car was still parked in the same place.

'I want to take a drive,' Myron said. 'Alone.'

Win wiped his eyes with two fingers. Then he stepped out of the car without a word. Myron slid into the driver's seat. His foot pressed down on the accelerator. He passed trees and cars and signs and shops and homes and even people taking late-night walks. Music came from the car speakers. Myron did not bother turning it off. He kept driving. Images of Brenda tried to infiltrate, but Myron parried and sidestepped.

Not yet.

By the time he reached Esperanza's apartment, it was one in the morning. She sat alone on the stoop, almost as though she were expecting him. He stopped and stayed in the car. Esperanza approached. He could see that she had been crying.

'Come inside,' she said.

Myron shook his head. 'Win talked about leaps of faith,' he began.

Esperanza stayed still.

'I didn't really understand what he meant. He kept talking about his own experiences with families. Marriage led to disaster, he said. It was that simple. He had seen countless people get married, and in almost every case they ended up crippling one another. It would take a huge leap of faith to make Win believe otherwise.'

Esperanza looked at him and kept crying. 'You loved her,' she said.

He closed his eyes hard, waited, opened them. 'I'm not talking about that. I'm talking about us. Everything I know – all my past experience – tells me that our partnership is doomed. But then I look at you. You are the finest person I know, Esperanza. You are my best friend. I love you.'

'I love you too,' she said.

'You're worth taking the leap. I want you to stay.'

She nodded. 'Good, because I can't leave anyway.' She stepped closer to the car. 'Myron, please come inside. We'll talk, okay?'

He shook his head.

'I know what she meant to you.'

Again he closed his eyes tight. 'I'll be at Win's in a few hours,' he said.

'Okay. I'll wait for you there.'

He drove off before she could say more.

37

By the time Myron reached his third destination, it was almost four in the morning. A light was still on. No surprise really. He rang the doorbell. Mabel Edwards opened it. She was wearing a terry-cloth robe over a flannel nightgown. She started crying and reached out to hug him.

Myron stepped back.

'You killed them all,' he said. 'First Anita. Then Horace. And then Brenda.'

Her mouth dropped open. 'You don't mean that.'

Myron took out his gun and placed it against the older woman's forehead. 'If you lie to me, I'll kill you.'

Mabel's gaze veered quickly from shock to cold defiance. 'You wired, Myron?'

'No.'

'Doesn't matter. You have a gun pointed to my head. I'll say whatever you want.'

The gun nudged her back into the house. Myron closed the door. The photograph of Horace was still on the fireplace mantel. Myron looked at his old friend for a brief moment. Then he turned back to Mabel.

'You lied to me,' he said. 'From the very beginning. Everything you told me was a lie. Anita never called you. She's been dead for twenty years.'

'Who told you that?'

'Chance Bradford.'

She made a scoffing noise. 'You shouldn't believe a man like that.'

'The phone taps,' Myron said.

'What?'

'Arthur Bradford tapped your phone. For the last twenty years. He hoped Anita might call you. But we all know she never did.'

'That doesn't mean anything,' Mabel said. 'Maybe he just missed those calls.'

'I don't think so. But there's more. You told me that Horace called you last week while he was hiding. He gave you this dire warning about not trying to look for him. But again Arthur Bradford had a tap on your phone. He was looking for Horace. Why didn't he know anything about it?'

'Guess he messed up again.'

Myron shook his head. 'I just paid a visit to a dumb thug named Mario,' he went on. 'I surprised him while he was sleeping, and I did some things to him I'm not proud of. By the time I was through, Mario admitted to all kinds of crimes – including trying to get information from you with his skinny partner, just like you told me. But he swears he never punched you in the eye. And I believe him. Because it was Horace who hit you.'

Brenda had called him a sexist, and he had been wondering lately about his own race issues. Now he saw the truth. His semilatent prejudices had twisted on him like a snake seizing its own tail. Mabel Edwards. The sweet old black lady. Butterfly Mc-Queen. Miss Jane Pittman. Knitting needles and reading glasses. Big and kind and matronly. Evil could never lurk in so politically correct a form.

'You told me you moved into this house shortly after Anita disappeared. How did a widow from Newark afford it? You told me that your son worked his way through Yale Law School. Sorry, but part-time jobs do not pay that kind of money anymore.'

'So?'

He kept the gun trained on her. 'You knew Horace wasn't Brenda's father from the beginning, didn't you? Anita was your closest friend. You were still working at the Bradfords' home. You must have known.'

She did not back down. 'And what if I did?'

'Then you knew Anita ran away. She would have confided in you. And if she had run into a problem at the Holiday Inn, she would have called you, not Horace.'

'Could be,' Mabel said. 'If you're talking hypothetically, I guess this is all possible.'

Myron pressed the gun against her forehead, pushing her onto the couch. 'Did you kill Anita for the money?'

Mabel smiled. Physically it was that same celestial smile, but now Myron thought he could see at least a hint of the decay looming beneath it. 'Hypothetically, Myron, I guess I could have a bunch of motives. Money, yes – fourteen thousand dollars is a lot of money. Or sisterly love – Anita was going to leave Horace brokenhearted, right? She was going to take away the baby girl he thought was his. Maybe she was even going to tell Horace the truth about Brenda's father. And maybe Horace would know that his only sister had helped keep the secret all those years.' She glared up at the gun. 'Lots of motives, I'll give you that.'

'How did you do it, Mabel?'

'Go home, Myron.'

Myron lifted the muzzle and poked her forehead with it. Hard. 'How?'

'You think I'm scared of you?'

He poked her again with the muzzle. Harder. Then again. 'How?'

'What do you mean, how?' She was spitting words now. 'It would have been easy, Myron. Anita was a mother. I would have quietly shown her the gun. I would have told her if she didn't do exactly as I said, I would kill her daughter. So Anita, the good mother, would have listened. She would have given her daughter a last hug and told her to wait in the lobby. I would have used a pillow to muffle the shot. Simple, no?'

A fresh flash of rage surged through him. 'Then what happened?'

Mabel hesitated. Myron hit her with the gun again.

'I drove Brenda back to her house. Anita had left a note telling Horace she was running away and that Brenda wasn't his child. I tore it up and wrote another.'

'So Horace never even knew that Anita had planned on taking Brenda.'

'That's right.'

'And Brenda never said anything?'

'She was five years old, Myron. She didn't know what was going on. She told her Daddy how I picked her up and took her away from Mommy. But she didn't remember anything about a hotel. At least that's what I thought.'

Silence.

'When Anita's body vanished, what did you think happened?'

'I figured that Arthur Bradford had shown up, found her dead, and did what that family always did: threw out the trash.'

Another rage flash. 'And you found a way to use that. With your son, Terence, and his political career.'

Mabel shook her head. 'Too dangerous,' she said. 'You don't want to stir up those Bradford boys with blackmail. I had nothing to do with Terence's career. But truth be told, Arthur was always willing to help Terence. Terence was, after all, his daughter's cousin.'

The anger swelled, pressing against his skull. He

wanted so much simply to pull the trigger and end this. 'So what happened next?'

'Oh, come now, Myron. You know the rest of the story, don't you? Horace started looking for Anita again. After all these years. He had a lead, he said. He thought he could find her. I tried to talk him out of it, but well, love is a funny thing.'

'Horace found out about the Holiday Inn,' Myron said.

'Yes.'

'He spoke to a woman named Caroline Gundeck.'

Mabel shrugged. 'I never heard the woman's name.'

'I just woke Ms. Gundeck out of a sound sleep,' Myron said. 'Scared her half to death. But she talked to me. Just like she talked to Horace. She was a maid back then, and she knew Anita. You see, Anita used to work hotel functions to make a little extra money. Caroline Gundeck remembered seeing Anita there that night. She was surprised because Anita checked in as a guest, not a worker. She also remembered seeing Anita's little daughter. And she remembered seeing Anita's daughter leave with another woman. A strung-out drug addict is how she described the woman. I wouldn't have guessed it was you. But Horace would have.'

Mabel Edwards said nothing.

'Horace figured it out after hearing that. So he came charging over here. Still in hiding. Still with all that money on him – eleven grand. And he hit you. He got so angry that he punched you in the eye. And then you killed him.'

She shrugged again. 'It almost sounds like self-defense.'

'Almost,' Myron agreed. 'With Horace, it was easy. He was on the run already. All you had to do was continue to make it look like he was in hiding. He would be a black man on the run, not a homicide. Who would care? It was like Anita all over again. All these years you did the little things to make people think she was still alive. You wrote letters. You faked phone calls. Whatever. So you decided to do the same again. Hell, it worked once, right? But the problem was, you weren't as good at getting rid of the dead as Sam.'

'Sam?'

'The man who worked for the Bradfords,' Myron said. 'My guess is that Terence helped you move the bodies.'

She smiled. 'Don't underestimate my strength, Myron. I'm not helpless.'

He nodded. She was right. 'I keep giving you these other motives, but my guess is that it was mostly about money. You got fourteen thousand from Anita. You got eleven thousand from Horace. And your own husband, dear, sweet Roland whose picture you wept over, had an insurance policy, I'd bet.'

She nodded. 'Only five thousand dollars, poor soul.'

'But enough for you. Shot in the head near his very own home. No witnesses. And the police had arrested you three times the previous year – twice for petty theft and one for drug possession. Seems your downward spiral began before Roland was killed.'

Mabel sighed. 'Are we done now?'

'No,' he said.

'I think we covered everything, Myron.'

He shook his head. 'Not Brenda.'

'Oh, right, of course.' She leaned back a bit. 'You seem to have all the answers, Myron. Why did I kill Brenda?'

'Because,' Myron said, 'of me.'

Mabel actually smiled. He felt his finger tighten on the trigger.

'I'm right, aren't I?'

Mabel just kept smiling.

'As long as Brenda didn't remember the Holiday Inn, she wasn't a threat. But I was the one who told you about our visit there. I was the one who told you she was having memories. And that's when you knew you had to kill her.'

She just kept smiling.

'And with Horace's body found and Brenda already a murder suspect, your job became easier. Frame Brenda and make her disappear. You kill two birds with one stone. So you planted the gun under Brenda's mattress. But again you had trouble getting rid of the body. You shot her and dumped her in the woods. My guess is that you planned on coming back another day when you had more time. What you didn't count on was the search party finding her so soon.'

Mabel Edwards shook her head. 'You sure can spin a tale, Myron.'

'It's not a tale. We both know that.'

'And we both know you can't prove any of this.'

'There will be fibers, Mabel. Hairs, threads, something.'

'So what?' Again her smile poked his heart like a pair of knitting needles. 'You saw me hug my niece right here in this very room. If her body has fibers or threads, they'd be from that. And Horace visited me before he was murdered. I told you that. So maybe that's how he got hairs or fibers on him – if they even found any.'

A hot bolt of fury exploded inside his head, almost blinding him. Myron pressed the barrel hard against her forehead. His hand started quaking. 'How did you do it?'

'Do what?'

'How did you get Brenda to leave practice?'

She didn't blink. 'I said I'd found her mother.'

Myron closed his eyes. He tried to hold the gun steady. Mabel stared at him.

'You won't shoot me, Myron. You're not the kind of man who shoots a woman in cold blood.'

He didn't pull the gun away.

Mabel reached up with her hand. She pushed the barrel away from her face. Then she got up, tightened her robe, and walked away.

'I'm going to bed now,' she said. 'Close the door on your way out.'

He did close the door.

He drove back to Manhattan. Win and Esperanza were waiting for him. They did not ask him where he'd been. And he did not tell them. In fact, he never told them.

He called Jessica's loft. The machine answered. When the beep sounded, he said that he planned on staying with Win for a while. He didn't know for how long. But a while.

Roy Pomeranz and Eli Wickner were found dead in the cabin two days later. An apparent murder-suicide. Livingstonites speculated, but no one ever knew what had driven Eli over the edge. The Eli Wickner Little League backstop was immediately renamed.

Esperanza went back to work at MB SportsReps. Myron did not.

The homicides of Brenda Slaughter and Horace Slaughter remain unsolved.

Nothing that happened at Bradford Farms that night was ever reported. A publicist for the Bradford campaign confirmed that Chance Bradford had recently undergone knee surgery to repair a nagging tennis injury. He was recovering nicely.

Jessica did not return the phone message.

And Myron told only one person about his final meeting with Mabel Edwards.

Epilogue

The cemetery overlooked a schoolyard.

There is nothing as heavy as grief. Grief is the deepest pit in the blackest ocean, the bottomless ravine. It is all-consuming. It suffocates. It paralyzes as no severed nerve could.

He spent much time here now.

Myron heard footsteps coming up behind him. He closed his eyes. It was as he expected. The footsteps came closer. When they stopped, Myron did not turn around.

'You killed her,' Myron said.

'Yes.'

'Do you feel better now?'

Arthur Bradford's tone caressed the back of Myron's neck with a cold, bloodless hand. 'The question is, Myron, do you?'

He did not know.

'If it means anything to you, Mabel Edwards died slowly.'

It didn't. Mabel Edwards had been right that night: he was not the type to shoot a woman in cold blood. He was worse.

'I've also decided to quit the gubernatorial race,' Arthur said. 'I'm going to try to remember how I felt when I was with Anita. I'm going to change.'

He wouldn't. But Myron didn't care.

Arthur Bradford left then. Myron stared at the mound of dirt for a while longer. He lay down next to it and wondered how something so splendid and alive could be no more. He waited for the school's final bell, and then he watched the children rush out of the building like bees from a poked hive. Their squeals did not comfort him.

Clouds began to blot the blue, and then rain began to fall. Myron almost smiled. Yes, rain. That was fitting. Much better than the earlier clear skies. He closed his eyes and let the drops pound him – rain on the petals of a crushed rose.

Eventually he stood and trekked down the hill to his car. Jessica was there, looming before him like a translucent specter. He had not seen or spoken to her in two weeks. Her beautiful face was wet – from the rain or tears, he could not say.

He stopped short and looked at her. Something else inside him shattered like a dropped tumbler.

'I don't want to hurt you,' Myron said.

Jessica nodded. 'I know.'

He walked away from her then. Jessica stood and watched him in silence. He got in his car and turned the ignition. Still, she did not move. He started driving, keeping his eye on the rearview mirror. The translucent specter grew smaller and smaller. But it never totally disappeared.